STRIKES IN FRANCE, 1830–1968

STRIKES IN FRANCE
1830–1968

EDWARD SHORTER
Associate Professor of
History, University of Toronto

CHARLES TILLY
Professor of History and
Sociology, University of Michigan

CAMBRIDGE UNIVERSITY PRESS

Published by the Syndics of the Cambridge University Press
Bentley House, 200 Euston Road, London NW1 2DB
American Branch: 32 East 57th Street, New York, N.Y. 10022

Library of Congress Catalogue Card Number: 73-80475

ISBN: 0 521 20293 0

First published 1974

Photoset and printed in Malta by
St Paul's Press Ltd

TO THE MEMORY OF IAN WEINBERG

Contents

Tables

APPENDIX B TABLES

Maps

Figures

Figures

Preface and acknowledgements

French strikes have changed enormously in form over the last hundred and fifty years. They have altered somewhat as well in the basic objectives for which they were waged. And they have increased manyfold in frequency. To explain why these changes took place is the task we set ourselves in this book.

We try to find answers in places that people might not normally think of looking, such as the struggle for political power, the nature of big-city life and the matrix of associations that bind men together away from the workplace. And we challenge many of the explanations other scholars have customarily found in familiar places, for we don't think that technical systems of 'industrial relations' are very important in accounting for the big changes in strikes from one epoch to the next, or from place to place; nor do we think that narrow accounts of 'economic interest' explain much about conflict either. Finally, we peer with dismay into that old closet of 'psychological' explanations, and have written this book so that writers will at least swallow hard once before they put down in the future, 'The workers struck because they were angry.'

To do all this challenging, confronting and affirming we have compiled a record of all strikes we could find out about between 1830 and 1968. Sometimes the record could be built up from chronicles of separate disputes; in other years we were dependent upon aggregate figures. Before 1890 simply enumerating the individual strikes was difficult in the absence of official statistics, and so we have relied heavily upon other researchers who have conducted painstaking archival investigations. Our indebtedness to material collected by Jean-Pierre Aguet and Michelle Perrot and to the men who around the turn of the century wrote the *APO* is manifest in the text. (We are further indebted to Professor Perrot for having permitted us to read a manuscript copy of her magisterial *thèse*, and for having given our manuscript a close critical reading as well.) After 1935 individual strikes cease entirely to represent the building blocks of the analysis, for the government released only summary statistics in often inconvenient aggregates (years, industrial sectors, regions).

It is between 1890 and 1935 that the bulk of the evidence presented in this book lies. In those years the Labor Ministry published annually the *Statis-*

tique des grèves. This marvelous source lists for each year every strike to have come to official attention – some 36,000 all together – telling where it took place, how long it lasted, what occupation was on strike, how many were the strikers, how large the plant they worked in and sometimes whether a union was present.

We have recorded in machine-readable form standardized kinds of information on each of these thousands of strikes in order to construct from this massive base of evidence a kind of demolition platform for arguments about industrial conflict, politics and social change. Our exact procedure is to take ideas on these subjects, both our own and other scholars', and hurl them against this giant rock of strike statistics. The notions which survive this battering turn up as struts in the argument of this book; those which don't the reader will find out about as well.

This mischief would have been impossible without the help of others. And a large number of people, many of whom are now teaching and writing in other universities, have assisted us from 1963, when the research began in the little library of the Harvard – MIT Joint Center for Urban Studies above Sage's Grocery, to 1971, when the Institute for Advanced Study gave us adjoining offices overlooking the Olden farm in Princeton, so that the manuscript could be written.

Back in 1963 a small band of workers started the study off: Judy Carter wrote the initial codebooks for recording strike statistics; Lutz Berkner readied the labor-force data; Lynn Lees and David Hunt did most of the coding; and Cyrus Stewart caused the tape drives of Harvard's old IBM 1401 computer to spin before this awestruck gaggle of research assistants, among whom one of the principal investigators was to be found. Later in Toronto Cindy Aron, Joan Baker and Glen Jones supplied both computer programs and ideas. Muhammad Fiaz and Abdul Quaiyum Lodhi found time alongside their own graduate work to aid us. Edna Birkenbaum, Regina Lam and Kathy Orkin waltzed among coding, tabulating and digging in the library. At the University of Michigan, David Snyder, Dan Ayres and Priscilla Cheever aided with the statistical and the machine analysis. Finally, Carolyn Connor took care of some last-minute queries, and Cecile Sydney typed the manuscript.

An initial grant from the Social Science Research Council financed the work on industrial conflict, as part of a larger investigation of social change and political conflict in modern France, directed by one of the authors. The National Science Foundation supported later stages of the research. And it is to the patience and generosity of that magnificent patron of Canadian scholarship – The Canada Council – that we owe the completion of the study.

At the end of the road, as we beamed upon our completed manuscript, Val Lorwin expunged numerous small errors and warned of larger ones as well. Some of his comments fell upon deaf ears, but at least he can say that he *tried* to save us!

Whatever beams of lightheartedness and insight there are in this book may recall the spirit of our colleague Ian Weinberg, who in his brief lifetime offered to us so much of both.

EDWARD SHORTER   CHARLES TILLY
Toronto, Ontario   *Ann Arbor, Michigan*

Abbreviations

APO	Ministère du commerce, Office du travail, *Les Associations professionnelles ouvrières*, 4 vols. Paris: Imprimerie nationale, 1894–1904.
CFDT	Confédération française démocratique du travail.
CFTC	Confédération française des travailleurs chrétiens.
CGC	Confédération générale des cadres.
CGT	Confédération générale du travail.
CGT-FO	Confédération générale du travail – force ouvrière.
CGTU	Confédération générale du travail unitaire.
ILO	International Labour Office.
INSEE	Institut national de la statistique et des études économiques.
PCF	Parti communiste français.
PTT	Ministère des postes et télécommunications.
RFT	Revue française du travail.
SFIO	Section française de l'internationale ouvrière.
SG	Ministère du commerce, Office du travail, *Statistique des grèves et des recours à la conciliation et l'arbitrage*, annually 1890–1935. Paris: Imprimerie nationale, 1892–1939.
SPD	Sozialdemokratische Partei Deutschlands.

1   The significance of industrial conflict

Two weeks after the July Revolution, the government's prosecutor in Douai wrote his superior in Paris:

> I hasten to inform you that on the night of 10–11 August, a riot of textile workers occurred in Roubaix; they wanted a raise in pay. There were many crowds in the streets. They broke the windows of the main shops, where they went in force to ask for written agreements about the raise.
>
> My deputy at the tribunal of Lille, informed of this untoward event in the middle of the morning of the 11th, went immediately to Roubaix, where they had made a great many arrests; in cooperation with the justice of the peace of Roubaix, he ordered the release of everyone who was being held except four who had been identified as the most guilty; them he had taken to Lille. The National Guard of Lille and the gendarmes went to Roubaix, where people feared that the crowds would gather again the evening of the 11th; but there is reason to believe that this show of force will hold back the rebels.
>
> I will let you know the result of the inquiry my deputy is now conducting as soon as he gives it to me. This riot, according to my deputy's report, does not appear to have any political overtones.[1]

Despite the revolution, most of the larger industrial conflicts of 1830 resembled the 'riot' of Roubaix: sometimes workers in one shop walked off the job for a while, and sometimes they tried to get work stoppages in other shops of the same industry; but the core of their action was a show of strength coupled with the presentation of collective demands concerning the conditions of employment in a particular set of shops. The law of the time forbade almost any sort of collective action by workers. The usual results were intervention by the local authorities, exemplary arrests, a few workers fired and the immediate return of the rest to their jobs. Meanwhile, the government watched the action nervously to make sure there was no connection between the workers and Republicans, Bonapartists, Legitimists or other subversives.

Almost 140 years later came the largest wave of strikes France has ever known: the strikes of May and June 1968. Events at the big Renault factory in Cléon, near Elbeuf, give the flavor of the action. Something less than half the workers there joined the one-day protest strike against the government which went on through much of France on 13 May, ten days after the struggles between students and police began in Paris. A one-hour walkout to support demands for reforms in social insurance laws had long been scheduled for 15 May, and did take place that morning. During the day, the news spread that the workers of Sud-Aviation, near Nantes, had occupied their factory and 'sequestered' some of the company's high officials. That afternoon

> At three o'clock a small group of workers . . . launched the action. Young people were again in the lead, sparking the movement. This time the strikers asked that the management receive delegates to discuss their demands.
>
> The management refused the first time.
>
> The movement continued, gaining strength. The people involved would no longer consider going back to work before representatives of the work-force had an interview with the management.
>
> Management still refused to talk.
>
> At the delegates' third request, the top management and some of the staff . . . barricaded themselves in their offices, latched their doors and shut themselves in with three plant guards. 'The management does not receive delegates under pressure.' News of the event spread through the factory. There were further marches through the shops to call out the remaining workers resisting the strike; all the workers joined the move-ment. From that point on it was irreversible. Since the management refused any dialogue and since its sole action was to lock itself into offices, the workers enthusiastically decided to occupy the factory. By six o'clock nothing was running in the shops any more.[2]

The strikers kept the plant manager and some other executives closed in for three days, and remained on strike over a month. When the strike ended on 17 June, the workers had won a wide variety of concessions over and above the national settlement – the Grenelle agreements – which issued from the conflicts of May and June.

The giant strikes of 1968 differed from most other industrial conflicts of the 1960s in more ways than size. Although sitdown strikes played an impor-tant part in the previous record strike wave of 1936, it was unusual for French strikers to take over their shops, offices and factories; that happened widely in 1968. What is more, over the country as a whole proposals for institutionalized power of workers over the operation of the workplace acquired great prominence. Young workers appear to have taken an excep-tionally large responsibility in the movement of 1968. These special features were obvious enough to start all sorts of observers talking about the new pattern of conflict emerging with 'post-industrial society.'

Yet some of the things which separate Cléon in 1968 from Roubaix in 1830 reflect long-run changes in the whole pattern of industrial conflict in France. In between 1830 and 1968, French workers mounted some 110,000 separate strikes. The great majority, however, occurred after 1900; the highest annual levels by far came after the Second World War. The high frequency and large scale of strikes in the 1960s, the way in which multiple labor unions were involved without being in complete control of the strike, the combination of national politics and local economic issues, the frequent use of the short strike of protest, sympathy or emphasis, the hovering presence of the government, the existence of standard routines for starting, conducting and ending strikes, the sheer legality of the basic forms of strike activity – all these features formed the characteristic pattern of French industrial conflict in the mid-twentieth century. The pattern was far different from the one which prevailed before France's deep industrialization began in the 1850s.

In this book, we describe that transformation and try to explain it. Our descriptions emphasize the broadest patterns, especially the ones which can be counted, tabulated and shown to occur over and over. We rarely stop to analyze individual strikes, however great their political impact or symbolic significance. Our explanations deal mainly with big, crude transformations of economic and political organization. We have little to say about doctrines, leaders, particular craft traditions or the day-to-day hopes, fears, frustrations and routines of specific groups of workers. Our book will not replace Georges Duveau's sensitive reconstructions of the orientations of major types of workers under the Second Republic and the Second Empire, or Georges Lefranc's skillful tracing of the doctrines, organizations and leadership of French labor since 1870, or Maurice Agulhon's masterly presentation of the organization of work in nineteenth-century Toulon. We hope it will complement those books, and others like them. It could do so by providing limits and setting frames for the fine patterns of industrial conflict.

We have not, however, prepared our book as background reading for other studies. We are attempting to single out the strike itself as a distinctive form of collective action, and to ask whether its variations in one industrializing country correspond to what we imagine we know about the transformation of all sorts of collective action under industrialization. For those purposes, it is much less important to portray any particular event, person, setting or idea precisely than to get the gross patterns right, and to pursue their alternative explanations seriously. That is what we have tried to do.

No doubt concerted work stoppages date back as far as organized work itself. But that form of work stoppage we call the strike only became a standardized and frequent form of collective action in western countries with the industrialization of the nineteenth and twentieth centuries. It is fascinating to watch the emergence of a relatively standard sequence of actions from the mixture of brawl, demonstration and walkout which preceded the strike we know today. It is instructive to compare the evolution of the strike with the development of the demonstration over the same period. In most western countries, both forms of collective action went from being illegal and subject to severe repression early in the nineteenth century to being tolerated, within limits set by the state, in our own time; both acquired standard ways of starting, stopping, articulating demands, laying claims to operating space and so on; both increasingly involved associations one of whose major specialities was the organization of precisely that form of collective action.

The strike clearly underwent a greater standardization than the demonstration: a literature, a set of bureaucracies, a jurisprudence and a population of specialists all devoted to the production, regulation and resolution of strikes came into being, while for the demonstration all these features remained fleeting and shadowy. In the case of the strike, employers, governments and workers' organizations actually collaborated in the production of common expectations and operating rules. Yet it was like presidential succession, boxing or courtship: the existence of well-defined rules did not keep the struggle from sometimes being deadly serious, painful, angry or violent.

In concentrating on the strike, we exclude a number of the other forms of conflict and of collective action (the two are by no means synonymous) in which French workers engaged over the course of industrialization. That is convenient, since the strike is one of the easier forms of action to identify, trace and describe. The other forms of conflict, protest and self-expression which one might plausibly use to get some sense of the changing orientations of workers include machine-breaking, sabotage, brawling, demonstrating, pamphlet-writing, perhaps turnover and absenteeism as well; all of them are much harder to pin down than strikes. The other forms of collective action workers have employed to accomplish common ends include the organization of political parties, mutual aid societies, conspiratorial groups, labor unions, insurance plans and many other cooperative ventures; these, too, resist the massive, systematic analysis we are attempting here.

We try to relate strike activity to other forms of conflict and collective action where we can. An important part of our effort, for example, goes into studying the impact of unionization on strikes in France. (Despite the fabled instability and ineffectiveness of French trade unions, that impact turns out to have been important.) By making these connections carefully and by conducting a thorough, skeptical review of the changing patterns of strike activity, we hope to help answer a very large question: how does industrialization transform the major forms of collective action men have at their disposal?

Industrialization and collective action

The answer we give to that question will depend, first of all, on the definitions of 'industrialization' and 'collective action.' By industrialization we mean simply the processes by which occurs a shift of production (a) away from agriculture toward manufactured goods and services, (b) away from house-holds, kin groups, communities or individual entrepreneurs, toward spe-cialized formal organizations. Any net movement of production in either of these directions counts as industrialization. By these criteria France was already a relatively industrial country in 1830. Close to half the French labor-force, for instance, was already working in manufacturing and services by that time.[3] The high proportion often comes as something of a surprise to French historians, accustomed to treating their country as a nation of peasants and noting in support of their view that in 1830 almost 80 percent of the population lived in rural communes (places with fewer than 2,000 people in the central settlement). The apparent contradiction is due to the fact that before the rapid urbanization of French industry began in the 1840s and 1850s, a great deal of manufacturing went on in the countryside, the work of small entrepreneurs and individual craftsmen. After that France as a whole industrialized, but the countryside deindustrialized. Both processes dragged on through the nineteenth century. Only by the end of the century (as we shall see in detail later on) was a substantial proportion of the French labor force in technologically advanced industries like engineering or steel-making.

The 'collective action' which interests us consists of the application of some population's pooled resources on behalf of that population's common objectives. The simple notion has a lot of trouble hidden in it. Many analysts of western political systems have assumed that it is natural and inevitable for groups of people who have common interests, are aware of each other and can communicate without great cost to act collectively on behalf of those interests. Mancur Olson has shown how dubious that assumption is; in fact, the collective interest and the individual interest frequently point in different directions; any particular individual will often do better for himself by assuming that everyone else will look out for the collective interest.[4]

Finding out exactly what population lies behind any collective action also turns out to be tricky: for how many American Blacks do the Black Panthers, the Black Muslims, the Black Caucus speak? It is usually hard, furthermore, to decide just what *are* a given population's common interests and objectives, not to mention whether the interests and objectives coincide; hence innu-merable arguments over the 'false consciousness' and 'true interests' of workers as a class.

We have no ready general solutions for these difficulties. Let us borrow a strategy from the ostrich; let us bury our heads at least part way in the sand, limit our attention to a small set of relatively unambiguous resources and refuse to ask too insistently why people should ever bother to pool those resources and apply them to common ends. Collective control of labor, land, capital, technique and organization interests us most. How does indus-trialization affect which populations wield such collective control, how they do it and to what effect? In particular, what about different groups of workers?

The available answers to these questions differ considerably depending on the time-scale we adopt. Long-run theories of industrialization frequently build some statements about the transformation of collective action into the very definition of their subject: the formation of factories, the growth of large formal organizations, the concentration of capital and so on. Beyond definitions, we have a plethora of theories of the long run: trend statements like those which have the importance of kin groups as vehicles of collective action declining over the course of industrialization, phase theories identifying, say, 'traditional,' 'transitional' and 'modern' forms of collective action and a great many others. In the medium run there are plenty of theories which associate the extent or character of collective action – the choice, for instance, among inactivity, rebellion or involvement in electoral politics – to the current pace of structural change, the current configuration of power or some other such feature of the social situation. When it comes to variation from day to day, month to month or year to year, we encounter another sort of theory in which cues like government edicts, price fluctuations, decisions by managers and harvest failures play a major part. The time span makes a considerable difference to the sort of theory and the kind of variable it makes sense to consider.

At each time-scale, however, we can find the same three broad classes of argument linking collective action to industrialization: breakdown arguments, deprivation arguments and interest arguments. Under the heading of *breakdown* come ideas of collective action (or, more likely, particular forms of collective action) as a consequence of the dissolution of existing social bonds and controls by industrialization. Thus Neil J. Smelser theorizes that industrialization proceeds via a master process of structural differentiation: differentiation introduces discontinuities into the lives of the people most directly affected; discontinuities produce strain, disorientation and *anomie*; people respond to those unpleasant conditions by producing or joining movements of protest.[5]

Within the category *deprivation* we find a variety of arguments starting from the miseries and constraints imposed by industrial organization and ending with some form of collective resistance to those miseries and constraints. Thus Clark Kerr proposes a natural history of 'labor commitment' in industrialization which includes this sequence:

> The form of protest also shifts from the individual's protest expressed through turnover and absenteeism, to the guerrilla warfare of the quickie strike or boycott over immediate dissatisfactions, to permanently organized economic or political action or both, and finally to the petty and covert sabotage of the trained bureaucrat whose chains can be rattled a bit but never lost. This is the normal life cycle of protest and it is closely related to the normal life cycle of the process of commitment.[6]

Kerr assumes that dissatisfactions are inevitable in industrial work, but that 'protest' in response to them gives way to more durable forms of collective action as industrialization goes on.

Interest arguments, unlike arguments from breakdown and deprivation, locate the source of a group's collective action in its relation to other groups and larger structures. One might imagine an isolated population acting together in response to breakdown or to deprivation, but interest articulation requires the existence of some sort of arena within which groups are contending. As applied to industrialization, these theories characteristically treat rearrangements of the structure of power and of communication as crucial, and have the new units which are created (or, for that matter, the old units which are threatened) by the rearrangements organizing around a collective perception of their interests.

Many origins have been proposed for the collective perception: diffusion of beliefs from elsewhere, gradual awakening to an objective reality, spontaneous or charismatic generation of new ideologies, invocation of ideas already belonging to the group's tradition but previously inactive, and so on. Thus E. P. Thompson offers two interdependent arguments concerning the collective action of English workers during the early nineteenth century: (1) those whose communities had not yet been dissolved by the expansion of the market insisted vigorously, in the face of threats to their social survival, on rights to land, work and bread due to them under the 'moral economy' which had prevailed in the eighteenth century; (2) true working-class consciousness, and action on the basis of that consciousness, grew from the very process of opposition to the demands and pressures placed on workers by the emerging class of capitalists.[7]

As Thompson's analysis should remind us, the arguments from breakdown, deprivation and interest are not mutually exclusive; they simply assume quite different weights in different theories. Nor are the boundaries among long-run, medium-run and short-run theories at all precise. Nevertheless, putting the two classifications together produces a useful matrix for sorting the ideas available to us for the task at hand:

	Short-run	Medium-run	Long-run
Deprivation	Kerr		
Breakdown		Smelser	
Interest			Thompson

By and large, the most plausible treatments of deprivation as a spur to collective action have been short- to medium-run; the most plausible breakdown arguments, medium-run; the most plausible interest theories, medium- to long-run.

Despite the neat opportunity this pattern offers us to save *all* available hypotheses, most of the arguments we lay out in this book will weigh against both breakdown and deprivation as promoters of collective action at any time-scale. We shall offer much argument, and some evidence, to the effect that breakdown of social bonds and controls tends to reduce rather than to increase the capacity of the affected population for collective action. We will concede somewhat more to deprivation, especially in the short run, but will generally insist that it only spurs collective action where organization of the deprived population is already extensive and its interests well articulated. On the whole, our line of arguments runs along the interest row of the matrix: short-run interest, medium-run interest, long-run interest as well.

Even after the exclusion of breakdown and deprivation, 'interest' covers quite a territory. We have economic interests, organizational interests and political interests all in mind. Let us save the details of the arguments for later; a silhouette will do here. In the long run, changes in the organization of production, including the effects of technical innovations on work routines and supervision, shape both (a) the features of the work situation which workers seek to improve, eliminate or control and (b) the opportunities and constraints affecting collective action on the part of workers and of managers. Prosperity, governmental toleration and the mobilization of their opponents all promote collective action by the one party and the other. Largely as a result of their own collective action (which never ceases, but still accelerates into critical bursts from time to time), organized groups of workers acquire places in the national structure of power.

The strike becomes the principal means by which those organized groups display their strength and exert pressure on the other chief participants in the power structure – both employers and the government. As a consequence of these multiple long-run changes, strikes become more frequent and larger in scale, their responsiveness to changes in the national political position of labor increases and acquiescence or even collaboration on the part of government officials plays a growing part in the outcome of strikes. Strikes are power struggles; organized workers use what power they have to economic advantage, of course; but strikes expand as workers organize and as their organizations acquire increasing stakes in the national structure of power.

If so, neither absolute nor relative deprivation is likely to heighten strike activity. Indeed, long deprivation should depress the propensity of workers to strike; *a fortiori*, long-run immiseration of workers should be antithetical to strike activity. At this time-scale, we emphatically reject explanations of strikes as responses to deprivation.

Our argument likewise forbids the appeal to 'breakdown' as the origin of the strike. To the extent that a given reorganization of production actually dissolves social bonds and controls personally affecting workers, our argument leads us to expect a decline in strikes because of the increasing cost of collective action among those workers. There is an interesting qualification: if we consider direct restraints on collective action such as legal penalties for organizing or striking to be the critical 'social controls,' then our argument does anticipate an increase in strike activity as controls dissolve. That is, however, a long way from the conception of strikes as a form of protest or disorder generated by the strains of extensive or rapid social change.

As the book proceeds, we will elaborate these broad arguments about the long run of strike activity in four ways: (1) by specifying their implications for particular durable features and long transformations of strike activity in France (such as the chief demands actually made by strikers), (2) by relating those specifications to the arguments and findings of other students of strike activity – both those we agree with and those we reject, (3) by laying out great slabs of data concerning the durable features and long transformations of French strike activity from 1830 to 1968, (4) by looking closely at the correspondence between the data and the specific implications of our arguments, reformulating or rejecting our reasoning where necessary. To be informative and fair, we will provide enough data so that a defender of one of the many arguments we reject will be able to try out his favorite formulations on our own materials.

For the most part, our arguments make little distinction between the medium and the short run. That is because neither our arguments nor our data offer much specification of the precise sequences of events by which strikes begin and end. Those sequences surely depend on the character of local leadership, the political coalitions currently prevailing among managers, labor leaders and government officials, the response of the government to the threat or actuality of industrial conflict and a number of other fast-shifting variables which only depend in part on such matters as current wage levels or the unionization of the labor force. Let us therefore sketch our ideas concerning the short and medium runs at the same time.

Economic, organizational and political interests operate at these time-scales as well, but not in quite the same fashion as over the long run. For one thing, organizational efforts take some time to pay off; at any particular point in time, the experience of the labor force with unions, mutual aid societies and the strike itself over a string of years will have a greater effect on its propensity to strike than will the amount of mobilization that has just occurred; this effect of prior organization will show up, among other places, in a tendency for surges of strike activity to come disproportionately from increased involvement on the part of the sectors of the labor force which were *already* involved, rather than from the drawing in of aggrieved but previously unorganized workers. Great crises will, indeed, draw new workers into the movement, but their involvement will weigh more heavily on the next crisis, not the current one.

In the short and medium run, we expect changes in the organization of production to have much weaker effects on the opportunities and constraints affecting collective action than in the long run. Over a long period of time, we reason, a shift like the subdivision of labor in processes previously handled by individual craftsmen will promote fundamentally new divisions, solidarities and communications within the affected industries, but the people involved will try for considerable periods to accomplish their ends with existing rights, laws and organizational forms. Organizational inertia and the time required for the development of new orientations and socialization of workers to them will slow the impact of changes in production on strike activity.

We expect, on the other hand, that the relative movement of prices, wages, profits and other outcomes of economic activity which are fairly visible to workers, managers and government officials will have a larger impact on strike activity in the short and medium runs than in the long run. They will supply cues to each of the parties, affecting their estimates of the probable outcomes of striking, resisting and so on. Nevertheless, our basic expectation for the short run corresponds to that for the long run: that prosperity will favor strikes and economic hardship will hinder them. (We will eventually make two concessions to deprivation arguments on this point: first, noting that a threat to the survival of a well organized segment of the labor force tends to incite a wide variety of defensive actions, including strikes; second, reviving the notion that a short-run economic downturn in the midst of prosperity promotes strike activity.)

Finally – and least conventionally – we expect changes in the national political position of organized labor to cause strikes to increase. What is more, we expect the political dimension of the strike to expand over time, as the labor movement nationalizes. Here we part most definitively from breakdown and deprivation accounts of strike activity. Strikes have an important role in the struggle for power. We go beyond the vast majority of interest accounts as well, since they treat strikes as relatively direct expressions of changing economic interests. In our account, economic interests only find their expression in strike activity in so far as they are mediated and supported by organization for collective action. The existence of that organization, moreover, involves workers in the struggle for political power, and makes the strike available as a political weapon. How widely it is used for that purpose will vary from time to time and country to country, depending on the nature of the accommodation the leaders of organized labor have made with other wielders of power. But once labor has organized on a national scale, we expect the capacity to strike to be its most important weapon in the struggle for power.

We will refine all these arguments about the medium and short run as the book moves on. Later chapters will attach them to groups, times, places and events. We will also make a zealous effort to bring in the previous authors who have made the most powerful relevant arguments on these matters. As compared with the evidence concerning the long run, the appropriate evidence on these matters will more often take the form of time-series analyses, comparisons of specific bursts of strikes and studies of particular industries or regions. But again we will try to make the evidence sufficiently abundant to permit a skeptical reader to cross-check our conclusions.

Major changes in the organization of production

The evolution of industrial technology provides a way of periodizing the history of strikes into major blocks; several important shifts in the character of strike activity (as Chapter 3 will show) coincide neatly with changes in the technology and organization of industry. One could isolate such other components of industrialization as the degree of industrial concentration, the intensity of the economic exploitation of the worker or the level of wages as variables strategic in shaping the nature of conflict. For the set of arguments we have just laid out, however, it is crucial to have two broad chronologies in place: (a) the major phases in the organization of production, (b) changes in the organization and national political position of labor. The second will occupy an important part of our next chapter, not to mention two subsequent chapters on unionization and its impact. The first we sketch here, and fill in later.

Industrial sociologist Alain Touraine sees the major change in industrial technology over the last century and a half as the passage from a 'professional' system of work to a 'technical' one. In Touraine's view the crucial questions are whether a system of production possesses 'unity' – whether the individual worker understands his task as a comprehensible part of a greater whole, whether the worker derives some feeling of creativity and responsibility from his particular task. Both professional and technical systems provide this unity; the problems come in the transitional phase. Touraine gives all this a nice concreteness in his typing of the evolution of industrial technology into the famous phases A, B and C.[8] Here we label them:

A: artisanal phase
B: mass-production phase
C: science-sector phase

In 1830, the artisanal organization of production prevailed, and only a glimmer of the assembly line had appeared. By 1968, artisans were mainly a memory, and the science sector was achieving great importance both in the organization of production and in the character of industrial conflict.

Touraine refuses to assign exact dates to his phases, preferring to think of them more as types of production than exact historical periods. For convenience, we might place the artisanal phase in the years between 1800 and

1880. The initial steps in industrial growth replaced the decrepit guild system with the concentration of production in small factories. In the early mills (except for textiles) worked artisans whose productive techniques, social arrangements and awareness of historical tradition were pretty much the same as those of former guild craftsmen, except that these skilled factory hands did not own the means of production. Rather they were in the employ of some provincial family firm. In the early factories these transplanted artisans processed the raw materials directly through their own skill and labor, or with the aid of some uncomplicated machines which demanded considerable judgment and initiative on the part of the operator. This is, in Touraine's terms, a 'professional' system of work.

Social relationships within such small factories are normally close, partly because the very smallness of scale permits a frequency and intimacy of intercourse lacking in large establishments. This means that informal networks of friendship and communication will tightly enmesh the workers, setting up little hierarchies of control and organization, with leadership going to the most senior or the most skilled workers. But the workers are also closely knit because formal networks, whose membership coincides closely with that of the informal ones, command the employees' allegiance with a constancy reminiscent of the guild system. In a moment we will suggest the characteristics these organizations take on.

The artisanal phase does not create the mythical 'happy worker.' Not that the factory artisan is necessarily unhappier than any other kind of worker. We believe that such emotional qualities as worker 'happiness' or 'contentment,' if in fact they vary over the years or from one kind of technology to another, are of little importance in explaining conflict. What counts is people's desire and ability to act collectively. This ability is already substantial in the small cohesive plants of the artisanal phase; the desire is enhanced by the specific kind of discontent early factories generate within their skilled workforce. Skilled artisans in this phase are mainly upset that the master-entrepreneur profits by the capitalist system from his exploitation of their labor and creativity. His ownership of the means of production spotlights the glaring permanence of the journeyman's inferior status, which stands in violation to the theoretical premises of the guild system from whose ruins most skilled labor in the artisanal phase emerges. Formerly differences between masters and journeymen were largely generational (or at least that was how it was supposed to be); in early factories the journeyman's inferiority is enshrined in the structure of the class system.

Early industrial glassmaking firms exemplify the artisanal phase. The master glass blowers adhere to a self-conscious artisanal tradition dating far back in time, and consider themselves master craftsmen; the shop has a rigid hierarchy based on professional qualification and training; mechanization is minimal, and the work demands a maximum of skill from the workers. The shop is well organized in terms of both formal unions and informal solidarity.[9]

Coalmining is an artisanal heavy industry, different from glass blowing mainly in the absence of a formal apprenticeship. The technology of mining, at least before the advent of the automatic cutter–ripper machines, places the worker in direct contact with his raw materials, evoking from him great skill and effort if the coal is to be smoothly manipulated from seam face to conveyor buckets. So miners take pride in their professional traditions, and the web of organization within the pits, both friendship groups and regular unions, gives them a powerful capacity for collective enterprise. Without institutional apprenticeship programs, which serve other artisanal phase occupations well as valves for the regulation of labor competition, the miners are more at the mercies of economic fluctuations, liable to lay-offs and pay slashes. Yet in other key respects they are identical.

In summary, then, the artisanal phase means a particular constellation of worker organization at the shop level and of social and professional discontent formed by an artisanal factory technology in which the 'unity' of production prevails: the worker has immediate contact with and control over his materials.

The thoroughgoing industrialization of the late nineteenth century, and especially the changes in production technology introduced during the First World War, caused a radically different form of production, the 'mass-production phase,' to overshadow the artisanal. The epitome of phase B technology is the conveyor belt, tended by anonymous ranks of semi-skilled workers ('O.S.s' in the parlance of French industrial sociology: *ouvriers specialisés*) who pass their days in endless routinized, repetitive movement. Imaginative, skillful contact with production gives way to the mindless performance of some narrowly standardized task. The efficiency which large industrial concerns demand forces the parcelization of work, the subdivision of production into a number of discrete, specialized steps which can be performed by machines.

Training for such machine-tending may be acquired on the job, obviating the need for regular apprenticeship or for the maintenance of professional traditions of competence and artistry. And the technology of production means the individual workers are isolated one from another at their separate posts, rather than working collectively at some productive task. Hence even though the plant is gigantic, commensurate with the expanded scale of enterprise which the costly new technology requires, the worker within it is essentially alone. The high degree of specialization means the job itself becomes meaningless, a random point on a seemingly endless line having neither beginning nor ending. The worker's needs for imaginative participation in his work and for seeing things as a whole are lost; and the unity of production is shattered, with important organizational consequences.

In the new mass-production plant formal organizations do indeed exist, as we shall see when we examine interwar labor unions in detail later on. But they are divorced from informal networks of communication and control. Contrary to what Marx predicted, the spirit of solidarity is reduced in these plants, and with it the capacity for effective collective action. Worker grievances center more on the inequitable distribution of wealth within society as a whole, that is from one social class to another, than on the unfairness of the particular employer's exploitation of skilled labor to make a profit. Early in the mass-production phase the loss of job control which new forms of industrial organization entail elicits an outburst of concern over shop issues. However, the ineluctable demands of technology soon smother this protest and the classic semi-skilled proletarian becomes resigned to the dehumanization of the industrial environment.

A paradigm of assembly-line industry is the great Renault plant in Boulogne-Billancourt which Touraine studied, just as in North America the automobile assembly line represents the extreme case of assembly-line production. Textiles are the classic mass-production industry, for since their very inception spinning and weaving mills have employed unskilled workers as interchangeable parts standing before whirring spindles and looms. In general, mass-production technology became important in French manufacturing during the 1880s, drawing scads of migrating peasants to the worker suburbs of the great industrial cities. Management's enthusiasm for Taylorism around 1910, combined with the productive exigencies of the First World War, gave assembly-line industrial organization a considerable boost. The spirit of specialization and mechanization dominated the industrial environment in the interwar years.[10]

A new stage in industrial technology whose hallmark is automation has commenced since the Second World War. Touraine identifies it as phase C, and sees as its salient characteristic a restoration of the former unity of production through technical progress. We call it the 'science-sector' phase. What this means is that the worker in an automated plant has a very different attitude towards his work than a worker in a mechanized plant. The supervisor of automated equipment enjoys the same overview of the productive process from start to finish the artisanal worker once had. And the job of operating self-regulating machinery calls for a vastly higher degree of responsibility and participation in the productive process than does assembly-line work. The science-sector worker himself is no longer the untrained proletarian of the automobile assembly plant but an employee of whom substantial formal education is required and who receives an intensive on-the-job training.

The quality and cohesiveness of organization in science-sector establishments is reminiscent of the small, artisanal shops of the artisanal phase. Yet the *basis* of organization is quite different, which is what Touraine had in mind when he talked about the passage from professional to technical systems of work. The old consciousness of membership in craft communities, of course, is lacking in the science-sector phase because, except for repairmen and mechanics, no handwork competence or preparation is necessary for employment: the principal job qualifications are good education, intelligence and a capacity for responsibility. The nature of the work itself, however, gives the employees a sense of *integration into the plant*: they see their own functions as vital in the success of some larger whole; they are given some power and responsibility and have scope for the exercise of initiative and creativity, and they are bound to the firm through liberal personnel policies, such as high wages and generous pensions and fringe benefits. All these ties uniting them to the company and to their fellow workers evoke a state of mind roughly similar to that of the early factory craftsmen. In Chapter 7 we examine in detail the consequences of this reintegration into the enterprise for formal worker organization.

The best examples of science-sector technology are the so-called con-tinuous-processing industries, which convert a raw material into a finished product in one smooth flow of production, from ingestion into the plant to packaging of a marketable commodity in cardboard boxes. Most chemical plants function in this manner, requiring almost no semi-skilled workers to perform standard, repetitive tasks but instead a labor force able to man-ipulate complex dials and levers and to take responsibility for intricate, expensive flows of material from one stage to another. The gas and electric industries operate on a comparable principle.

Let us not overdo the determinism of technology. In the science-sector phase some fundamental changes in the structure of industry take place quite independently of shop-floor organization. There is, to start with, a growth in the scale of enterprise, as partly for technological reasons, partly for other considerations, the percentage of the workforce concentrated in great industrial establishments far exceeds interwar levels. As a result, authority in industry begins to shift from the single employer, supervising the shop floor from his little office high above, to the paid executives of bureaucratized modern management. And the pressure points of industrial relations become more centralized than ever before. Secondly, the services sector encompasses an increasing share of the labor force, growing along centralistic, bureaucratic lines, and thus augmenting the concentration of industrial authority. Finally, a great share of France's industrial plant has become nationalized since the war: railroads, coalmines, electricity, gas, transport and important manufacturing plants in the automobile and air-craft industries. Parts of the tertiary sector, including some of the banks and insurance companies, have been nationalized as well. The government therefore becomes a direct participant in industrial disputes. As the nature and concentration of control in the economy change, the style and thrust of working-class collective action change as well.

Changing forms of labor organization and industrial conflict

A certain style of labor organization accompanies each of these phases of technological change. The typical worker organization of the artisanal phase is the craft union. Consciousness of membership in occupational communities which have long historical traditions, which must regularize the transmittal of skills and which aim to choke off the influx of super-numerary apprentices, moves early skilled factory workers to band together formally in such cooperative, non-combative associations as mutual aid societies. (As we shall see in the following chapter, trade unions in the proper sense were illegal before 1884.) The informal solidarity of workers is also strong, nourished by a constant cross-flow of people in a given occupation throughout France. Virtually no organizations for the non-craft laborer or unskilled factory worker exist in the artisanal phase; the informal ties binding unskilled workers to one another also appear tenuous.

In the mass-production phase the characteristic form of organization is the industrial union, significantly different from the narrowly craft-based occupational union. In contrast to the decentralized, casually constituted craft unions, industrial unions are heavily bureaucratized at the top, with a powerful central seat in Paris. Yet at the base they are weakly organized with membership subject to wild fluctuations and locals whose existence is ephemeral, again in contradistinction to craft unions. For reasons we shall later explore, such unions attempt to secure advantages for the working classes more through political action than through collective bargaining.

Some writers attribute a special propensity for political action to the mass-production phase. That is, in our view, only half right. At all periods in the course of industrialization the worker movement has been political, organizing for the explicit sake of obtaining advantages for the working classes through access to the polity. Yet the form and intensity of this action change from one era to another. In the mass-production phase unions use revolutionary rhetoric to mobilize support for an assault on the central strongholds of political power. In the artisanal and science-sector phases strategy is different.

During the science-sector phase the worker movement undergoes a great split in the pattern and objectives of union organization. Pace-setting new confederations such as the CFTC (which became after 1964 the CFDT) represent a harkening back to the artisanal phase, for they play down extreme centralization and ponderous bureaucratic superstructures in favor of active plant-level organizations. Indeed a major development in unionism since the war has been the spread of locals among individual industrial establishments, a process tied in with the new integration of the worker into the firm. In politics the progressive unionism of the science-sector phase is more concerned with expanding worker power downwards from the central base in Paris to the area of job control in single establishments than with endless demands for wage hikes. All this happens among workers involved in the new 'unified' technology.

The production-line segment continues to dominate manufacturing in science-sector industry, yet such plants in France have changed since the war through a centralization of ownership and an increase in size. The workers in this sector remain in top-heavy industrial federations of the assembly-line phase model, loosely affiliated with frail local organization. For these workers and unions, the only difference the postwar period has made is a new emphasis on political action at the center, a consequence of the government's enormous leverage in labor relations and of the imperviousness of the private corporate sector to the normal sticks and carrots of collective bargaining.

The configurations of industrial technology, shop-floor social relations, and working-class institutions one finds for each of these phases produce substantially different styles of strike activity. Much of the effort in later chapters of this book will go into documenting and distinguishing those styles. Still it may be helpful to give preliminary illustrations of each of them.

–The strike of Marseille tailors in September of 1843 is typical of the artisanal phase. Organized in a 'philanthropic society,' the tailors throughout the city demanded wage increases. A notice they had published in *Le Peuple Souverain* gives some insight into their orientations: 'Their labor and energy safeguard them no future but the poorhouse, while they enrich their masters with at least 6,000 francs of income acquired without effort and without risk.' In the course of the strike the tailors subjected non-strikers to some 'pressures.' Troops were summoned, apparently to replace the striking tailors in several establishments.[11] The commonplace features of the dispute are clear: the workers in a skilled occupation upset about exploitation, a formal organization providing coordination among the individual shops and government intervention to suppress the dispute.

–Characteristic of prewar mass-production phase strikes is a dispute at the Cochet shoe factory in Fougères from 7 to 24 July 1903. A worker, who happened to be the president of the cutters' union, was fired for 'improper work.' The union of shoemakers, which together with the cutters' union constituted the Federal Union of Shoe Workers of Fougères, decided upon a solidarity strike, and all 505 workers in the Cochet factory walked off their jobs.

Now the negotiating began. The strikers asked the justice of the peace to convoke a meeting of a conciliation committee, and on 17 July worker delegates and employer's representative convened. The workers insisted the employee be rehired, the delegate of the owner argued he had made too many mistakes in the past. After this meeting and another like it had proved fruitless, the employers' union threatened to lock out all the workers in the city unless the Cochet strike was ended. Thereupon the subprefect intervened, again with no result. On 22 July the two opposing unions met at the labor exchange and succeeded in settling the strike in principle. On the following day the parties again convened at the justice of the peace's office and worked out the details. The fired worker was not rehired but the Cochet employees could select someone to take his place. The employer promised to treat the cutters 'with greater consideration' and to fire no one without good cause.[12]

This strike is characteristic of mass-production disputes in several ways. For one thing, semi-skilled industrial workers are involved, shoe cutters and stitchers who maintain only vestiges of the old artisanal traditions in an industry in the throes of technological change. (Strikes over the introduction of new machinery were frequent in Fougères throughout the twenty years or so preceding the First World War.) For another, we are dealing with an industrial union, not a craft organization, which brings together all the different shoe specialties in the city. The union has a strike fund (not so typical of these years), and is able to pay benefits to its members. Of additional interest is the effective employer organization. Further typical of the mass-production phase in these years is the grievance occasioning the walkout: unjust dismissal of a worker. The strike clearly emerged from a matrix of tension over authority on the shop floor; treating the workers with respect, letting them decide on the fired worker's replacement and the like. Finally, the extensive government participation in the strike is worthy of note. The role of the justice of the peace is prescribed by the collective bargaining law, and the sub-prefect enters the dispute seemingly as a matter of course. It was not, after all, a serious strike, yet two different officials attempted to help settle it. Subsequent mass-production strikes would differ from this example mainly in their obsession with wage issues to the exclusion of shop-floor complaints.

– A four-hour nationwide walkout in the public electricity and gas sectors on 20 March 1963 illustrates a science-sector strike. The conflict occurred in the midst of a strike wave dominated by the collieries, but which had been gathering support from numerous other industries. Sponsored jointly by three different labor federations, the strike's purpose was to force the government to recognize officially that wages in the electric and gas utilities were lagging. Discussions were to ensue.[13]

The extreme brevity, the enormous compass, the deft central direction of the dispute and the immediate pressure on the highest echelons of government it brought to bear, epitomize the postwar strike movement. They display the growing influence of science-sector industries on the whole pattern of industrial conflict in France. They represent a sharp break with the forms of the artisanal strike, by now a faded memory. They differ from those of the mass-production strike as well.

These three cases are, of course, only illustrations. It remains to see how close is the correspondence among forms of industrial conflict, forms of labor organization, and forms of production. It also remains to trace out the causal relations among them. Those are the essential tasks before us.

Making sense of the changes

We stand at the crossing of two roads. One of them leads toward an understanding of the ways in which industrialization transforms collective action, especially the collective action of workers. We have laid out some preliminary notions of those processes already, and will develop them as the book moves on. The second road heads toward a comprehensive explanation of changes in industrial conflict in France. We have suggested how we plan to travel that road, but the real journey has still to begin. Eventually the two roads lead in different directions, as good roads should; in order to produce solid or even interesting conclusions concerning the impact of industrialization on collective action, one would have to consider many places, times and activities beyond modern industrial conflict in France; in order to explain all the peculiarities of French industrial conflict, one would have to examine a number of factors only distantly related to industrialization. Fortunately, the two roads run together for quite a space. We plan most of our traveling for that common ground.

Our effort to remain in that common ground explains some special features of this book. We have not constructed a continuous narrative history of the French labor movement, or even of French strikes. We have not assembled extensive case studies of particular industries, localities, periods or types of conflict. We have relied little or not at all on memoirs, interviews, surveys, newspaper accounts, court proceedings, correspondence or even the police reports with which French archives abound.

We have instead poured our energy into making as complete an enumeration as possible of the 100,000-odd strikes which occurred in France from 1830 to 1968, putting together uniform descriptions of their characteristics, likewise assembling as standard a body of information as possible concerning the settings and periods in which they occurred, translating the sorts of questions this chapter has raised into systematic comparisons and statistical analyses and interpreting the results of the analyses. (Appendix A describes our principal sources and methods.) The book swarms with tables, maps, graphs and equations. It contains enough supporting evidence, enough negative findings, enough sheerly descriptive material to make it possible to do three important things: (1) verify the arguments and interpretations of findings we offer; (2) try out alternative arguments; (3) make meaningful comparisons with times, places and forms of action not dealt with in our own analysis. We hope our readers will put the book to all three uses.

The chapters which follow center on analytic problems, not on periods, regions or industries. We begin by introducing the actors – employers, workers and state officials – and the changing rules within which they acted (Chapter 2). The following section of the book (Chapters 3 to 5) takes up changes in strike activity over time: the general transformation of the strike

from the 1830s to the 1960s, the nature of year-to-year variation in strikes
and the character of strike waves. Chapters 6 and 7 move on to labor organization and its impact; first how unionization occurred in France, then the
impact of unions on the character and extent of strike activity. The next
chapter (8) takes a close look at the links between industrialization and
shifts in industrial conflict, as they show up in particular sectors of the labor
force, some individual occupations and establishments of different sizes.
A trio of chapters (9 through 11) then goes at the explanation of geographic
variation in strike activity: regional differences, differences among communes and their interaction with the distributions of industry and of unionization. Chapter 12 compares the broad patterns of French industrial conflict
with those of a number of other countries for which comparable documentation exists. And Chapter 13 lays out our conclusions from the entire analysis.

2　The parties and the rules

We must bear in mind that in France an industrial dispute customarily involves three parties, for in addition to labor and management, the state also participates because of its eager interest in conflict of all sorts. The purpose of this chapter is to introduce these three parties by rapidly sketching the objectives each tried to accomplish and the anxieties each tried to allay in industrial conflict. We shall also briefly review the legal restrictions on the parties' freedom of action, and the legislative institutions designed to bring them together.

The rules

First, the rules of the game must be established, both the rules governing how management and labor were permitted to organize themselves, and the rules of negotiation in collective bargaining. Their history is such a familiar one that we need do little more than remind the reader of its highpoints.

During the first two-thirds of the nineteenth century unions and strikes were illegal. The Le Chapelier law of 1791 had forbidden workers to meet together, 'to appoint a president, secretaries or syndics, to keep records, to make decisions or deliberate, or to regulate their purported common interests.' Nor were there to be strikes or work stoppages. The workers might not 'make among themselves agreements for the concerted refusal of work, or for supplying at a fixed price the efforts of their industry or labor . . .' Employers' organizations were forbidden as well. The purpose of this rigor was, as article 1 of the law explained, to preserve revolutionary accomplishments: 'The destruction of all kinds of corporations of citizens of the same estate and occupation is one of the fundamental bases of the French Constitution; it is forbidden to reestablish them in fact, under whatever pretext or form.'[1]

But subsequent legislation made clear that these anti-union provisions were more an attempt to stifle a class movement than a manifestation of revolutionary vigilance. For employers' organizations were treated much less harshly than workers'. The law of 12–22 April 1803 stipulated that only those associations of employers aiming to 'compel unjustly and abusively the reduction of wages' were to be suppressed, whereas all worker combinations were outlawed; the penalties against employer associations were not to exceed a month in prison, those against worker organizations not to exceed three months. These differentials in harshness were then enshrined in the penal code of 1810, which stipulated six days to a month in prison for members of employers' coalitions, one to three months for worker members. Worker leaders were to be jailed for two to five years. The code further forbade all associations of more than twenty members, save by express consent of the authorities. This made it difficult to establish any kind of working-class organization, not just *syndicats ouvriers* aiming at strike activity. A law of 10 April 1834 completed the edifice of repressive legislation by further sharpening some of the penal code's anti-assembly and anti-association provisions.[2]

Thus the 1791 Le Chapelier Law and the 1810 penal code were linchpins in a train of legislation which in theory made it impossible for workers to act collectively against their employers: they could not meet in large numbers in public places except by official permission; they could not under any circumstances found organizations whose purpose it was to launch concerted action against employers; and only with the express consent of the authorities could they mount formal organizations of any kind, even of the most innocuous mutualist nature. We shall see in Chapter 6 that despite these forbidding laws the working classes managed to carry on a rich organizational life between 1830 and 1884, mainly through mutual aid societies and producers' associations. Yet the state could intervene and repress with this legislation virtually any worker group it feared was getting out of hand.

Then things turned around. Between 1864 and 1884 the working classes secured the two rights necessary to their freedom of action in industrial conflict: the rights to unionize and to strike. The law of 25–7 May 1864 modified articles 414 and 415 of the penal code, making strikes legal by deleting the general prohibition of 'toute coalition de la part des ouvriers pour faire cesser en même temps de travailler . . .' From now on, as long as 'violent' or 'fraudulent' interference with the 'free exercise of industry or labor' was not attempted, work stoppages would be legal. Having a 'concerted plan' behind the walkout – which meant a union – continued however to be illegal.[3]

Two further breaches came in 1868. One was the law of 6–10 June permitting public meetings without the preliminary authorization of the authorities. (A notification of the meeting had to be filed; meetings on political or religious matters were not included in this liberalization.) And late in March the Emperor decreed that as a matter of equity worker organizations be tolerated in the same way that those for employers had been for some time. This 1868 edict of toleration meant that the state would not dissolve *syndicats ouvriers*, and would cease arresting and fining their members, as long as the unions submitted their statutes for official approval, gave the authorities copies of their minutes, and permitted 'un agent de police' to attend their meetings.[4]

In 1884 all unions were legalized. The modern legal framework of union organization was laid out in the law of 21 March, called occasionally the Waldeck-Rousseau law after the minister who sponsored it. The key article said: 'Occupational unions, appropriately constituted on the basis of the prescriptions of the present law, may establish themselves freely for the consideration and protection of their economic, industrial, commercial and agricultural interests.' To come into existence, a local union had merely to give to the proper authorities a copy of its statutes and a list of its officers. The union would then have a civil personality, which meant it could own property. The only meaningful restrictions in the law were directed at federations of unions: they were denied a judicial personality and the ability to own property. Articles 414–15 of the penal code still protected free access to work, and so reduced the efficacy of picket lines, but otherwise legal sanctions against the right to strike and organize had been completely dismantled.[5] The legal basis of worker organization laid out in the 1884 law did not change in any substantial way until 1946, save for the short-lived experiments of the Popular Front.

A delphic clause in the preamble to the Constitution of 1946 stating 'the right to strike may be exercised within the limitations of the laws which regulate it' was taken by the courts to mean that dismissing strikers from their jobs was illegal. And in 1950 a law stated explicitly that striking workers might be fired only for committing 'serious abuses' (*fautes lourdes*), interpreted in the courts to mean principally political strikes and slowdowns.[6] This law completed the strikers' legal protection.

The right of public servants to unionize and strike floated in a twilight zone from 1884 to 1950, determined by administrative decree rather than by law. (Workers in state industries, such as tobacco and ammunition factories, were thought to come under the provisions of the 1884 law just as did workers in private industry.) Until 1894 the government insisted that state employees had not been given the freedom to organize against 'the nation itself' that private workers had against private employers. Then in 1894, upon a request from the Chamber of Deputies to let workers in the public sector organize themselves, the government agreed to tolerate unions in the post office (PTT).[7] Other functionaries then seized upon the 1901 law on associations as a legal basis of their organization. From this time on the government authorized public service unions as long as they did not arrogate the title 'syndicat ouvrier' with accompanying pretension to Bourse du travail membership, and as long as they did not strike. Administrative decrees forbade strikes in the public services. Though punishment and repression were not uniform, the two chief sanctions applied to striking public service workers were dismissal and mobilization into the army. (The justification for mobilization was that such strikes threatened the national security.) The right of public employees to organize like the private sector was finally secured with the 'Statut général de la fonction publique' of 19 October 1946, and the right to strike was guaranteed in the Dehaene decree of 7 July 1950, on the basis of the preamble to the Constitution.[8]

The point of this recital of legislation is that after 1884 there were no important legal limitations on the workers' freedom of action in either industrial conflict or political contest. Even though the 1884 law had emphasized that the union be of 'occupational' nature, it did not bar political activity. Nor did it rule out such worker tactics of conflict as blacklisting or the slowdown. Whatever weaknesses afflicted the worker movement were thus a consequence of factors other than legal inhibitions.

Laws on collective bargaining constitute the other part of the legal matrix in which strikes were situated. All modern states try to fix the rules of the game by, at a minimum, specifying tactics which are not permitted and by facilitating the coming together of the parties for negotiation. The French state has fixed fewer rules and limits than most western countries, and compared to the United States, for example, the only real law in French labor relations appears to be the law of the jungle; yet some knowledge of the mediation procedures made available by the state through law is important because these procedures determine the initial steps the three parties in industrial conflict might take towards one another.

Before 1892 no legal procedures were available for aiding negotiations between employers and strikers. Unless the government chose for reasons of state to intervene in a dispute, the parties would make their own peace as any two private citizens settle a quarrel between themselves.[9]

Believing that formal mediation would reduce the frequency, acerbity and duration of strikes, the Chamber passed in 1892 a 'Loi sur la conciliation et l'arbitrage en matière de différends collectifs entre patrons et ouvriers ou employés.'[10] Because frequent use was made of this law, it is worth pausing for a moment to review its provisions. The justice of the peace (*juge de paix*), a cantonal official, was to be the basic mediator. Workers and employers could ask him to head a committee of conciliation to negotiate any collective disagreement, which meant in the main a strike. (Disputes between individual workers and their employers were to go before the local *conseil de prud'hommes*.) After a strike had broken out, three different procedures could bring into action the good offices of the justice of the peace: (1) the workers could ask him to mediate; (2) the employer could do the same; (3) the j.p. could voluntarily offer his services as a mediator. His assignment was to get both workers and employers together at the same table (*comité de conciliation*), and so after receiving a request for conciliation from one party, the j.p. would ask the other party if it wanted to be conciliated. If both parties were agreeable, each could name up to five members of the conciliation committee, which the j.p. would chair. The committee would meet in a locale 'warmed and lighted at the cost of the commune';

the j.p. would head the meetings and keep the protocols, writing up and witnessing the final agreement.

If no agreement emerged from the conciliation committee, the 1892 law foresaw an arbitration committee. If the parties wanted arbitration each would name several arbiters, or agree upon a common arbiter, to whom the disagreement would then be submitted. If the arbitration committee itself could not reach agreement, it would either appoint a new third arbiter, or ask the president of the local civil tribunal to appoint one. This third echelon of mediation would then presumably reach some Solomonic judgment, which the parties were free to accept or reject as they chose, just as they could ignore decisions of the mediation panel. This elaborate machinery was merely to bring people who otherwise might not talk to each other together for discussion; no decision reached at any stage was binding upon anybody. In a moment, by seeing what vicissitudes the law met, we shall discover how day-to-day industrial relations in France actually worked, and the balance of forces which normally prevailed.

What turned out to be a minor alteration in the legal matrix of collective bargaining came in the law of 25 March 1919 on *conventions collectives*. The law gave to collective agreements between organized labor and management the status of civil contracts, binding on the parties and enforceable in the courts. But both workers and employers had good reasons for avoiding committing themselves in such agreements, and little use was made of the *convention collective*.[11]

The regime of the 1892 law therefore continued undisturbed until the radical but short-lived experiment with compulsory arbitration in 1936. This new law came at the behest of the CGT itself, for once the working classes had begun to entrench themselves in political power they could easily dispense with the traditional strike. The law of 31 December 1936 seriously curtailed the right to strike by making arbitral sentences binding, by stipulating that there be no strikes against the collective agreements imposed by the arbiters and by providing for substantial penalties against employers and worker leaders who violated the terms of the agreement (stiffened in a decree-law of 12 November 1938). The law also provided that collective agreements reached in a single strike could be extended under certain conditions to cover an entire industry. Compulsory conciliation and binding arbitration were applied to many of the conflicts of the 1936–9 period, and Hélène Sinay pronounces the effects of the law 'extremely positive, indicating the confidence placed in it by the working classes . . .' (p. 437). The war swept the entire edifice away.

Postwar legislation changed patterns of collective bargaining mainly by accelerating the state's involvement in labor relations. The first law came on 23 December 1946, giving the state the power to convoke national mixed commissions for the sake of drawing up nationwide agreements covering an entire industry. No collective agreement was to be valid without the

consent of the Labor Ministry. A High Commission on Collective Agreements was to be created to specify where ministerial intervention was
necessary and to facilitate the formulation of such agreements. Georges
Lefranc concludes of this legislation that 'state control [*étatisme*] was thriv-
ing.'[12]

The 'liberation' of wages from government controls in 1949 required a
revision of collective agreement legislation. The law of 11 February 1950,
which set the terms of collective bargaining for the 1950s and 60s, had as
its most interesting feature the extension within a given industry of collective agreements reached at the national or regional level of the industry.
If the most representative employers' and workers' organizations of an
industry reached a collective agreement, the Labor Ministry could make
the adoption of the terms of that agreement obligatory for all the enterprises within the territory those organizations covered. The Labor Ministry
could also convoke on its own initiative employers' and workers' organizations to form a mixed commission for the sake of elaborating such a collective agreement.[13]

The 1950 law also provided for 'compulsory' conciliation and for 'ad-
visory' arbitration, but these concepts meant in practice little departure
from the conciliation procedures of the 1892 law. Although all disputes
were to be submitted to conciliation, the parties were under no obligation
to reach an agreement, to accept the judgments of the conciliation committee or to accept arbitral sentences. Indeed the only compulsory feature
in the entire process was that within a month of the strike's outbreak the
parties had to seek conciliation. The parties were first to ask the departmental prefect to mediate, then to form a regular conciliation committee,
headed by a state official within the Labor Ministry hierarchy. Whereas in
the old justice of the peace system judicial officials mediated industrial
conflict, now that responsibility went to state administrative officials.[14]

The upshot of these legislative changes was a heightening of the echelon
at which bargaining would take place and an increase in the state's involvement. The assumption of the 1892 conciliation law, made explicit by the
1919 *convention collective* law, was that bargaining would occur between
local unions and individual employers or employers' organizations. The
state would enter the process only by offering its good offices via the justice
of the peace. The postwar legislation changed things by assuming that
bargaining would take place among 'multiple syndical organizations' of both
workers and employers (a consequence of the fragmentation of the worker
movement) sitting at the regional or national levels, though local agreements
were not ruled out. The law further assumed that ministerial officials and
national commissions and councils (such as the High Commission on
Collective Agreements) rather than the humble j.p. would bring the parties
together, and that the government would extend agreements to cover all
the establishments in the industry, whether or not the workers and owners

of some of those establishments were represented at the bargaining table where the agreement was reached.

We must bear in mind that the 1950 law scarcely affected shopfloor labor relations as such, for the parties were free to ignore the recommendations and decisions of the whole mediation apparatus. National agreements left unregulated many areas of industrial life. And the wage contracts of national accords turned out to be the equivalent of minimum wage legislation, pulling up wage floors but not setting actual rates. Thus the postwar legislation little affected shop-floor relations.[15]

We have given the formal institutions of collective bargaining rather short shrift because we do not think they are very important either in accounting for changes over time in patterns of French strikes, or for explaining why strikes in France are different from those in other countries. The modifications over the years in collective bargaining have not been substantial, consisting mainly of minor improvements in the mechanics of mediation. The readiness of the parties to accept such intervention has changed very little, save in the public sector. And there has been little change over the years in the willingness of the parties to enter into collective agreements at the plant level. In other words, the whole North American apparatus of grievance procedures, government labor relations boards, binding arbitration and judicial rulings is simply absent in France. The only change of importance over time has been the government's greatly enhanced willingness to step into disputes.

At first sight, therefore, one might conclude that the singular French pattern of strikes results from the lack of institutions for collective bargaining, such as those the Wagner and Taft–Hartley Acts established in the United States. But at second view it becomes clear that the conjunction of a certain style of strike activity with a certain style of industrial relations does not mean that the latter causes the former. There is within industrial sociology a tendency to attribute mechanically all that happens within the plant to the system of industrial relations prevailing there. Yet is it not more reasonable to assume that both strikes and collective bargaining systems are determined by wider social and political forces? Likewise, is it not slightly unrealistic to assume that the institutions of labor relations have a life of their own, and that they intervene like a *deus ex machina* in the power struggles of industrial life? A society gets, after all, the labor relations system it deserves.

So to get at the roots of things we must ask why the French deserved institutions of collective bargaining characterized by:

(1) arbitrary and haphazard intervention by the government rather than by the routinized mediation of bureaucratic public agencies;

(2) the law of the jungle at the level of the individual enterprise: no formal rules for good-faith bargaining and no collective agreements to resolve day-to-day grievances.

To answer this question we must specify the hopes and fears of each of the three participants in industrial conflict.

The workers

Of the three parties the motives and ambitions of the workers are most difficult to determine, for the worker (as opposed to the worker leader) has left almost no written indication of his aims and purposes behind him, whereas this material is abundant in state and firm archives for the other two parties. Evidence on labor relations taken from strike statistics, in addition to a few anecdotes of single strikes in the *SG*, compose an indirect way of discovering what the workers thought they were doing when they went on strike. The argument of this section will be that strikes were more an instrument to force the intervention of the state in labor relations than a tool for, say, belaboring employers at the bargaining table.

There were in France few shop-level worker unions. Factory locals have seldom succeeded in implanting themselves, outside the nationalized sector, because private employers by and large have never recognized unions as the legitimate representatives of their workers. The basic unit of worker organization was, therefore, not the plant but the municipality.

Why this weakness of plant-level unionism? We advance two explanations: (1) the employer refused to negotiate with the unions, and harassed them in every possible way; (2) the unions, in any event, had other objectives in mind than plant-level wage agitation, and did not imagine their primary mission to be representing their members in collective bargaining. It goes without saying that the second explanation may be merely a rationalization for the state of affairs created by the first: the unions could accomplish nothing with individual employers, and so perforce turned to other objectives. Yet we think that the political thrust of French unionism had a life of its own, independent of shop-floor success. In this chapter we explore those sources of political unionism within the system of industrial relations, namely worker powerlessness in the face of management supremacy. Then in Chapter 7 we discuss larger influences, especially industrial technology, which made for the French pattern of centralized, politicized unions, weakly implanted at the plant level and fundamentally indifferent to shop-floor matters.

Even though they had little luck within the plant gates, unions abounded. Within a given municipality a number of militant unions were likely to be present. And these organizations, with headquarters perhaps in the local Bourse du travail, would be instrumental in persuading the workers to strike and in coordinating their actions once the conflict was under way. As we shall see in Chapter 7, a worker union was present in three-fourths of all strikes just before the First World War. But the role of that union was to mobilize and direct, not to settle and negotiate. Official statistics reflect the minimal incidence of direct negotiation between workers' unions and employers (or employers' unions) in strikes.

Between 1898 and 1914, to take the period for which the most complete data are available, worker unions formally negotiated with employers in only 6 percent of all strikes ('Grèves ayant reçu leur solution par les syndicats professionnels,' or some similar formula). We have no reason to think that this minimal share was much different in either the years before or after this time. And in only 1 percent of all strikes in 1905–14 did employers' and workers' unions actually negotiate together to end a dispute. It is thus clear that local worker unions had no chance to represent their members at the plant level.

So hopeless was the prospect of compelling employer recognition of shop-level unions that the workers did not attempt it through strikes. Virtually no disputes were waged for the purpose of forcing union recognition: only 1 in 1895–9, 36 in 1910–14 and 11 in all of 1915–34.[16]

Another indication of worker helplessness against the individual employer was the minuscule number of collective agreements. Statistics on this mode of settlement begin with the 1919 law on collective contracts. Between 1919 and 1924 a meager 5 percent of all strikes ended with *conventions collectives*; this figure rose to 8 percent in 1925–9, and then declined to an insignificant 3 percent in 1930–5. And a fifth of all these *conventions collectives* between 1920 and 1935 came in consequence of arbitral sentences, rather than from collective bargaining between the two parties.

A final sign of worker powerlessness at the shop level was the low percentage of strikes ending in out-and-out success, rather than in compromise or failure. We shall follow in detail the results of strikes over the years in the next chapter; let us remark here that between 1830 and 1965 only one-fifth of all disputes whose outcome is known resulted in complete success for the workers (6,510 strikes out of 37,010, or 17.6 percent). For the workers the strike would bring victory not by wresting concessions from individual employers but by exerting pressure upon the government and the legislature, for the central state could influence the *patron* far more effectively than could the workers themselves.

It followed, then, that a prime objective of a strike was to compel government intervention. If the departmental prefect could be induced to mediate, or if the attention of the Labor Ministry could be drawn, the workers' chances of getting at least a compromise from the dispute were greatly enhanced.[17]

One way to demonstrate the strikers' fundamentally favorable attitude to the state, and their eagerness to see its agents intercede, is to examine statistics on who initiated the conciliation procedures prescribed in the 1892 labor relations law. There were four possible ways, as we have seen, to invoke the justice of the peace's good offices: either the employer, the workers or both together could ask him to arrange conciliation, or the j.p. himself could approach the parties. The relative frequency of each of these possibilities in 1893–1909 is shown in the accompanying table.[18]

Requests for mediation of justice of the peace, 1893–1909

Made by	(%)
The employer	2.6
The workers	48.3
Workers–employers jointly	2.9
Justice of the peace himself	46.2
	100.0

The table shows that of the two combatants, the workers were twenty times as inclined as the employers to ask the government to mediate. It also indicates that the government, in the person of the justice of the peace, was as anxious to offer its services as the workers were to receive them. To be sure, conciliation by the j.p., a judicial official, was not the same thing as intervention by the local police commissioner or subprefect, to say nothing of intervention by the Labor Ministry – all administrators. We must also bear in mind that this 1892 law was invoked in only a quarter of all strikes between 1893 and 1909 (in 2,702 of 12,412 strikes, or 22 percent, to be exact). Yet to the extent that the procedures of the law were used at all, it was the workers who were most avid to take advantage of them.

It is our impression, though we do not have exact statistics on the matter, that the workers also asked the intervention of higher authorities in strikes, save when these officials stepped in on their own accord. The descriptions of disputes in the back of each volume of the *SG* before the First World War contain many references to worker requests to the departmental prefect or to the central government in Paris to help settle the dispute by arranging negotiations with hitherto mute employers. Here is a typical instance of strike requests for government intervention:

In April of 1900 the journeymen carpenters of Angers decided to ask the employer carpenters for an increase in the pay tariff, the rates of which had been first established in an 1881 convention, and then revised in 1897. The journeymen carpenters appointed a delegation of five of their members with plenipotentiary powers to negotiate on their behalf, but the entrepreneurs refused even to receive the delegation. The workers asked the prefect of the Maine-et-Loire to talk with the employers, who once again 'refused any negotiation.' The employers also rejected the overtures of the justice of the peace. The strike dragged on until July, when the workers finally asked the Minister of Commerce to intervene, having exhausted all other public authorities. The Minister thereupon asked the prefect to intercede once more: the prefect proposed to both parties a compromise 'tarif de Tours,' which resulted in a 5 centimes per hour increase for the journeymen carpenters; and on 23 August work resumed.[19]

Yet unless the government were truly goaded to act, not merely requested to do so, its intervention might lack sufficient force to make recalcitrant employers pliable. The government, after all, expended political capital every time it prevailed upon employers to make concessions to strikers, creating debts or dribbling away influence which on some other occasion would have to be repaid or reclaimed. To force the government's hand, striking workers often chose the instrument of public demonstrations. Because of this circumstance French strikes often seemed on the verge of spilling into violence.[20] Here an illustration or two of how the government might be moved will suggest the point.

Although the anti-worker bias which marred the *SG*'s reporting until about 1894 obscures exactly what happened, it appears that the coalminers of the Haute-Loire basin of Sainte-Florine were able to bring about official intervention on their side by threatening to create public disorder. The mining firm which owned the six Sainte-Florine concessions dismissed two union leaders for agitating among the workforce. This action provoked a strike at the two concessions of Taupe and Grosmenil, and through threats and picket-line disorders the strike was soon general in the entire basin. The prefect came on the scene, and unsuccessfully attempted to conciliate the parties. Thereupon the subprefect of Brioude counseled the workers to propose arbitration to the mining company, but the company rejected the worker delegation's proposals. 'Socialist agitators' arrived; arrests were made 'pour atteinte à la liberté du travail.' A riot appeared to be in the offing. At this point 'The subprefect of Brioude, seeing how tempers were inflamed and fearing for the public order, realized he would have to use his influence to obtain concessions from the company.' The company began to yield: an indemnity would be paid to the two dismissed unionists. Yet the workers, acting on the advice of a delegate from the Bourse du travail in Paris, demanded the rehiring of the two men. The strike dragged on, accompanied by further violence and the threat of major trouble (boxes of dynamite found alongside the dwellings of those strikers who had drifted back to work). Finally, at the insistence of the subprefect, the company agreed to increase the idemnity from 400 to 500 francs, and the strike was settled.[21]

The Sainte-Florine strike was a specific illustration of what appears to us a standard sequence. The strikers threaten disorder and violence in order to galvanize the government to pressure the employer into making concessions. Of course violence and demonstrations had other uses for the workers in addition to the acceleration of sympathetic government intervention. The point is that the workers could summon, in some fairly unconventional ways, the power of the state to help right the balance of forces in an otherwise highly unequal struggle with their employers.

The final proof of this argument is that government intervention in strikes paid off in results. If an official within the government hierarchy, or indeed a mere justice of the peace, could be persuaded to take a hand in the strike, the chances were vastly improved that the strike would end either in victory for the workers or in compromise – also a happy result; and the chances were greatly lessened that the strike would end in failure or indeed in the workers' dismissal. Government intervention had not always benefited strikers, for during the July Monarchy exactly the opposite relationship prevailed: the government stepped in to repress conflict, and its intervention substantially lessened the chances of success. The following table demonstrates this change over time from official intervention against the workers to intervention on their behalf.

Thus during the July Monarchy success for the workers was likely if the government stayed out, and the failure of the strike was a high probability if the government intervened. During the Third Republic, on the other hand, official intervention increased the chances of a happy outcome (either success or compromise), and reduced the chances of failure. In 1910–14 only 9 percent of the strikes in which the government intervened were failures, while 52 percent of those without intervention failed. And whereas 11 percent of the non-intervention strikes ended in firings in 1910–14, only 1 percent of the intervention strikes did so. The same was true for 1895–9; the opposite was true for the July Monarchy.

Thus there is a pattern: if Ministry of Interior officials or other high agents of authority stepped into a strike, the chances were significantly increased that the strike would neither end in failure nor in disaster with massive firings. The chances were only slightly improved that the strike would end in outright success. But the chances were *greatly* increased that the strike would end in compromise. The implication of these findings is that higher government officials intervened when forced (or urgently requested) by the workers to do so, to turn failure into compromise, to salvage lost situations.

Table 2.1: *The impact of government intervention upon the outcome of strikes, 1830–1914*

	1830–47	1895–9	1910–14
% of strikes failing when the government intervened	58	13	9
% of strikes failing when the government *did not* intervene	38	51	52
% of strikes succeeding when the government intervened	22	27	21
% of strikes succeeding when the government *did not* intervene	32	23	19
% of strikes ending in compromise when the government intervened	20	60	70
% of strikes ending in compromise when the government *did not* intervene	29	26	29

N.B. The intervention of *juges de paix* is not included in these figures.
SOURCE: Our own coding of strike data.

The intervention of justices of the peace was only slightly less efficacious for the strikers. We shall dispense with a table, and merely report that for 1910–14, whereas 52 percent of the non-intervention strikes ended in failure, only 31 percent of the j.p. intervention strikes so ended. Whereas 11 percent of the non-intervention strikes ended with the participants' dismissal, only 4 percent of the strikes where the j.p. intervened so ended. Justice of the peace interventions did not elevate the chances of worker success, but they skyrocketed the likelihood of compromise. The employers had therefore good grounds to avoid j.p. overtures for conciliation, for even this humble official could exert nearly irresistible pressures for compromise and against ruthlessness.

The chief implication of these findings is to explode a myth in the historiography of the French labor movement. The myth is that the government invariably repressed strikes, bringing wherever possible the power of the state against worker militants on behalf of employers.[22] Our data show that the government stepped into a strike reluctantly, but that when it did so, it acted to moderate employer repressiveness and to restore industrial peace to a region by pressuring both sides for compromise. The strikers, conscious of how meager their strength was in the face of employer power, were eager to compromise so as to gain at least some of their demands. The employers were reluctant to give in at all, and so from the government's viewpoint, the nut to crack in a strike was the employer, not the union.

We begin to see how strikes had the very immediate political objective of compelling government intervention on behalf of the strikers, and against the employers. If the intercession of the state was of such importance in day-to-day militancy, how much more urgent would the acquisition of membership in the national polity become to the workers, permitting them to enlist routinely the resources of the state in their struggle against the employers. Yet precisely this drive for control meant the rhetoric of class struggle and the ardor of 'revolutionary' political activity. Hence working-class militants were able to curse the state from one side of their mouth, and plead for its intervention in their affairs from the other.

The employers

Statistics on the settlement of disputes give us a few partial insights into the mentalities of the second party in industrial conflict, the employers. It goes without saying that management preoccupations and ambitions may be thoroughly plumbed only by an intensive study of company archives, correspondence with the government, public declarations and similar evidence.[23] Yet quantitative strike data may tell us a little about how employers viewed organized militancy among their employees, and how they felt about the government's intervention.

Employers were to some extent organized as they met the strike threat, though not as many strikes involved a *syndicat pour les patrons* as did a *syndicat pour les ouvriers*. In 1895–9 27 percent of all disputes had employer organization, 48 percent by 1910–14. There was no tendency for the owners of large firms to organize themselves any more readily than the owners of small firms, for in 1910–14 the percent of strikes involving employers' associations was roughly comparable at all sizes of plant.[24]

The one objective the employer attempted at all costs to reach in labor relations was the protection of his *patronal* authority. Indeed, keeping his position as master of his own house from encroachment by organized labor or by the state appears even to have triumphed over the profit motive. In this section we wish to demonstrate the relentless hostility of the French employer to worker militancy.

Paramount was his reluctance to negotiate with his workers. The very idea of 'collective bargaining' is inappropriate to French labor relations, because the typical *patron* vastly preferred arrangements with individual employees to group bargaining. Much better to abide by the dictates of custom in shop organization, or to be guided by collective agreements reached at the municipal or regional levels, than to treat with unions.

As we saw in table 2.1, the employers initiated virtually none of the appeals to the justice of the peace for conciliation under the 1892 law. And as the prewar years passed, the handful of requests for conciliation that did emanate from the employers became fewer and fewer. Statistics are not available on who initiated the appeal to the justice of the peace in the interwar years.

Almost as often as not, the employers would refuse the j.p.'s offers of conciliation, even though the workers or the official himself had initiated the request. Of all recourses to the j.p. between 1893 and 1909 41 percent failed to result in the formation of a conciliation committee, and the vast majority of those failures must be attributed to employer refusal. Of the 1,015 rejections of the j.p.'s good offices in those years, 859, or 85 percent, came from the employers. And even if the employers agreed to sit on a conciliation committee, they were most unlikely to accept arbitration in the event that conciliation failed. There were between 1893 and 1909 340 'refus

Table 2.2: *Percent of requests for conciliation through justice of peace initiated by employers, 1893–1914*

Period	(%)
1893–4	4.3
1895–9	2.5
1900–4	3.3
1905–9	2.0
1910–14	1.5

SOURCE: Information in preface of yearly *SG*, 1893–1914.

de recourir à l'arbitrage,' 49 percent of them from the employers, 15 percent from the workers and 36 percent from both parties together.[25] Thus the employers had to be dragged, kicking and screaming, along every step of the formal mediation procedure prescribed in the 1892 law.

And even when we leave the formal procedures to the side and look at strikes in general we identify an unmistakable employer hostility to negotiations with workers in any form. For the years 1895–9 and 1910–14 we took special note in our coding of how the strike was settled, whether the employer undertook collective bargaining with his workers in any form. Table 2.3 shows how strikes were settled during these periods.

The major message of table 2.3 is that collective negotiation simply did not go on in most strikes, and that this tendency became more, not less, pronounced, as time went on (at least, until the First World War; thereafter, the data give out). The minor message is that labor unions came increasingly to represent the workers in whatever negotiations did take place.

Again, we see the singular inappropriateness of a term like 'collective bargaining' for what happened in French strikes. There was little bargaining at all. In order to communicate with each other the parties resorted to public announcements, notices placarded on the plant gate or the door of the town hall or printed in the local newspapers. Typically, an employer who wanted to end a strike by meeting his workers halfway, or by giving in to their demands, would post the new pay schedule in a public place. And if the workers were inclined to accept, they would appear on the job the next morning; if not, they would continue to stay away until a new *affiche* was displayed, or until the employer had replaced them with new workers. Strikers appeared to most employers as they appeared to M. Jacquet, the owner of a Clermont-Ferrand foundry whose workers struck in December of 1902: 'He considered the cessation of work among his employees in no way as a strike, but as a mutiny.'[26] And you don't bargain with mutineers (although in fact he did so later).

Anecdotes of disputes in the *SG* give a more concrete sense of employer

Table 2.3: *Modes of negotiation, 1895–9 and 1910–14 (in percent)*

	1895–9	1910–14
Miscellaneous	2	—
Employer negotiates with union	15	19
Employer enters into conciliation–arbitration	7	6
Employer negotiates collectively with non-unionized workers	12	2
Employer does not participate in collective negotiations of any sort	64	73
TOTAL	100	100

SOURCE: Coding of individual strikes from *SG*.

anxieties over authority than is possible from numbers alone. It is worth pausing for a moment to see how jealousy over employer prerogatives could envenom the daily course of labor relations. (The struggle for control extended into the most private areas of workaday life, as the employees of a wool weaving mill in Roubaix learned in 1910, when the owner installed steam vents in the toilets 'dans le but d'y empècher les séjours trop pro-longés.' They struck to have the devices removed.)[27] Now if these disputes over authority masked the conflict of economic interests that would be one thing; the struggle would not be symbolic but over real francs and centimes. Many disputes which appeared to be clashes over the shadow of prestige turned out to concern the substance of material interest, as for example strikes over the hiring of women: male workers protested not because they feared for their masculine dignity (we believe) but because women were paid less and would drag the entire rate structure down with them. Rather, we have in mind a large range of disputes arising from the injured pride, not the injured purse, of the employer. And what is pride in the local arena gets writ large as Power in the national.

Management fear of losing control lay behind a Oise weavers' strike in 1894. On 4 October the director of a weaving mill in Esquennoy issued the directive: 'The workers must sweep behind their looms every day at 10 a.m.' Sport was made of this:

> In the afternoon a note written in big letters on brown paper circulated in the workshops: 'At 10 a.m. it is necessary to stop the looms in order to sweep up.' [Hard, they thought, to imagine such a waste of time.] This joke displeased the director of the mill, who began an investigation to discover the author; unsuccessful at this, he dismissed five workers who had passed the note on instead of stopping it.

The following morning all two hundred workers of the establishment went on strike to protest the dismissals, appealing to the justice of the peace to intervene. At the j.p.'s behest, the director agreed to take back four of the fired workers, yet insisted that the ringleader would not be rehired under any circumstances; the strikers found this proposal unacceptable. That following Sunday at a general meeting chaired by the secretary of the weavers' union of Amiens, the strikers voted to return to work, provided that the ringleader's wife be taken back. The director's acceptance of this face-saving compromise ended the strike.[28]

How sternly these paternalistic employers reproved impoliteness from their workers! Witness a St Quentin weaving mill strike of 1900. It all started when a worker was dismissed who had been caught chatting once too often with his wife (who worked in the same plant). The five shop delegates demanded several times that the worker be rehired. Finding their insistence intolerable ('de n'avoir pas une tenue suffisamment correct à son égard'), the employer fired the five along with two of their wives. At that point all

219 weavers in the mill walked out. The wife of the first fired worker thereupon died, her passing 'attributed to the emotion caused by the dismissal of her husband.' After the passions stirred up by this unfortunate event had subsided, the justice of the peace attempted to conciliate the parties, but the employer refused, 'saying that questions of internal discipline could be handled only by himself alone.' Four days later the strikers returned to work in failure.[29]

Example could be piled on example of employer sensitivity to symbolic questions of status and authority; yet while this anecdotal technique might suffice to make a point about a commonplace state of mind, it is inadequate as a measure of change over time. Did employers become more or less hostile to unions and to collective action by their workers with the years? Whereas the accumulation of impressions will not answer this question, a quantitative index of employer ferocity towards strikers might be devised that will: the percentage of all strikes in which the strikers were not rehired. We reason that employers who viewed walkouts more as a mutiny than a valid bargaining technique would be disinclined to rehire the strikers. And there is plenty of evidence in the written descriptions of embittered disputes between 1893 and 1914 that this logic was true, for many accounts conclude with such phrases as 'Les ouvriers n'ont pas été repris.' The index is not entirely a pure one of employer antagonism to organized militancy, for many managers – enraged or not – may have had little alternative than to rehire the workers. (The *SG* seems to have excluded from these figures strikers who found permanent employment elsewhere during the strike.) Nonetheless it should be a rough guide.

Table 2.4 suggests a diminution in employer hostility to collective action within the *maison* over the years. The downturn was not linear, for especially in 1925–9 the percentage of dismissals approached prewar levels. Yet the conclusion is probably warranted that in the 1930s the employers felt more comfortable with industrial conflict than in the 1890s.

Abundant anecdotal evidence indicates that these generalized employer anxieties about authority led them to repress unionism among their em-

Table 2.4: *Percent of strikes in which a majority (at least two-thirds) of the strikers were not rehired, 1895–1934*

Period	(%)
1895–9	12.6
1910–14	9.2
1915–19	2.5
1920–4	3.9
1925–9	7.4
1930–4	6.4

SOURCE: Coding of individual strikes from *SG*.

ployees systematically. Quantitative indicators of these matters are not available, but a few examples may indicate the nature of the phenomenon.

In the summer of 1892 the newly unionized quarry workers of Comblanchien (Côte-d'Or) won through striking a pay increase from their employers. But for the employees of one quarry owner, at least, the victory was ominously clouded: 'I am obliged to give in today, because I have rock to deliver, but in January accounts will be settled [*nous nous retrouverons*].' Sure enough, in January 1893, the owner declared that he would no longer employ workers who belonged to the union. To ensure that his intentions were understood, he posted publicly an extract from his letter to the mayor of Comblanchien:

> Work will resume immediately after the thaw; I will employ only non-union workers. Consequently, you should request that my shops be protected by the gendarmerie or the army, as the subprefect promised me.
> I ask you to tell the union workers that it is useless to believe that I shall take them back, at least until they resign from the union.

Naturally, this assault elicited a strike; official intervention and conciliation took place; and the employer backed down, agreeing to tolerate the unionists.[30] The story characterizes garden-variety employer attempts to purge unionists through outright dismissal.

A second commonly used tactic to rid oneself of unionists was not to rehire the leaders of a strike. The workers tried to protect themselves against this by stipulating in the agreement that *all* strikers were to be rehired; yet if the strike were unsuccessful, or ended in a draw, the employer might well avoid having to take back the main unionists. (If this question became a serious obstacle to settlement, the worker leaders would renounce their own return for the sake of the commonweal, a gesture thought to raise class consciousness.)[31]

A final theme in employer hostility to worker organization was spun around the question of one's employees holding public office. Many bosses found absolutely intolerable the notion that members of their workforce should acquire the authority and influence accompanying, for example, election to the municipal council. And so worker candidates and councilors from time to time found themselves without jobs. The issue of workers in politics triggered several famous strikes, notably the Carmaux mining strike of August–November 1892.[32] But as a typical example let us take a walkout of Besançon shoeworkers in May of 1900. Forty-three workers struck when one of their fellows, the secretary of the union and candidate for the municipal council, was dismissed. The employer responded to the strike by replacing twenty-nine of the strikers, telling the justice of the peace that all the workers who left his employ had been replaced, and that no disagreement existed between him and his present-day workforce. The local shoeworkers' union lost three-fourths of its members 'as a result of this incident.'[33]

In attempting this sketch of mentalities we are not saying that employers behaved 'irrationally.' On the contrary, an antipathy to unions and strikes fitted well into an integrated, coherent view they possessed of the social and political order. Yet to the extent that such hostility prolonged or precipitated work stoppages, it would hurt profits, 'irrational' only in the narrow context of economic rationality. The desire to be absolute master within one's own house (factory) which so keynoted labor relations was part and parcel of a larger pattern of entrepreneurial mentalities which scholars such as David Landes have identified as peculiarly French.[34] What may not be singularly Gallic, however, is the larger fabric of political struggle into which employer hostility to unions was also woven. For employers just as much as workers sensed that resources and authority were disputed in a regular continuum of political arenas running from the workshop to the national legislature. M. Jacquet was right: the strike was indeed a mutiny.

The state

It makes sense to treat the government as a party in labor disputes because it was a contender for power in its own right, following goals and banishing spectres of its own choosing. State administrators had their own objectives, and their own means of pursuing them. To some extent, to be sure, the government danced to the tune of the most powerful members of the polity; yet in many matters the bureaucrats acted independently of external influences. And important among the latter matters were labor relations.

Only careful archival research will establish if the government was, as Marxist scholars claim, the tool of the business class, moving repressively to put down worker movements which threatened the profitability of the capitalist system. The evidence we know about, indistinct and ambiguous though it may be, points away from that hypothesis. Strike data suggest that the government's main preoccupation in labor relations was the preservation of public order, rather than the strangulation of working-class political movements. And the maintenance of order, like a two-edged sword, could work against the interests of those demanding repression just as against those creating disorder.

The question of the government's motives for intervening in strikes has been dreadfully beclouded with partisan rhetoric. The Left continues to be astonished that ministers who themselves sprang from the bosom of the worker movement ended up as strikebreakers: witness the scorn even now heaped upon Briand, Viviani and Millerand.[35] And the Right has similarly turned aginst ministies for their pro-labor sympathies: witness the animosity employers directed against the Waldeck-Rousseau government in 1899–1902, and against the Blum governments of the Popular Front. Sorlin's biography of Waldeck-Rousseau is in fact one of the few archivally based monographic studies we have of the response of the governmental apparatus to industrial unrest; and Sorlin makes clear that the ministers and civil servants were anything but the tools of the bourgeoisie.[36] Aside from a handful of such investigations, we have at present no knowledge of what the bureaucrats thought of industrial conflict, as distinct from revolutionary political movements. (It's evident enough the government was opposed to them.)[37] Data from *SG* supply some indirect illumination.

The government was on the whole reluctant to intervene in strikes, yet this reluctance diminished with the passage of time. That at least is the message of official statistics on official intervention. A low level of government involvement in disputes, entailing few political risks, was the justice of the peace's self-initiated intervention under the 1892 law. Not a functionary himself, the j.p. was nonetheless responsive to suggestions and exhortations from the ministerial pipelines. Between 1893 and 1913 self-initiated interventions of j.p.'s in industrial disputes increased by 9 percent, as shown in table 2.5.

But the most important variety of intervention was that of government officials themselves, for the efforts of labor inspectors and subprefects give us an exact idea of general governmental involvement in industrial conflict. The official statistics mirror instances in which officials were instrumental in the actual resolution of a dispute, excluding the numerous less formal applications of suasion, confidential conversations with the parties, letters exhorting moderation and the like. Accordingly, these *SG* statistics reflect more the tip of the iceberg than the true dimensions of governmental involvement in disputes. We classify as 'governmental' all the following officials: prefects, subprefects, ministers, labor inspectors, police commissioners and the administrators of special agencies such as the marine bureau and the regional placement office. We exclude mayors, other municipal officials, senators and deputies from the category 'government.' Table 2.6 gives government intervention in strikes, 1898–1935.

These figures point to a marked increase in governmental willingness to intervene in strikes after the First World War, coming possibly in consequence of more effective strike tactics intended to compel intervention

Table 2.5: *Percent of conciliation attempts initiated by justice of peace* (recours formés sur l'initiative des juges de paix), *1893–1914*

Period	(%)
1893–4	42.8
1895–9	39.1
1900–4	40.8
1905–9	50.2
1910–14	51.8

SOURCE: Statistics in preface of each volume of *SG*, 1893–1914.

Table 2.6: *Percent of strikes in which the government formally intervened, 1898–1935*

Period	(%)
1898–9	3.7
1900–4	5.2
1905–9	5.6
1910–14	2.9
1919–24	14.0
1925–9	13.8
1930–5	12.3

SOURCE: Statistics in preface of yearly volumes of *SG*, 1898–1935.

(more of that in the next chapter on increasing size and frequency of strikes), possibly in consequence of successful worker political pressures for greater *dirigisme*. The 1920s marked official intervention in many more areas of economic life than before the war, among which was industrial relations.

Over the years an ever wider range of officials came to intervene in disputes, as is shown in table 2.7. Between 1898 and 1914 the prefects and subprefects were the group of administrators most frequently involved in labor disputes; a residual category identified in the source as 'others who intervened' also bulked large in this decade (this category was in fact composed largely of state administrators, plus some justices of the peace and deputies). Then after the war the labor inspectors and various ministers joined prefectoral officials (whose own activities were unabated) in mediating strikes. Thus a higher rate of government intervention in general after the First World War meant a broader band of officials to whom the workers could appeal for intervention. We should also like to infer – though our evidence is indirect – that this increase in government intervention meant the strike movement was paying off in solid political gains. That part of the working classes which had launched the strike movement, the skilled artisans, was now reaping its political benefits and was on the verge of demobilizing, as we shall see in Chapter 8.

Table 2.7: *Officials who intervened in strikes, 1898–1935*

	Police commissioners (%)	Labor inspectors (%)	Sub-prefects (%)	Prefects (%)	Ministers (%)	Others (%)	TOTAL
1898–1914	4.1	1.0	37.6[a]	30.8[a]	–	26.0	99.5
1919–35	3.6	24.1	24.9	30.4	11.2	5.7	99.9

[a] 1898–1902 prefects and subprefects lumped.

SOURCE: Statistics in preface of yearly volumes of *SG*, 1898–1935.

What the government did when it intervened in a strike is a question we know both a little and a lot about. The descriptions of strikes at the end of the yearly *SG*s go into detail about the mechanics of official mediation: first the subprefect would talk with the strikers, then with the employers, then try to bring the two together; failure; then the prefect would attempt etc. This information is not of absorbing interest because it is so obvious, being precisely what any mediator would do to reconcile two disputants. What we know little about, on the other hand, is the kind of pressure the government could exert against either party to force them to abandon fixed positions and settle quickly. From time to time we get a glimpse into the *dessous* of official intervention, but such insights are rare.

There was, for example, the use of troops as a lever on *employers*, not on workers. It often happened that the government would send detachments of soldiers into a municipality where a large strike was in process. Violence flared easily in labor disputes, and administrators would be at great pains to guarantee public security – which meant to their minds stationing troops in the town. If soldiers were near the strike-bound plants, the employers needed not fear striker violence against strikebreakers, nor physical assaults on the struck establishments themselves, and so could hold out longer. Yet the government could use the threat of withdrawal of these troops to bring the employers to a quicker settlement.

This threat was used in the bitter smelting and forge workers' strike in Rive-de-Gier (Loire) in 1893. The strike began in January in the forges of the Marrel brothers over a squabble about the timing of the lunch hour. The Marrels refused to receive a worker delegation on the subject, and fired a union leader when he answered affirmatively to the question: 'Is it true that if we fire one of you, the others will go on strike immediately?' Thereupon a strike broke out, which the newly formed worker union, incorporating around 1,400 of the 1,750 smelting workers in the Rive-de-Gier, made general in all metallurgical establishments. At this point a three-way dialogue began in which the workers appealed to the prefect of the Loire for help, in which the prefect had conversations with the master of the forges, but in which the masters refused to negotiate with the workers. There were some disturbances, clashes between the strikers and the authorities, assaults of strikers upon scabs. 'Mort à tous les gros voleurs et à leurs soutiens!' said a placard. The strikers held great public meetings; Jaurès came to speak, thundering against the sending in of troops. Still, the masters of the forges would not negotiate, and the Marrel brothers would not take back the dismissed unionist.

On 27 February, two months after the strike had begun, some of the strikers began returning to work, having reached a partial entente with their employers. The union dropped some of its more objectionable demands, such as the recognition of union commissions within the plants. Yet certain employers still refused to negotiate because the document with the revised moderate demands was written on union stationery and bore the stamp of the union on the first page. The *SG* explains:

> This intransigence could have aborted the resumption of work, the success of which had been accelerating. Hereupon *Monsieur le préfet* decided he would have to go to Rive-de-Gier. He immediately convoked the employers, and the first interview took place the morning of 3 March.
>
> The prefect began by declaring to the employers that if the majority of them demonstrated themselves opposed to the conclusion of an agreement, he would be obliged to refer the matter to the minister, who, perhaps, would not judge suitable the maintenance of so many troops in Rive-de-Gier.[38]

We cannot know if the prefect put the threat so delicately in his actual conversation with the employers. But it was superbly effective, for the employers became malleable and granted salary increases (even though the Marrels did not rehire the fired worker); three days later the strike was virtually over.

In this strike we see governmental administrators playing a familiar part. They are galvanized to action by the threat of violence and of large unruly crowds (a worker was killed in the strike and boxes of dynamite kept turning up). Of course they arrest individual strikers, sometimes put the leaders behind bars, and try to assure the 'liberty of work.' But their actions are ultimately directed at the avoidance of a large social explosion, such as a wave of riots in the proletarian St-Etienne region; and so they attempt to restore peace by leaning on stubborn employers.[39]

The *dessous* of governmental intervention had other facets too. A coal-mining strike broke out in 1896 at La Vernarède (Gard) over a wage reduction. It was settled when the Minister of Public Works prevailed upon the directors of the P-L-M railway to reduce the Gard–Marseille coal freight charges, so that the mining company was able to revoke the pay cut by cutting its shipping costs.[40] One can proceed through the annals of industrial conflict, picking such examples here and there. Yet we forbear this exercise because the haphazard selection of isolated instances gives no systematic information about typicality or change. The major point is that government intervention meant shifting the balance from failure to compromise for the workers; exactly how the officials managed to accomplish this awaits further investigation.

What are the broader implications of the increase over time in official willingness to intervene? In conclusion we may speculate about one possible consequence. Heightened government intervention, rather than increasing animosities between employers and workers, was probably behind the growing desuetude of the 1892 collective bargaining law. Although in the first years of its existence the 1892 law was applied to a sizable proportion of all conflicts, after the First World War its use became rare, as table 2.8 shows.

Table 2.8: *Percent of strikes in which strikers, employers or justices of the peace tried to invoke the 1892 conciliation law, 1893–1935*

Period	(%)
1893–4	20.5
1895–9	24.2
1900–4	25.0
1905–9	18.9
1910–13	17.4
1919–24	8.9
1925–9	8.5
1930–5	5.4
1950–64[a]	6.0

[a] This statistic refers to the yearly average percentage of strikes examined by conciliation commissions in accordance with the 1950 conciliation law. The percentage is based on a figure Hélène Sinay presents in *La Grève*, p. 421.

SOURCE: 1893–1935 statistics in preface of yearly volumes of *SG*, 1893–1935.

The percentage of strikes in the postwar period subject to formal conciliation appears about the same as in the interwar years, which suggests that in the 1950s modes of settling labor disputes were about the same as in the 1920s, and that the extensive postwar legislation on the subject made little real difference. We hypothesize that formal conciliation declined because of increasing government intervention in strikes, for the parties would be unlikely to bargain freely if an outside force might suddenly come to the aid of one or the other. Labor relations experts claim that government intervention in disputes customarily disrupts what is called in North America 'free collective bargaining.' And there may be something to that. An alternative explanation for the disuse of the 1892 law during the twenties is that tensions between labor and capital were being exacerbated during these years.[41] Yet both a rising percentage of strikes ending in collective agreements during the twenties, and a sagging percentage of employer dismissals of strikers, cast doubt on this alternative. The explanation we prefer is that the growing disuse of formal settlement procedures betokened an increase in informal – but nonetheless real – worker influence with the government bureaucracy, and in formal worker political power.

In this chapter we have introduced the actors by suggesting what aims and worries set each of them – employers, workers and government – into motion. Limitations of evidence have confined the discussion to a small segment of the total period we attempt to cover. But the postures and preoccupations the exceptionally rich documentation point to for the years 1890 to 1914 probably held true for both earlier and later periods, for they were determined more by cultural reflexes and responses than by structural features in the economy and society. In the following chapter we try to turn from these more abiding characteristics to consider how changes in the structure of economic life and industrial organization brought about changes in the pattern of strikes.

3 The transformation of the strike

The last hundred and fifty years have seen profound changes in the form and frequency of strikes, and indeed in the very purpose of industrial conflict itself. So that the Marseille construction workers who walked off the job in November of 1947 as the Ramadier government abolished the coal subsidy would have recognized very little in common with the coopers in nearby Roquemaure (Gard) who stopped work a hundred years earlier – in April of 1847 – to obtain a wage increase. This chapter sets out to sketch these grand changes, and to account for them in terms of the evolution of worker organization and of national patterns of political action. We intend to show how the strike has become transformed from a means of maintaining local political influence and job control to a device for pressing at the national level working-class claims to political representation.

The data on the outbreak and character of strikes we present in this chapter will in themselves not suffice to 'prove' this case. A number of alternative explanations would be consistent with the bare facts on duration, grievance, strike propensity and the like that we offer here, and the reader has no basis for assuming that our 'political' hypothesis is necessarily the correct one. But the argument will be fleshed out in coming chapters, as we examine variation in industrial and territorial patterns, as we look at the major eruptions of strike waves and as we examine the nature of French worker organization. And at each of these points we add a further strut to the political action argument. What we are doing here, then, is to specify a series of explicanda, facts requiring further explanation.

To preview the major shifts in the structure of conflict, strikes have passed from isolated occurrences, confined in scope to a few artisanal shops, to everyday events in working-class life, reaching across the industries of entire cities and regions. Their length has dropped from the middling duration of ineffectual shop-floor action to the brevity of symbolic political demonstration. Finally, they have been ever less successful, from July Monarchy to Fifth Republic, in achieving the strikers' stated demands, but evidence on the other hand an emerging spirit of compromise in industrial relations. In the following pages we look carefully at each of these major changes, locating the turning points in time and speculating about the reasons for the transformation.

Changes in the incidence of strike activity

The single most compelling fact of French strike history is the enormous increase in the sheer number of strikes during the last century and a half. The incidence of strikes, both in absolute numbers and relative to the labor force available for participation in conflict, rose almost steadily from the 1880s, when concentrated working-class organizational efforts began, until after the Second World War. What are the major stepping stones in this upward progression?

In the years from 1830 to 1880 the number of strikes fluctuated at a low level, as fig. 3.1 points out. No startling changes occurred from one five-year period to the next, and no trend is apparent. A directionless up and down, with the troughs not widely separate from the peaks of the graph, characterizes these early years. In the late 1870s, for example, the average annual number of disputes was close to that of the early 1840s. And both were, compared to later years, minuscule. To be sure, the 1830–63 series may not be entirely comparable to the 1864–84 series. We have considered in Appendix A deficiencies in each, concluding that the two series probably mirror the approximate course of events, though not too much importance should be attached to short-term fluctuations. The important point here is that no long-term changes of note occurred before 1880 in the incidence of conflict.

Then in the early 1880s, as fig. 3.1 further reveals, the great take-off in militancy commenced. Twice as many strikes took place in 1880–4 as in 1875–9, or in any other previous period. A slight slackening occurred in 1885–9 but thereafter the rise was almost uninterrupted. The *belle époque* saw a yearly average of over a thousand strikes; the post-Second World War era witnessed double that number.

Each of the principal increases in strike activity was tied to an increase in the organizational capacities of labor. As we shall see in Chapter 6, the 1880s were the start of the great mobilization of working classes for political action. And there is little doubt that the efflorescence of strikes came in direct consequence of this improved associational foundation. Unionization progressed steadily until the First World War, and throughout this period the number of strikes became ever greater.[1]

Then in the interwar years the pace of union growth stopped; indeed within manufacturing a certain deunionization took place. Significantly, the level of strike activity between 1915 and 1935 stabilized at roughly its prewar plateau. Between 1890 and 1914 a yearly average of 791 strikes occurred; between 1915 and 1935 an average of 793. (When the three restored departments of Bas-Rhin, Haut-Rhin and Moselle are subtracted from the interwar figures, the average drops slightly to 761.) The years 1936–8 then experienced another major upward leap, coincident with a new advance of unionization.

Between 1946 and 1964 industrial conflict rode a much higher plateau, with each five-year period showing an average of almost exactly 2,000 strikes

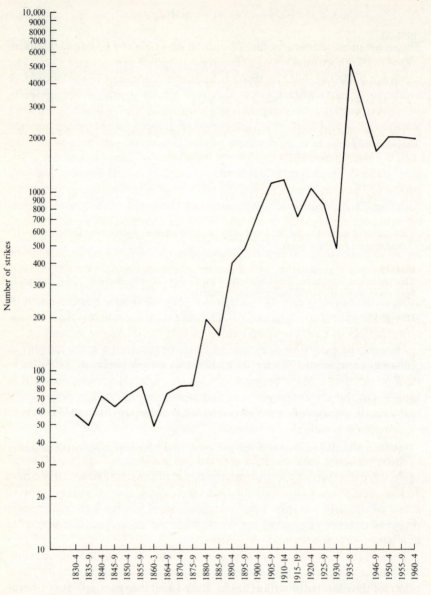

Fig. 3.1: Number of strikes, 1830–1964

a year. Of course, considerable year-to-year variation went on within the postwar era, yet over broader periods of time a constant outline of intense conflict is visible. Coincident with this postwar advance in strikes was an increase in unionization, and in the bureaucratic grasp of centralized union structures.

NOTES

1830–63
Figures refer to the number of *coalitions poursuivies*, taken from *APO*, I, pp. 27, 40. We consider this series the best available proxy for the actual number of strikes.

For the reader's convenience in estimating the reliability of this series on repression, the actual number of strikes Aguet (p. 365) reports are by annual average:

1830–4	22	1840–4	24
1835–9	11	1845–7	33

The only objective source of the frequency of strikes after the July Monarchy is an enumeration published in the *Statistique annuelle*, covering the years 1852–84 (*SA*, 1889, p. 134). These annual averages over five-year periods are:

1852–4[a]	2	1870–4	13
1855–9[a]	8	1875–9	39
1860–4	22	1880–4	121
1865–9	22		

[a] *SA* reported no strikes for 1854 and 1855; we have inserted figures compiled from the *APO* enumeration for these years.

1864–89
This series has been taken from Michelle Perrot's *Les Ouvriers en grève*, p. 61. Perrot drew both upon archival sources and published material.

1890–1935
The source for these years was our coded enumeration of strikes in the *SG*. Our annual totals differ slightly from those the *SG* published because (a) we considered every separate line in the *SG* to represent a separate strike, whereas the *SG* would occasionally count as a single dispute a number of substrikes for which information was given separately, line by line, and (b) we excluded Algerian strikes.

1936–8, 1946–53
Tabulation of annual numbers of strikes published in the *Annuaire statistique*, 1966, p. 120.

1954–64
Tabulation of annual numbers of strikes published in the International Labour Organization's *Year Book of Labour Statistics*, 1957 (p. 496) and 1966 (p. 714).

Annual totals were available to us for 1965–7. The *Annuaire statistique* covering 1968 left blank the rows for May and June, so data for the crucial year are incomplete. The *Annuaire statistique* gives strike totals for the years after 1964 (where fig. 3.1 stops) as follows:

1965	1,674	1966	1,711	1967	1,675

Yet if the number of strikes has increased over the years, is that not merely because the number of workers has also increased? The answer, to put things simply, is no. The active population in industry in 1881 was 4,444,000 workers; by 1959 their number had increased 60 percent to 7,092,000. The workforce of industry and services combined (the non-agricultural labor force) was 8,580,000 in 1881. Their number climbed by 66 percent to 14,300,000 in 1959. Yet over this same period the number of strikes increased by over a thousand percent, from a yearly average of 140 in 1880–4 to 2,040

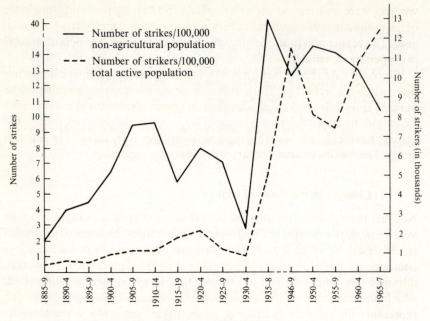

Fig. 3.2: Strike and striker rates, 1885–1967

NOTE
Strike rates per 100,000 total active population over long time blocks are:

| 1890–1914   4.0 | 1915–35   3.7 | 1946–66   9.6 |

in 1955–9. It is thus evident that the *propensity* to strike has risen alongside the absolute number of strikes.

Fig. 3.2 presents strike rates beginning only with 1885, because before that date strikes were neither plentiful enough, nor labor-force data sufficiently accurate, to warrant the computation of rates. The intensity of conflict, measured by the number of strikes per 100,000 non-agricultural active population, increased in steady progression from 2.0 in 1885–9 to 9.6 in 1910–14. Strike rates thereupon rose sharply at the conclusion of the First World War, but tapered off during the 1920s; finally, the propensity to strike soared to the high, steady level we have already noted in the post-Second World War period. By 1960–4 the chances that a strike would break out among a group of average workers were more than six times greater than in 1885–9.

The number of workers participating has risen with the sheer incidence of outbursts. Data are poor before 1885, but for the years thereafter, when most strikes took place, we may determine the number of workers involved. In 1885–9 a yearly average of only 27,000 workers went on strike, not very many considering the non-agricultural workforce numbered eight and a half million. (Not all of them, of course, could strike because the number includes self-employed and isolated workers.) By 1960–4 a yearly average of 2,069,000 workers were walking out on strike, which, in a non-agricultural labor force of 14 million means that one in every seven workers struck during a typical year. The reader will find information on annual average numbers of strikers in Appendix B, table 1.

We could cast the figures on strike incidence and participation in other dramatic ways, reflecting from different facets the staggering reality of the passage from low worker involvement in sporadic disputes to massive participation in commonplace events. The essential message is that strike activity has increased manyfold from nineteenth-century levels to become an integral part of twentieth-century worker collective action.

Changes in the shape of strikes[2]

Not just the volume, but also the actual shape of strikes changed over the long span of the nineteenth and twentieth centuries. In order to grasp that transformation, we have to break aggregate strike activity down into three components: duration, size and frequency. The first dimension is the average duration (for which we will use the median, to avoid the distorting effect which one interminable strike can have on the mean). The second dimension represents the number of strikers; mean strikers per strike is the statistic. These two dimensions give us the shape of the typical strike. We might imagine them as forming a rectangle whose height represents mean strikers, whose length represents median duration and whose area approximately represents the man-days absorbed by the strike. Strike A is therefore long but small, Strike B short but large, Strike C both long and large.

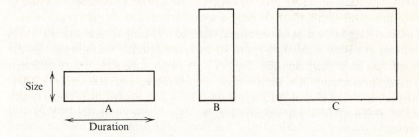

To represent aggregate strike activity in a period, region or industry, we need a third dimension: the number of strikes. Here we express it as a rate, the number of strikes per 100,000 workers in the appropriate segment of the labor force. The third dimension turns the rectangle into a solid. Industry X has few strikes, but they tend to be long ones and fairly large. Industry Y has many large, short strikes.

To restate the problem: we are asking how the shape of this three-dimensional box changed in France from the 1830s to the 1960s. In the 1830s, the shape of strikes was middling long, low and paper-thin. In the 1960s,

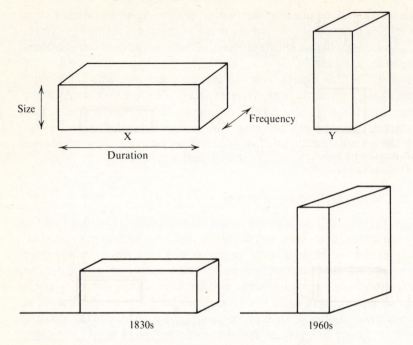

when such episodes as the general strike of May-June 1968 often over-shadowed other forms of labor relations, the shape of strikes was short, high and wide. The diagram shows the general difference. The two shapes correspond to different phases in the economic development of France. The early industrial strike tended to involve few workers because the scale of enterprise was small, plants widely dispersed and workers poorly organized. The early strikes we have examined were of middling length, and so few in number as to make calculations of strike rates virtually meaningless. So the shape has little thickness. By the 1960s strikes had become a very different sort of phenomenon. On the average, they involved over 500 workers. Their normal duration shrank to a single day. They had passed from being small-scale, intense, unusual occurrences to large-scale, calculated everyday events.

The images in fig. 3.3 permit us to follow the evolution of strike physiognomy in greater detail. The boxes make it clear that the general shape of strikes in France changed little from the July Monarchy to the First World War. At that point the average size of strikes more than doubled. The most drastic modification in shape, however, took place some time after 1935. Let us examine the development of the three dimensions of strike activity separately.

When did the typical duration fall off so sharply, from six days to one? Median duration stayed steady at five or six days from the mid-nineteenth

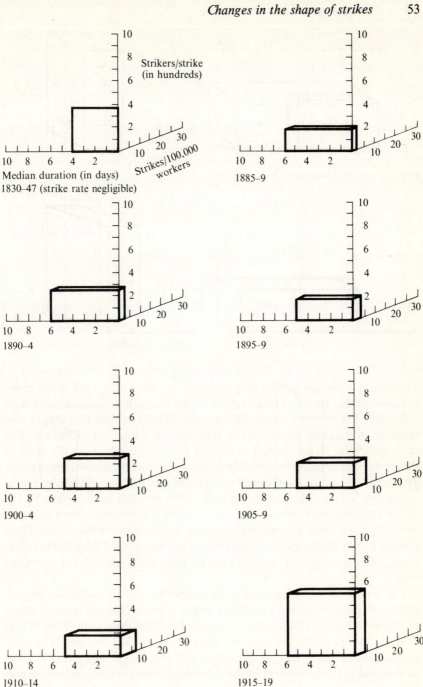

Fig. 3.3.: National strike shapes, 1830–1964

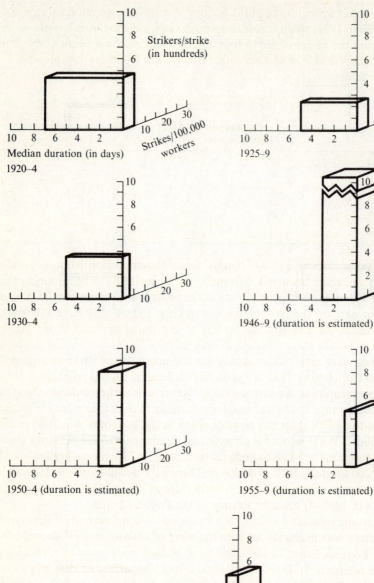

Strikers/strike
(in hundreds)

Median duration (in days)
Strikes/100,000 workers

1920–4

1925–9

1930–4

1946–9 (duration is estimated)

1950–4 (duration is estimated)

1955–9 (duration is estimated)

1960–4 (duration is estimated)

Fig. 3.3 (*continued*)

century until the beginning of the Second World War, except for the period from 1920 to 1924, when it rose to seven days. Nor did mean duration swerve much from the range of ten to fourteen days during those years. Only after the Second World War can we detect the decline. Consider the accompanying little table.

Period	% of strikes lasting 24 hours or less	Weighted average duration (man-days per striker)
1890–1914	19	16.6
1915–35	16	14.3
1946–9	36	4.6
1950–4	44	3.4
1955–9	48	2.3
1960–4	51	2.7

This table does not show exactly when the transition from moderate to short duration occurred. It could just as easily have been during the Popular Front as during the storms of the years just after the Second World War. But data on the late thirties are lacking, and we shall have to consult other indices for the precise timing of the transformation in the strike pattern.

Second, what major fluctuations has the mean size of strike undergone? The data from before 1885 are probably misleading on this point, since they surely overrepresent the larger strikes. Nevertheless they indicate that the size of the average strike was much more uniform over the century from the 1830s to the 1930s than the large changes in the economy would have led us to believe. What we find is an apparent decline of strikers per strike from the 300 range in the 1830s to under 200 in the 1880s. The mean then seesawed around 200 until the First World War. During the decade from 1915 through 1924 the figure climbed to 500. Another drop (237 in 1925–9) and another rise (368 in 1930–4) brought France to the Popular Front.

Now, some time after 1935 a shift to the brief but massive strike occurred. The pattern was probably set with the wave of sitdown strikes accompanying the Popular Front in 1936, followed by two more years of turbulence in labor relations. In formal statistical terms, the strikes of 1936 had a low amplitude (2,423,000 strikers in 1936, distributed over 16,907 separate strikes, yields 143 strikers per strike). The same goes for 1937. In 1938 the average strike size rose to over a thousand. Ratios are probably misleading here. Identifying some 17,000 separate 'strikes' in 1936 is a registration device. In reality a single seamless net of conflict lay upon France in the agitated summer days of the Popular Front. We are actually dealing with only a handful of truly separate conflicts, each of which involved tens of thousands of workers.

Postwar strikes were bigger than those before the Second World War, even though their average size declined steadily from the great heights of the late 1940s. There were 396 strikers per strike over the period 1915–35, 740 over the period 1946–64. The expanding size of industrial firms may finally have inflated the strike as well. But the timing of the major increases in strikers per strike suggests that changes in the level of unionization of the French labor force were at least equally influential. The periods 1918–21, 1936–8 and 1946–8 were, after all, the heroic days of unionization and of labor-based political action in France. In those years French workers came closest to the general strike advocated by Sorel.

Finally, the reader will recall the evolution of the strike rate itself. The number of strikes per 100,000 workers increased sixfold in a fairly steady progression from 1885 through 1914; the rate in 1885–9 was 1, in 1910–14 6 per 100,000 workers. During the First World War, for obvious reasons, the rate dipped very low. In the postwar explosion of labor militancy it rose a point or two. However, the simultaneous increase in the average size of strikes meant a great rise in man-days of strike activity: 17 per 100 workers in 1915–19, 30 per 100 workers in 1920–4. The Great Depression cut the strike rate to half its level of the 1920s. The movement of 1936 brought an unparalleled increase in the strike rate, unmatched even after the Second World War until May–June 1968.

On the whole the postwar strike rate ran at record levels. It began at 8.5 strikes per 100,000 workers in 1946–9 and climbed farther in the 1950s: 10.7 in 1955–9, 10.5 in 1960–4. Again the use of man-days per 100 workers gives a rather different picture:

1946–9	53	1955–9	12
1950–4	25	1960–4	15

What happened, of course, is that strikes decreased in length even faster than they increased in number. They grew larger, shorter and more frequent. The data from France, in sum, provide no support at all for the idea that strikes dwindle as industrialism advances. They do strengthen the hypothesis of an association between large, short strikes and politically active unions, but with the qualification that the pattern only became predominant in France with or after the Popular Front.

It is noteworthy that political disturbances evolved in a similar direction in France. We have made a detailed study of 674 disturbances occurring in the three decades from 1830 to 1860 and another 595 disturbances occurring between 1930 and 1960. A 'disturbance' is an event in which (a) at least one group of fifty or more persons took part and (b) some person or object was damaged or seized over resistance. The two samples consist of every such event trained readers encountered in the examination of two national newspapers for each day in the six decades. The descriptions of the disturbances come not only from the newspaper accounts but also from archival materials, court-reporting journals like the *Gazette des tribunaux*, yearbooks like the *Année politique* and secondary historical works.

From 1830 on, disturbances ended faster than strikes. In a direct parallel to strike reporting, our procedures count as a man-day any day *on which* an individual took part in the disturbance, however briefly. Even by this rather undemanding criterion, the median disturbance in all periods studied lasted only a day. If, however, we employ man-days per participant as the measure of duration, a definite shortening of the average disturbance appears over the 130-year span. The table gives figures for the three dimensions of disturbances. Fig. 3.4 graphs the figures in a form comparable to the strike diagrams. Disturbances not only got shorter, they got bigger. In both respects, their evolution paralleled that of strikes.

Period	Number of disturbances	Disturbances per million population	Man-days per participant	Mean participants
1830–9	259	7.7	1.6	1,131
1840–9	292	8.2	1.9	1,751
1850–60	114	3.2	1.6	927
1930–9	333	7.9	1.0	2,214
1940–9	93	2.3	1.0	2,403
1950–60	302	7.1	1.0	2,197

They also differed in important ways. First, in all periods disturbances tended to involve more people than strikes did. Because they also tended to be shorter, the curious result is that the man-days in the average disturbance and the average strike in each period resembled each other much more than their durations or sizes did. Second, there is no tendency for disturbances to become more frequent, while the strike rate definitely rose as the twentieth century advanced. (Nor, incidentally, did disturbances fade away with time.) Third, the timing of the changes in the two forms of collective action appears to differ considerably. By 1930, for example, the man-days per participant in disturbances was already down to one, while the sharp reduction in the duration of strikes began at least six years later.

In pointing out the gross similarities in the changes of shape of strikes and political disturbances, then, we do not mean to say that they are the same phenomenon. We suggest instead that in both cases the emergence of new, complex and relatively effective forms of organization made it increasingly possible to mobilize a considerable number of men for a show of strength, carry out some common action and then demobilize quickly. In the early nineteenth century, the natural networks of neighborhood or shop brought relatively few men out for a strike or a protest, but once men were committed

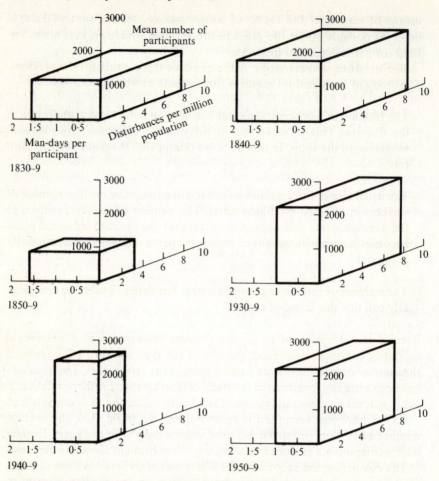

Fig. 3.4: Magnitudes of collective violence, 1830–1960

to either one they found it hard to withdraw before winning or being smashed. With the twentieth century, they organized on an increasing scale and developed more flexible means of collective action. Hence in strikes and disturbances alike size increased as duration went down.

Changes in patterns of mobilization

The reason the number of strikers and the number of strikes do not vary in perfect rhythm, then, is that the number of workers participating in a typical strike varies from one time or place to another. The average number of strikers per strike indexes worker involvement in strikes, as distinct from the number of strikes as such. Because we use strikes in this book as a means of getting at the fabric of working-class life, we want to learn as much as possible about the mechanisms through which workers are mobilized for participation in disputes.

The measure strikers/strike is the result of three quite different factors. The study of mobilization requires the separate examination of each:

– The fraction of workers in an establishment on strike who actually join in the dispute. This is measured as the number of strikers/100 workers employed in the shop. In this book we often call it the plant participation rate.

– The usual size of the establishment on strike (mean or median number of workers in affected establishments). The number of strikers involved in the average strike will appear to increase if the average industrial plant becomes larger, without any change in the percent of workers customarily going out.

– The number of establishments per strike. For variety's sake, we occasionally call this the scope of strikes.

Even if the structure of enterprise remains the same, and if plant-level solidarity continues unaltered, the size of the typical strike will increase if the number of establishments participating in the strike rises. This measure has been virtually forgotten in the study of North American labor relations;[3] yet it indexes an essential feature of worker mobilization in French strikes.

As we have just seen (and is again pointed out in fig. 3.5), the average number of strikers per strike has risen substantially over the years. Exactly which components of worker mobilization have brought about the increase?

The rise before the Second World War does not seem to have been a result of increasing plant participation rates, that is, in the median percent of workers in affected establishments actually going on strike. We have refined figures for 1895–9 and 1910–14, and in those two periods the median strikers/worker percentage was stable (see notes to fig. 3.6). The plant participation level after the First World War was, at the median, eight percentage points higher than before the war; yet the *trend* from 1915–34 was downwards. There is not, in any event, any long-term parallelism between the two, and so for the years before the war we may rule out the notion that changes in strike size were caused by changes in plant participation levels.

Higher strike size *after* the Second World War, however, may well have come from participation by a greater number of workers within the struck establishments. Plant participation rates, though at an absolute level lower than for interwar years, climbed from a yearly average of 33 strikers/100 workers in struck establishments in 1952–5 to 44 percent in 1955–9, to 49 percent in 1960–4. Possibly the steadily growing science sector of the 1950s

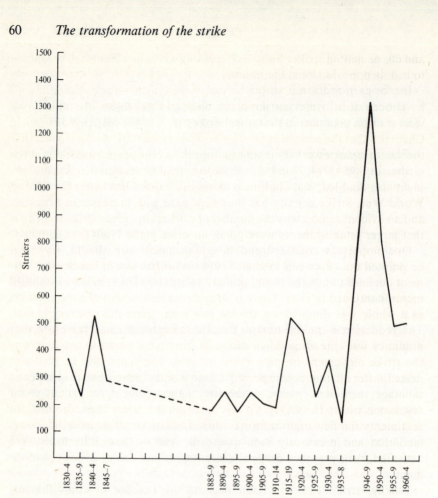

Fig. 3.5: Mean size of strikes (strikers/strike), 1830–47, 1885–1964

NOTES

APO data for the years 1848–84 were excluded from this table because the source is biased towards large, important strikes. For the reader's information, however, we reproduce here the average number of strikers/strike calculated from the *APO* enumeration. In parentheses is the number of strikes on which the calculation is based, that is, for which the number of strikers was known. Only 2 cases existed for 1848–9, and 1 for 1850–4.

Strikers/strike, 1855–84

1855–9	486	(6)	1870–4	237	(4)
1860–4	474	(7)	1875–9	1,914	(10)
1865–9	1,173	(16)	1880–4	1,868	(31)

In computing mean strikers/strike for 1830–47 and 1885–1935 only those strikes were included in the denominator for which striker information was available in the numerator. This precaution could not be applied to aggregate data after 1935, it goes without saying. Yet presumably the number of strikers was invariably known in later years.

The mean here, as everywhere in this book unless otherwise indicated, is a weighted mean, computed by adding up all the strikers, all the strikes, and then dividing one by the other.

and 60s cemented striker unity by increasing worker awareness of belonging to a skilled, professional community.

Increases in industrial scale (the size of the typical struck establishment) have been at all times an important factor in increasing the number of workers who take part in the typical strike (fig. 3.7). We shall demonstrate in Chapter 8 that the scale of enterprise has risen since 1901. And it is a fact that the size of *struck* establishment has gone up over the years: 59 workers at the median in 1895–1914, 74 in 1915–35. During the Depression struck establishment size doubled, and continued at a high constant level after the Second World War. Strike activity has thus kept pace with increases in firm size, and an evident reason why the number of workers in a given strike went up is that larger establishments were going on strike in the 1960s than formerly.

One important counter-trend in establishment size should, however, be pointed out. Between 1895 and 1914 the *median* size of struck establishment declined (while the mean, pulled upwards by a few very large establishments, continued to rise). There is no evidence that industrial concentration as a whole was diminishing around this time; quite the contrary in fact. This reduction in the size of struck establishments indicates, therefore, that militancy was spreading down the scale from large plants to small ones as the strike movement became more frenetic. The years 1895 to 1910 witnessed, after all, the 'heroic period' of the worker movement: the anarchist sabotage, the well publicized clashes with the government, defiant talk about revolution within the CGT. All this agitation doubtless conveyed militant sentiments and new organizational capacities into small shops in the hinterland that had previously been quiescent. And as these little firms were activated, their presence dragged down the median size of struck establishment.

Finally, strike size has risen because the number of establishments involved in a single strike has gone up, or, at least, rose until the Depression (fig. 3.8). In the July Monarchy 3.3 establishments participated in the average strike. (This figure is probably too high because Aguet doubtless missed a number of single-establishment strikes.) The scope of strikes then climbed between 1890 and 1914 from 4.8 to 8.5 establishments, which averages out to 8.4 establishments/strike in 1890–1914, and to 9.5 in 1915–35.

During the Depression this trend began a reversal (at the same time as plant participation rates were suddenly turning upward, and as the size of establishments on strike was also rising). In 1930–4 establishments/strike dropped to 5.5. Then in the postwar era the scope of strikes, while starting out at a high plateau in 1952–4 comparable to the level of the 1920s, more than halved itself by the early sixties. In 1960–4 the scope of French strikes was back at July Monarchy levels.

The measure *median* establishments per strike refines the picture a bit more. Median strike scope climbed unmistakably from the late eighties to the turn of the century, the period of the initial acceleration of militancy, and thereafter leveled off. This means that post-1900 increase in *average*

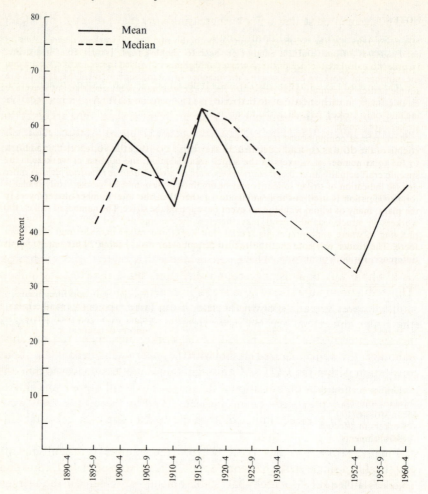

Fig. 3.6: Percent of workers who join strike in affected establishments, 1890–1934, 1952–64

establishments was due to a few very large citywide strikes which encompassed enormous numbers of firms. The across-the-board surge had completed itself by 1900.

We consider the rising scope of strikes a consequence of unionization. A central municipal headquarters, say a Bourse du travail, coordinates the actions of individual militants scattered among the industrial firms of the town. These union organizers will be unlikely to recruit majoritarian support within any single plant, but when a large number of such shops act together, the number of strikers they contribute is very large. The emergence of centralized unions with the requisite bureaucratic coordination made such an extension of the scope of conflict possible.

NOTES

Not until 1895 did the *SG* begin reporting both the number of workers *occupés dans les établissements atteints*, and the number of separate establishments participating in a strike. In order to calculate the size of the average establishment involved in each strike, we divided the number of workers employed by the number of establishments involved. It is then a simple matter to compute what percent of the workers actually went on strike in the average establishment in each strike, and to determine median percentages for five-year periods. We include only strikes for which the numbers of establishments, of workers in them and of strikers are known.

More refined computations may be made for 1895–9 and 1910–14, the periods when our coding of the *SG* was especially detailed. In the years 1895–1919 the *SG* reported, in addition to the total number of workers in the struck establishment, the number of workers in the specific craft actually on strike, *if craftworkers were on strike within an industrial plant*. A more precise indication of striker solidarity may be obtained if the number of workers truly available for participation is used in the denominator, rather than the total number of employees in the plant, many of whom would in no event have joined the strike. The number of strikes/100 workers in struck establishments may therefore be recomputed for 1895–9 and 1910–14, plugging in where appropriate this special craft workforce, rather than the total plant labor force. The reader will note that the refined denominator makes about 20 percentage points difference, for both means and medians:

	Only regular plant workforce used in denominator	Special craft workforce used where appropriate (and regular plant workforce used where not) in denominator
	1895–9	
Median strikers/100 workers in affected establishments	42	69
Mean strikers/100 workers in affected establishments	50	70
	1910–14	
Median strikers/100 workers in affected establishments	49	69
Mean strikers/100 workers in affected establishments	45	58

To ensure comparability the special workforce has been ignored in all calculations for 1895–1935 in fig. 3.6.

Data for 1952–64 are taken from the *Annuaire statistique*, 1966, p. 121, and represent the five-year total *effectifs en grève* divided by the *effectifs totaux des établissements touchés par les grèves*.

These time series suggest that two distinct patterns of mobilization have alternated during the last century and a half to bring workers out on strike. And it is the kind of industrial technology and accompanying union organization that determine which pattern will be dominant.

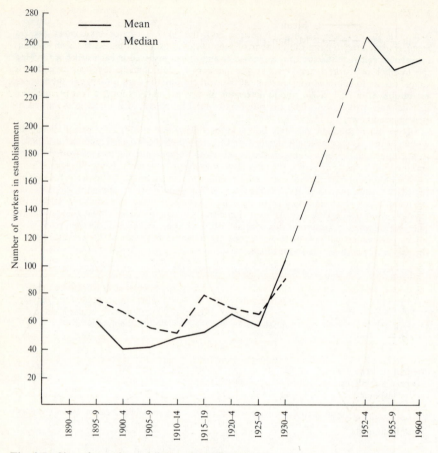

Fig. 3.7: Size of struck establishments, 1895–1964

NOTE

Size of struck establishment was computed in 1895–1935 by dividing the number of workers *en établissements atteints* by the number of establishments involved, for each strike, and then aggregating to five-year means and medians. For 1952–64 we took already aggregated annual numbers of establishments on strike, and workers employed in those establishments, and divided one by the other to compute average size of struck establishment. The data are in the *Annuaire statistique*, 1966, p. 121.

One pattern combines limited areal scope with high plant participation, and seems to come from workers and unions with an articulate awareness of occupational solidarity. There are hints of this pattern at work in the July Monarchy. In the 1830s artisanal craftsmen coalesced in informal groups which owed their high cohesiveness to a remembrance of guild traditions and to a sense of professional community. We have no solid data on plant participation during the July Monarchy, but given what we know about the later strikes among the kinds of workers who formed the core of the

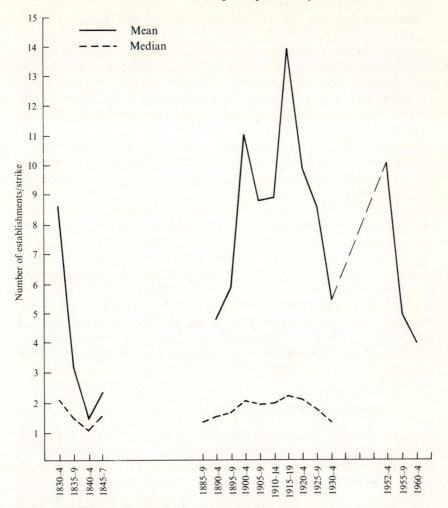

Fig. 3.8: Number of establishments per strike, 1830–1964

NOTES
The source of data for 1890–1935 is, of course, the *SG*. For 1952–64 we have relied on the annual totals published in the *Annuaire statistique*, 1966, p. 121.

With such a measure as establishments/strike the reader must especially bear in mind that the 'median' we use throughout is really the geometric mean, not the true median. In both 1890–1914 and 1915–35, 72 percent of all strikes were confined to a single establishment, and so, of course, the true median would be one establishment per strike. The geometric mean reflects, therefore, the strong upward pull of the multi-establishment strikes.

1830–47 strike movement, it seems reasonable to speculate that high plant participation rates characterized these early strikes (even though these strikers did not maintain their solidarity long once on strike). And we are confident that these early strikes were limited to a few establishments.

Our trend data hint that this pattern began to recur after the Second World War. Plant participation rates rose after 1946. Correspondingly, the territorial extension of strikes contracted. We raise, following Serge Mallet, the intriguing possibility that the return of this classic artisanal mobilization pattern reflected the postwar increase of skilled professional workers within the labor force, especially within the science sector. If this interpretation has any validity, a major structural shift in conflict would have had at its origin technological change.

The alternative pattern of mobilization combined a wide areal extension of strikes with low plant participation. In the 1920s the proletarian workers in the great *bagnes industriels* were organized, if at all, only nominally by ideologues from union central offices; of professional community there could be no talk, and of corporate traditions no shred remaining. The plant was giving way to the neighborhood as the axis of worker collective action, and new solidarities were replacing old ones. If this analysis is correct, the number of establishments per strike would rise as worker organization shifted from shop-level sodalities to centralized associations at the level of the municipality, region or nation. Such intensely political unions compounded the desolidarizing effects of assembly-line technology by frightening many workers away; hence a further reason for low plant participation rates. This pattern of mobilization came ever more into prominence in the first third of the twentieth century, and thus, squarely in the middle of the strike movement, has shaped our image of the 'classic' French strike.

Changes in aims and achievements

Alvin Gouldner has shown that the poorest way of knowing what workers want in strikes is to go by what they say they want.[4] To get at the real emotional and conflictual roots of an Ohio gypsum plant strike, Gouldner interviewed actors on the scene. Now this option is foreclosed to the student of French strike history, and those who wish to penetrate the surface of *demandes d'augmentation de salaire* must choose less direct and confident ways. In coming chapters we attempt through various statistical devices to establish what additionally the strikers had in mind beyond their stated grievances. Here we review how the grievances have chan~ed over the years, and try to mortar stated demands into the context of the strike as a whole.

Overwhelmingly, strikers said they wanted wage increases, or else such wage-related matters as shorter hours without pay reduction. And at most points in time wage demands so overshadowed all others as to make concern over work rules, worker organization and like questions scarcely worth considering. Yet at one point in time the latter variety of grievance did swell to prominence, though by no means achieving majoritarian status. The data in table 4 of Appendix B tell the story.

In the beginning the strike movement was preoccupied with wage issues.

During the July Monarchy, 80 percent of all disputes aimed at pay questions, another 8 percent were over 'mixed' matters, most of which concerned pay and hours, and a trifling 3 percent concerned worker organization. (The remainder were unclassifiable.) In our view this 'economism' is not evidence of poverty or economic deprivation; workers who were pushed to the rim of existence were unlikely to have possessed the associational resources to go on strike in the first place. This concern over wage issues reflects instead, we believe, the skilled worker's resentment at the uneven distribution of the resource pie, an unfair share going to the man who put up the capital, an unjustifiably small share to the men from the sweat of whose brows the entrepreneur existed. Job control questions were seldom at issue because most employers had not yet begun a systematic campaign upon hallowed shop-floor routines and prerogatives. Industrial organization and technology were transmitted and sanctioned by custom.

During the next half-century the modernization of industry precipitated a fierce struggle for job control at the shop-floor level (we further hypothesize). Mechanization and increases in scale forced the employer to rationalize his establishment, by subdividing the steps of production, by introducing machinery – therewith changing those artisanal routines and customary procedures which were incommensurate with mechanization – and by hiring unskilled labor for tasks formerly executed by polyvalent professional craftsmen.

Evidence for this interpretation is the steadily increasing percentage of strikes over worker organization questions. By 1885–9 12 percent of all strikes concerned such matters, by 1910–14, 25 percent. In Chapter 8 we shall discover that the workers on strike over job control were in fact the skilled professionals, who bitterly resented the loss of status and influence that new hiring policies and employer powers represented.[5]

Then after the First World War, the struggle was abandoned, though the skilled artisans were by no means driven to the wall. What changed was the nature of union objectives; whereas before the war struggling worker federations embraced these emotional questions of control as useful ways to mobilize support and consciousness, after the war the federations came to shun such issues. This growing antipathy to worker organization disputes was, we argue in Chapter 7, a direct consequence of union bureaucratization. Strikes waged over job control issues tended to fail more often than strikes in general, and a lost strike could devastate a struggling union.[6] Bureaucratization meant for union leaders a greater concern for preserving the integrity of the organization above all other objectives, and leaders who thought this way would avoid the explosive authority issues that could shatter their unions into fragments.[7]

A second factor in the abandonment of job control demands was the growth of the machine-tending proletarian labor force, workers who lacked all sense of occupational solidarity or professional identification. Such proletarians – the great auto assembly plants outside Paris come at once to mind – were glumly resigned to dehumanization of their industrial environment that came with assembly-line production. Advanced mechanization brought with it a sense of the hopelessness of the job control struggle. For both the logic of the situation and the overwhelming power of the employer commanded Taylorism, the rationalization of work and the subdivision of labor. In such circumstances it was impossible for the new proletarians to carve out a substantial realm of job control, and so, guided by their bureaucratized unions, they mounted demands for salary increases.

Such an emphasis upon wages does not exclude the possibility that other non-wage issues motivated these strikers as well. We would argue, with Michelle Perrot and Rolande Trempé, that wage demands in themselves symbolized a larger range of worker aspirations, giving a nice concreteness to struggles which outside the local level must have seemed mysterious and blurred. Michelle Perrot writes: 'In fact the range of the strike was not measured solely in its immediate results. Workers felt more or less confused when they situated their local struggle within the tableau of a play of several acts, as an episode in a campaign on several fronts.' Wage demands thus crystallized more diffuse, less articulated political ambitions. More important than the content of a grievance was the fact that it had been advanced at all. It seems to us, therefore, a mistake to take these wage demands at their face value. And Peter Stearns's assertion that French workers were essentially moderate because their demands – mostly wage-related – seldom exceeded the bounds of reasonableness, seems to us downright wrongheaded. Wage demands were not a substitute for revolution, but instead, as Rolande Trempé has recently argued, a way-station on that road.[8]

There was no change from the 1920s to the 1950s in the overwhelming preponderance of wage claims. Only in the 1960s did some signs of a turning set in. Yet here is not the place to describe new directions in which the CGT–FO or the CFDT led worker demands, or to chronicle the outpouring of job control grievances in May–June 1968. These tasks await Chapter 5.

The main movement among grievances over the last century and a half has thus been parabolic; a slow rise of job control demands commenced with the advance of mechanization late in the nineteenth century, peaking just before the First World War, then declining to the infinitesimal levels characteristic of the July Monarchy. A complex interaction between technology and organization lay behind this smooth arc.

The outcomes of French strikes have been so dismal over the years, and their growing lack of success so palpable, that one wonders why the workers bothered (fig. 3.9). Indeed, anyone who insisted that the true purpose of strikes was to achieve the stated grievances would be absolutely at a loss to explain why in the 1960s workers still struck at all, so few of their demands were ever met.

If one looks at complete successes, strikes of the July Monarchy were the

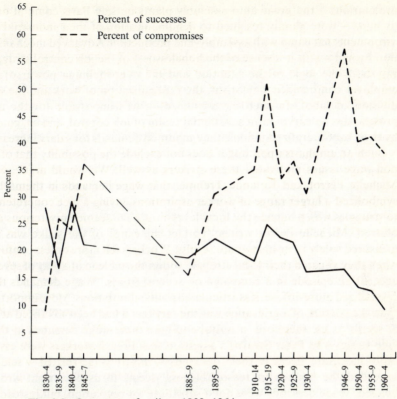

Fig. 3.9: Outcomes of strikes, 1830–1964

NOTES

The standard outcome categories the *SG* used were:

        Réussite (R) – success
        Transaction ou réussite partielle (T) – compromise
        Échec (E) – failure

To these we added a fourth: strikers dismissed, in the event that more than two-thirds of the strikers were not taken back. Unless otherwise stated we treat both the *échec* proper and the fired strikers as 'failure.'

The *RFT* retained the three standard categories. Percentages after 1946 in fig. 3.9 are based on the number of strikes for which the outcome was known.

For reasons already indicated, we are reluctant to present *APO* data because of the source's overpowering biases. For what it's worth, here is the *APO* outcome series (the number of cases in parentheses):

The percentage distribution of outcomes in the APO, *1848–84*

	Success	Compromise	Failure
1848–9	56 (5)	0	44 (4)
1850–4	0	0	100 (3)
1855–9	13 (2)	13 (2)	73 (11)
1860–4	52 (12)	17 (4)	30 (7)
1865–9	28 (13)	30 (14)	41 (19)
1870–4	48 (11)	17 (4)	35 (8)
1875–9	27 (7)	8 (2)	65 (17)
1880–4	38 (22)	17 (10)	47 (28)

most successful of all. Thereafter it was downhill. Only in 1920–4 did disputes briefly again achieve the high success rates of 1830–4 and 1840–4. The percentage of strikes ending in victory oscillated between 16 and 25 percent in the years 1885–1949, plunging definitively downwards in the 1950s. Between 1950 and 1965 the win rate dropped from 13 to a meager 9 percent of all strikes. Fluctuations in the success rate between 1885 and 1934 were probably more due to market conditions in the price and supply of labor than to the concerted efforts of the labor movement. But the shifts over the very long pull, from the July Monarchy to the 1960s, we consider the result of conscious changes in labor's strategies of conflict.

The win rate fell partly because some successes were turning into compromises. The proportion of successes fell by only 3 percentage points from 1830–47 to 1915–35, but the compromise rate increased by 15 points, from 23 percent to 38 percent. And then in 1946–9 the compromise rate rose again to nearly 60 percent of all strikes. So on balance strikes over the long haul had ever happier outcomes, if one counts both success and compromise as essentially favorable results for the workers. Most compromises should be considered partial successes rather than partial failures, because most strikes are 'offensive' worker-initiated challenges to employers rather than 'defensive' responses to employer-initiated changes.[9] Therefore we may read the rising compromise rate, combined with the falling success and failure rates, as evidence that workers and employers were, perhaps, more willing to bargain and to avert the *grève-illimitée* as the years passed.

This interpretation will not, however, hold for the period 1950–65, when the success and compromise rates have trended downwards together, and the failure rate has risen. It is true that after the Second World War a higher percent of strikes ended in compromise than before the war; but the direction of change within the postwar period has been towards failure. At the same time, strike rates have risen to unprecedented levels. Why did the workers trouble to strike at all if the likelihood of success was steadily receding? We argue that in the postwar years the worker movement became ever more indifferent to the actual outcome of strikes, that is, to whether the stated objectives were achieved, because the purpose of strikes had become increasingly not to wrest wage concessions from individual employers but to mount a symbolic protest for the sake of impressing the political elite.[10] Strikes would, in fact, have a substantial pay-off, but it was intended to come via the executive order or legislative *projet* rather than via collectively negotiated wage increases.

The alternative explanation for the rising failure rate after 1950 is that the worker movement was becoming increasingly powerless and its strikes ever more ineffectual. The fragmentation among the confederations was taking its toll in results, and underorganization among the manufacturing workers grew increasingly serious, with the consequence that the likelihood of either success or compromise diminished steadily. The falling success and compromise rates, according to this interpretation, would stem not from deliberate indifference to shop-floor gains but from a painful working-class defeat in a desperate struggle over real wages. There may be something to this interpretation, for there is no doubt of the enervating effects of the extreme subdivision of labor in modern factories. Yet we feel this alternative hypothesis is inconsistent with the course the next characteristic of strike activity – duration – has followed.

As we have seen, strikes started out in the July Monarchy quite short, climbed around the *belle époque* to a middling duration, and then after the Second World War declined in length to such an extent that in 1960–5 their median duration was only one day (fig. 3.10). Yet the brevity of strikes in 1830–47 came from quite different reasons than in 1946–65.

Before we consider the detailed evolution of strike duration, let us consider for a moment the possible inferences one might make from brevity in strikes. They are essentially three:

– If the strike is short, it may mean that the workers lacked solidarity and organizational resources, and therefore were simply unable to hold together for long. Even with the strike barely under way, striker unity would dissolve and the workers straggle back to their jobs, more intent upon pursuing individual economic advantage than benefits for the commonweal. A variant of this interpretation might be that the strikers were desperately poor, and that economic want forced them back to work, their children crying for bread, their wives berating them for misadventure.

– If the strike is short, it may mean that the strikers had intended only a symbolic gesture by walking out, not an endurance contest with their employer to see whom financial distress would drive first to making concessions. Once the symbolic protest is effectively presented to the surrounding public and to attentive political authorities, no further reason exists for remaining out and the strikers return to work.

– Finally, if the strike is short, it may mean that the employer was unable to hold out, as precariously balanced profit margins dictate quick surrender to striker demands. But in the realities of industrial conflict in France such situations came seldom to the fore. Not many employers had overhead costs so high, or were in markets so restless, that production delays of a few days would have forced them to their knees. And indeed the strikers' whole strategy was to call down community and government pressures for compromise upon the unbending employers. The strikers were well aware that employer resentment of their insurgency would prolong resistance long after profit considerations had counselled compromise.[11]

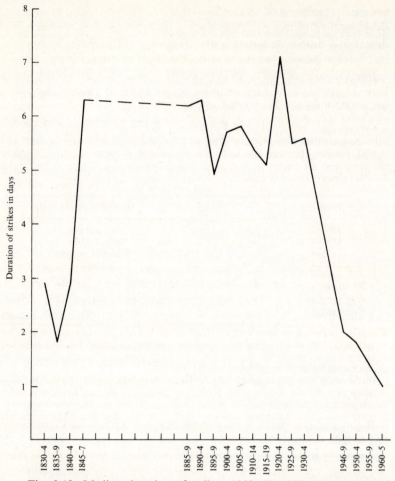

Fig. 3.10: Median duration of strikes, 1830–47, 1885–1934; estimated for 1946–64

The median duration of strikes during the July Monarchy was 3.8 days. How should that be interpreted? As we have seen, strikes of that era tended to be successful, evidence that we are not dealing with the wretched of the earth whom financial penury prevents from enduring past a couple of days on strike. Also, independent evidence will be presented in later pages to the effect that these July Monarchy strikers were probably the elite of the labor force, highly skilled craftsmen in jobs giving them considerable leverage upon their employers. Two factors may have converged, however, to limit the duration of their strikes. Although their informal solidarity was doubtless high, their formal organizations were weak, indeed not proper labor unions at all but mechanisms for coordination and devices for meeting together that were concealed as innocuous self-help societies and mutualist

NOTES

We used the *SG* method of calculating duration by subtracting the beginning date of the strike from the ending date. Holidays and Sundays are included in the duration figures. Both strikes lasting less than a single shift, and those which began on one day and ended the following, are treated as having lasted a single day. When the need arises, however, we are able to distinguish the less-than-a-shift from the full-day variety for the years 1915–35.

The *RFT*'s duration categories changed from time to time. When the relevant data are given at all, it is always possible to determine the percent of strikes lasting a day or less. But in 1952–9 the next duration category up the scale was 1–5 days, rather than 1–6 days as in other years. And between 1946 and 1958 the top duration category was 25 days and more, rather than the +30 days adopted in 1959.

No duration data were available in the *RFT* for 1954, 1955, 1957, 1958 or 1962.

APO duration data are manifestly not comparable to those of other sources because the compilers' net tended to catch only long, prominent strikes. Here is the *APO* median duration series (number of cases for which data available in parentheses):

Period	Median duration in days
1848–9	only 1 strike
1850–4	only 1 strike
1855–9	3 days (4 strikes)
1860–4	3 (6)
1865–9	29 (19)
1870–4	17 (10)
1875–9	28 (11)
1880–4	27 (34)

Assuming that the compiling bias remained constant for all periods, these data indicate a lengthening of strikes during the last half of the nineteenth century. Such a movement fits with what we know from Aguet and the *SG*.

The 'median' duration reported in fig. 3.10 is, as always, the geometric mean. Yet the median duration of 1 day we cite for 1960–5 is in fact the genuine median. In order to allay reader uneasiness about the comparability of these two measures of central tendency, we reproduce here the three different duration series for 1890–1934. It is clear that the geometric mean and the true median are close to interchangeable in these distributions (though theoretically they are quite distinct).

	Average duration[a]	Geometric mean duration[b]	Median duration[c]
1890–4	14	6	6
1895–9	10	5	5
1900–4	13	6	5
1905–9	14	6	5
1910–14	13	5	5
1915–19	10	5	5
1920–4	15	7	7
1925–9	12	6	5
1930–4	12	6	5
1960–5	–	–	1[d]

[a] Computed by taking the total number of duration days in the five-year period and dividing by the number of strikes for which duration information is available. The number of days each strike lasts is its 'duration days.'

[b] Computed by totaling the logarithms of the number of duration days in each strike, dividing by the total number of strikes and then finding the antilog of that result.

[c] Computed by finding the mid point in the frequency distribution.

[d] By inference, because 50 percent of all strikes lasted a day or less.

associations. A labor union has resources in experience and command to keep workers together in a strike action that a mutualist society simply does not possess. Secondly, the state intervened quickly in many strikes to bring them to an end. No dispute of any magnitude could long continue before the government would step in, often arresting the leaders. The judicial suppression of the strike movement might therefore help explain the brevity of disputes.

Strike duration rose over the next hundred years as both parties organized themselves with increasing completeness. At all points in time before 1936, organization of both employers and workers is associated with lengthy duration.[12] And thus as the disputants acquired the capacity to resist interminably, their disputes dragged out increasingly. Median duration reached its plateau late in the nineteenth century, and then stayed at around six days from 1885 to 1934, exceptionally shooting up to seven days in 1920–4 (the result of the long strikes of 1920 and 1921).

After the Second World War a great decline in duration set in as we earlier noted. By 1960–5 median duration was one day.[13] A reduction of this dramatic nature manifestly makes everything about the strike different: participation patterns, objectives and collective bargaining modes. When seen in connection with other developments, this great decline in duration supports the case that strikes in France completed after the Second World War their long 'nationalization,' becoming a means of political action on the part of a working class avid for representation within the magic circle of center-stage politics.

Let us step back a couple of paces and try to place these various elements in the transformation of the strike in a wider perspective. Why have these changes – the enormous acceleration in strike rates, the widening scope of disputes and their simultaneous fall in duration – occurred? We argue that the transformation of the strike took place in a four-stage process. And the reader will be better able to follow the subsequent analysis if we here outline this process of change. All four steps in the strike's transformation concern politics, yet from one epoch to another worker notions of the seat of political power and of the proper forum for the advance of one's political interests have shifted.

Strikes started out in the July Monarchy as a means used by scattered groups of skilled craftsmen to negotiate for themselves a larger share of the profits pie of individual firms – whose total profitability, they could clearly see, was being increased by dint of their own talent and effort. Why their collective efforts should have galvanized in the early 1830s, rather than in the 1820s or the 1840s, is unclear to us. Inevitably, a combination of circumstances came together whose exact identity a study at this level cannot disentangle. The participants in these early strikes do not seem to have intended their agitation to convey messages to anyone beyond the confines of the local community. But since the scale of political action was small, and because contests for power unfolded in this localized arena, we are unwilling to call these strikes non-political. Whether the early strikers wished to accomplish purposes going beyond the redistribution of the profits of individual entrepreneurs remains an open question. This ideal type of the July Monarchy strike, in any event, was the point of departure, the status quo that subsequent events would transform.

The second stage in the transformation came in the years 1880–1910, a period we call the great mobilization of the working classes. The principal participants continued to be artisans. At this time formal organizations were constituted across the country, and these local associations became linked to national networks. The avowed purpose of such organizations was political: revolutionary syndicalism, the exhortations of the Charter of Amiens to transform society and other features of the labor movement long familiar to French historians. Not all of these unionists were 'revolutionary,' but the bulk of their strikes were nonetheless fundamentally political. They were challenging the distribution of resources and authority within two different arenas: (1) within the plant, where mechanization was shattering the carapace of artisanal custom and perquisite; (2) within the national polity (rather than the municipality), where control of critical resources was becoming increasingly lodged.

The third stage in the transformation of the strike may be dated at the Popular Front. During the 1920s a new stratum of workers had been accumulating who had little organization, and little influence in any arena, be it local or national. As we have seen, such workers abandoned thoughts of job control or shop-level influence. The processes of mechanization and industrialization that called these new proletarians into existence had ruled out such concerns from the outset. The new proletarians were interested solely in acquiring power at the national level, and finally in 1936 they rushed into organizations and confederations that promised to do just that. For these men the strike was becoming a symbolic act, designed to impress their case upon decision-makers in the ministries and legislature, not to force individual employers to compliance or local mayors to greater sympathy. And the decline in duration and the increase in scope testify to this new purpose.

Our post-Second World War data suggest that a fourth stage in worker protest may be under way. Skilled professional workers within the science sector, and within white-collar bureaucracies, appear determined to use nationwide worker organizations as a means of acting through the center to solve local, office-floor issues. Their preoccupations, as with the objectives of the artisans of the July Monarchy, concern rewards and gratifications within the individual firm, but their tactics in treating with their nationalized or nationwide employers compel them to press demands at the center.

Outfitted with an argument, we now pass beyond the frontier of national aggregates into the thicket of the strike movement.

4 Year-to-year variation in strike activity

We have stressed the political role of the French strike. We don't mean that strikes had nothing to do with the condition of the economy. Both the capacity of workers to strike and the probability that a strike would win depended on the current levels of prices, wages, employment and production. On the whole, contrary to any simple notion of industrial conflict as an outgrowth of economic deprivation, prosperity brought higher levels of strike activity. The generalization holds, of course, over the very long run. Both the general prosperity of the French economy and the real incomes of French workers have risen greatly during the same century which has brought strikes from rare events to everyday occurrences. It holds at the medium run as well: despite important contrary cases like 1936, periods of cyclical depression like the later 1870s or the 1930s tended to produce fewer strikes than periods of growth like the later 1890s or the 1920s.

As this chapter will show, the generalization also holds in the short run of year-to-year variation. Yet this chapter will also show that factors, not so obviously 'economic' in character, influence the rise and fall of strike activity; those factors have to do with the organization and political position of labor. The elementary model with which we are working takes something like the form of fig. 4.1.

A model such as this indicates schematically how things hang together, what general relationships among industrial conflict, economic activity and political action our argument anticipates. To put our anticipation in English, we hope the data in this chapter will reveal:

(1) a tendency for the prosperity of employers and workers to rise together as production expands;

(2) a tendency for worker organization to increase as workers acquire more resources (real wages) to devote to their movement or as the political position of labor changes, possibly through threats to labor's existing power, possibly through new opportunities for the further expansion of worker political influence;

(3) a tendency for changes (especially improvements) in the political position of labor, for increases in worker organization and for rises in the prosperity of management all to raise the level of strike activity.

Furthermore, we expect the political and organizational components of

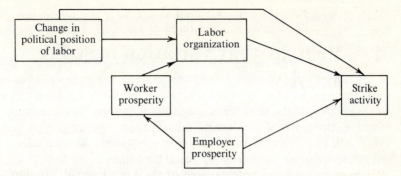

Fig. 4.1: A preliminary model of the argument

the model to acquire more weight as time goes on. These expectations follow fairly directly from the tentative analysis we offered at the end of the last chapter.

Our techniques and their limitations

Obviously, the argument requires a good deal more specification. Alas, it also calls for some compromises and some modifications. Compromises, because data to represent all its ramifications simply do not exist at present. Modifications, because we shall find that shifts from period to period were more irregular than our statement indicates, and because 'prosperity' presents greater complications than we have said.

In order to treat year-to-year variation at all, we have to do some radical simplifying. For one thing, we must take the calendar year as our unit of analysis, although we know that in some industries work and conflict follow a different schedule. Agriculture is a clear example. Yet the calendar year represents the only common ground of the varied data we have to consult.

We simplify even more aggressively by dealing with all strikes for France as a whole instead of making separate analyses by locality or by industry. In so doing, we surely obscure some of the relationship between political or economic fluctuations and the movement of strike activity; industries, localities, individual plants vary in their vulnerability and responsiveness to price swings or political crises. Furthermore, the summing of all strikes gives greater weight to the industries with the most strikes: metalworking, textiles and construction count more than foods or chemicals. Because the proportions of the labor force and of total strike activity in these various industries have changed significantly since the nineteenth century, we can't distinguish with great confidence between (a) changes in relationships among strike activity and political or economic fluctuations which affected *all* industries and (b) the changing prominence of different segments of the labor force which respond to economic or political fluctuations in significantly different ways. All these complications mean that to pin down firmly some of the relationships which interest us we would have to examine different industrial settings separately.

Yet we have little choice. The task of collecting and codifying data on prices, wages, unionization, unemployment and the other variables which we must consider year by year for separate industries and localities would be staggering. If the data were magically to appear in our mailbox one morning, the work of conducting separate analyses category by category would still exceed by far any of the large analyses we have actually carried out. Many of them, furthermore, would be pointless; the usual annual frequency of strikes in a particular industry within a particular locality is too small for sustained statistical analysis. We must aggregate.

Finally, we simplify by concentrating separate analyses on a series of relatively short periods, all of them since 1869. Before 1870, the data are too sparse and unreliable to deserve year-to-year study at a national scale. We break the period from 1870 onward into sections partly because the available data are more homogeneous and less vulnerable to the shifts in the composition of the labor force we have just mentioned than are the data covering the entire span from the 1870s to the 1960s; partly as well because we can thereby match our work to that carried on by other scholars.

The reader must keep in mind some important kinds of variation left entirely unexamined by this year-to-year analysis, such as fluctuations in strikes from one month to the next. Just as strikes display certain regularities over the years, such as the movement with the cycle of profits and wages, they show as well marked seasonal regularities. As fig. 4.2 indicates, conflict tended to accelerate during the spring, coasting then downhill through the summer and fall to stabilize at a low plateau in the winter. This pattern became attenuated as time went on, for workers in a modern industrial economy grow, presumably, less sensitive to whatever the seasonal fluctuations are – the weather, the harvest, the sap in the trees – that evoke strikes. That is just the point: our annual data make inaccessible the study of the motors of these month-to-month oscillations in conflict. An accounting of seasonal movement in strikes might turn out to be as promising as that of annual movement. Yet our data compel us to address the latter variety of fluctuation alone in this chapter.

We begin with the period 1870–90, which Michelle Perrot has studied in far greater detail. We continue with the overlapping period 1890–1913, which corresponds to the analyses of Edgard Andréani. Our next series covers 1920 to 1938, the *entre-deux-guerres* of Robert Goetz-Girey and other students of industrial conflict. Finally, we take up 1946–67 – a period less sanctified by the attention of scholars, but covering the postwar years for which we have continuous data.[1]

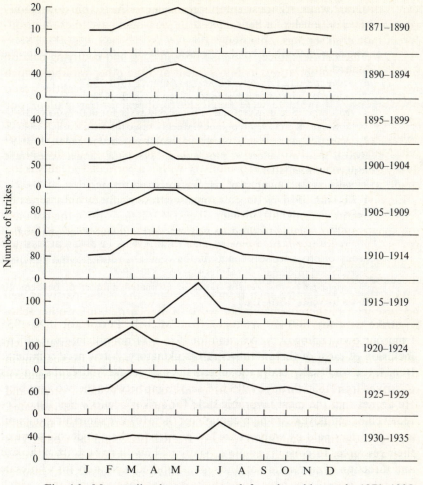

Fig. 4.2: Mean strikes begun per month for selected intervals, 1871–1935

Correlates of year-to-year variation

Let us begin simply: by correlating the number of strikes and the number of strikers in a given year with a set of variables representing fluctuation in France's political and economic life. We concentrate on variables for which we have data covering most of the period from 1870 through 1967. We thereby sacrifice some refinement and gain some comparability. Here are the eleven variables:[2]

> 1. *unemployment*: number of persons registered jobless each year, 1920–67 (for 1890–1913 we have borrowed a correlation coefficient calculated by Andréani from data unavailable to us)

2. *cost of living*: Singer-Kérel 213-item index for Paris, 1870–1938; INSEE retail price index for Paris, 1946–67

3. *wholesale prices*: Statistique générale de la France index, France as a whole, 1870–99; INSEE index, France, 1900–67; former series transformed to meet latter

4. *wholesale/retail ratio*: variable 3/variable 2, 1870–1967

5. *money wage*: Singer-Kérel index, France, 1870–1954

6. *real wage*: Singer-Kérel index B, weekly wage for male worker, 1870–1938; Singer-Kérel 213-item index, weekly wage for male worker, 1946–54

7. *industrial production*: Crouzet industrial production index, 1870–97; INSEE index of industrial production, 1898–1967; former series transformed to meet latter

8. *unionization*: number of members of *syndicats ouvriers*, 1890–1914, 1920, 1921, 1926–38 (to get a smooth series, data for four of the interwar years have been interpolated)

9. *cabinet changes*: number of formal changes of government in the year

10. *violent conflicts*: estimated number of events involving at least one group of fifty persons or more in the course of which persons or objects were seized or damaged over resistance, 1870–1960

11. *participants in collective violence*: estimated number of participants in such events, 1870–1960

Strike data for 1871–90 are taken from Michelle Perrot, for 1890–1935 from our own coding of the *SG*, and for 1936–67 from official sources. The inclusion of most of these items is self-explanatory. A few need comment. Item 4, the wholesale/retail ratio, enters the list because Andréani's analysis of strikes from 1890 through 1913 stresses the gap between the two variables. He argues that the most favorable time for strikes occurs when the prices received by employers are high enough for them to have something to spare, and the prices paid by workers are low enough for them to devote some of their resources to collective action. Andréani himself reasons from the size and direction of correlation coefficients computed separately for wholesale and retail prices. We have done the same, and then added a ratio which represents the *gap* more directly.

Item 9, annual cabinet changes, rarely figures in quantitative analyses of French history, but often appears implicitly as the major index of political instability. We don't attach quite such broad significance to French changes of government, since the 'cabinet crisis' became a more or less routine way of doing political work in France, and since most governmental activity continued unperturbed by crisis after crisis. Yet each cabinet crisis did provide an opening for a redefinition of the relative positions of the actors in the national political structure, including the representatives of organized labor. For that reason, we consider their frequency a possible approximation of a variable which is very hard to index directly: changes in the national political position of labor.

Finally, we include our own counts of violent conflicts and of participants in collective violence in order to close in on the same relationship from another direction. (In correlating violent conflicts with strikes, we are not merely measuring the same thing twice, since less than a sixth of the conflicts in question involved groups which we know to have been on strike at the time of the violence; to turn the same question around, we have been able to establish the presence of collective violence in only a tiny proportion of the roughly 36,000 strikes reported from 1890 through 1935.[3]) Again, our analysis of these variables takes for granted something which must eventually be proved independently: that collective violence rises and falls with other forms of political conflict.[4] The most we can say with any confidence is that since the 1890s the times of extensive collective violence in France have also been the times of hostile demonstrations, mass meetings, explicitly political strikes and calls for revolution. Even if other forms of political conflict follow other rhythms, it will be useful to know whether strikes and these sorts of mass actions fluctuate together. That much, at least, our analysis can establish.

The table of simple correlations between these variables and the number of strikes in a year (table 4.1) displays some strong relationships in each period. Nevertheless, the pattern changes considerably from one period to the next, and the average magnitude of the correlations falls off after the First World War. The relationship between the number of strikes and the cost-of-living index, for example, falls from $+0.75$ in 1870–90 to $+0.35$

Table 4.1: *Zero-order correlations of selected variables with strikes per year*

Variable	Period			
	1870–90	1890–1913	1920–38	1946–67
Unemployment	—[a]	-0.32^b	$+0.40$	$+0.10$
Cost of living	$+0.75$	$+0.35$	0.00	-0.05
Wholesale prices	-0.61	$+0.74$	-0.10	-0.03
Wholesale/retail	-0.67	$+0.79$	-0.12	-0.03
Nominal wage	$+0.69$	$+0.85$	$+0.07$	$+0.13^b$
Real wage	$+0.75$	$+0.79$	$+0.14$	-0.36^b
Industrial production	$+0.81$	$+0.81$	-0.02	-0.04
Unionization	—[a]	$+0.88$	$+0.58^b$	—[a]
Cabinet changes	-0.14	$+0.07$	-0.03	-0.06
Violent conflicts	-0.15	$+0.44$	$+0.43$	$+0.63^b$
Participants in collective violence	-0.32	$+0.47$	$+0.19$	$+0.69^b$

[a] Data unavailable for this period.
[b] Calculated over period shorter than indicated because of missing data; see variable descriptions. The correlation for unemployment over 1890–1913 is the coefficient reported by Andréani over 1895–1913.

in 1890–1913 to 0 after the First World War. Some wild switching occurs from period to period. The most notable is the movement of the whole-sale/retail ratio from −0.67 in 1870–90 to +0.79 in 1890–1913.

Generally speaking, however, the economic indicators display strong positive relationships with strike activity from 1870 to the First World War, and decline to insignificance thereafter.[5] The partial exceptions are unemployment (correlated +0.40 with number of strikes in 1920–38) and real wages (correlated −0.36 with number of strikes in 1946–54, after having been strongly and positively related to strikes before the First World War).[6] In the two periods for which data exist, unionization and strikes show a strong tendency to fluctuate together. The number of cabinet changes turns out to be essentially unrelated to strike activity in any period. But the number of violent conflicts and the participants in them goes from a weak *negative* relationship with number of strikes in 1870–90 to fairly strong positive relationships thereafter. In fact, the two violence variables correlate more highly with the number of strikes after the Second World War than do any other variables on the list.

The correlations with number of participants in strikes (given in table 4.2) differ considerably in detail, but describe the same general pattern. As Andréani observed in his study of 1890 to 1913, the relationships tend to be weaker than the corresponding relationships with the number of strikes. Yet the same drift of the economic relationships from strongly positive to insignificant occurs. Unionization again shows a strong positive relationship with strike activity. Cabinet changes still display little association with industrial conflict. And the indicators of collective violence again go from

Table 4.2: *Zero-order correlations of selected variables with strikers per year*

	Period			
Variable	1870–90	1890–1913	1920–38	1946–67
Unemployment	—[a]	—[a]	+0.33	−0.23
Cost of living	+0.52	+0.16	+0.02	−0.07
Wholesale prices	−0.39	+0.59	+0.03	−0.10
Wholesale/retail	−0.46	+0.71	+0.05	−0.07
Nominal wage	+0.40	+0.62	+0.04	+0.13[b]
Real wage	+0.47	+0.61	+0.06	−0.47[b]
Industrial production	+0.49	+0.58	−0.21	−0.02
Unionization	—[a]	+0.63	+0.63[b]	—[a]
Cabinet changes	−0.22	+0.20	+0.09	+0.10
Violent conflicts	−.0.20	+0.63	+0.32	+0.29[b]
Participants in collective violence	−0.30	+0.65	+0.05	+0.24[b]

[a,b]   See notes to table 4.1.

weakly negative in 1870–90 to substantially positive thereafter; the strongest relationship between year-to-year variation in collective violence and in number of strikers appears in 1890–1913.

Some of these correlations of strikes and strikers with other variables, however, reflect a common trend rather than a causal connection. During the years from 1890 through 1913, for example, both the number of strikes and industrial production rose almost continuously; it is the joint movement over the entire period, instead of the shifts from one year to the next, that accounts for most of their correlation of +0.81. A common trend often reflects the influence of a third factor rather than a genuine interdependence of the two phenomena correlated. Inflation moves most price series upward, and rapid inflation produces very high correlations among them; common trends in a wide variety of social indicators come from a general increase in population size; in a time of general economic decline, many distantly related economic indices swing down together. In order to examine the relationship between yearly fluctuations in strike activity and the immediate economic and political situation, we must remove the effects of trend.

Our simplest, most general attempt to detrend the correlations appears in tables 4.3 and 4.4. There we report the partial correlations of the same pairs of variables after removing the effect of the linear regression of each variable on time – that is, the number of years from the start of the period being analyzed. The higher the correlation with time, the stronger the trend. The correlation coefficients at the bottoms of the two tables indicate that a simple linear regression produced a good fit to the trend from 1870 through 1890

Table 4.3: *Correlations of selected variables with strikes per year, partialed for time*

Variable	Period			
	1870–90	1890–1913	1920–38	1946–67
Unemployment	—[a]	—[a]	+0.30	−0.04
Cost of living	+0.44	−0.03	−0.38	−0.04
Wholesale prices	+0.27	+0.38	−0.11	+0.02
Wholesale/retail	+0.08	+0.08	−0.34	−0.05
Nominal wage	+0.13	+0.25	−0.53	+0.38[b]
Real wage	+0.41	+0.15	−0.24	−0.37
Industrial production	+0.61	+0.04	−0.11	+0.03
Unionization	—[a]	+0.29	+0.60[b]	—[a]
Cabinet changes	−0.13	+0.08	−0.09	−0.18
Violent conflicts	+0.15	+0.34	+0.33	+0.64[b]
Participants in collective violence	+0.02	+0.43	+0.06	+0.70[b]
r, strikes × time	+0.70	+0.87	+0.29	−0.04

[a,b] See notes to table 4.1.

Table 4.4: *Correlations of selected variables with strikers per year, partialed for time*

Variable	Period			
	1870–90	1890–1913	1920–38	1946–67
Unemployment	—[a]	—[a]	+0.33	−0.22
Cost of living	+0.41	−0.16	−0.20	+0.06
Wholesale prices	+0.17	+0.26	+0.03	−0.05
Wholesale/retail	−0.05	+0.49	+0.33	−0.12
Nominal wage	−0.08	+0.10	+0.35	+0.05[b]
Real wage	+0.12	+0.13	−0.22	−0.58[b]
Industrial production	+0.19	−0.06	−0.28	+0.55
Unionization	—[a]	−0.06	+0.73[b]	—[a]
Cabinet changes	−0.22	+0.22	+0.24	+0.05
Violent conflicts	−0.04	+0.58	+0.26	+0.18
Participants in collective violence	−0.10	+0.62	−0.04	+0.17
r, strikers × time	+0.46	+0.65	+0.19	−0.08

[a,b] See notes to table 4.1.

and from 1890 through 1913, a poorer fit from 1920 to 1938, and no fit at all after the Second World War. (In the first three periods the trend ran upward, less decisively so after the First World War than before; from 1946 through 1967, the very high levels of strike activity in the first few years produced something of a downward trend, but the movement from year to year was so great as to produce a zero correlation. The correlation coefficient, of course, measures the scatter about the best-fitting regression line rather than the slope of the line itself.) We should therefore be unsurprised to find the partialing procedure making large differences in the coefficients before the First World War, and little difference after the Second World War.

In all periods the removal of trend attenuates most of the correlations. The most dramatic changes in the pattern appear in the period 1890–1913. There, common trend seems to account for much of the zero-order relationship between unionization and strike activity, and almost all of the relationship between industrial production and strike activity. (At this point our findings differ somewhat from those of Andréani; his correction for trend via a five-year moving average left a correlation of +0.25 between the number of strikes and his index of industrial production; he concluded from other analyses that unionization had no independent effect.)

Before the Second World War the relationships between strike activity and all the wage-price indicators appear due in large measure to common trend. Nevertheless, the partialing leaves a significant relationship between wholesale prices and strike activity up to 1913, a shift of the relationship between real wages and industrial conflict from positive before the First

World War to negative thereafter and a substantial tendency for strikes and strikers to abound when the cost of living was high from 1870 through 1890. We have no year-by-year data on unemployment before 1920. After then, the figures go from a moderate positive relationship between unemployment and strikes in the 1920s and 1930s (a relationship strongly affected by the wave of strikes in the high-unemployment years after 1935) to a weak negative relationship after the war. The political variables emerge relatively unaffected by the correction for trend because they themselves have little trend.

On the whole, the new coefficients reinforce strongly the impression – already given by the zero-order matrix – of an increasing association after 1890 of strikes with collective violence, and thus by inference, with political conflict.

The elementary model which began this chapter proposed three direct determinants of the level of strike activity: (a) employer prosperity, (b) worker organization, (c) change in the political position of labor. It suggested that the prosperity of workers depended to some extent on the prosperity of employers and facilitated the development of labor organization, but had no significant independent effect on strike activity. We have indexed all the elements of the model – especially change in the political position of labor – rather indirectly. If our indicators do represent the main clusters of variables in the model adequately, we have to introduce more change in the weights and directions of the relationships than our original statement of the argument permitted.

The prosperity of employers, for example, began by being an important condition for strike activity, but faded after the First World War, if we may take wholesale prices and industrial production as fair indices of such matters. Worker organization (or, at least, the unionization of workers) displayed an increasing synchronization with strike activity during the two periods for which we have the necessary statistics, but we must plead ignorant before 1890 and after 1938. Change in the political position of labor – to the small extent that one can infer it from collective violence – acquires greater importance as a predictor of strike activity after 1890. The prosperity of workers does, indeed, show a tendency to rise with that of employers. Whether unionization tends to rise as a function of the well-being of workers seems more dubious, but deserves closer attention later in this chapter. In any case, the preliminary study of correlations reveals an unexpectedly strong positive relationship of strike activity with real wages before the First World War, moving to a negative relationship thereafter. We encounter, that is, more complications than our model gives us any right to expect. Some of the complications will later turn out to result from the spurious relationships produced by dealing with only two variables at a time while other variables lurk in the background. All of our subsequent analyses, however, will indicate that over the period from 1870 to 1967 both the character of the strike and the conditions favorable to strike activity changed fundamentally. A static model does not do justice to that transformation.

Before trying to sort out the complications by means of multivariate analyses, let us look at a few other features of strikes. Our model provides a more plausible account of the offensive strike – the strike which conquers new ground for workers – than of the defensive strike, the one which resists the speedup, the wage cut or the imposition of new work rules. If we separate offensive and defensive strikes, the ability of the model to differentiate should show up as a difference in the pattern of relationships for the two classes of strikes. In particular, defensive strikes ought to show some tendency to occur in times of economic contraction. The model also suggests that those strikes which *do* occur in times of contraction have a smaller chance of success.

We have detailed information on the outcomes of strikes and the issues involved only from 1890 to 1935. During those forty-six years, 22 percent of all strikes were successful in terms of the initial demands of the workers, 37 percent ended in compromise and 41 percent failed.[7] The rate of success declined from 1890 to the First World War, rose again into the early 1920s, and then fell even lower after 1926; its maximum was 34 percent in 1891, its minimum 14 percent in 1930. Failure also declined from 1890 to the First World War, only to rise abruptly after 1919; but the failure rate rose even higher after 1929. Its minimum was 16 percent in 1917, its maximum 58 percent in 1931. As the accounts of success and failure suggest, compromise was becoming a more frequent outcome of strikes as the 1890s and 1900s moved on, and only suffered a temporary decline in the early 1920s. The smallest proportion of compromises – 21 percent – came in 1890, while the largest – 56 percent – arrived during the First World War, in 1917.

There are gaps in our data on the offensive or defensive nature of strikes, for before the First World War we coded this information only in 1895–9 and 1910–14, recording it consistently however in 1915–35. During the interwar period offensive grievances appeared in a whopping 76 percent of all strikes, defensive grievances in another 11 percent. From a prewar plateau, offensive strikes rose steadily until the end of the 1920s, broken by a crevasse in 1921 and 1922: maximum offensive 90 percent in 1910, minimum 26 percent in 1921. Defensive strikes moved in the opposite direction. Obviously, we have some strong trends to sort out.

Table 4.5 presents the zero-order correlation coefficients between a number of features of strike activity and a set of economic and political indicators for the two periods from 1890 to 1935. (The last year for which we have this kind of detail concerning strikes is 1935. The great strike wave of 1936 drowned the reporting system.)

The years from 1890 to 1913 show a strong upward trend (as measured by the regression of the variable in question on the number of years since 1885)

Table 4.5: *Zero-order correlation coefficients between aspects of strike activity and selected political and economic variables, 1890–1935*

Item	Number of strikes	Number of strikers	Number of man-days	Mean duration	% offensive	% defensive	% success	% compromise	% failure	Trend
1890–1913										
Cost of living	+0.35	+0.16	−0.10	+0.28	—	—	−0.41	−0.13	+0.24	+0.42
Wholesale prices	+0.74	+0.59	+0.31	+0.10	—	—	−0.42	+0.23	+0.16	+0.70
Nominal wage	+0.85	+0.62	+0.52	+0.05	—	—	−0.51	+0.53	+0.14	+0.92
Real wage	+0.39	+0.26	+0.27	+0.04	—	—	−0.39	+0.44	+0.11	+0.45
Industrial production	+0.81	+0.58	+0.30	+0.24	—	—	−0.60	+0.43	+0.03	+0.92
Unionization	+0.88	+0.63	+0.42	+0.21	—	—	−0.58	+0.58	+0.06	+0.98
Violent conflicts	+0.44	+0.63	+0.75	−0.13	—	—	−0.06	+0.26	−0.10	+0.33
Participants in collective violence	+0.46	+0.65	+0.82	−0.16	—	—	−0.11	+0.25	−0.02	+0.31
Trend	+0.87	+0.65	+0.45	+0.21	—	—	−0.59	+0.60	−0.03	1.00
1920–35										
Unemployment	−0.60	−0.48	−0.29	−0.18	−0.68	+0.67	−0.11	−0.21	+0.17	+0.76
Cost of living	−0.29	−0.47	+0.46	−0.11	−0.08	+0.06	−0.57	+0.07	−0.03	+0.74
Wholesale prices	+0.55	+0.18	+0.07	+0.07	+0.70	−0.70	+0.04	+0.60	−0.66	−0.15
Nominal wage	−0.44	−0.60	−0.58	−0.06	−0.25	+0.23	−0.60	−0.03	+0.10	+0.92
Real wage	−0.62	−0.66	−0.71	+0.24	−0.57	+0.55	−0.33	−0.48	+0.45	+0.81
Industrial production	+0.10	−0.36	−0.55	+0.22	+0.45	−0.48	−0.32	+0.29	−0.31	+0.39
Unionization[a]	+0.65	+0.57	+0.50	−0.11	+0.55	−0.53	+0.39	+0.65	−0.80	−0.50
Violent conflicts	−0.26	−0.18	−0.02	−0.14	−0.34	+0.35	−0.26	+0.07	+0.07	+0.55
Participants in collective violence	−0.29	−0.26	−0.12	+0.14	−0.34	+0.34	−0.35	−0.11	+0.20	+0.46
Trend	−0.59	−0.67	−0.59	−0.09	−0.44	+0.41	−0.49	−0.11	+0.15	1.00

a For 1920, 1921, 1926–35.

in almost every aspect of strike activity. The mean duration of strikes increased less regularly than their other features, but nonetheless increased as well. The absolute numbers of successful, unsuccessful and compromised strikes all rose considerably, but the rise of compromise was so much greater and more regular as to produce a negative correlation between time and the *proportion* of all strikes ending in success for the workers.

The economic and political indicators, likewise, follow a definite upward trend. Obviously, the zero-order correlations between different aspects of strike activity and the economic–political indicators therefore also contain a strong element of common trend. Despite that, the table brings out a marked difference in timing among successful, unsuccessful and compromised strikes. In those years from 1890 to 1913, a higher proportion of strikes tended to fail when prices were high. During the same period, compromise was taking over from out-and-out success so rapidly that all the correlations with proportion successful are negative and all the correlations with proportion compromised positive. There is therefore no point in looking too closely at those relationships until we have controlled the effects of trend.

The second panel of table 4.5 presents parallel observations for the years from 1920 to 1935. This time we also have information on the number of man-days expended in strikes, on their mean duration, on the proportion presenting offensive grievances and on the proportion defensive as well. We can also add information on unemployment. From the strike wave of 1919–20 to the rare strikes of the early 1930s, the trend runs decisively downward. (If we were to include the enormous conflicts of 1936, 1937 and 1938, to be sure, we would reverse the overall trend completely.) As a consequence, all the correlations of basic strike indicators with time are negative. It would be too simple to attribute that downward drift of all but unsuccessful strikes to the Depression. The full weight of the Depression arrived late in France, and strike-filled 1936 was a true Depression year. In fact, the overall movement of every economic indicator except wholesale prices goes upward from 1920 to 1935.

Over the period from 1920 to 1935, as before, the correlates of man-days in strikes resemble the correlates of number of strikers; that is unsurprising, since man-days is essentially a compound of duration and number of strikers. This time we find negative relationships of man-days to most of the economic indicators, a positive relationship to unionization and no relationship to collective violence. All except the positive correlation with unionization reverse the relationships which prevailed from 1890 to 1913. No strong relationship of the average duration of strikes to any variable shows up in table 4.5.

When it comes to the proportions of strikes around offensive and defensive grievances (which are not simple complements, since we have omitted those which were neither clearly offensive nor clearly defensive), on the other hand, we find signs of a tendency of offensive strikes to occur in years of high production, low wages and extensive unionization. Defensive strikes come in years of low production, high wages, high unemployment and weak unionization. The removal of 1936–8, with their high unemployment and great strike activity, from the years treated in the earlier correlational analysis completely reverses the relationship between unemployment and strikes. Now we see a strong tendency for strikes to decline with high un- employment.

In these years there are also some indications of an association between defensive strikes and collective violence. The association comes to a con- siderable extent from the concentration of Right versus Left violence in the early 1930s, which were also years of economic contraction and defensive strike activity.

The conditions for success and failure in strikes show an interesting change from the years before the First World War. Before the war, the great upward trend of compromise left success associated with economic decline and failure faintly associated with economic expansion – at least as measured by prices and wages. In those years, success was more frequent in those years in which unionization was low (which means the 1890s), compromise pre- valent when unionization was high (which means after 1900). But after the First World War we discover a considerable association between economic contraction, as represented by wholesale prices and the industrial produc- tion index, and the failure of strikes.

Indeed, unsuccessful strikes tended to occur in 1920–35 when there was relatively little strike activity; the zero-order correlation between the percent of strikes which failed and the total number of strikes from 1920 to 1935 was −0.64, while the correlations for percentage successful and compromise were +0.40 and +0.75 respectively. The conditions for frequent compromise resembled the conditions for extensive strike activity: economic expansion, low wages, high unionization. Through all this comes a suggestion of an association of widespread union membership not with *success* in strike activity, and certainly not with failure, but with a tendency to work out com- promise settlements. In fact, the zero-order correlations with union member- ship run like this:

Total strikes	+0.65
% offensive	+0.55
% defensive	−0.53
% successful	+0.39
% compromise	+0.65
% unsuccessful	−0.80

It is as if the presence of unions made both strike activity and negotiation more likely.

As in the earlier periods, we find in 1920–35 a close relationship between strike activity and wages. But whereas before the First World War strikes and wages rose together, thereafter they moved in opposite directions. In this regard, the correlates of success and failure did not change so much as the correlates of compromise. Compromise was more prevalent in high-wage years before the war, more prevalent in low-wage years after it. In other respects, the conditions for compromise remained roughly the same: extensive unionization, wholesale prices high relative to the cost of living, comparatively high industrial production.

Obviously common trends, rather than shifts from one year to the next, account for some of these relationships. The computation of partial coefficients with the effect of the linear regression on time removed will again provide a sharper picture of short-run covariation. In table 4.6 we provide those partial coefficients for 1890–1913 and 1920–35. The results come out differently from the previous effort to remove the effects of trend, because this time the great strikes of 1936–8 are not there to bend the curves upward.

The analyses of man-days and duration add little to what we already know, except to highlight (a) a strong relationship between the amount of collective violence and the total man-days in strikes before the First World War, followed by a moderate relationship after the war, (b) the characteristic shift from a positive relationship between wages and man-days before the war to a negative relationship thereafter, (c) an indication of a stronger relationship between unionization and the total volume of strike activity, as measured by man-days, than we had detected before. The tendency of offensive strikes to occur in years of economic expansion and defensive strikes to occur in times of contraction comes out even more clearly after correction for trend; likewise, the general similarity of the conditions for extensive strike activity and for offensive strikes becomes more obvious after the trend is removed. The partialing attenuates the relationship of collective violence to defensive strikes, and reveals a previously hidden association of defensive strikes with low (rather than high) nominal wages.

Once again the removal of trend for the years from 1890 to 1913, when almost all the indices were rising so rapidly, generally reduces the correlations. The apparent effect of unionization before the First World War washes out with the trend, except for a surprisingly high partial correlation between unionization and the *failure* of strikes. Andréani's wholesale/retail price scissors appears to have been operating, especially for the likelihood of compromise – but there is now a negative relationship between the industrial production index and the proportion of strikes ending in success or compromise.

After the First World War, partialing does not affect the pattern of correlations very greatly. It simply accentuates the association of compromise outcomes with relative prosperity; the one exception in this regard is the positive association between unsuccessful strikes and real wages. The analysis merely reaffirms the association of success and compromise, rather than failure, with unionization after the First World War. And it dilutes

Table 4.6: *Correlations between aspects of strike activity and selected political and economic variables, partialed for trend, 1890–1935*

Item	Number of strikes	Number of strikers	Number of man-days	Mean duration	% offensive	% defensive	% success	% compromise	% failure
1890–1913									
Cost of living	−0.03	−0.16	−0.10	+0.28	—	—	−0.22	−0.52	+0.28
Wholesale prices	+0.38	+0.26	+0.31	+0.10	—	—	−0.02	−0.34	+0.26
Nominal wage	+0.25	+0.10	+0.52	+0.05	—	—	+0.10	−0.06	+0.43
Real wage	−0.02	−0.05	+0.28	+0.04	—	—	−0.17	+0.23	+0.14
Industrial production	+0.04	−0.06	+0.30	+0.24	—	—	−0.19	−0.40	+0.15
Unionization	+0.29	−0.06	+0.52	+0.21	—	—	−0.02	−0.06	+0.55
Violent conflicts	+0.34	+0.58	+0.72	−.013	—	—	+.017	+.009	−.010
Participants in collective violence	+0.43	+0.62	+0.82	−0.16	—	—	+0.10	+0.08	−0.00
1920–35									
Unemployment	−0.28	+0.07	+0.30	−0.17	−0.60	+0.61	+0.46	−0.19	+0.09
Cost of living	+0.28	+0.05	−0.04	−0.06	+0.41	−0.41	−0.35	+0.24	−0.21
Wholesale prices	+0.58	+0.11	−0.03	+0.05	+0.72	−0.71	−0.03	+0.59	−0.65
Nominal wage	+0.32	+0.05	−0.10	+0.06	+0.42	−0.40	−0.43	+0.18	−0.11
Real wage	−0.29	−0.27	−0.53	+0.40	−0.41	+0.41	−0.01	−0.55	+0.48
Industrial production	+0.45	−0.14	−0.43	+0.28	+0.76	−0.76	−0.16	+0.36	−0.41
[a]Unionization	+0.50	+0.34	+0.21	−0.10	+0.45	−0.45	+0.22	+0.61	−0.80
Violent conflicts	+0.10	+0.29	+0.46	−0.10	−0.14	+0.17	+0.01	+0.16	−0.01
Participants in collective violence	−0.03	+0.08	+0.22	+0.21	−0.17	+0.19	−0.16	−0.06	+0.15

[a] For 1920, 1921, 1926–35.

any suggestion of an association between the outcome of strikes and the extent of collective violence.

Let us try to bring these last findings together with the earlier ones. The chief tentative inference about year-to-year fluctuations we can reasonably draw from the full set of correlational analyses are:

(1) Up to the First World War, strike activity tended to be more intense when employers were prospering; that was probably because the number of offensive strikes rose in such years. After the First World War, the association with employer prosperity continued to be true of offensive strikes, but defensive strikes were sufficiently frequent to weaken the general relationship between employer prosperity and strike activity.

(2) In the years from 1890 to the First World War, strike activity and unionization went together; nonetheless, strikes were more likely to fail when unionization was high. From 1920 to the Second World War, strong positive associations among unionization, total strike activity and the likelihood of success or (especially) compromise appeared. Before and after these periods, we have no information concerning this set of relationships.

(3) Before the First World War, strikes tended to be more frequent when wages were high, even though strikes were also more likely to fail in those years. After the First World War, strikes tended to be more frequent when wages (especially real wages) were low.

(4) The overall level of industrial production was a less powerful factor in strike activity at any time (except possibly the 1870s and 1880s) than prices, wages and other economic fluctuations more directly affecting the fates of individual workers.

(5) After the Second World War, the synchronization of strikes with economic fluctuations (except wages) practically disappeared.

(6) Although cabinet changes never displayed much correspondence to fluctuations in strike activity, there was a mild but persistent tendency for strike activity and collective violence to vary together, especially after 1890.

Our model, then, emerges from the pummeling a trifle battered, but still recognizable. The correlational analysis gives us some ground for associating offensive strikes with economic expansion. It gives us additional ground for associating defensive strikes with economic contraction. The conditions for successful strikes, however, do not correspond at all closely to those for offensive strikes; there is a much greater parallel between offensive strikes and compromise as an outcome. Our analyses suggest that French workers went through an important organizational change around the First World War: striking often, and offensively, but also unsuccessfully, in times when employers were prospering before the war; striking often, and offensively, but now successfully, in times of prosperity after the war.

The analyses also suggest that unionization went with failure before the war and with success (or, more precisely, a tendency to arrive at negotiated settlements) after the war. To the extent that we can infer changes in the political position of labor from the intensity of collective violence, we have evidence of a substantial relationship between strike activity and political change from 1890 to the First World War, and of a weaker but persistent relationship after the war. We have not directly examined the hypothesis that the prosperity of workers varies as a function of the prosperity of employers; the general patterns of the correlations make the hypothesis quite plausible. Nor have we looked closely at the relationship between the prosperity of workers and the extent of labor organization, or between change in the political position of labor and its organization. On the effects and correlates of changing political position, we shall not be able to offer more than argument and indirect evidence. On the organization of labor, we shall have a good deal more to say.

Some simple multivariate analyses

The trouble with leaving the analysis where we have brought it, of course, is that a number of our explanatory variables are themselves related to each other. The trend over time isn't the only confounding factor. Nominal wages, real wages and industrial production, for example, rise and fall together to some extent. Perhaps we have incorrectly attributed independent influence to one of them, when it is acting as a shadow of the other.

The simplest way to face that uncertainty is to place the variables together in the same equations and examine their relative contributions to multiple-regression predictions of strike activity. The basic model is still linear, but now it is multivariate. We have only permitted ourselves to try an equation when an available argument – our own or someone else's – gave a rationale for that combination of variables. But the available arguments, as the reader has no doubt noticed, are quite loose. We have actually tested a great variety of plausible hypotheses in the multiple-regression manner.

Here we report only the survivors of our scrutiny: the equations within each set which (a) produce the best fit (by a linear least-squares criterion) to the time series of strikes under examination, (b) contain individual relationships each of which is statistically reliable, as measured by conventional tests of significance, (c) leave low serial correlation of the unexplained variance from year to year. In order to blunt the effects of a few extraordinary years, we have used the logarithm of the number of strikes in a given year – rather than the raw number of strikes – as the dependent variable. We have continued to detrend by using the linear regression of strike activity on time as an independent variable in each analysis.

As it turns out, the multivariate results support all the general conclusions we have drawn from the correlations; they simply modify our interpretation of particular relationships in particular periods. For the years from 1870 through 1890, for example, the best-fitting equation is:

log(strikes) = 327.2 − 0.176(time) − 0.163(nominal wage index)
                 + 0.126(industrial production index)

The coefficient of determination (R^2) for that equation is 0.81. Here and henceforth, the results will be easier to interpret if we standardize the regression coefficients. In standard form, the equation above reads:

log(strikes) = − 1.915(time) − 0.858(nominal wage) + 1.240(industrial
                 production)

During the years 1870–90, that is, once the strong effect of rapidly rising industrial production is taken into account, both time and the nominal wage level predict negatively to strike activity. We had already detected a strong relationship between strike activity and industrial production in that period. But the preliminary findings gave greater weight to real wages and price fluctuations; their effects now appear to depend on changes in production. Low nominal wages, on the other hand, appear to have acted as a sharper spur to strike than the first analysis indicated.

Over the years from 1890 through 1913, the best-fitting equation includes real wages and industrial production for the year previous to the one under observation; in standard form:

log(strikes) = 0.882(time) + 0.242(wholesale/retail ratio) + 0.254(real
                 wages for previous year) − 0.334(industrial production for
                 previous year)

$$R^2 = 0.89$$

The relationship of strikes to industrial production, once their strong common upward trend is removed, reverses the one observed for 1870–90; it is negative. Once again it appears that the strong positive relationship Andréani found between the two resulted from trend rather than from a direct causal connection. The analysis confirms, on the other hand, Andréani's conclusion that the widening of the gap between wholesale and retail prices (which he interprets as meaning that employers are prospering while workers escape, to some extent, from the struggle for survival) encouraged strike activity in that period.

If we compute regression equations separately for the proportions of strikes from 1890 to 1913 ending in success, failure or compromise, we arrive at the following results:

$\dfrac{\text{success}}{\text{total strikes}}$: no reliable equation

$\dfrac{\text{compromise}}{\text{total strikes}}$ = 2.381(time) + 0.343(wholesale/retail ratio) − 1.077
                 (nominal wages) + 0.349(real wages) − 1.243 (industrial
                 production)

$$R^2 = 0.61$$

$$\frac{\text{failure}}{\text{total strikes}} = 0.625(\text{nominal wages}) + 2.558(\text{union members}) - 2.902 \\ (\text{time})$$

$$R^2 = 0.38$$

In none of these cases does lagging the variables add to their explanatory power. The prominent variables in the equation for compromise are the same as those for total strikes, although their timing is different. In those years from 1890 to 1913, unionization and *failure* in strikes went together, as the earlier partial correlations suggested.

The years from 1920 through 1938 (or, more precisely, 1920, 1921 and 1926–38, the years for which we have data on unionization) bring many more variables into the picture:

$$\log(\text{strikes}) = 0.365(\text{industrial production}) - 0.529(\text{time}) - 0.311(\text{real} \\ \text{wages}) + 1.000(\text{union members}) + 0.385(\text{violent conflicts})$$

$$R^2 = 0.88$$

Lagging the variables generally diminishes their explanatory power in this period; no lagged equation yields significant results. As we noticed before, our political and organizational variables begin to take on weight after the First World War. A negative relationship of strike activity to real wages reverses the prewar connection between the two. And once the effects of other variables are sorted out, strike activity now runs higher in years of high industrial production than in other years. There may well be a joint effect of fluctuations in production and in wages which our measurements don't quite catch, for in these first three periods where the coefficients of the wage variables are positive the coefficient of the production variable is negative, and vice versa.

As for success, failure and compromise over the period from 1920 to 1935, our best-fitting equations take the following form:

$$\frac{\text{success}}{\text{total strikes}} = 2.11(\text{time}) - 1.22(\text{industrial production}) - 0.69(\text{violent} \\ \text{conflicts}) + 2.03(\text{wholesale/retail ratio})$$

$$R^2 = 0.75$$

$$\frac{\text{compromise}}{\text{total strikes}} = 1.51(\text{time}) - 0.27(\text{real wages, previous year}) + 1.63 \\ (\text{wholesale/retail ratio})$$

$$R^2 = 0.73$$

$$\frac{\text{failure}}{\text{total strikes}} = - 0.86(\text{time}) - 0.52(\text{union members}) - 1.06(\text{whole-} \\ \text{sale/retail ratio})$$

$$R^2 = 0.90$$

These results call for some skepticism. The number of years under consideration – especially when lags enter the equation – is very small. The coefficients are high enough to suggest considerable instability. What is more, the one-year serial correlation of the third equation is −0.45, which suggests a strong year-to-year alternation unaccounted for by the variables we are considering. We should therefore resist paying excessive attention to the high coefficients of determination (R^2).

The wholesale/retail ratio enters these equations most persistently: positively related to the proportions of strikes ending in success or compromise, negatively related to failure. During this period, unionization appears to have been a bar to failure more than an open door to success. When other variables are taken into consideration, we discover a hidden tendency for the likelihood of success or compromise to increase from 1920 to 1935. But the differences between the equations for success and compromise leave the roles of production, wages and political conflict in all this ambiguous.

Because our predictor variables cover such different sets of years, we can't run a reliable analysis of this sort for the years from 1946 to 1967. We can, however, examine the relationships among a number of the predictors from 1920 to 1954, with the war years omitted. (The most serious loss is our inability to represent the effect of unionization over this period.) For 1920–38 and 1946–54 combined, the best-fitting equation simplifies again:

$$\log(\text{strikes}) = 0.784(\text{time}) + 0.497(\text{unemployment in previous years}) + 0.709(\text{wholesale/retail ratio})$$

For this equation, however, R^2 is only 0.48. It happens that unemployment in the same year produces almost as good a prediction as unemployment in the previous year. This remarkable positive association between strikes and unemployment is due mainly to the mass of strikes in the high-unemployment years of the 1930s. As we noticed before, if we reduce the earlier period to 1920–35, the relationship of strikes to unemployment turns negative. We are inclined to take the radical alteration of the whole equation when the years from 1946 to 1954 join those from 1920 to 1938 as supporting our earlier contention that a substantial shift in the whole pattern of French strike activity occurred around the Second World War.

Finally, let us study the longest span for which we have simultaneous data on unionization and almost all the other variables: the years 1890–1913, 1920, 1921 and 1926–38. (Unemployment data are now the only serious loss.) This period is of particular interest to us; it corresponds approximately to the years dealt with by most of the analyses of individual strikes, regions and industries reported later in this book. Here we arrive at an equation containing seven separate variables:

$$\log(\text{strikes}) = 0.495(\text{time}) - 0.046(\text{wholesale/retail ratio}_{-2}) - 0.792(\text{nominal wage}_{-1}) - 0.465(\text{real wage}) + 0.466(\text{industrial production}) + 0.756(\text{union members}) + 0.168(\text{violent conflicts})$$

(Here the subscript -1 means for the previous year, -2 for the year before that.) Now $R^2 = 0.87$.

The grafting of the years before the First World War onto those between the two wars adds the lagged wholesale/retail ratio and the lagged nominal wage to the interwar equation – wholesale/retail with a weak negative effect and nominal wage with a strong negative effect. By assigning the lagged wholesale/retail ratio a negative value over this long run, the 1890–1938 equation raises the possibility that periods of *recovery* from a price squeeze on employers are especially favorable to strike activity. With these additions, the equations for 1890–1938 and for 1920–38 bear a strong family resemblance. Both tell us that with allowance for the long-term trend strikes tend to be more frequent when employers are prospering, wages are low, union membership is extensive and violent conflict is widespread. At this general level, the conclusions rejoin those we have already drawn from the study of correlations.

The best-fitting equations for the proportions of success, failure and compromise over the entire period (now 1890–1913, 1920, 1921, 1926–35) involve many fewer variables:

$$\frac{\text{success}}{\text{total strikes}} = 0.369(\text{time}) + 0.404(\text{wholesale/retail ratio}) - 0.539(\text{industrial production}) - 0.580(\text{union members})$$

$$R^2 = 0.53$$

$$\frac{\text{compromise}}{\text{total strikes}} = 0.736(\text{union members}) - 0.239(\text{time})$$

$$\frac{\text{failure}}{\text{total strikes}}: \quad \text{no reliable equation}$$

Over the long haul, an important part of the variation in the outcome of strikes remains unexplained. Taking the half-century as a whole, unionization appears to have acted as a strong force for compromise, despite its stimulation of failure in the 1890s. The negative association between success and industrial production over the four decades repeats what we found for 1890–1913 alone. It actually represents the tendency of the total volume of strike activity *and* of the proportion of compromises to rise when industrial production is high. The wholesale/retail ratio again shows up in association with successful strikes. So our statistics cut into a nexus bringing together employer prosperity, low wages, political conflict and unionization as correlates of extensive strike activity, with unionization promoting compromise as the outcome of those strikes that occur.

Revamping the model

Back at the beginning of the chapter, we proposed an elementary model relating strike activity, worker organization, changes in the political position of labor, worker prosperity and the prosperity of employers. None of the information we have encountered so far has flatly contradicted the model. Perhaps the greatest doubts have arisen around our proposal that the prosperity of workers indirectly favors strike activity by directly promoting the organization of labor. Even leaving that problem aside, however, we can hardly claim that the model has been persuasively confirmed. First, the model itself is too imprecise for decisive confirmation as it stands. A number of different variables, lags and forms of relationship could all fit into its framework. Second, variables which ought, by the argument, to be equivalent, or at least closely related to each other, sometimes move in different directions; our effort to index 'changes in the political position of labor' indirectly by means of cabinet crises and collective violence, for example, produces contradictory results. Third, the relative weights of the variables in question change considerably from one analysis to the next. Those rapid shifts result to a considerable degree from the shortness of the separate periods under study; with short spans of years, one strike wave or one big measurement error will skew all the results. Finally, we have some evidence that the underlying pattern of relationships was changing from 1870 to 1967. Some indications have come in, for example, that before the First World War strikes tended to rise with real wages, while afterwards strikes tended to be more frequent when real wages were low. Our model provides no means of anticipating that kind of result.

Some of these defects and uncertainties will only disappear as better data come into existence. We need longer, uniform series for the same variables, data concerning shorter intervals like months or quarters, better indices of the basic elements of the model, year-to-year information for particular groups of workers. Other uncertainties in the argument require more refined arguments rather than new data. Might it be, for example, that the apparent association between unionization and negotiated outcomes to strikes (instead of simple victories or defeats) results partly from the increased likelihood that representatives of the government will step in and press for a settlement when labor is relatively strong? Or that labor itself will force them to intervene? We have left all such complexities out of the argument so far.

Later chapters of this book will take up some of these issues, but not with time-series data. Here the best we can do is (1) identify the most durable relationships that have shown up in our time series by glancing back at the longest periods for which we have uniform data, and (2) summarize the interrelationships of our primary variables by studying them all simultaneously instead of two by two. We can accomplish the first objective by consolidating the analysis into two overlapping periods: 1890 to 1938 and 1920 to 1954. The first stretch of years (which, to be exact, consists of 1890–1913, 1920–1, and 1926–38) includes all those for which we have estimates of union membership. The second (actually 1920–38 and 1946–54) covers the maximum span of uniform data on wages, prices, unemployment and strike activity. We can accomplish the second objective by recasting the multiple regressions presented earlier – and some not discussed so far – in the form of path diagrams. The diagrams describe our closest approximations to our basic model. The paths from variable to variable are labeled with standardized partial regression coefficients; they represent essentially the number of standard deviations of change in the dependent variable associated with a change of one standard deviation in the independent variable, once the effect of the other variables in the same set has been taken account of. This way of describing the relationships has the advantage of making them comparable.

In the analyses the diagrams report, we have adopted a different method of dealing with the effects of trend. We have computed the linear regression of each variable on time over the period in question, and then used the residual – the deviation of the year's actual value from the value predicted by the regression – in the analysis. Since time was one of the explanatory variables in the earlier multiple regressions, the effect is to produce lower multiple correlations than have appeared in the rest of this chapter. The coefficients of determination (R^2) for the logarithm of the number of strikes in the four diagrams are, in order, 0.68, 0.69, 0.33 and 0.30 instead of the 0.88 and 0.48 produced by most closely comparable earlier equations.[8]

For each set of years, we present two somewhat different models. In each case the first, somewhat simpler model sums up the joint effect of the well-being of workers and the prosperity of employers in the old, reliable wholesale/retail ratio. The second substitutes separate measurements of industrial production and real wages for that joint effect. In both periods the explanatory powers of the two models are quite similar. (The paths leading from outside the diagram to particular variables represent the unexplained portion of their variation.) In any case, it is the pattern of relationships which interests us here.

During the period from 1890 to 1938, model 1 (in fig. 4.3) indicates a substantial effect of the wholesale/retail ratio on the number of strikers and, especially, on the number of strikes. The extent of collective violence and the size of union membership predict to the number of strikes, but (once that relationship has been taken into account) not to the number of workers involved in them. Union membership rises, to some extent, with the frequency of collective violence, but shows no relationship to the wholesale/retail ratio. To the extent that these variables do represent changes in the political position of labor, the prosperity of employers and so on, they conform to the prescriptions of our general model.

When we separate our indices of the well-being of employers and workers in model 2 for 1890 to 1938, however, some embarrassment for the general argument appears. There is the minor difficulty of a moderate negative relationship between union membership and industrial production; we anticipated no relationship at all; a negative relationship suggests a closer

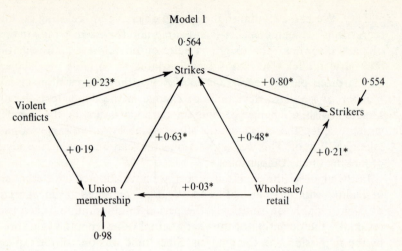

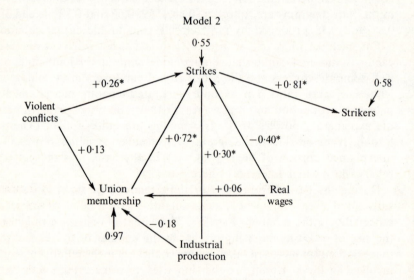

* Starred coefficients are greater than two times their standard error

Fig. 4.3: Revamping the model, 1890–1938

connection between unionization and economic contraction than our line of argument finds comfortable. More important, real wages have no significant effect on unionization, according to this analysis; we anticipated more extensive union membership as workers had the resources to devote to organization. Finally, we discover a fairly strong *negative* relation-

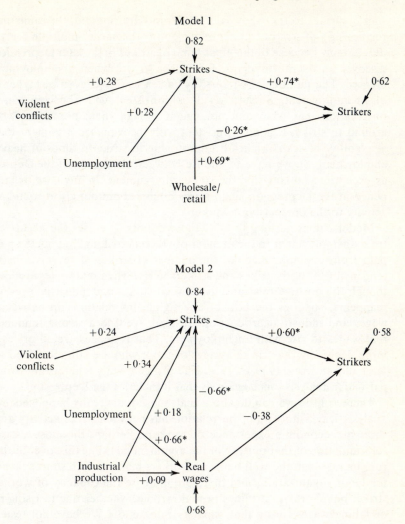

* Starred coefficients are greater than two times their standard error

Fig. 4.4: Revamping the model, 1920–54

ship between the number of strikes and real wages, which counters our expectation of no relationship between them. The rest of the model runs more or less as expected.

In moving to the second period, from 1920 to 1954 (fig. 4.4), we lose the ability to deal with unionization, but gain information about the effects of unemployment. Model 1 repeats the positive relationship between the number of strikes and violent conflicts. It also reiterates the positive relationship of strikes to the wholesale/retail ratio. It brings out the same unusual relationship of strikes to unemployment as the earlier multiple regression did. Largely because of the great lump of strikes in the later Depression, we discover an overall tendency for strikes to *rise* when unemployment increased. The number of strikers, by contrast, was reduced by higher levels of unemployment. Such a result is consistent with the common-sense observation that when unemployment is high there are fewer workers around to strike. It is not consistent with the standard argument that the availability of scabs makes it unprofitable to strike in times of heavy unemployment. So we have to choose between shrugging off the Depression as exceptional or revising the standard argument. In any case, what happened in the Depression again raises doubts about our effort to link strike activity to the prosperity of workers.

Model 2 does nothing to allay those doubts. It erases the negative path from unemployment to the number of workers striking, but not the positive path from unemployment to the number of strikes. It reveals substantial tendencies for both strikes and strikers to rise when real wages are low. Although the positive relationship between strikes and industrial production reappears, so does the lack of any significant relationship between real wages and industrial production. Instead, we find a strong tendency for real wages to *rise* with unemployment. That is because retail prices drop more decisively than do the wages of those who are still employed – or at least did so from 1920 to 1954. The problem with generalizing from this particular analysis, once again, is that it includes the Depression.

There is little we can do about that; those years really happened. So our analysis leaves uncertain the relationship between strike activity and the short-run economic experience of workers. Perhaps the most reasonable reformulation of that portion of the argument goes like this: over the longer run, increases in the well-being of workers make more resources available for labor organization, and therefore increase the capacity of workers to strike; but short-run declines in real income, whether due to rising prices or falling wages, bring that capacity into action. We have not tested the reformulation.

In other regards, the 1920–54 diagrams serve well. Although some of the coefficients involved are statistically unreliable because of their high standard errors (the great fluctuation of violent conflicts from year to year being the clearest example), the models support the association of strike activity with the prosperity of employers and with violent conflict. The pattern repeats what we found for the overlapping period 1890–1938. Considering that the new period brackets both the Depression and the Second World War, it is almost surprising that those relationships should continue to show up.

We need, then, to modify the argument with which we began . . . but not

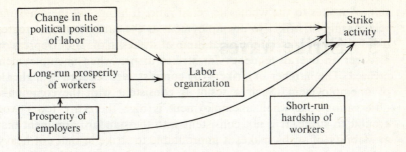

Fig. 4.5: A revised model of the argument

to abandon it. To take only the most general features of the argument, we might now sketch it this way, as in fig. 4.5.

The new sketch does not dispose of all the problems our analyses have raised. The relationship between change in the political position of labor and the development of labor organization is surely reciprocal over the long run. The model says nothing about the effect of previous failures or successes. Nor does it predict to the success or failure – even the defensive or offensive character – of strikes. For these purposes we need more complex models, better data and some analysis of issues this chapter has not even touched. What the sketch does, however, is to bring the politics and the organization of labor squarely into the explanation of strike activity. While focusing on the lineaments of the strike itself, the remaining chapters of this book will return again and again to the political and organizational context. In fact, we begin at once. Chapter 5, in singling out major strike waves for analysis, will bring us immediately to the politics and organization of labor. And Chapter 6, on unionization, will hardly let questions of politics and organization go.

5 Strike waves

The importance of strike waves

This chapter is intended to do two things: to tell the story of the major eruptions of strike activity in France during the last century and a half and to add a couple of struts to the central argumentation of the book. We trace the narrative of strikes by looking briefly at the massive strike waves which march as exclamation marks in labor history from late in the nineteenth century to 1968. And we support the logical structure of the book by using these strike waves to support two larger points: (1) that timing of outbursts of strikes may be partly explained by the timing of political crises, and (2) that organization is essential to the successful launching of such forms of large-scale collective action as strike waves.

By hooking together politics and strikes we do not intend to say that political crises 'cause' strike waves to happen, for one may point in French history to many political upheavals which left the surface of working-class life mirror-smooth. Instead, it seems more sensible to claim that politics constitutes an important kind of precondition for the eruption of large-scale worker movements, though not being in itself a sufficient one. Doubtless other major moments must be considered as well before one can understand what essential circumstances conjoin to produce a strike wave, and the more complete the explanation, the greater would have to be the number of factors adduced. Our claims are more modest. Rather than 'predicting' in time the occurrence of strike waves, we are pointing to a sense of political crisis as a prime factor in bringing a large number of men together for collective action. When men act together, we think it is usually for political reasons; an awareness that pushing and shoving outside the charmed circle of the polity had reached some critical point should enhance by a good deal their willingness to move momentarily in unison.

Because we feel that politics and organization dovetail, we pay special attention in this chapter to the standard assumption in historical writing that strike waves spread 'spontaneously,' as the fiercely independent unorganized workers who occupy such a prominent place in the mythology of French social history suddenly leap up from their café tables and cry, 'Hey, let's go on strike!' This view sees the important instances of industrial conflict as galvanic explosions of accumulated fury, an Old Faithful theory of working-class history in which the geyser splashes the landscape with sulphurous waters, then subsides into impotent fuming and sputtering. Our claim will be that the great mobilizations of participants in a strike wave would be impossible without a preexisting cadre of militant unionists or grass-roots politicians. To make this point we shall consider closely the structure of strike waves, noting both the evolution of various characteristics of conflict from wave to wave, and the differences distinguishing such waves from other less synchronized forms of strike activity. By observing both the political antecedents and the structural features of strike waves we may thus link up the history of major episodes of conflict to the unifying themes of this volume: politics and organization as inherent features of collective action.[1]

We preview the exact argument to be made so that the reader will know what to watch for as we take up the narrative of 150 years of strikes. The timing of strike waves depends largely on the timing of political crises, but their form is the result of somewhat more complex combinations of circumstances. Some aspects of waves are determined by such variables as technological change, which operate in a rather *cyclical* fashion, going from artisanal to mechanical, then back again in the post–Second World War period to a modern adaptation of the classic artisanal. Other aspects of waves are determined by changes in French society that seem to go in a *linear* way, becoming more and more pronounced with the passage of time, instead of oscillating. We have in mind here: (1) the 'nationalization' of working-class politics, a process which commenced with the mobilization of the 1880s and 90s; and (2) an increase in the scale of those institutions regulating working-class life which has been in progress since the days of Louis Napoleon.

How do these independent changes alter the nature of strike waves? Technology affects the way in which strikes cluster together in two ways. (1) The form of industrial organization modifies the willingness of workers to follow the directives of nationwide, centralized organizations, for in the classic artisanal economy, where local organizations are strong and national ones weak, little coordination or direction among outbursts exists; in the mass-production economy local unions are weak, and in their absence rise highly centralized industrial federations and confederations which carefully channel and control strike waves from industry to industry, and city to city; in the science-sector economy local unions and political groups reacquire some of their lost importance, and their members become indifferent to instructions radiating out from the central headquarters.

(2) Industrial organization determines what kinds of workers shall set the tone of the entire labor movement, providing models of action and organization for others to emulate. In the classic artisanal phase skilled craftworkers are the pacesetting groups; in the mass-production phase the leaders are proletarian, semi-skilled operatives in manufacturing or the

providers of rough, dirty services, such as stevedores or tramway conductors; in the modern technology phase the pacesetters are the skilled professionals of the office building or plant headquarters.[2]

Other structural changes in French society and the economy, beginning approximately during the Second Empire, have influenced strikes in a linear way. The drive for worker political representation at the center became ever more powerful between the late 1860s and 1950s. And it was this thrust for membership in the polity that provided the initial motor of the strike wave. Then too, over the years the institutions which bound working-class life together have simply become bigger: the cities where they live have become larger; the factories where they labor have grown in size; the organizations they belong to have become increasingly extensive; and the media with access to them have come to sprawl across the nation. These increases in the scale of life meant that every successive strike wave has involved a larger number of participants than the preceding one, a measure of the impact of scale upon patterns of mobilization.

Table 5.1 demonstrates the steady upward progression of strike and striker rates from 1893 to 1948 (1968, we must assume, would register the highest levels of all, if only data were available for the calculations). Data on the yearly number of strikes and strikers, and on strike rates for five-year periods, are available in Appendix B, tables 1 and 2.

A final independent influence upon the form of strike waves which has grown more pronounced over the years is the role of Paris. With time the center has come increasingly to dominate the periphery – *le désert français* – and the workers of Paris to set the pacing and form of events, models for the provincials. Before 1870 strikes were as much provincial as Parisian affairs, but thereafter, especially after 1906 with the completion of labor's centralization, Paris would call the tune.

Which of the highpoints within the long series of strikes deserve recognition as waves? Let us begin with a simple but helpful criterion: a 'strike wave' occurs when both the number of strikes and the number of strikers in a given year exceed the means of the previous five years by more than

Table 5.1: *Rising intensities in strike waves, 1893–1948*

Year	Strikers/100,000 total active population	Strikes/100,000 total active population
1893	900	3
1899–1900	1,000	4
1906	2,100	7
1919–20	5,600	9
1936	12,000	83
1947–8	23,000	9

SOURCES: 1947–8 strike data from International Labour Office, 1936 data from the *Annuaire statistique*, 1966, p. 120. Data for previous years from our own coding of *SG*.

50 percent. If the mean strikes per year over the last five years has been 1,000 and the mean strikers 200,000, we will not recognize this year as a 'wave' year unless it has more than 1,500 strikes and 300,000 strikers. Once a year qualifies, however, we include all the year's strikes and strikers in the wave. By that standard, the years of strike waves from 1890 on were:

1890	1904	1936
1893	1906	1947
1899	1919	1948
1900	1920	1968

In the following pages we analyze in detail the conflicts of each of those years except 1890 and 1904. The strike wave of the former year we exclude as a possible artifact, owing to the improvement of strike reporting with the first volume of the *SG* in 1890. And because we dissected the 1906 wave at considerable length, we felt discussing the lesser upsurge of two years previous a bit superfluous.

In the absence of reliable information on the number of strikers before 1890, we took for waves in 1830–89 quite simply the obvious highpoints in the graph of strikes.

We divide these various strike waves into four blocks: 1830–1900, roughly coterminous with the artisanal system's prime years of dominance; 1906–35, the take-off of proletarian mass-production industry; 1936, an episode worthy of a separate section; and 1947–68, when the encroachment of science sector patterns upon strike waves began. Finally, we shall present some summary statistics to draw these discrete historical events together.

1830–1900

The strike waves of these years were mounted by skilled artisans in small shops whose contacts with one another were tenuous and informal. The apparent slackness of connecting ties and the transitory existence of formal worker organizations in this period must not be read as 'disorganization,' or 'absence of associations.' In the towns and shops where these people found employment, closely knit networks born of long-standing familiarity and an awareness of common traditions provided the basis of collective action.[3]

1833

A period of political instability preceded the first strike wave of modern times: the Revolution of 1830, an uprising in Lyon in 1831, a peak in the number of disturbances in 1832 which would be surpassed only in 1848, and in the summer of 1833 renewed activity from the Society of the Rights of Man.[4]

The curve of strike activity shows a distinct peak in the early thirties, and in 1833 above all. That year the government initiated 90 prosecutions against strikes, as opposed to 51 the previous year and 55 the following year. Jean-Pierre Aguet's data on strikes in the July Monarchy confirm 1833 as a *crise ouvrière*, with 72 strikes registered in archival materials, as opposed to 8 in 1832 and 14 in 1834. Reliable data on the number of participants are not available.

Of those 55 identifiable by municipality (map 5.1), 13 took place in Paris, 9 in Lyon, 4 in le Havre, 3 apiece in Lille and St-Etienne, the rest dispersed across the land in both large and small towns. There was a clustering of strikes around Rouen; otherwise no regional concentration of any kind is to be seen, hundreds of miles of territory often isolating one from the next. The bulk of strikes were thus in the principal cities, spread across the entire country.

The individual strikes did not bunch up during a particular month, but were scattered throughout the year: Lyon tullemakers in January, Anzin miners in May, Paris stonecutters in September. Almost all strikers were in skilled occupations, and the only participants obviously factory operatives were the spinning mill workers on strike in Ste-Marie-aux-Mines (Haut-Rhin), a dispute which turned into a disturbance when the strikers of one plant, unsuccessfully attempting to persuade the workers of another to join them, clashed with police. Reassembling later in the day, they marched through the town singing the *Parisienne* and shouting 'Vive la misère! Vive le drapeau noir!'[5] Of the 55 strikes 19 were in the textile sector, the others distributed largely among printing, woodworking and building materials.

The strikes of 1833 were tied, at least in part, to the politics of the July Monarchy. The government affected to see the specter of political unrest behind these industrial disputes, and in fact Republican sympathizers seem to have been involved in Lyon, Paris and St-Etienne. A recent study of silk-weaver organization and the July strikes in Lyon makes crystal-clear the nexus of political rivalries whence these disputes emerged: powerful merchant-industrialists, aided by the state, encroaching constantly upon the corporate autonomy and economic profitability of that city's thousands of independent master weavers.[6] All together, 1833 marks the first instance of a pattern we shall find recurring for the next seventy years. Skilled workers backed by dimly articulated local organizations strike with approximate simultaneity. No nationwide federations exist to steer the movements, and what happened in the provinces is largely autonomous of Paris.

1840

A second peak in the number of strikes came in 1840, when prosecutions 'for the act of striking' rose from an average of 49 (1833 excluded) during the 1830s to 130, and the number of strikes Aguet counted from an average of 10 to 37. The wave had two components: an exceptional frequency of isolated conflicts here and there in the provinces throughout the year, and a

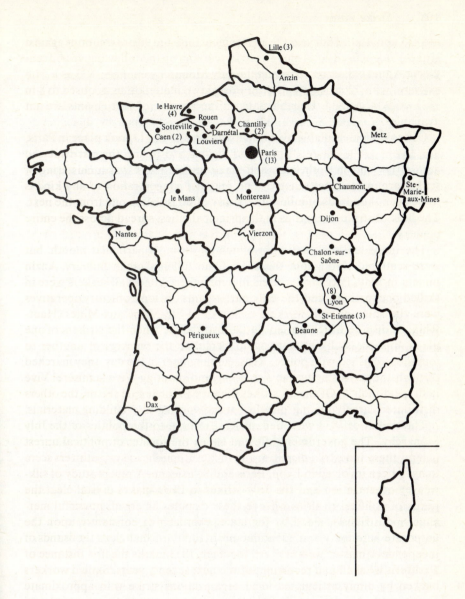

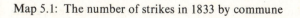

Map 5.1: The number of strikes in 1833 by commune

concerted series of disputes in Paris from June through September. In the political background of labor relations stood turbulent 1839, notably the Society of the Seasons' attempted Parisian coup in September. Then during the summer of 1840 the Republicans staged a banquet campaign in Paris and the provinces, culminating in a great gathering on the *plaine de Châtillon* on 31 August, attended by 'several thousand democrats'; speakers dilated upon the need for the 'organization of labor.' Several days thereafter one of the greatest mass movements in the working-class history of this period broke out in Paris, likened by Aguet to the Lyon uprising of 1831. Tanners, bakers, building trades, wagonmakers and metalsmiths (*serruriers*) – to name some of the participants – went out during the first week in September, numbering twenty to thirty thousand at the height of the movement. There were disturbances through the first ten days of the month; troops were rushed in; but by 10 September it was all over.

What did the riots and strikes of September 1840 mean? May we associate them with political events, specifically with the banquet campaign? Thureau-Dangin, of course, sniffed the guiding spirit of the radicals behind the September events, as behind all tumult during the July Monarchy.[7] Aguet, hoping to lay to rest the conspiracy theory of strike activity, is at pains to disclaim any linkages between political action and the worker movement; yet he tells us that workers attended the banquets, and suggests that the authorities intervened in striker demonstrations of 2–3 September because they feared the Republicans were attempting to channel the movement to their own ends.[8] How did these great numbers of workers happen to find themselves together at the same time and the same place, acting to the same apparent end? Aguet believes the 'unanimity of opinion among the workers participating in these movements' (p. 220) sufficed to mobilize them for a series of separate conflicts which were isolated one from another though simultaneous. Everything we know about working-class life in these years suggests this hypothesis is incorrect; yet proving its obverse is impossible with available evidence, namely, that the workers of Paris were moved to joint action by an informal leadership structure which was concerned to furnish evidence of mass support for Republican demands for the 'organization of labor.' But circumstantial evidence in the timing alone of banquets and worker protest suggests some interaction between national politics and bread-and-butter issues in worker daily life.

1869–70[9]

In 1869 for the first time a foreshadowing of proletarian participation in a strike wave may be noted, isolated outshoots in a movement still largely dominated by small-shop artisanal strikes. For the first time there were coordinated walkouts among semi-skilled laborers in large plants, chiefly in smelting, metalworking, textiles and railroading. The number of strikers rose from an 1864–8 average of 23,000 to 41,000 and to 88,000 in 1870; strikes also climbed to a peak in 1870.

Fernand L'Huillier's monograph is our principal guide to the period. In the parts of France that L'Huillier studied carefully, the elections of May 1869 and February 1870 seem to have revived worker interest in political affairs.[10] The severe defeats Louis Napoleon's government suffered in the 1869 election doubtless made the composition of the polity appear to be newly fluid, therewith suggesting that worker representation within the political arena would benefit by grassroots agitation.

The summer of 1869 is noteworthy not for widespread walkouts but for a few giant disputes. On 11 June 1869 in the Loire basin 15,000 miners stopped work, guided, L'Huillier believes, by a strike central in St-Etienne.[11] The movement spread at once to the miners of Carmaux, then to the carpenters of Vienne in August, the weavers of Rouen and the wool spinners of Elbeuf, finally to the miners of Aubin in October. During the Loire strike on 16 June, the famous 'massacre of the Ricamarie' took place, leaving thirteen workers dead.[12] In January of 1870 the first of the great strikes in the Schneider metalworking shops and forges at le Creusot broke out; the second took place late in March, spreading from the mines. In both disputes political slogans and discussions helped tie the workers together, though of course the stated grievances concerned the shop floor.

Alongside these historic disputes, artisanal strike activity continued apace, setting the tempo of the actual wave of strikes in June and July 1870. First in the sequence seems to have been a well organized walkout among the coppersmiths (*chaudronniers*) of St-Etienne, whom mechanical construction workers then followed into the streets, late in May. In mid-June the well established weavers' association in Lyon staged a large strike. Early in July the metalworkers and the railroaders of Rouen stopped work. Here and there members of the International turned up to exhort and direct, but there was, as far as one can tell, no question of the central orchestration of strikes across regions.

Early in July the wave took up in Alsace among the building trades and textile plants around Mulhouse, thence among masons, stonecutters, cloth printers, metalworkers. Important among the organizing cadres were, according to L'Huillier, members of the First International. 'The International was effectively present in Mulhouse, if not in the principal industrial agglomerations of the department; it was there through its program, which inspired various worker demands . . . One may reasonably assert that the worker movement in Mulhouse came into life under the influence of the International, and even that the strike within metalworking arose under it . . .'[13] Whatever the role of the International, it would be inaccurate to claim that striking workers thought they were making a statement about national political representation. As the Carmaux miners' strike over local authority issues demonstrates, worker ambitions in 1869–70 were sooner directed at struggles with employers and municipalities.

On balance the strikes of 1869–70 were still part of the artisanal pattern, despite the intermittent involvement of what appear to have been machine-tenders in the *grande industrie*. Skilled trades within building or metal-working, such as the *chaudronniers*, called the tune during the piling up of strikes in the summer of 1870; no central federations or agencies coordinated events from one region to the next, but solid local unions and associations such as the fellowship fund (*caisse fraternelle*) in St-Etienne, were very much in evidence; and proceedings in Paris did not statistically overwhelm those in the provinces.[14]

1893

In 1893 the first major upsurge of industrial conflict since 1870 took place, with 634 strikes (compared to an 1871–92 average of 157 yearly) and 170,000 strikers (compared to an 1871–92 average of 47,000 yearly). Whereas the 1869–70 wave had come near the front end of the long transition from artisanal to mechanized production, the 1893 strike was located near the rear, for in the future waves of strikes (as opposed to workaday industrial conflict) would reflect the styles and forms of the proletarian cadres of the CGT.

The spring of 1893 was a time of political unsettledness. The Panama Affair caused in March the downfall of the Ribot government; the campaign for the August elections had begun; in April the Dupuy government closed the Paris Bourse du travail because the constituent unions had failed to comply with the provisions of the 1884 law; the capital saw riots on 1 May.[15]

As these events were in progress a strike wave broke out: in April the numbers of strikes and strikers tripled from first quarter levels, remaining high through June. But already in January the walkouts had begun – wood-cutters in the Nièvre and silk throwsters in the Ardèche. Linkages to political events were clear. The *SG* noted, for example, of a long weavers' strike in Bousies (Nord): 'Public opinion in the area attributes the prolongation of the strike to the agitation of the electoral campaign.'[16] In the coming months conflicts would sweep across all industries save agriculture and smelting, and most regions save Brittany and the southwest.

The occupations which carried the wave along were textiles and construction, within each the skilled workers, not the machine-tenders or laborers. The lacemakers of St-Quentin in March; the dyers, cotton spinners and garment workers of Amiens in April and May; the dyers of Roubaix in May, and the wool spinners of Vienne in August represented the textile sector. Throughout the spring and early summer skilled construction trades such as carpenters, joiners and cabinetmakers walked out, each dispute confined to a single municipality but within that town twenty or so estab-lishments striking together. These disputes piled up more in the south and west than elsewhere.

Yet the 1893 wave had something of a proletarian caste, for the *mécani-ciens–constructeurs* of Nantes and the *métallurgistes* of the Rive-de-Gier stopped work, as did a number of laborers in the transportation sector:

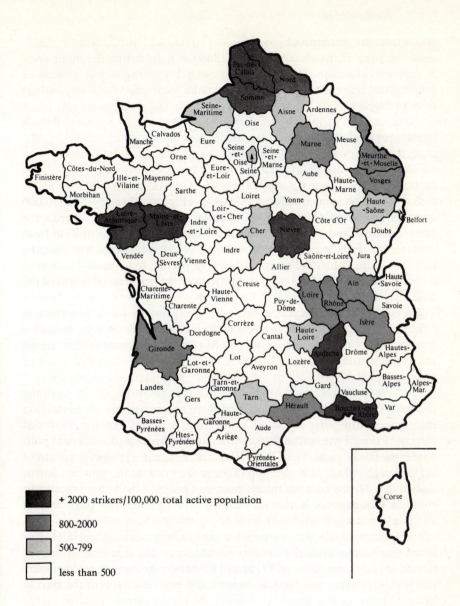

Map 5.2: Striker rate, 1893

Legend:

- ■ + 2000 strikers/100,000 total active population
- ▨ 800-2000
- ▨ 500-799
- □ less than 500

coal unloaders, carters and the like in the south and Paris. There was also a great strike of Parisian coachmen in June and July. Finally, among the proletarians of heavy industry were the miners, who in Béthune in September went out some 39,000 strong. Map 5.2 shows which departments had highest rates of activity.

Three features of the strikes of 1893 show that year as a bridge between two eras of conflict. For one thing, skilled trades such as cabinetmaking and cloth dyeing figured prominently, a characteristic of artisanal strike waves which would be on the wane thereafter. A related feature is that, secondly, centralized federations (to say nothing of the CGT) did not attempt to co-ordinate and channel the disputes, and locally autonomous skilled trades arranged their own informal synchronization. The low Parisian striker rates accompany provincial autonomy, an artisanal-wave feature. (In 1893 the department of the Seine had approximately the same proportion of France's strikers – 17 percent – as its normal 1890–1914 share of 15 percent). Thirdly, the participants in the 1893 wave appear to have lacked the explicitly political objectives that were to characterize strike waves after the First World War. The wave's political content probably did not exceed the implicit supporting of one's own boys; strikers didn't want to topple with revolutionary tactics anyone else's boys. Further research will reveal how influential the various socialist and anarchist groups were in mobilizing the participants.

1899–1900

If we take the phrase 'political crises' to mean opening up to redefinition the composition of the national polity, then 1899 qualifies ideally, for in June of that year the first socialist, Alexandre Millerand, joined a bourgeois government, the ministry of René Waldeck-Rousseau. It was the climax of the Dreyfus Affair, and the Republicans feared a coup from the Right, especially after the harassment of President Loubet at the Auteuil racetrack. June 11 saw a great Republican demonstration at Longchamp, and on 22 June Waldeck-Rousseau formed his 'government of national defense,' reaching as far to the Left as possible. The rank and file, in contrast to the union and socialist leaders, were highly enthusiastic about Millerand's access to power, and from all over France small worker groups, sometimes even single workers, sent him requests to speak, letters of encouragement and the like.[17]

Connections between the intense strike activity of 1899–1900 and a gov-ernment thought to be sympathetic to the working classes are not difficult to find. For one thing the peak number of strikes in the whole twenty-four–month period came in July 1899, just after the ministry was formed. Also, the strikers themselves turned often to the government for arbitration, mani-festly anticipating that the Waldeck ministry and the prefects would side with them against their employers. They also increasingly sought aid from their deputies. The September–October strike of Creusot smelting workers, with their successful appeal to the ministry for arbitration, is a case in point. The employers and their organizations turned against the ministry for its worker sympathies.[18]

What was the actual course of events? The sheer number of strikes to appear in waves after 1899 makes the discovery of patterns difficult because in these agitated years virtually every industry in every department was likely to experience some conflict throughout the wave period. Tracing the spread of disputes is before 1899 as simple as watching water trickle over dry sand, thereafter more difficult. Yet the main movements are clear. Unlike later years, when the bulk of a year's strike activity would pile up within the same month or two, in 1899–1900 conflict ran at high levels over a period of eleven or twelve months. The first great walkouts began with the masons of Marseille on 1 May 1899, spreading then to the 9,000 smelting workers of le Creusot late that month, and to the 10,000 miners of nearby Montceau-les-Mines early in June. The impressive multiplication of separate strikes, however, as opposed to these isolated giant stoppages, commenced only in July after the Waldeck government had formed. Thereafter not a month until December 1900 saw fewer than 10,000 strikers or 60 strikes.

Some sectors were more enthusiastic about the wave than others. Table 5.2 shows which had higher-than-usual striker rates in 1899–1900. When striker rates are viewed on a year-to-year basis, all sectors except agriculture evidenced a rapid upturn in 1899–1900, a fact the table conceals, for the

Table 5.2: *Striker rates by industry, 1899–1900*

	Strikers per 100,000 active population	
	1899–1900	1890–1914
Agriculture	—	100
Mining–quarrying	15,700	13,800
Food industries	700	500
Chemicals	7,300	5,300
Printing–paper	1,000	1,500
Leather–hides	2,200	1,600
Textiles–garments	2,200	1,400
Smelting	17,800	4,600
Metalworking	3,000	1,900
Construction–building materials	1,700	2,500
Transport–residual[a]	3,200 (500)	3,000 (400)
National	1,000	800

[a] The strikers in the 'transport–residual' sector were mainly in transportation industries, but a few belonged to otherwise unclassifiable occupations, mostly of a tertiary nature. The figures in parentheses, therefore, are the rates of all strikers in *SG* category XI (*transport et manutention*) plus XI *bis* per 100,000 members of the total tertiary labor force: transportation proper, commerce, office work, government service and such. The left-hand figure is the rate of all strikers in 'XI' and 'XI *bis*' divided by the labor force of transportation alone.

sectors which in 1899–1900 did not improve dramatically upon their 1890–1914 average performance were those which later on experienced great volumes of strike activity, making their 1899–1900 returns seem paltry by comparison.

Among individual industries, exceptionally active were coal mining (in most basins), chemicals, shoemaking (the major component of the leather-hides sector), cotton and wool spinning mills within textiles, and mechanical construction in the metalworking sector. Artisanal industries and occupations which formerly had figured prominently in waves were now remaining quiescent.

Map 5.3 tells better exactly what happened. Principal strike activity in Flanders came in textiles and mining, the spinners, wool combers and dyers of Roubaix and Tourcoing striking throughout the winter and spring at intervals, the dockers of Dunkerque in August of 1900 and the miners of Pas-de-Calais in October of 1900. In the Somme the jute workers of Berteaucourt, and in the Aisne the cotton spinners and weavers of St-Quentin, went out.

Although in the Seine-Maritime a November strike of the le Havre stevedores took place during the first crest of the wave, an August walkout of seamen, dockers and metalworkers in le Havre and Rouen represented the major activity in that department. In the Aube the stocking knitters of Troyes took part in a great dispute during February of 1900.

In 1899–1900 eastern France experienced its first important strike activity. From September through November of 1899 the machine builders, ironworkers and watchmakers of such little industrial towns as Beaucourt and Dampierre-les-Bois, and in larger Belfort city, went out. Later in 1900 the cotton spinners of Giromagny struck as well.

The 1899–1900 wave in the Saône-et-Loire was a historic event. The miners of Montceau-les-Mines, ten thousand in number, struck three times, in June of 1899, in January of 1900 and in January of 1901. The last of these strikes ended in absolute disaster: 1,200 workers fired. Next, nine thousand metallurgists of neighboring le Creusot struck twice, in May and September of 1899, dismissals and repressions following both of these disputes as well. The upshot of the failure of this great push was the end of militancy for the next thirty-five years in the Schneider empire.

The St-Etienne industrial region formed an important part of the winter 1899 wave, as 21,000 ribbon weavers stopped work on 18 December, followed by 13,000 miners on 26 December. Finally, in the south the Carmaux miners struck in February of 1900, and the sailors, dockhands and carters of Marseille, numbering all together around 10,000 men, followed in August.

Those were the principal conflicts. What may be said in general about this bridge year between the old- and new-style strike waves?

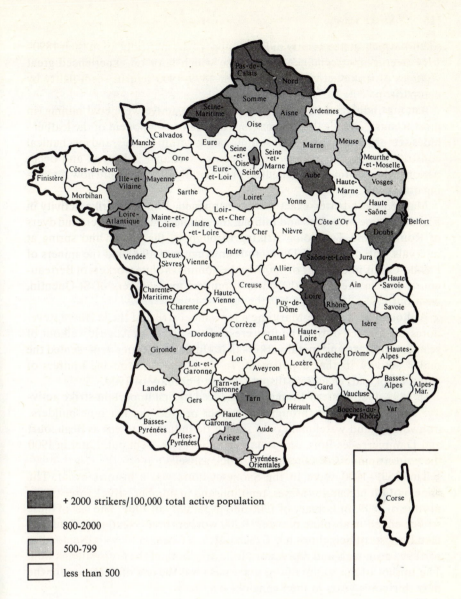

+ 2000 strikers/100,000 total active population

800–2000

500–799

less than 500

Map 5.3: Striker rate, 1899–1900

–The pace-setting industries of 1899–1900 were for the first time modern mass-production plants and the proletarian service occupations, though at the same time older skilled trades were substantially in evidence. Noteworthy is that in 1899 for the first time under any circumstances the machine-tenders and machinists in metalworking plants (*mécaniciens–constructeurs* in *SG* parlance) went out in large numbers in many different places.

–No evidence whatsoever of national coordination of the movement has been found. The customary pattern of informal synchronization among local organizations continued to prevail, each of which probably had clearly in mind some notion of the *grève générale*; yet such simultaneity had so long existed that one must be cautious in attributing the 1899–1900 events to the newly popular ideology of the general strike.[19] The CGT at this time was still in disarray from the disastrous railway strike of 1898.[20] Confusion among the several socialist parties about the proper response to ministerialism prevented them from following a clear line on mass strike movements.[21]

–Paris continued, as in 1893, to lag behind in militancy: 11 percent of all strikers in 1899–1900, compared to 15 percent in 1890–1914. This was probably tied into the silence of the central organizations, whose action slogans were normally heard most loudly in their immediate environs.

1906–20

The winter of 1905 and spring of 1906 seemed to many a political hinge. Socialist cooperation with the government ended in November of 1905 over the question of the schoolteachers' right to strike. In January 1906 Senate elections occurred and a new President of the Republic was selected; in March there was a cabinet crisis over church–state relations; and on 6 and 20 May the new elections for the Chamber of Deputies took place. In 1906 for the first time the Unified Socialist Party was able to present candidates in almost all electoral districts, and to an electorate fundamentally divided over social issues. A number of questions of concern to the workers figured in the election campaign: worker retirement plans, nationalization of some railroad lines and the like. These events combined to open up the question of working-class representation in political life at the center.[22]

In addition to events within the arena of national politics, changes within labor's internal politics conspired to give the 1906 strikes their compass and form. The proximate origin of the 1906 wave, of course, was a decision reached at the CGT's national congress at Bourges in 1904 that on 1 May 1906 a great general strike for the eight-hour day be staged. A special commission was created at that time within the CGT's executive body to coordinate the agitation. The amplitude of the 1906 wave, however, must be traced to the completion of the labor movement's centralization in Paris. The two worker *industrial* organizations converged into a structure unified at the top when the *Fédération des bourses* joined the CGT in 1902 at the Montpellier Congress. And the three chief worker *political* organizations combined to form the SFIO at the Paris Congress of Unification in 1905. For the first time, then, in 1906 the actions of local organizations would be coordinated from the center.

But events did not go quite as the organizers had planned. The 1906 wave was triggered not on 1 May as the CGT had wished, but by the Courrières mine disaster of 10 March 1906. On that date 1,200 miners in five pits near Lens were killed by a gas explosion. Four days later the anarchist *jeune syndicat* of miners, a rival to Emile-Joseph Basly's Guesdist *vieux syndicat*, took the lead in a protest movement. Soon 61,000 miners in the north, horrified by the disaster and by the mining company's carelessness, were on strike for higher wages.[23] Throughout the remainder of March the mining strike spread slowly across the Nord and Pas-de-Calais, leaping then in April to basins in the Loire and the Gard.

Other federations jumped the gun in April, among them typographers in Paris and Lille, smelting workers in Villerupt (Meurthe-et-Moselle) and Parisian coachmakers. But the bulk of the wave unfurled in the first week of May as citywide walkouts in one place after another, and strikes in virtually all the important nationwide federations not already out, swept across France. The 158,000 strikers registered in May were a quarter of the year's total.

Table 5.3 gives a systematic look at striker propensities by industry in

Table 5.3: *Striker rates by industry, 1906*

	Strikers per 100,000 active population	
	1906	1890–1914
Agriculture	200	100
Mining–quarrying	31,700	13,800
Food industries	1,000	500
Chemicals	4,200	5,300
Printing–paper	12,100	1,500
Leather–hides	4,300	1,600
Textiles–garments	2,200	1,400
Smelting	31,800	4,600
Metalworking	8,600	1,900
Construction–building materials	8,200	2,500
Transport–residual[a]	2,400 (400)	3,000 (400)
National	2,100	800

[a] See note to table 5.2.

1906, showing that every sector save chemicals and transport had an unusually high level of conflict in that year. This is the first wave in which all sectors, agricultural workers included, joined in simultaneously and with a sense of concert.

Four main regions of conflict (map 5.4) may be identified: the north, the ring of departments around Lyon, the Mediterranean coastal departments and Paris. Let us take them one at a time.

Striker rates in the north were driven up largely by the miners, as we have seen, but textile workers of various kinds and the dockers of Dunkerque – both groups of enduring militancy – must also be mentioned. A new note was struck in the walkouts of the automobile workers and machine builders in Lille, an instance of the general participation of the heavy metalworking sector throughout France in 1906.

In Lyon a great strike wave gathered force in metals and textiles. Both the older artisanal metalworkers, the thousands of coppersmiths, tinsmiths, ironworkers, polishers, moulders, metalsmiths and turners of the city went on strike, in addition to the newer automobile assemblers. But also in textiles: 3,000 tullemakers walked out in February, joining a spasm of conflict in that industry which stretched eastward into the Ain and Savoy. And on 2 May thousands of dyers and garment workers walked out.

High striker rates in the construction sector offered a common theme in the south. From the construction laborers of Toulon and Nice to the masons of Perpignan, construction workers supplied the big battalions, a familiar pattern in the Midi where the building trades were consistently more militant than their confreres in northern France. Otherwise numerous different industries struck in Marseille, miners in the Gard, and agricultural and transport workers in the Hérault and Pyrénées-Orientales. (The orange loaders in Cerbère had three separate strikes in the course of the year.)

Finally, Paris. This was the first wave led from and dominated by the capital. Most of the 126,000 workers who went out in Paris came from construction–woodworking and from metalworking. An unprecedented 72,000 construction strikers were recorded, and while a few of them took part in the premature mid-April strikes, most walked out on 2 May: 20,000 masons and bricklayers, 10,000 housepainters, 8,000 navvies, 6,000 carpenters and so on.[24] The metalworking sector accumulated some 37,000 strikers in the year, most of them appearing in a few great strikes during April and early May: some skilled metals crafts, of course, such as 1,800 braziers, 5,100 moulders, 5,000 metalsmiths and 3,000 jewelry workers (*bijoutiers*). But most noteworthy is the first massive participation of the Parisian automotive industry in strike activity: a preliminary 1,200 autoworkers in Billancourt early in April, then on 30 April a walkout of 10,000 in Paris and its nearby suburbs.[25] This 1906 strike was the parturition of militancy in a sector which ever after would symbolize proletarian protest.

Yet while the wave of 1906 served to diffuse conflict to hitherto quiet sectors, it recruited for the most part from industries and areas militant in

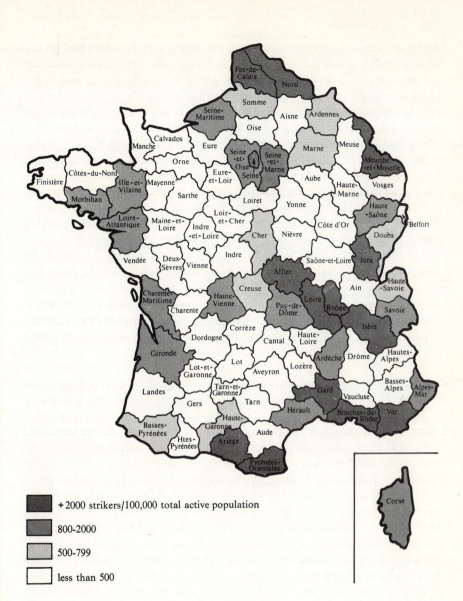

Map 5.4: Striker rate, 1906

Legend:

+2000 strikers/100,000 total active population

800-2000

500-799

less than 500

the past. A quick way of demonstrating this is to compute correlations between past and present strike activity for each industry within each department. Let us represent past activity by the average striker rate 1890–1905 by industry–department, present conflict by the 1906 striker rate in each industry–department. The correlation between the two was a substantial 0.50 for the strike rate and 0.37 for the striker rate.[26]

The component parts of a proletarian strike wave fit together neatly in 1906:

– It was the first centrally directed wave, planned carefully in advance for 1 May and guided from Parisian central bureaus.

– It was the first in which proletarian workers would keynote the timing and form of the action, as did the autoworkers in Paris and the Nord or the construction workers in the Midi.

– It was the first since 1840 in which Paris overshadowed the provinces, for the commands of the federations were heard most audibly close up. In 1906 Paris had 29 percent of all strikers, compared to 15 percent in 1890–1914 as a whole.

– It was the first since the July Monarchy involving a direct confrontation between worker organizations and the established government, for the mining leader Pierre Monatte, the CGT secretary Griffuelhes and treasurer Lévy were arrested, and the Paris CGT headquarters searched. The Parisian bourgeoisie, fearing revolution, began to stockpile food, a somewhat overwrought course in view of the absence of putschist ambitions on the part of either CGT leaders or rank and file.[27]

1919–20

The nature of the political crisis in 1919–20 can be stated quite simply: furious at their betrayal at the hands of corrupt politicians and reformist labor leaders, the working classes streamed back from the trenches in 1919 determined to make the proletarian voice count for something; the example of successful Red Revolution in the East said that if all else failed violent revolution would provide the highroad to political representation. Annie Kriegel has summed it up: 'In 1919 the masses of workers, exhausted from the bloody tasks of war but excited by the wind from the East, put an enormous dynamism at the service of the revolutionary Left.' This revolutionary thrust would find its foremost channel in the strike waves of 1919–20.[28]

The strike wave is remembered in political chronicles as the genesis of the French Communist Party, for severe disillusionment with the policies of the CGT met the failure of its great actions. In the history of strikes, 1919–20 is notable not so much for an establishment of new patterns of action as for a continuation of those already laid down in 1906.

The volume of conflict in 1919–20 was a midpoint between that of 1906 and 1936: 2,000 strikes in 1919 and 1,800 in 1920, as opposed to 1,400 in 1906 and 16,000 in 1936. The number of strikers in 1919–20 also fell between the two stools: 1,300,000 in 1919 and again in 1920, as opposed to 400,000 in 1906 and 2,400,000 in 1936. The progress of a trend in the expansion of waves is thus evident.

The history of the events of 1919–20 may be organized about four great single disputes.[29] Only a modest level of conflict was seen in 1919 until 1 May, when the CGT called a nationwide general strike demanding the immediate application in the factories of the eight-hour-day legislation signed into law just a week earlier. (The eight-hour day, of course, had provided the occasion for the 1906 wave as well.) During the first week in May, therefore, a large number of walkouts over pay increases and shorter hours occurred in many industries.

The month of May also saw an agitated debate within the metalworkers' federation over the role of politics in a general strike. This discussion stimulated a series of metals disputes later in May, and triggered the second major event of the period: a general strike of 165,000 machine builders (*mécaniciens–constructeurs*) in the Seine from 20 to 30 June. This gigantic dispute evoked simultaneous walkouts in most other industrial cities and sectors, notably a nationwide coal strike beginning 16 June. Over 500 strikes were registered in June all together.

The pace of conflict then slackened somewhat until the third major upheaval of these years, the series of railway strikes running from 23 February 1920 to 4 March. The largest of these was the 26,000-man walkout of Parisian railworkers. These disputes commanded nationwide attention, and cued another burst of walkouts in other industries and departments: 333 strikes in February of 1920, 452 in March and a commensurately high number of participants. Many of these, of course, were sympathy strikes.

The fourth punctuation point was the famous second railway strike of 3 May 1920, over which militants and historians have wrung their hands until this day. The moderate success of the February strike, combined with rank-and-file irritation that the companies were not respecting the agreement, brought the April congress of railway workers to agree to a second strike. May 1 was set as the date, and on 28 April Léon Jouhaux vowed the CGT's support. The strike was a terrible failure. On 29 May the 93,000 railworkers returned to the job after the Briand government arrested union militants and threatened to mobilize the strikers into the army. Eighteen thousand railroad employees were dismissed for having participated in the strike. The *élan* of the great postwar wave had been shattered.

In the second rail strike the CGT orchestrated waves of support in numerous other sectors, calling out miners, seamen and dockers on 1–3 May 1920; metalworkers, construction workers, aircraft builders and the remainder of ports and docks on 10 May; a third wave in furniture and gas on 11 May.[30] All together at that time some 380,000 sympathy strikers were recorded in the *SG*, without more precise designation of place or sector.[31] Further shops and plants in city after city joined in support for the railworkers, even though not directly commanded to do so. This vast mobilization made the late spring of 1920 a historic high point of the worker movement. Strike activity subsided to a minimal level after the failure of the rail strike, and the rest of 1920 experienced relatively token amounts.[32]

How may we find regularities among these thousands of separate disputes, coordinated in time around four central events though they may be? Table 5.4 indicates the pattern of striker rates by industry. The national frequency was in 1919–20 four times higher than usual, and each industry multiplied its normal striker rate by a factor of at least two. Rates in 1919 of 51,000 smelting workers on strike per 100,000 mean that in effect every other member of metalsmelting walked out, every other chemical worker and miner and every fourth metalworker. In the following year virtually every smelting worker in France struck, to go by the rate of 96,000 strikers/100,000 workers, although doubtless some struck more than once, others not at all. The statistics which say that in 1920 every third transport worker struck are measuring primarily the impact of the two railway strikes, and the numerous sympathy strikes which mushroomed about them. We have come to expect high rates in these sectors during strike waves, so these findings are not a surprise.

More unexpected is the broad geographical extension of the strike movement in 1919–20. A comparison of map 5.5, which charts 1919–20 striker rates, with map 5.4 of 1906 rates, demonstrates that in 1919–20 many more departments experienced top rates of conflict than in the earlier wave. Just after the First World War the southwestern departments of Landes and

Table 5.4: *Striker rates by industry, 1919–20*

	Strikers per 100,000 active population			
	1919	1920	1919–20	1890–1914
Agriculture	100	300	200	100
Mining–quarrying	41,100	57,200	49,200	13,800
Food industries	10,600	4,600	7,600	500
Chemicals	47,700	12,400	29,400	5,300
Printing–paper	6,100	10,600	8,400	1,500
Leather–hides	9,000	8,600	8,800	1,600
Textiles–garments	9,400	7,800	8,600	1,400
Smelting	50,900	96,500	73,600	4,600
Metalworking	28,100	5,600	16,700	1,900
Construction–building materials	14,700	7,500	11,100	2,500
Transport–residual[a]	15,200 (2,700)	32,300 (5,900)	23,800 (4,300)	3,000 (400)
National	6,000	5,200	5,600	800

[a] See note to table 5.2.

the Gironde (agricultural strikers), Finistère and other Breton departments (metalworking) and the eastern departments of Ardennes (metalworking), Aube (textiles), Marne (construction), Vosges and Haute-Saône (both textiles) and Doubs (smelting and metalworking) came to life with an intensity notably absent in 1906. In general most departments struck in 1919–20 much more intensively than in 1906.

Finally of note from map 5.5 are the high striker rates in the lost departments now returned: Bas-Rhin, Haut-Rhin and Moselle. Several general strikes supplied the large numbers of participants which sent these rates soaring. Details here are unnecessary, but one might speculate that renewed contact with the militants of the lost provinces gave the impetus to other workers in eastern France to join the great waves.

Yet conflict was *not* extended into territories hitherto entirely quiescent and unorganized. In only a couple of local industries with peak rates of activity in 1919–20 had conflict been rare before the war. In 1919 the construction industry in the Ardennes struck massively, yet had been passive in 1890–1914 as a whole. And in 1920 the great smelting strikes in Lyon had been prefigured by no especial prewar militancy. But it was typically Parisian metalworking, Pas-de-Calais coalmining, Marseille stevedoring that supplied the big battalions in 1919–20, and these are precisely the areas and industries whence most militancy stemmed before the war. We may statistically confirm this conclusion by correlating (as for 1906) the previous strike histories of each industry in each department with its performance in 1919–20. Again, high correlations emerge: 0.56 for the strike rate by industry–department between 1890–1914 and 1919–20, and 0.43 for the striker rate (480 industry–departments).

The magnitude of the influx of new workers into the existing industrial structure after demobilization has been a standard theme in the history of this period. What we have just said about patterns of persistence means that only in those industries in those places with a preexisting tradition of conflict would all the new workers actually swell the ranks of the strikers. Where the new industrial recruits found no extant tradition of collective action (or structure of association) awaiting them, they would remain isolated and unmobilized for the great waves of 1919–20.

To sum up, 1919–20 continued some themes now familiar to us in the study of strike waves:

(1) In quantitative terms the center dominated the movement, for in 1919 Paris (the department of the Seine) contributed 32 percent of all France's strikers, as opposed to that city's normal share in 1915–35 of 20 percent.

(2) Paris was also dominant metaphorically as the seat of the central federations and confederations which mobilized the ripples of disputes criss-crossing the country: the CGT, the railworkers' federation, the metalworkers' federation and so on.

(3) Strikers themselves were drawn most heavily, in both relative and ab-

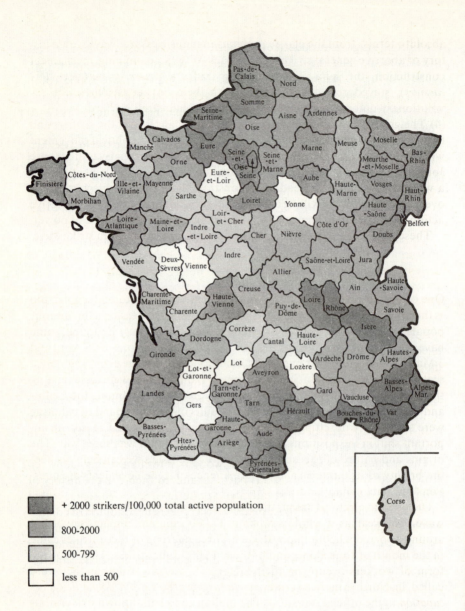

Map 5.5: Striker rate, 1919–20

■	+ 2000 strikers/100,000 total active population
▨	800–2000
▧	500–799
□	less than 500

Corse

absolute terms, from the classic proletarian industries – railways with a history of abortive general strikes dating back to 1898, coalmining, mechanical construction, the semi-skilled building trades (*ouvriers du bâtiment, terrassiers*), stevedores and the like – with their class-conscious, often revolutionary unions and their long histories of industrial warfare.

(4) The government, bourgeois society, and perhaps half of the strikers and their leaders thought of the wave as a revolutionary political movement whose purpose was not to improve wages or hours (how trivial was the excuse Jouhaux provided for the 1 May 1919 strikes: immediate implementation of a week-old law!), but instead to demonstrate that rank-and-file workers all over the country were willing to surrender substantial resources to collective action in order to influence the political struggle at the center of power.

These four features together are the epitome of a proletarian strike wave.

1936

One of the most compelling problems in recent French historical scholarship is the 'social explosion' of 1936. In the depths of the Depression a tumultuous popular movement uncoiled for which a counterpart may be found, some have claimed, only in the *grande peur* of 1789. The elections of 26 April and 3 May 1936 gave the Left parties a stunning victory: increases in Communist seats from 11 to 72 and in Socialist from 131 to 147; there were losses among the Radical Socialists of 51 seats (from 157 to 106), and among the Center and Right of 44 seats (120 to 76).[34] The results of the first round of balloting were sufficiently upsetting to cause a brief financial panic. Clearly, an important shift in the positions of the contenders for power was under way. The origins and nature of this surge from below are issues we can help resolve; the brevity of its duration and impermanence of its achievements are questions our data cannot address.

Outside the electoral arena, the social explosion took the form of a strike wave. The year as a whole saw some 17,000 separate conflicts, involving around two and a half million strikers. Three quarters of these strikes came in the month of June alone, and of those 12,000 June strikes, 9,000 took the form of workers occupying their factories – sitdown strikes as they were called in North America (*grèves sur le tas*, or *grèves ayant donné lieu à occupation* in the official statistics). The million and a half sitdown strikers thus represented the heart of the 1936 strike wave, and any effort to deal with the conflicts of the year as a whole must treat in the first place these factory occupations.

The first four months of 1936 were absolutely placid, a slight revival of strike activity noticeable only in May. More interesting, in May the first hesitant sitdowns took place, apparently directed by the metalworkers' federation in provincial mechanical construction plants, and then brought in mid-May to the Paris region when the tactic proved effective.[35] By 28 May the movement had spread to the entire Parisian automobile industry, and after a brief pause for Pentecost, radiated out from Paris to the provinces, and from the metalworking industry to all other sectors. On 5 June Léon Blum's Popular Front government was installed, whereupon Blum immediately began broadcasting appeals to stop the sitdowns. Negotiations between workers' and employers' organizations commenced at the Hôtel Matignon on Sunday the 7th, and that very night the famous Matignon agreements were signed. Accord meant the abatement though not the end of the strike movement, for factory occupations continued to break out well into November, reaching nearly a thousand in October alone. In 1937 and 1938 some sitdowns took place, although numerically they represented only a fraction of the total of strikes. The question of the social explosion of the Popular Front is essentially a question of what happened in June 1936.

To retain perspective in the following discussion the reader must have a sense of the magnitude and dispersion of conflict in 1936 as a whole. Whatever territorial differentials existed, it must not be forgotten that in 1936 strikes spread with hitherto unprecedented intensity into virtually every corner of France. Map 5.6 of striker rates for 1936 as a whole shows that only a handful of departments fell into *less than the maximum* category of conflict, on the basis of the scale we have been using for earlier wave years. A few districts in Aquitaine, the Midi-Pyrénées and the Pays de la Loire had only middling striker rates, but everywhere else at least 2,000 strikers/ 100,000 total labor force (usually our highest category of intensity) prevailed. And some top scores were previously unheard of: 34,000 strikers for every 100,000 active population, including agriculture, in the Aube; 43,000 in the Nord; 46,000 in Belfort. So the agitation of 1936 as a whole was nationwide.

Yet when we plot those disputes specifically involving factory occupations, and when we examine the distribution of the highest *intensities* of conflict, a pattern appears startlingly different from any past strike wave. Map 5.7 indicates the distribution of factory occupations per 100,000 industrial workers. (In this and the following two maps solely industrial workers provide the denominator.) The sitdowns were centered in the departments around Paris, Lyon and Marseille, to go by their sheer number alone. Although a sprinkling turned up in most other departments as well, the highest frequencies were manifestly confined to a few regions. (The highest rates of *non*-sitdown strikes were also recorded in those areas, so in 1936 it is not a matter of one style of dispute predominating in one area, a different style in another.)

The number of disputes alone misleads, for a single sitdown could involve tens of thousands of workers, others merely dozens. When therefore we estimate the distribution of participants a rather different, though still not familiar, pattern appears.[36] As may be seen from a map of estimated sitdown strik*ers* in June of 1936 (map 5.8), the most intense conflict took place north

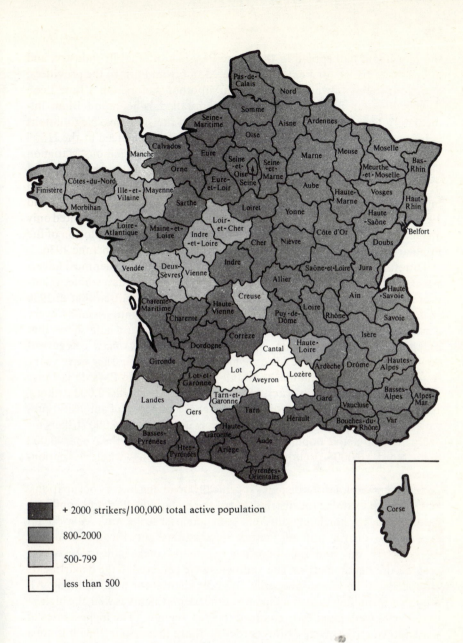

████	+ 2000 strikers/100,000 total active population
▓▓▓▓	800-2000
░░░░	500-799
□□□□	less than 500

Corse

Map 5.6: Striker rate, 1936 (agricultural and tertiary labor forces included in denominator)

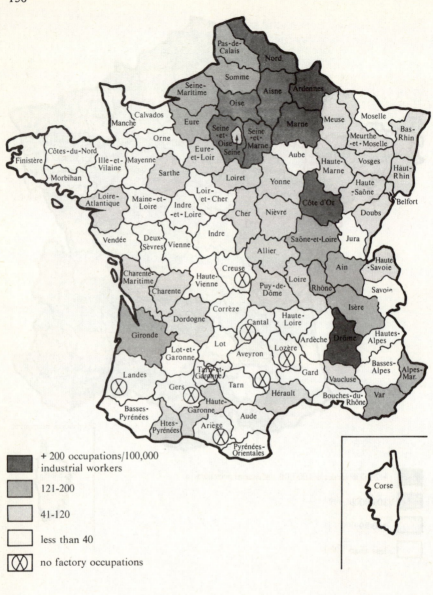

Map 5.7: Number of factory occupations in June 1936 per 100,000 industrial workers

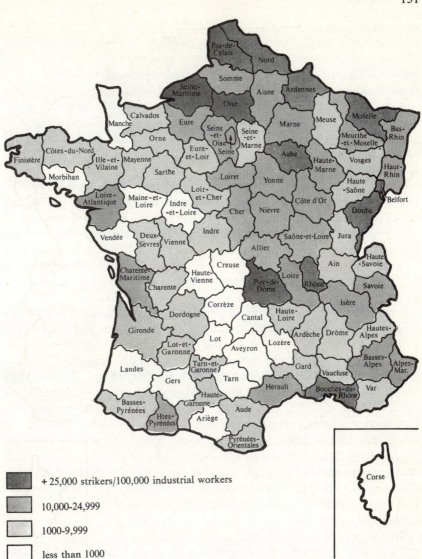

Map 5.8: Estimated sitdown striker rate, June 1936

and east of a line drawn from le Havre to Marseille; the departments to the south and west of that line were distinguished by low intensities, or by the absence of factory occupations. Centers of past worker militancy and firm association in the Gard and Aveyron, Haute Vienne, and Maine-et-Loire, Finistère and Ille-et-Vilaine remained *comparatively* silent, while industrial communities in northern and eastern departments hitherto passive flared up with fierce intensity: the Oise and Ardennes, the Eure, Cher and Yonne, the Savoie and Basses-Alpes. We may note that the highest incidences of participation in June sitdowns occurred in customary centers of militancy: Rouen and le Havre, the north, the iron mining and smelting towns of the Moselle, the mechanical construction plants of the Doubs, Lyon, Clermont-Ferrand and Marseille. (Data are at the departmental level, and the singling out of individual municipalities is informed guesswork.) Yet the watershed nature of the le Havre–Marseille line means that the usual associations between union organization, worker concentration and strike propensity we have identified in the past did not hold up in 1936, for the north and east did not have a monopoly on militant, solidary proleterians. Quite the contrary, in fact.

It rarely happens in areal analysis that a complex country divides into two such homogeneous groups. What accounts for the pattern? Antoine Prost in an important original analysis of union growth in 1935–7 has given us some clues. He says most rapid to increase in union membership were the departments of 'dynamic France,' where the modernization of manufacturing had been proceeding apace (map 5.9). The areas where union organization had previously been strongest, however, were those of 'static France,' old, traditional industrial centers where (a) time had implanted the roots of union locals, and (b) the highly unionized tertiary sector was strong – teachers, *fonctionnaires*, postal and telegraph workers and the like. Prost argues that the surge of unionization occurred precisely in the underunionized manufacturing sectors of dynamic France, among semi-skilled factory workers, touching with greatly reduced pressure the established centers and tertiary industries of static France.

The argument that industrial modernization in the 1920s led to high unionization after 1936 and sitdown participation is neatly confirmed by the fact that the large industrial establishments lay mainly north and east of the le Havre–Marseille line. Map 5.10 shows the percentage of industrial workers employed in establishments over 500 workers in 1936; and the reader will note how closely this predicts (a) the areas of intense sitdown activity and (b) the areas of rapid unionization.[37]

Thus four different kinds of phenomena coincide with amazing exactness in the summer of 1936: the explosion of new union recruits, the concentration of workers in great industrial establishments, the intensity of sitdown strikes and the absence of previous union organization. (In Paris, the Nord, Marseille and some other important industrial centers of the northeast, it goes without saying, strong local unions had existed for a long time; but in many other areas of the northeast which saw ferocious sitdown activity, such as Lorraine or the Champagne, they had been lacking.)

One further fact about the sitdowns. They seem to have been mobilized by informal local political groups and single militants coming from the areas of political rather than union action. Georges Lefranc has sketched the small groups who got the sitdowns off the ground. Emerging from the shadows to take the leadership of the movement, flying in the face of regular local and national unions, these militants were sometimes professional organizers, sometimes members of political sects and discussion circles. 'Anarchists, Trotskyists, Communists of strict obedience and Pivertistes furnished the essential cadres: there was a temporary conjunction of activists, coming from different orientations and for the most part hitherto without union responsibilities, but who almost always took over the function of workshop representative.'[38] Marcel Schulz thought that young Communist propagandists in the plants had steered the movement in a political direction.[39]

Not only does a comparison of various maps tell us about a relationship among these several variables, the statistical technique of multiple regression reveals the pattern of causation as well. We plugged into a regression analysis quantitative data representing the various logical chains in our explanation of the sitdowns: information on previous militancy and unionization, information on leftist voting in 1936, on the percentage of the workforce in large establishments ($+500$ workers), on the position of the departments relative to the le Havre–Marseille line and of course on the sitdowns themselves. Here are the independent variables which best 'explain' the variation in the rate of sitdown strikes from department to department (measured per 100,000 non-agricultural labor force):

Dependent variable: sitdown strike rate in June 1936

Significant independent variables:	Standard regression coefficient
– Percent of votes on the Left (SFIO or PCF)	0.237
– 'Northeastness' (department's position north of le Havre–Marseille axis)	0.484
	$R^2 = 0.34$

Slightly different independent variables best account for the distribution of the strik*er* rate:

Dependent variable: estimated number of sitdown strikers per 100,000 industrial labor force in June 1936:

Significant independent variables:	Standard regression coefficient
– The number of workers in establishments larger than 500	0.310
– 'Northeastness'	0.524
	$R^2 = 0.45$

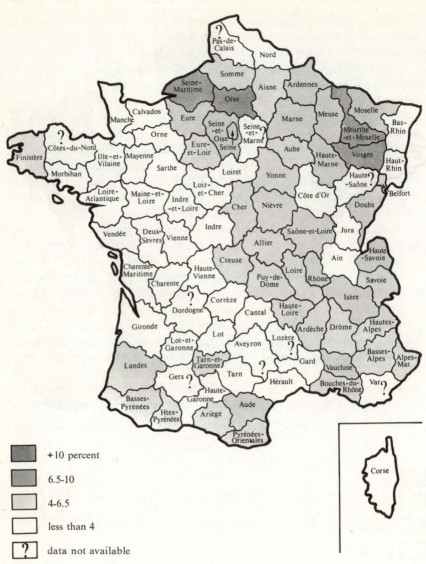

Map 5.9: Percentage increase in union membership, 1936–8 (adapted from Prost, *La C.G.T. à l'époque du Front Populaire*, p. 98)

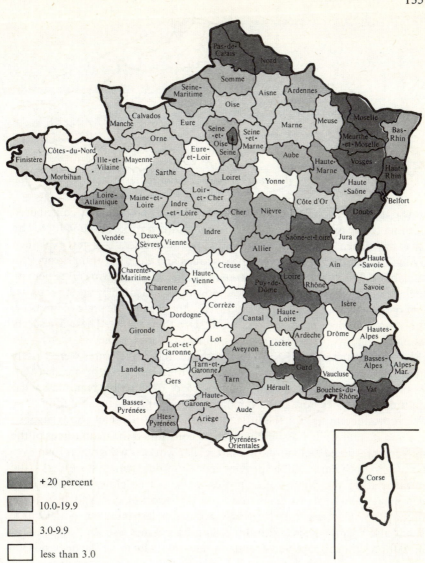

Pas-de-Calais
Nord
Somme
Seine-Maritime
Aisne
Ardennes
Oise
Calvados
Manche
Eure
Seine-et-Oise
Seine-et-Marne
Marne
Meuse
Moselle
Bas-Rhin
Meurthe-et-Moselle
Orne
Seine
Côtes-du-Nord
Finistère
Ille-et-Vilaine
Mayenne
Eure-et-Loir
Aube
Haute-Marne
Vosges
Haut-Rhin
Morbihan
Sarthe
Loiret
Yonne
Haute-Saône
Belfort
Loire-Atlantique
Maine-et-Loire
Indre-et-Loire
Loir-et-Cher
Cher
Nièvre
Côte d'Or
Doubs
Vendée
Deux-Sèvres
Vienne
Indre
Allier
Saône-et-Loire
Jura
Charente-Maritime
Haute-Vienne
Creuse
Ain
Haute-Savoie
Charente
Loire
Rhône
Savoie
Corrèze
Puy-de-Dôme
Isère
Dordogne
Cantal
Haute-Loire
Gironde
Lot-et-Garonne
Lot
Aveyron
Lozère
Ardèche
Drôme
Hautes-Alpes
Landes
Tarn-et-Garonne
Tarn
Gard
Vaucluse
Basses-Alpes
Alpes-Mar.
Gers
Hérault
Bouches-du-Rhône
Var
Basses-Pyrénées
Haute-Garonne
Aude
Htes-Pyrénées
Ariège
Pyrénées-Orientales

Corse

+ 20 percent
10.0-19.9
3.0-9.9
less than 3.0

Map 5.10: Percent of workers in establishments larger than 500, 1936

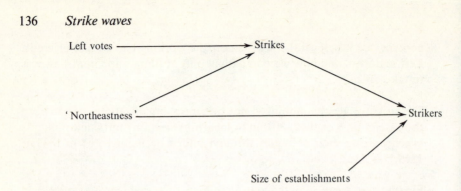

Fig. 5.1: A model of worker participation in the sitdown strikes of 1936

These numbers say that previous unionization and militancy contributed nothing to the propensity to participate in sitdown strikes in June 1936. The sheer incidence of conflict, as measured by the strike rate, is best explained by the distribution of Leftist political groups and electoral enthusiasm. Presumably the political organizers in each locality urged the workers to occupy their factories. Participation in the sitdowns, as measured by the striker rate, emerges as a function of large enterprises: the greater the scale of industry, the more willing would workers be to seize their plants. These are surely assembly-line workers, who in the summer of 1936 streamed massively into the newly reunited CGT.[40] Both the strike and striker rates were closely grouped according to region, indicating that residence in northeastern France would predispose workers to factory occupation regardless what political influences bore upon them or what size firm they labored in.

We reproduce in fig. 5.1 the little model these statistical measures suggest.

Even if semi-skilled assembly workers constituted the main forces of the movement, the participation of white-collar workers was greater than ever before. In both Paris and the provinces not only department store clerks (the proletariat of the white-collar professions), but employees of insurance companies and business firms took over their workplaces. And an occupation of the banks was only narrowly avoided in last-minute negotiations.[41] What also seems true is that in June shop-floor issues, especially the matter of worker control, received prominent mention, alongside the demands for wage increases which are intrinsic to mechanized workers and strikes.[42]

Although the personnel of the 1936 wave provide continuity with 1906 and 1919–20, in several ways the sitdown strikes were to foreshadow conflicts of the future:

– The strike wave was an explicitly political act, yet one directed as much at local problems (going via the center to unravel them) as at the central forum of national politics itself. One thinks of the collective bargaining provisions incorporated into the Matignon agreements. In Georges Lefranc's opinion the timing of the wave left little doubt as to its political content, for just several weeks earlier the working classes had elected a Left majority, and now were impatient only at Blum's apparent slowness to take office.[43]

– The strike wave was mobilized not by central organizations, as had been the case in 1906 or 1919–20, but by local organizations and single militants synchronizing their activities through informal channels, as in 1833 or 1869.[44]

– Finally, the unprecedented representation of trained professionals and of white-collar workers was to foreshadow the future. It marked the activation of the labor force at the leading edge of industrial change.

The postwar period

The post-Second World War period would see three major strike waves. Two different kinds of workers contributed in roughly equal proportions to these single episodes, and in general to postwar strike activity: the proletarians of manufacturing and transportation, whom we have seen in conflicts going back to 1869, and the educated professionals of the science sector (joined by the often indistinguishable white-collar workers from the tertiary) whose presence in labor struggles becomes massive and enduring after the Second World War. Just as proletarian machine-tenders set the style of conflict in prewar waves, these technicians and clerks provided archetypes for the post-war period.

1947–9

In the fall of 1947, and again in the autumn of 1948, a strike wave of such intensity welled up as to suggest civil war rather than the give and take of industrial relations. First, the political setting. In the spring of 1947 the coalition which had governed the nation since the Liberation was in dissolution. Cold War polarities were driving the Communists from the government, and De Gaulle stood in the wings. 'The straw that broke the loudly creaking back of *tripartisme*,' according to Alexander Werth, was a wildcat strike in the huge Renault Billancourt plant late in April.[45] The guideline 'no enemies on the Left' meant that the Communists were ultimately forced, somewhat against their will, to support the strike, thereby placing themselves in direct conflict with government policies on wage freezes. On 4 May the Communists in the Chamber decided no longer to back the government; thus commenced a period of probing and testing on the role of the Left in the governance of the nation, which, as with similar entries and exits in the past, provoked a strike wave.

Aside from two short walkouts in the nation's banks and a longer dispute in the newspaper industry, 1947 had been quiet until May. Then commenced the first of the two great bursts of conflict which were to occur in the course of the year. A rising drumfire of strikes in the Parisian metalworking industry throughout May was the prelude to three nationwide general strikes of railway workers, miners and bank employees, the former going out early in June, the latter two late in July. These great strikes, each involving hundreds of thousands of workers, pulled along many other smaller disputes. This wave, the smaller of the two in 1947, was without the benefit of central CGT orchestration.

The second peak came in November. On 10 November an increase in tramway fares in Marseille provoked a series of disturbances, culminating in general strikes in several industries. Simultaneously strikes erupted in the huge Parisian metalworking plants, spreading on 17 November to the miners of the Nord. Between 22 and 24 November the movement reached its maximum extension, general strikes in Parisian metalworking and construction, in all sectors of Marseille, in the ports, railways and many other places and industries. The powerful industrial federations had generalized the movement, especially the Federation of Metalworkers, and twenty Communist-led federations formed outside the CGT a temporary action coalition, the National Strike Committee.

The movement had immediate political overtones. The committee publicized: 'Bataille des 25 pourcent [pay increase] contre la politique du parti américain.' Lefranc states that the purpose of the expansion of general strikes was to challenge the Schuman government.[46] By 1 December the wave had turned into a general strike in entire departments, notably in the southwest. Factory occupations now ensued, along with efforts to occupy railway facilities. The movement had become insurrectional. Yet by 12 December it was all over. The government cajoled and threatened the strikers back to work, and the CGT, by now furiously split over both the wisdom of the entire adventure and union relations with the Communist Party, called things off.[47]

The thrust of the wave had spent itself, yet an account of major strike activity in these years would be incomplete without mention of the miners' strike the following year. In September 1948 the government issued decrees affecting in various ways the job status of miners. Thereupon the CGT's Federation of Miners polled the members about calling an 'unlimited strike' in response. The nationwide mining strike commenced 4 October and dragged on until the miners straggled back to work late in November, involving the occupation of the northern coalfields by the army, stretches of violent disturbances and a bitterness on both sides remembered vividly even at this writing. Nine million man-days of work were lost in the strike, three-fourths of the national total in 1948. At least fifty sympathy strikes took place in other sectors alongside the mining general strike; though contributions to the strike fund came in from all over France and Europe, the dispute failed completely, marking the end of the 1947–8 strike wave.[48]

On the one hand in 1947–8 we saw the persistence of traditional forms of mobilization: 'revolutionary' industrial federations calling out their forces in unison across the country to topple an unwanted government. This especially happened in November of 1947 and in the miners' strike of 1948. On the other hand we have white-collar workers going out by the hundreds of thousands, yet without the benefit of central orchestration and for reasons other than political confrontation. Two styles of strike wave had clearly come together momentarily, but for one it was an ending, for the other a beginning.

1953

There was in August of 1953 another ferocious little strike wave. As so often in postwar France, the movement arose to challenge a government change in the status of workers in the public sector; the precise issues are unimportant. On 5 August the Federation F.–O. of the Postal and Telegraph workers called an 'unlimited' general strike to force the government to revoke the decrees, and the other federations in that sector followed immediately. Even though many union leaders were on vacation, the wave spread rapidly to the other parts of the public sector, sometimes guided by a federation, sometimes not: railways, Paris métro, mines, municipal services, civil service and metalworking in the private sector. Only late in August did the strikers begin returning to work.

The wave came just after a series of cabinet crises of late May and June. Mendès-France delivered a widely publicized 'get-the-country-moving-again' speech in an effort to become premier, yet failed to receive a majority, as several other candidates for the post also failed. Much was made of this in Left circles, the SFIO for Mendès-France, the PCF against. It is difficult to say exactly what role this prolonged crisis played in giving the working classes a sense that an important political juncture was at hand, and that it counted to demonstrate worker enthusiasm for change. The evidence of synchronization in timing between politics and mass movements is only circumstantial. But once the August strike movement had become mobilized, its thrust was unquestionably at the center political stage: to embarrass and topple the Laniel government.[49] Here we have public servants, officials and salaried employees of various kinds leading a movement ostensibly over job status issues, rather than construction laborers walking out over wage hikes. Their mobilization was decentralized and informal rather than centrally directed. In 1953, for the first time since 1840, a major strike wave took place without the assistance of proletarians in manufacturing. This was an important new departure.

The August 1953 wave was perhaps the most broadly based and powerful surge of strike activity between 1948 and 1968, but it was certainly not the only movement in those years one might classify as a 'strike wave.' Indeed a characteristic feature of post-Second World War strikes has been their great amplitude. Almost every year in this period had at least one such movement, cutting across industries and regions, and we would have dwelt on these at length had they occurred before 1936. But chronicling such episodes as the public service strikes of 1962 or the coalminers' strike of 1963 would not contribute significantly to our purpose, presenting little more than a list, held together by speculation. The sad fact is that quantitative data are lacking for a more thoroughgoing study of postwar events. Departmental or regional data are terribly incomplete, and industrial data are limited to the series 'man-days lost,' an index which gives misleading weight to industries with long strikes, exaggerating or smoothing over differentials in the mobilization of participants. Consequently, a study of interindustry differences in single years, such as 1948 when the long coalminers' strike figured so prominently, is risky. The main point to note of these years is that the political role of the strike wave appeared to have changed. A new group of contenders for power was using the strike to advance its case, no longer the factory proletarians of the classic period of conflict, but the new professional classes whom industrial modernization had called into life.

May–June 1968
The May–June Days of 1968 are the end of the narrative. Conscious as we are of the problems of writing contemporary history, we cannot forbear placing those recent events within the framework of the argument of this book. A recapitulation of what happened would be pointless, for the general sequence of events is well known, and a scholarly analysis of what really *did* happen has only just begun. Here we wish to comment upon six features of the May–June Days, drawing both upon popular accounts and upon the emerging monographic literature.

For one thing, the May–June strike wave came in the immediate wake of the severest political crisis since the time in 1947 when everyone thought the Communists were trying to seize power in Marseille. There was the Night of the Barricades on 10–11 May, and Premier Pompidou's rush back to the capital from Afghanistan; there was a gigantic parade of 800,000 people through Paris on 13 May, and that evening the occupation of the Sorbonne. The next day, an aircraft plant near Nantes was occupied, beginning the sitdowns. On 16 May workers occupied the Renault Billancourt plant, launching pad of many earlier movements, and within four days the sitdowns had spread through all of France. The timing of events makes it clear that the sitdowns in themselves were not so much the creation *of* as the response *to* an existing political crisis, another jostling and maneuvering outside the portals of the polity, but with a more complex constituency this time: educated middle-class professionals in addition to the laboring masses.

Second point: the May–June sitdown strikes were the largest mobilization of workers in French history. An exact measurement of the movement is not possible because the government either did not know itself the sum total of participants and disputes, or was not telling.[50]

Third point: white-collar occupations engaged in the general strike more enthusiastically than ever before. This observation, of course, is an impression based on accounts of events rather than on solid statistical data by industry. Yet all observers agree that the white-collar employees within industry, to say nothing of the tertiary sector, were a fundament of the movement. That statement can be made of no previous strike wave save perhaps 1953.[51]

Fourth point: the strikers were mobilized along lines more reminiscent of 1833 or 1936 than of 1919 or 1947, that is, by local unions taking command at the outset, but in disregard of and in opposition to the wishes of the national federations and confederations. Erbès-Seguin's important research has demonstrated that in two of three possible patterns of mobilization, preexisting worker organization played a key role. Moreover, the two patterns involving unions were by far the most common.[52] In other words, it would be inexact to call the May–June Days 'spontaneous'; they were perhaps without overall direction from a central place, and they were certainly not planned in advance; yet they were guided by local structures rather than unfolding in some kind of 'Hey-boys-let's-go-on-strike' pattern.

An often-remarked lack of solid information prevents us from saying much about the styles of mobilization in these post-1936 conflicts, and we have avoided firm statements about the role of central federations in getting recent strike waves off the ground. The evidence of 1936, early 1947, 1953 and 1968 seems to be that for great musterings of force the coordinating functions of these confederations are in no way necessary, but that for actions of lesser scope, such as the great gas–electric strike of 1963, the central federation is of some import.

Fifth point: shop-floor issues, especially the question of worker control, clearly overrode wage grievances. Work is in progress by a number of scholars on the pamphlet literature, on worker preoccupations at the time of the sitdowns, and on other varieties of evidence. It shows that concern over participation in industrial decision-making, control over the pacing of work and the humanization of the shop-floor environment far outweighed concern over pay increases. Only when, at the end, the confederations captured control of events did wages appear to be the chief issue. But that is only because wage demands are the kind of *revendication* centralized organizations feel most comfortable with.[53]

Final point: the May–June Days created a number of interfaces in the political struggle besides their synchronization with a crisis in the nation's politics. They involved a political confrontation, by placing the sitdowners in opposition to the police and to the policy of the government, and by challenging the role of the employers in national politics. They also incorporated political objectives, the CGT especially aiming for the fall of the Pompidou government and perhaps the peacable replacement of the De Gaulle regime as a whole. (The CGT certainly did not desire an insurrection and violent revolution.) But the more central concern of the workers was for shop-floor, not national political matters. Given the involvement of the state in the national economy, any demand for 'co-administration' or 'worker control' anywhere in the public sector immediately became a political demand, because it challenged directly the authority of the state. That is the most innovative sense in which the May–June sitdowns cut into the fundamental logic of national politics, and yet departed from traditional 're-volutionary' proletarian movements.

These various observations help us to locate the 1968 strike wave within main themes of working-class history. The constant factors operating upon French society and economy since the beginning of this century made the May–June Days a logical extension of some decades-old trends in strike activity. The scale was larger than ever before because the scale of all the institutions which enmatrixed the participants – the establishments in which they worked, the cities where their paths criss-crossed, their ways of getting news about events elsewhere – had increased enormously, and so collective movements would swell larger than ever if only because countless new people had become available for simultaneous participation. The high white-collar participation was a consequence of yet other linear trends: the numerical expansion of the tertiary sector and the greater unionization of its workers. And the unmistakable political thrust of the May–June Days continued the process of nationalizing strike waves which went back to at least 1906.

But some variable features in French industrial life made the May–June Days different from recent waves and similar to some in the distant past. The advent of science-sector technology had weakened the control of central confederations over local movements. Strikes of trained draftsmen in 1968 resembled more the strikes of tailors in 1833 than of drill-press operators in 1947. Similarly, modern technology had placed a new emphasis upon worker control, also reminiscent of the guild craftsmen, but not of the *métallo* grimly resigned to the horror of his industrial environment and seeking compensation for it through wage increases.

Serge Mallet saw in the strikes of 1969 a continuation of the new themes struck in 1968. Whether future events will confirm these changes as enduring consequences of advanced technology remains to be seen.[54]

A statistical overview

A number of unverified assumptions about the form and origin of strike waves, and about their relative prevalence in industrial life, lie behind the argument of this chapter. We have assumed that strikes in waves mobilize more highly determined workers than do normal forms of strike activity; we have assumed that unions have an exceptional importance in this process, and we have assumed that the industrial environment makes a difference in the willingness of workers to participate in collective life. Now it is time to nail down statistically some of these assumptions.

How important was the strike wave in the average worker's experience with industrial conflict? One way of demonstrating its characteristic nature is to show that the years we have identified as 'strike wave' years accounted for a substantial amount of the total conflict of our period. The eleven wave years contributed 38 percent of all strikes between 1890 and 1960 (a sixty-four-year period, 1939–45 excluded). But of course many isolated disputes occurred in strike-wave years, not coordinated with any other activity or evoked by any external leadership. Similarly, in less frenzied times than those treated above as 'strike-wave years' identifiable strike waves took place quite often: a number of strikes synchronized within a given place. How characteristic are these?

Let us say we are dealing with a strike wave if more than ten establishments went on strike in the same industry in the same department in the same month. How important was strike activity within such establishments relative to the total number of establishments participating in strikes? Between 1915 and 1935 some *89 percent* of all establishments involved in strikes were swept along in such simultaneous disputes. And the separate strikes in which these establishments were registered constituted 32 percent of all strikes in this period. So the answer is that coordination and concentration of forces was the very essence of the strike movement: the isolated establishment on strike was a one-in-ten rarity.

How was the typical strike-wave dispute different from the typical non-wave dispute? One way to answer this is to see how disputes occurring during wave years deviated from other disputes in the same general period. Table 5.5 compares various features of strikes in wave years to strikes in the five-year period in which the wave took place. Some interesting regularities emerge, several which are obvious and predictable through common sense, several less so.

After 1900, strikes during wave years became longer than those during surrounding years, evidence that a concentration of forces increased the resolution of the participants to stick it through. The statistic probably shows the role of centralized federations in slowing the demobilization of local forces in a hard-fought dispute, for only after 1900 did these far-reaching agencies begin to intervene. As we shall see in Chapter 7, a close correlation existed between the participation of unions and the duration of disputes.

In all wave years the number of participants in the average strike was greater than during non-wave years (see table 5.5), reflecting the more extensive mobilization of strike-wave enthusiasm: if the air is full of talk about going on strike, the average walkout will attract more adherents than otherwise.

In all wave years (except 1899) the average number of establishments per strike was greater than in surrounding years, for the same effect which elicited more participants per dispute also drew in more establishments (see table 5.5).

The mobilization of workers within a given shop increased during times

Table 5.5: *Some characteristics of strike activity in wave years, 1893–1920*

Wave year and 5-year period	Median duration (days)[a]	Average size (strikers/ strike)	Scope (establish- ments/strike)	Average plant participation[b]	Union participation[c]
					(%)
1893	6	274	7.9	no data	67.2
1890–4	6	255	4.6	no data	63.8[d]
1899	5	230	5.6	56	59.6
1895–9	5	176	5.7	50	55.7
1906	6	369	14.8	61	76.6
1905–9	5	210	8.7	54	77.5
1919	7	637	19.9	77	16.3[e]
1915–19	5	516	13.0	66	11.8[e]
1920	8	554	14.1	60	8.9[e]
1920–4	7	459	9.7	58	6.3[e]

[a] Genuine median.

[b] Strikers/100 workers in struck establishments; figures uncorrected for craft strikes within industrial plants.

[c] Percent of strikes in which union involved.

[d] 1893–4; data not available 1890–2.

[e] The *SG*'s method of reporting whether a union was involved in the strike was much less complete after the First World War than before.

of political crisis, for in all wave years in table 5.5 the plant participation rate was higher than in surrounding years (number of strikers/100 workers in the struck establishment). All three of these mobilization statistics give us different aspects of the same truth: a strike wave is a more powerful magnet of support than is an isolated dispute.

Finally, the participation of unions during wave years was usually higher than in non-wave years, a simple statistical confirmation of the organizational theory of strike waves (see table 5.5). Good data are not available after 1914, but before then, in three of four wave years, unions were to be found more often than in neighboring years. An exception to this rule was 1906, which saw the extension of conflict to numerous unorganized areas; yet one must bear in mind that in absolute terms, unions led more conflicts during 1906 than ever before.

Much the same results turn up when we define strike waves not as entire years, such as 1906, but as concentrations of disputes in the same place, industry and time. Let us take as a 'mini-strike wave' any accumulation of ten or more strikes in the same industry, department and month. Some 1,700 strikes were involved in these mini-waves between 1915 and 1935 (111 mini-waves in total). How do they differ from non-wave strikes?

Just as disputes in wave years were longer than in non-wave years, so during 1915–35 were strikes in mini-waves longer (6.3 days at the median) than non-wave strikes (5.8 median). Like their wave-year counterparts, mini-wave strikes were also larger than non-wave strikes, an average of 445 strikers per strike as opposed to 390. Strikes in mini-waves were of *lesser* scope, however, than non-wave strikes: 8.3 establishments per strike as opposed to 9.7. The reader will recall that this relationship was exactly reversed in wave years, which generally pulled in more establishments per strike than non-wave years. Why this turnaround? Mini-wave strikes seem to have involved larger establishments than non-wave ones (median establishment size of 104 in mini-wave strikes versus 71 in non-wave disputes); no such distinction separated wave and non-wave years, however, for large establishments prevailed in some, small in other. Thus it appears that the specific sense of political purpose of wave years made the spread of a dispute from establishment to establishment easier. On the other hand, the impulse to participate in mini-strike waves centered more in large than in small shops, but did not transmit well from shop to shop.

Mini-wave strikes were distinguished from non-wave ones, just as wave years were distinguished from non-wave years, by high plant participation rates: at the plant level in 1915–35 61 percent of the workers in the typical struck establishment took part in a mini-wave as opposed to only 55 percent of the workers in an isolated dispute.[55] And, as one would expect, in mini-wave disputes the involvement of labor unions was greater than in non-wave disputes: 86 percent in 1910–14 mini-waves opposed to 73 percent in non-waves.

The organizational substructure of mini-waves also appeared in the stated grievances of such strikes. Pay issues in 1915–35 represented a higher proportion of the demands in mini-waves (80.5 percent) than in isolated strikes (75.4 percent), and worker organization issues correspondingly turned up more often in non-wave (14.0 percent) than in wave (9.2 percent) disputes. Salary issues, of course, made it easier for unions to bring out large numbers of participants by cutting across establishments.

Finally, mini-wave disputes tended to be less successful in achieving their stated demands than did non-wave disputes. A total of 46.1 percent of the former end in failure or the dismissal of the strikers, 39.2 percent of the latter. This makes our understanding of the political strike wave a little clearer, for the great wave-year mobilizations we have observed in this chapter were invariably rewarded with some kind of legislative success, the ultimate touchstone of the value of political action.

– The strike wave of 1899–1900 was followed by a succession of social laws and decrees, most of them from the pen of Alexandre Millerand. Notable were: the 10 August 1899 decrees regulating wages in public works projects, the 1 September 1899 decree reorganizing the *Conseil supérieur du travail*, which permitted unions to participate in choosing worker delegates and the law of 30 March 1900 establishing an eleven-hour day in manufacturing. Finally, the Labor Office (*Office du travail*) was elevated to the status of a *Direction*, with Arthur Fontaine at its head.

– The 1906 strike wave may have accelerated the passage of the Sunday rest law of 13 July 1906, and certainly contributed to the foundation of a separate Labor Ministry in October.

– Scurrying before the gathering strike wave of 1 May, the Chamber passed an eight-hour-day law in April 1919.[56] And on 25 July a law regulating occupational training was promulgated.

– The celebrated Matignon agreements of 7 June 1936 were, of course, a direct consequence of the sitdown strikes. They provided for collective bargaining, shop stewards and substantial pay increases.

– The 1947 strike wave is an exception; it resulted in no legislative achievements for the working classes; this is probably because the preceding two years had witnessed major improvements in social welfare progress, and because the Communist Party was on the way *out* of the polity rather than the way in.

– Finally, the May–June Days of 1968 issued in the Grenelle agreements, named after the street in which the Ministry of Social Affairs, site of negotiations between government, unions and employers, was located. This accord granted the working classes the largest single leap forward in modern times by establishing union representation at the plant level, improving pensions and family allowances and according gigantic wage increases.[57]

Clearly, then, workers have not been unsuccessful in political action on their own behalf, when they put their minds to it. But the question is, under what circumstances would they in fact resolve to turn strikes towards national politics? May we explain the important differences in politicization which appear from one period to the next in terms of industrial structure and technology? And what, exactly, is the relationship between organization and technology? The next three chapters address these questions.

6   The unionization of France

A challenger, to be effective, needs organization. And if the French working classes were to engage successfully in the contest for power, they would need organizations to pry loose time, money and commitment from small clusters of workers in local communities, organizations to focus prism-like these resources upon the arena of central state politics. The building of these organizations constituted the great mobilization of the working classes, which occurred in France – and in every other country in the industrial West – between around 1880 and 1914. To tell the story of how the strike became a weapon in this struggle for the national polity, we must pause to recount how labor organized itself as a challenger. The purpose of this chapter is, therefore, to examine first the actual spread of unions among the labor force, second to review the bureaucratization and centralization of the worker movement.

Union implantation: time, trade and territory

The salient fact of unionization in France is a fifty-fold increase in membership over the years. Around 1884, when unions first became legal, they numbered perhaps 72,000 adherents. By the 1960s over three million workers were dues-paying unionists. Expressed as a rate, that means an increase from 0.7 percent of the non-agricultural population to around 25 percent.

Fig. 6.1 presents the evolution of total union membership yearly between 1884 and the 1960s. There was a sharp upturn from the 1880s to the First World War, the major period of working-class mobilization; affiliation then leveled off at a middling plateau during the interwar period, at roughly its 1911 height; finally, after 1945 union membership commenced another upward crawl. Short-term fluctuations are, of course, ignored in this summary of long-term trends.

The aggregate membership statistics tell only part of the story, however, and taken alone a seriously misleading part, for the different sectors contributing to these great increases have changed over the years in fundamental ways. Table 6.1 shows how. In broad terms the explosive union growth of 1884–1914 came predominantly among the workers in mining and manufacturing; this was the time of initial union implantation and mobilization.

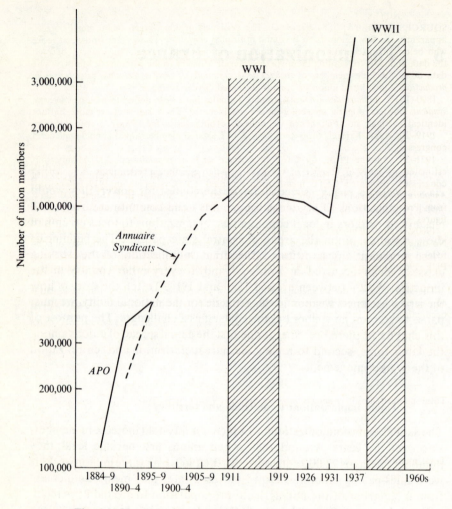

Fig. 6.1: Yearly number of union members, 1884–1960s

The modest net growth in total union membership 1921–35 conceals some dramatic gross changes: a deunionization among some key manufacturing sectors, and a powerful upsurge in white-collar and government service unionization. Table 6.2 pins down these grand sectoral changes to specific rates of unionization in 1884–97 and 1921–35. From it we may reconstruct the vicissitudes of four different labor forces.

(1) Small-shop artisans. The traditional craft associations suffered a serious decline over the years 1880–1935, partly because their members were

NOTES
SOURCES OF DATA: 1884–97: *APO*. The statistics include women union members, and apparently the few unionists to be found in French colonies in these years, or at least those who belonged to federations with headquarters on mainland France. The prefects collected the data annually, forwarding them via the Interior Ministry to the Commerce Ministry. The data do not include members of *sociétés de secours mutuels* or of *associations cooperatives de production*. Agricultural unionists are also excluded. 5-year averages.

1890–1911: *Annuaire des syndicats*, annual. Females have been added to male *membres de syndicats ouvriers*. Algeria and colonies are not included. These statistics are close, but not identical to those in *APO*; hence we reproduce both series for 1890–7. 5-year averages.

1919–20: Annie Kriegel, *Croissance de la C.G.T.*, stated membership at annual confederal congresses.

1921–37: Antoine Prost, *La C.G.T. à l'époque du front populaire*, p. 200. Membership estimated on basis of number of votes allocated to constituent federations at confederal congresses. Estimated CFTC membership included. CFTC strength in 1919 taken from *Annuaire statistique*, 1951, p. 100*, and then deflated. CFTC strength in 1934 and 1937 taken from Prost, pp. 49–50. CFTC membership for 1926 interpolated from above-mentioned figures.

1960s: Union membership data since the Second World War have been a disaster area. No time series worthy of mention are available. We have relied upon the estimates of confederal membership Georges Lefranc published for 1967 (*Syndicalisme en France* [Paris: PUF, 1968; Que-sais-je, 585], p. 119), taking the average of the highest and lowest estimates.

The data in fig. 6.1 do not include members of *syndicats ouvriers agricoles*. For the reader's convenience we present a series of union membership in the primary sector. The following occupations were included in agricultural laborers' unions in 1884–97:

Ouvriers agricoles	9%
Bûcherons	72%
Jardiniers	12%
Pêcheurs	7%
Total	100%

Total membership in *syndicats ouvriers agricoles* (*APO*, I, p. 284):

1884–9 average	355
1890–4 average	5,076
1895–7 average	8,171

Total membership in *syndicats ouvriers agricoles* belonging to CGT or CGTU (Prost, p. 200):

1921	5,803
1926	6,187
1930	4,957
1937	47,981

being absorbed into industrial federations, partly because technological change brought with it professional dequalification, which broke the backs of their organizations. Such downgrading of skill happened, for example, in leatherworking (especially to shoemaking), the garment industry (especially to hatmaking), woodworking and furniture making, and glassmaking. The rate of unionization dropped over time in all these industries. The principal crafts to survive this erosion of competency were the skilled construction trades and the printing industry.

Table 6.1: *Distribution of union members among major sectors (in percent of total union membership)*

	1884–97 average (%)	1911 (%)	1921–35 average (%)
Mining–manufacturing (includes construction)	67.4	65.7	33.7
Proletarian tertiary	23.1	23.3	35.4
White-collar tertiary	6.1	5.3	23.9
Various	3.2	6.3	7.1
Total	99.8	100.6	100.0
Total members	277,000	671,000	1,012,000

SOURCES OF DATA: For 1884–97, *APO*, I, pp. 328, 438, 552, 636; II, pp. 6, 235, 470, 668; III, pp. 8, 518; IV, pp. 8, 466, 744.
For 1911, Annie Kriegel, *Croissance de la C.G.T.*, pp. 204–5.
For 1921–35, Antoine Prost, *C.G.T. à l'époque du front populaire*, pp. 178–200.

NOTES
The figures for 1884–97 were computed from the government's union membership statistics published in *APO*. The figures for 1921–35 are compiled from stated membership at confederal congresses of the CGT and CGTU, and from estimated CFTC membership. The figures for 1911 are from the CGT's reported membership in that year. All figures include female unionists.

We are satisfied that the *APO* and Prost confederal data are essentially comparable because most people whom the *APO* picked up in the 1880s and 90s were likely to have become affiliated with one of the three great confederations in the 1920s. Also, the rates of union membership per 100 labor-force members presented in table 6.2 are remarkably close for both periods; and when they diverge, the differences are those one would anticipate from other kinds of reliable evidence.

Mining–manufacturing includes: *ardoisiers, argileurs, carriers, mineurs, alimentation, tabacs–allumettes, chimiques, livre–papiers, cuirs–peaux, textiles, habillement, bois, métaux–métallurgie, verre–céramique, bâtiment–travaux–publics–matériaux de construction.*

Proletarian tertiary includes: *cheminots, transports, ports–docks, établissements de l'état, PTT, éclairage–gaziers.*

White-collar tertiary includes: *enseignement, fonctionnaires, employés, services publics.*

(2) The factory manufacturing sector. In the years 1884–1914 all important occupations and industries within manufacturing, regardless of skill level, technology or any other factor, underwent widespread unionization. It is true that craft workers managed to put unions together somewhat earlier than did proletarian industrial workers, perhaps by fifteen or twenty years. But by 1900, and certainly by 1914, both craft and semi-skilled industrial workers were well on the way to a latticework of local unions spanning the nation. One important reminder: only a fraction of all the workers in any given manufacturing establishment became union members in these years; but this handful constituted itself in most industrial enterprises. The increase

in numbers of unionists in 1884–1914 reflects mainly the creation of this skeleton of militants.

Then in the 1920s came stagnation or collapse in manufacturing. Assembly-line production was inimical to thorough local union implantation. Therefore, as mechanization, the scale of enterprise and the subdivision of tasks progressed in industries like automaking and chemicals, rates of union

Table 6.2: *Union members per 100 active population by industry, 1884–97 and 1921–35*

	1884–97 average	1921–35 average	Change
Tobacco–matches	55	71	+16
Mining	12	20	+8
Ceramics	6	14	+8
Textiles	3	7	+4
Printing–paper	9	11	+2
Food industries	2	3	+1
Leather–hides	4	4	0
Garments	1	1	0
Building materials and construction	4	4	0
Wood	2	1	−1
Metals	4	3	−1
Chemicals	4	1	−3
Glass	11	6	−5
Mining–manufacturing	3	5	+2
Post–telephone–telegraph	0	30	+30
Utilities (*éclairage*)	44	72	+28
Railways	18	37	+19
Transport	9	16	+7
Ports–docks	1	6	+5
Proletarian tertiary	8	25	+17
(without PTT)	(9)	(25)	(+16)

NOTES

SOURCES: Labor-force data from J.-C. Toutain, *La Population de la France de 1700 à 1959* (Paris: I.S.E.A., 1963; Cahiers de l'I.S.E.A., No. 133); industrial codes from censuses of 1896 and 1931. In all cases *population active* of an industry.

Union membership data for 1884–97 from *APO*. Figures represent total membership in *syndicats ouvriers*, collected by the government bureaucracy. Women included.

Union membership data for 1921–35 are only for members of industrial federations belonging to CGT, CGTU or CFTC, reported in Prost, pp. 178–200. Figures represent the numbers of dues-paying members reported at confederal congresses of the CGT and CGTU in 1921, 1925, 1927, 1929, 1931, 1933 and 1935, averaged over the seven years. Data on CFTC membership by federation were also available for 1934 (Prost, p. 49). They have been included in the federation totals in weighted form to compensate for the abnormally low level of the strengths of some federations in 1934.

Notes to table 6.2 (*continued*)

Federation	1884–97	1921–35	Labor-force denominator in Toutain or *SG*, 1896 and 1931
Sous-sol	*Mineurs* **Carrières** *Ardoisiers* *Argileurs*	*Mines* *Minières* *Carrières* *Ardoisiers* (includes 13,000 CFTC)	*Industries extractives* (minus *pétrole extractive*)
Alimentation	Twenty various trades, most numerous being hotel workers, *bouchers, boulangers*	*Hôtel–restaurant–café* *Boulangers* *Cuisiniers* *Pâtissiers* *Bouchers*	*Alimentation* plus *hôtelleries, débits de boisson*
Tabacs–allumettes	*Tabacs–allumettes* (additional female membership estimated)	*Tabacs–allumettes*	*Tabacs–allumettes*
Chimique	*Industries chimiques* (minus *gaz* and *tabacs–allumettes*)	*Chimiques*	*Industries chimiques*
Livre–papier	*Papiers, cartons, industries polygraphiques*	*Livre–papier*	*Papier–imprimerie*
Cuirs–peaux	*Cuirs–peaux*	*Cuirs–peaux*	*Cuirs–peaux*
Textile	*Industries textiles, proprement dites* (additional female membership estimated)	*Textile* (minus *habillement* and *chapellerie*) (includes 38,000 CFTC)	*Industries textiles, proprement dites*
Habillement–chapellerie	*Habillement* (additional female membership estimated)	*Habillement–chapellerie* (CGTU *vêtement* membership est. 1926–30)	*Habillement*
Bois–tonneau	*Ameublement, travail de bois*	*Bois, ameublement, tonneau*	*Industries du bois*
Métaux	78 crafts in *métaux*	*Métaux*	*Transformation de métaux* plus *métallurgie*
Verre	5 *verre* crafts in *travail des pierres* (nos. 1, 9, 10, 16, 17)	*Verre*	*Verrerie, miroiterie*
Céramique	5 *céramique* crafts in *travail des pierres* (nos. 3, 6, 11, 14, 15)	*Céramique*	*Faïencerie porcelainerie*

Notes to table 6.2 (*continued*)

Federation	1884–97	1921–35	Labor-force denominator in Toutain or *SG*, 1896 and 1931
Building materials	7 crafts in *travail des pierres* (nos. 2, 4, 5, 7, 8, 12, 13)	Part of *bâtiment*	*Préparation des matériaux de construction*
Bâtiment (plus building materials)	*Industries du bâtiment* plus building materials	*Bâtiment* (minus *bois*)	*Bâtiment* and *travaux publics* plus *préparation des matériaux de construction*
Cheminots	*Chemins de fer*	*Cheminots* (includes 36,000 CFTC)	*Transports-fer* minus *tramways* (*tramways* figures estimated for 1931, 1896 on basis of 1936 ratio)
Transport	From *commerce, transport: bateaux– omnibus charretiers chauffeurs, cochers, omnibus–tramway services municipaux*	*Transport*	*Transport par terre* plus est. *tramways* labor force plus *transports fluviaux* (1901 and 1896)
Ports–docks	From *commerce transport: chargeurs– déchargeurs, coltineurs, hommes de peine, ports, quais, docks*	*Ports–docks*	*Manutention*
Etablissements d'état	—	*Etablissements d'état*	—
Postes– télégraphes	—	PTT	1936 PTT labor force
Enseignement	—	*Enseignement* (1926–35 only)	1936 *enseignement*– public labor force
Fonctionnaires	—	*Fonctionnaires* (1928–35 only)	*Services publics administratifs* minus PTT and teachers
Employés	From *commerce, transport: comptables, employés de commerce, voyageurs*	*Employés*	—
Services publics	—	*Services publics* minus *éclairage*	—
Éclairage	*Gaz*	*Éclairage* (rate may be overstated owing to indeterminate number of non-gas union members in *éclairage* and *force motrice*)	*Gaz*

membership fell off. This happened in chemicals because the new plants established in the interwar period simply failed to unionize before 1936. (Apart from gas and tobacco–matches, both kept separate from chemicals in table 6.2, there was little chemical industry to speak of in prewar France.) And this happened most remarkably in metalworking. The difficulty of breaking down highly aggregated sectoral union figures by type of technology and size of enterprise prevents us from viewing deunionization in other industries.

(3a) Proletarians in the tertiary sector. Virtually all the dirty, hard, unpleasant service jobs in the modern economy were part of the public sector in France, or at least closely regulated by public authorities: railroading (part public, part private), delivering mail, unloading ships and running the gasworks. The timing of unionization among proletarians in the tertiary was the same as in factory manufacturing, for the initial upsurges in railroading and, say, mining came together, as did those in clerical work and leatherwork. But tertiary workers achieved higher levels of unionization than manufacturing workers, for two interlocking reasons: (i) many of them were in government service, and were unlikely to be dismissed for union membership; (ii) all the workers in this sector were in great administrative bureaucracies (save perhaps taxi drivers and a few similar occupations); something about French bureaucracies compels the workers in them to organize, perhaps because the center of decision-making in maritime or railway companies is distant and inaccessible to informal, localized suasion; perhaps because for obscure psychological reasons workers simply hate the impersonal, rule-following corporation; perhaps because being situated within the complex of nationwide bureaucracies facilitates communication among workers in different places and categories, therewith making organization possible. At any event, the proletarian tertiary sector was more heavily unionized than the proletarian manufacturing sector.

(3b) White-collar occupations and government service. The high unionization rates in this sector may be ascribed to the circumstances just discussed for the proletarian tertiary sector. A tremendous leap in white-collar unionism began in the early twenties and continued through the 1950s and 60s.[1]

(4) The science sector. A rapid increase in the unionization of professionals and technicians in industry and in services has taken place since 1936. Solid data are absent, but most observers have the strong impression that this is so.[2] It is likely that a rise in this sector has been responsible for much of the major upward bound in total union membership since 1945.

All these developments are reviewed in fig. 6.2, the hypothetical course of unionization by sector, 1880–1960.

These time-series data on union membership, and on differences in unionization by industry, suggest that there is a lag between the initial appearance of an industry and the time its workers acquire an organizational

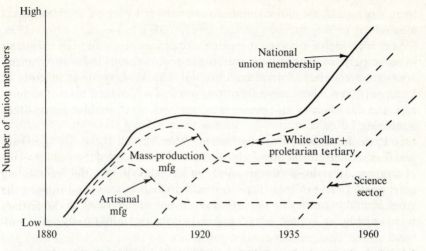

Fig. 6.2: Schematic representation of likely unionization by industrial sector, 1880–1960

capacity for collective action. This time gap held true for workers in the modern manufacturing sector, who were recruited into large, mechanized factories starting in the 1880s, yet who formed unions only late in the 1890s. The lag appeared for white-collar workers, who were heavily represented in the labor force by the *belle époque*, yet whose collective activities commenced only after the First World War. And it applied to technical employees in the modern sector, for which a time lag of at least a decade seems to have intervened between the formation of its labor force in the 1940s and 50s, and its organizational mobilization in the 1950s and 60s.

In addition to the development over time and industry, we must consider the spread of unionization over territory. Before the First World War the government reported total membership in *syndicats ouvriers* by department, and in the interwar years Antoine Prost has made that information available for the CGT and CGTU. We know no source of geographical data on unionization after the Second World War.

The years just before the First World War were the heyday of unionism, its base not yet eroded by assembly-line technology, its apex centralized in the CGT. Map 6.1 reveals certain basic features of unionization around this time (1911). Worker organization was most highly developed in the larger cities, for the departments containing the large urban agglomerations fall mostly into the solid black category: (+10% unionized): Gironde (Bordeaux), Haute Garonne (Toulouse), Bouches-du-Rhône (Marseille), Seine (Paris), Seine–Maritime (Rouen–le Havre), and Nord (Lille); nudging the bottom of this category are Rhône (Lyon) and Loire–Atlantique (Nantes–St-Nazaire) with 8 percent unionization apiece. Residence in a large city would, therefore, predispose a worker to formal membership in a union.

Secondly, map 6.1 reveals a regional skew in unionization. The industries of some parts of France were well organized, the same industries in other areas largely without formal unionization. The Mediterranean littoral, the Lyon periphery, the west and Brittany counted as classic centers of organization with histories of *compagnonnages* and other worker associations stretching far back in time. In contrast the northeast was startlingly under-unionized, for the textile departments of the Marne, Aube, Oise, Somme and Vosges, and the metalworking and metal-producing departments of the Ardennes, Meurthe-et-Moselle and Belfort all fell into the bottom two categories. Living in these regions would predispose a worker to stay away from formal membership in a *syndicat ouvrier*, be it because the employers were harshly set against worker unions or because traditions of association were not as strong as in the west and south.

Little changed in the territorial distribution of union membership during the interwar years before the Popular Front. Map 6.2 (1935) gives the picture. The large urban centers continued to fall in the upper range (though not necessarily in the top category), and there was a tendency, though somewhat reduced from 1911, for underunionization to continue in the northeast. Two lesser trends may be noted. One is a certain homogenization in the intensity of union membership, as disparities among departments were smoothed out and most departments glided into the range of 5–9 union members per 100 non-agricultural workers. This evening-up process probably resulted from bureaucratization of unions at the apex, for central control in the twenties meant much greater uniformity in organizing efforts and techniques than before. Consequently, most departments came up to their practical ceilings of unionization. (The practical ceiling was, to be sure, far beneath the theoretical ceiling.)

The second trend was toward modest deunionization in areas of mass-production manufacturing, especially within dynamic France. We must make allowances for the exclusion of some CFTC and independent union members from our statistics. Yet even so, such manufacturing departments as the Doubs, Loire and Seine-Maritime lost in union members relative to their non-agricultural population.

Most underunionized were those departments where union growth was most rapid during the Popular Front. Map 6.3 gives unionization in 1937, just at the height of the great inrush of new members. To be sure, all departments in 1937 had far higher rates of union adherence than previously, so if the scale of the maps of 1911 and 1935 were used in 1937, all France would be colored black. Yet relative differences in the intensity of unionization show a regional effect just as dramatic, *but the exact reverse*, of the regional effect we saw in 1911. In 1937 the departments of the north and east became the most heavily organized, those of the south and west the least so. This

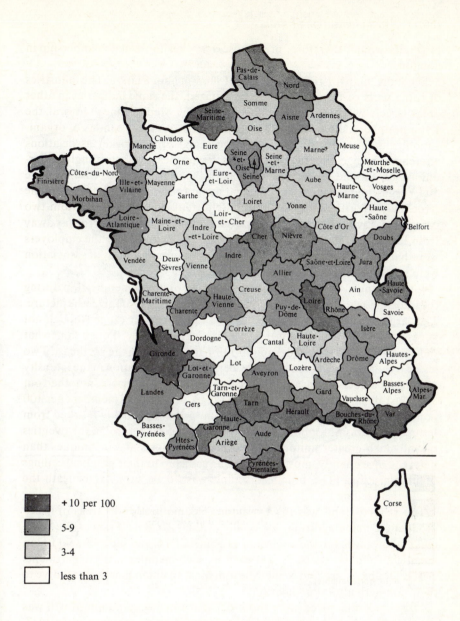

Map 6.1: Number of union members per 100 non-agricultural labor force, 1911
(see Notes on page 160)

158

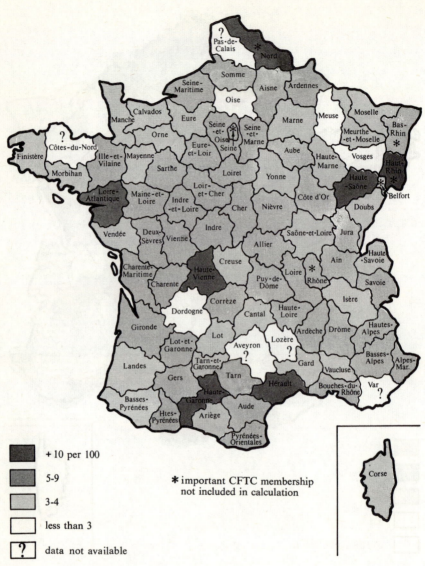

Map 6.2: Number of CGT members per 100 non-agricultural labor force, 1935 (see Notes on page 160)

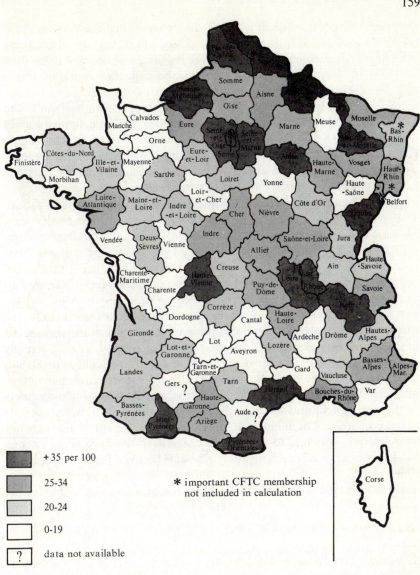

Map 6.3: Number of CGT members per 100 non-agricultural labor force, 1937 (see Notes on page 160)

illustrates the point made in the preceding chapter that the Popular Front meant for proletarian factory workers a period of catching up, of acquiring the firmly organized bases that craft workers had possessed before the First World War. Was this new unionization of the large metalworking, textile and chemicals plants to be an enduring feature of worker organization, or merely a transitory phenomenon, such as much of the enthusiasm at the base in 1918–20 had proved to be? Postwar data make a definitive answer impossible. We have as evidence only the testimony of such sensitive observers as Michel Collinet that large manufacturing plants, especially in metalworking, in the 1940s and early 50s were underorganized, having only one or two unionists to every couple of hundred workers.[3]

The very nature of industrial union organization in France, with its pattern of sparkplug locals allied with centralized federations, means that data on mass union adherence are misleading as a meaningful indicator of implantation. By 'meaningful' we understand the ability and desire of local unions to help organize strikes, for a local union which is not involved in conflict is probably of peripheral importance to the workers of the area. In 1895–9 and 1910–14 we know the percentage of strikes in which unions took part for each department through the *SG* category 'did a union exist for the workers?' This kind of union implantation is by no means the same as the union implantation measured by the percentage of workers who actually were union members. At the department level only a middling correlation turns up between the two indices: a coefficient of 0.30 between the percentage of strikes having unions in 1910–14 and the percentage of union members in the non-agricultural labor force in 1911, and of 0.24 between the percentage of strikers in unions and union members. The correlations are not uninteresting, which is to say they are significantly above zero; yet one would have expected much higher coefficients between these two variables, which on the face of it are just two different ways of measuring the same union implantation. The reason the relationship is so weak is that formal

NOTES TO MAPS 6.1, 6.2 AND 6.3

1911 (6.1). Union members are total membership in *syndicats ouvriers*, taken from *Annuaire des syndicats*, 17 (1911); females included. Labor force data from 1911 census, *population active totale* minus agriculture.

1935 and 1937 (6.2 and 6.3). Union members are CGT members in *unions départementales des syndicats*, as stated by Léon Jouhaux in a *rapport moral* of the 1938 CGT national congress. Reported membership was doubtless somewhat exaggerated in most departments. Labor-force data are from 1936 census, *population active totale* minus agriculture.

For the following pairs of departments only a single combined union membership figure was reported:

     Landes, Basses-Pyrénées
     Ain, Jura
     Drôme, Ardèche
     Puy-de-Dôme, Haute Loire
     Seine-et-Oise, Seine

unionization statistics encompass a large number of unionists who seldom strike, employees in white-collar occupations, railway workers and the like, while giving disproportionately small weight to the real activists out organizing in the plants. And these proportions vary from place to place.

Yet even this finer measure of effective union presence does not alter the rough outlines of geographical differences in organization we observed from map 6.1. The solidity of union activity in strikes along the Mediterranean coast, and up the Rhône valley to Lyon, appears even more dramatically from maps 6.4 and 6.5 (percent of strikes with union involvement, 1895–9 and 1910–14). So does the unionization of the west and southwest, and the lack of it in the northeast. Union implantation was also high in the Nord, the Seine-Maritime and the Paris region. A comparison of maps 6.4 and 6.5 permits us to reemphasize an important point about regional differences. The most organized areas on the eve of the great worker mobilization (1895–9) were 'static,' 'traditional' France, mainly in the west. Outside the west only Paris, Lyon and a few northeastern departments had important concentrations of union members – to go by the evidence of the participation of unions in strikes. Then by 1910–14, a dramatic diffusion had taken place throughout the remainder of 'traditional' France, and into a few of the newer proletarian industrial areas, such as Rouen–le Havre and the Mediterranean coast. Yet even by 1910–14 those departments which were later to be called modern, dynamic France remained relatively non-unionized. The great mobilization, therefore, occurred first within regional economies of a distinctly artisanal caste. Only in the middle third of the twentieth century did widespread unionization commence in areas of recent industrial advance.

A final question is which axis – the territorial or the industrial – was more important in the synchronization and coordination of strike activity? Which proved stronger, the ties of command running vertically within industrial federations, or the municipal and neighborhood networks of organization radiating out horizontally from the Bourses du travail and the territorial cells of the PCF? In other words, were industrial or geographical ties more important in linking together the strikers in different places and different occupations? And how did the solidity of these bonds change over the years?

Two simple indices provide clear answers to these questions, the percentage of all strikes coordinated by municipality, and the percentage of strikes coordinated by occupation (not aggregate industrial sector, but by specific industry and definite occupation). How to measure the extent of coordination? Let us take the standard of ten or more establishments on strike in the same month in the same *municipality* (regardless of the strikers' occupation) as indicating coordination at the communal level. Let us further take the standard of ten or more establishments on strike in the same month in the same *occupation* (regardless of the strikers' territorial location) as evidencing industrial coordination.

These tests of coordination are not meant to identify central planning or

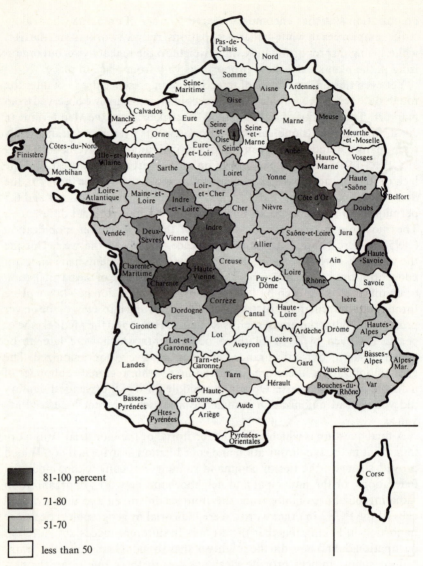

Map 6.4: Percent of strikes with union involvement, 1895–9

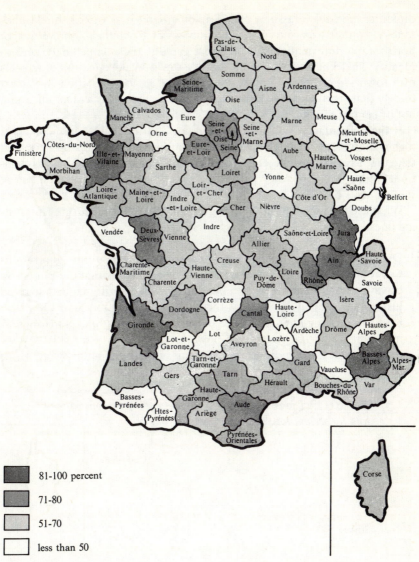

Map 6.5: Percent of strikes with union involvement, 1910–14

direction, nor do we assume that a guiding hand is at work behind simultaneity. Rather we are trying to spot along which channels – the vertical or horizontal – information travels most rapidly and compellingly, and to identify what kinds of workers – those in one's own occupation or in one's own town – represent the most powerful models for emulation. We assert merely that simultaneity of strikes is *prima facie* evidence of communication, not of central direction.

If the percentage of all strikes in France coordinated by municipality is higher than the percentage of all strikes coordinated by occupation, we shall take that as evidence that territorial municipal ties are stronger than associational industrial ones. And vice versa. Table 6.3 gives the results, comparing the two axes of coordination in 1895–9 and again in 1925–9.

What are the implications of the figures in table 6.3? We see three interesting ones:

1. During both periods the coordinating power of territorial organizations was roughly similar to that of industrial. This suggests that the Bourse du travail was approximately as effective a mobilizer of men and sparked just about as many conflicts as the industrial federation. The ties which held workers together who were in the same occupation yet in different municipalities were roughly as powerful as those which held together workers who were in different trades but in the same municipality.

Table 6.3: *The coordination of strike activity by commune and by occupation: which axis was stronger?*

	Coordinated by	
1895–9	Occupation (%)	Commune (%)
Establishments on strike	75.6	76.3
Strikes	24.2	20.2
Strikers	34.7	32.4
1925–9		
Establishments on strike	84.7	90.8
Strikes	25.8	31.8
Strikers	47.4	44.9

NOTE
If more than 10 establishments went on strike within a given occupation in a given month, that strike (and those strikers, and those establishments) were said to be coordinated by occupation. Likewise for communes: more than 10 establishments on strike in a given commune during a given month meant coordination. The percentages give the share of strikes thus coordinated relative to all strikes in France.

2. As the years passed all kinds of organizational ties grew more powerful, for the level of coordination along both axes rose from 1895–9 to 1925–9 by about 10 to 15 percent, depending on whether one is observing co-ordination among disputes themselves or among participants in disputes. The increase was not dramatic, but nonetheless noteworthy, showing that greater numbers of workers in unions, and greater numbers of Bourses du travail with more adherents, in fact produced greater synchronization and simultaneity. Thus better organization resulted in a pay-off in better collective action. (We have, of course, no way of ruling out the possibility that some of this increased coordination is an artifact of rising levels of strike activity, rather than a real consequence of expanding organizational networks. Yet we argue elsewhere that improved union action increased the strike rate, and if that is right, the problem is less serious.)

3. As the years passed, the communal axis became *more* important than the industrial (though not by a great deal). Coordination of strikes by muni-cipality came from behind to overtake industrial coordination. When establishments as such are viewed, the municipalities in fact increased their lead; and when strikers are taken as the index, municipalities kept abreast. In no case may one argue that over the years the industrial feder-ation became a more powerful synchronizer of collective action, nor that the territorial-based organization (be it Bourse du travail, PCF *cellule* or whatever) waned as a result.[4] All this helps us keep self-inflated chronicles of the histories of various industrial federations in proper perspective. It suggests as well that future research should concentrate on the terribly neglected histories of working-class neighborhoods, on how workers interacted with their neighbors, joined territory-based organizations and pursued an associational life outside the factory walls.

The centralization of working-class organization

If workers were to find representation at the center of political life, they would have to acquire centralized organizations capable of taking their part amidst the other squabbling contenders for power. The history of the great mobilization of the working classes between 1880 and 1914 may be written as the history of the knitting together of organizational threads in many communities to form a unitary tentlike structure with a single apex (or, like a circus tent, a series of apexes). A brief recounting of this network's history is important to the story of strikes because these nationwide organiza-tions actually guided and coordinated strike activity from time to time, and, perhaps more importantly, gave participants in labor disputes the sense that their actions would reverberate in far-distant centers of power.

Essentially, there were three kinds of national worker organizations: horizontally, the Bourses du travail, labor exchanges in most industrial

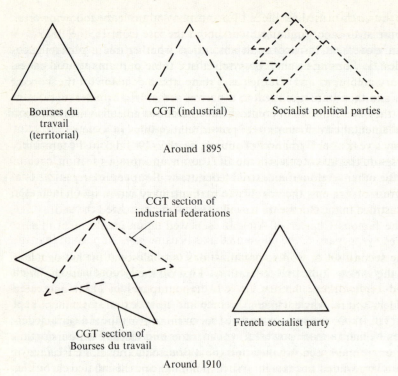

Bourses du travail (territorial)   CGT (industrial)   Socialist political parties

Around 1895

CGT section of industrial federations

French socialist party

CGT section of Bourses du travail

Around 1910

Fig. 6.3: Nationwide working-class organizations around 1895 and 1910

cities; vertically, the *syndicats professionnels*, that is, the labor unions proper, a separate federation for each industry; and running along both axes, from city to city and from trade to trade, the socialist political parties, separate from the organizations of industrial conflict yet an intimate part of the worker struggle for political representation. Fig. 6.3 shows these three nationwide networks schematically around 1895, when the knitting-together process was at midpoint, and around 1910, when the process was complete.

The associations which joined together all the workers in a single locality, regardless of their occupation, were called Bourses du travail. They existed by 1914 in 144 cities. Although exact arrangements varied from place to place, the basic pattern was that a municipality would give a small monetary subvention to a local alliance of labor unions to help pay for a local headquarters. This Bourse would aid the population at large as a labor exchange, a clearing-house for the seekers of work and workers; in return the local unions would have space for meetings and a place to hang their hats. Each Bourse governed itself, the local unions cooperating to keep things running smoothly and providing additional funds beyond the municipal contribution. The first Bourse was founded in Paris in 1887, a second in Nîmes that same year, a third in Marseille in 1888 and many others in the following years. In contrast to other organized workers in the late eighties, the Bourse du travail movement insisted upon abstention from action in parliamentary politics; as libertarian anarcho-syndicalists, these militants viewed parliamentary ambitions and rivalries as a snare and a delusion for the working class, and thus were apolitical in a narrow sense. In a broader sense, however, they were intensely political, for anarcho-syndicalism insisted upon a fundamental transformation of power relationships in society.

Only a year after Fernand Pelloutier's death in 1901 did the Federation of Bourses du travail vote to join the CGT as an autonomous section, coequal with the other section of industrial federations. Four years later at the 1906 Congress of Amiens, the hostility to parliamentary action which Pelloutier had instilled in the Bourse du travail movement conquered the entire CGT, for the famous Charter of Amiens eschewed union involvement in party politics.[5]

The second set of worker organizations to coalesce at the national level were the various industrial federations. First off the ground were the highly skilled craftworkers: hatters in 1870, typographers in 1881, and metal moulders and railway engineers, firemen and conductors, and miners, all in 1883. The 1890s then saw a wave of formations of national organizations: bakers, joiners, ceramists, all kinds of shoe and leather workers, textile workers, coopers, coachmakers, glass blowers and so on. It is misleading to name a large industrial category, such as mining, and then to suggest by linking it to a single date that a powerful nationwide apparatus bounded smoothly upwards, propelled by the enthusiastic cooperation of local organizations all over the country. The histories of some of these federations in the 1890s and early 1900s are full of dissolutions, false starts, schisms and crippling rivalries.

Mining and construction are classic examples. In mining a national federation was founded in 1888, only to split in 1902 as the miners' locals of the Nord, Pas-de-Calais, Anzin, Montceau-les-Mines and Loire formed an independent federation. Then the Nord itself was pulled between Emile-Joseph Basly's Guesdist *vieux syndicat* and Benoît Broutchoux's anarchist *jeune syndicat*. Unity once more in 1910, then in 1912 the Nord, Pas-de-Calais and Anzin locals again split off. Unity reestablished in 1919, then in 1921–2 again rupture as the CGT divided in two. A similar chronicle could be told for construction, which united in an industrial federation only in 1906.[6]

Moreover, the administrative reality of these federations was considerably less imposing than their grand titles. Commonly a federation would have only one or two paid permanent officers running its national headquarters (usually in Paris); there would be a national newsletter of some kind, a national biennial congress, often at the same time as the CGT congress to save delegates' traveling expenses. There would be endless difficulty over collecting dues from local constituent unions across the country, over preventing fragile locals from falling apart entirely and over the allocation of whatever meager strike fund the federation happened to possess.

To place the founding of the CGT in proper historical perspective we must go back to the first nationwide confederation of unions of any kind, the loosely organized National Federation of Worker Unions, founded in 1886 at a Lyon meeting of 160 delegates of local unions. A majority of those assembled declared themselves in favor of Guesdist Marxian socialism, foredooming the young confederation to failure because the Guesdists thought labor unions useless in the political struggle and because this explicit ideological statement alienated non-Guesdist workers. The federation had, in any event, little contact with local labor unions or national industrial federations, and was in 1892, after six national congresses, virtually without achievements.

At the seventh congress of this National Federation in Limoges in 1895 the CGT (*Confédération générale du travail*) was born. The delegates realized that close ties to the volatile, schismatic political parties meant the kiss of death for a stable, wide-reaching union movement, and so resolved to establish a confederation of unions that would be independent of the parties. The delegates had come from a variety of different local organizations: some from Bourses du travail, some from municipal or departmental alliances of labor unions (*fédérations locales*, *départementales* or *regionales*), some from industrial federations, some from a single craft within a single municipality. This confusion of constituencies was also mirrored in the organization they laid down for the CGT, as single local unions could adhere and vote, just as could territorial and industrial federations. Nonetheless most of the local groups belonging to the CGT in these years identified themselves on the industrial dimension rather than the territorial. (The important thing about them was their occupation or industry, not where they came from.)[7]

Between 1895 and 1912 the CGT attempted steadily to rationalize its structure. In 1902 it distinguished between territorial and industrial axes as the Federation of Bourses du travail merged with it; simultaneously the CGT resolved to admit only industrial or territorial federations: no longer could single local unions adhere directly. In 1906 the CGT decided to admit no more craft federations; henceforth only industrywide federations would be allowed, and existing craft organizations were urged to transform themselves into industrial groupings. In 1912 it tried to make of its territorial wing a neat bureaucratic hierarchy by prescribing that the local Bourses du travail form departmental federations, which then were to converge at the national headquarters. By 1914 in place of the 153 Bourses du travail which formerly had belonged directly to the CGT, there were 82 departmental federations and 52 industrial federations.

Fig. 6.4 shows the various administrative instances which would interpose themselves between a particular *syndicat* in a given municipality and the

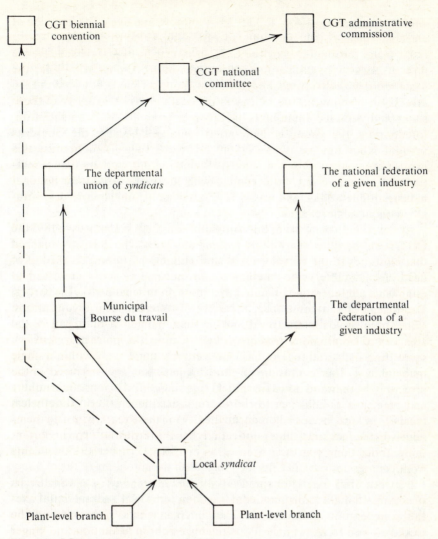

Fig. 6.4: CGT organization around 1912

national CGT. To take Marjorie Clark's example, the metalworkers' union of Nîmes would belong first to the Bourse du travail of Nîmes (a territorial federation), then to the departmental federation of the Gard (in some cases the departmental federation would be identical with the municipal federation of the department's major city, in some not), then finally to the national *Fédération des métaux*. The departmental federation (before 1912 the Bourse du travail) and the *Fédération des métaux* would both be members of the national CGT, and so local Nîmes metalworkers would find national representation through two different pipelines.[8]

The CGT was thus a coordinating committee for the various industrial and departmental confederations. 'Legislation' was to stem from the confederation's biennial conventions, to which local unions sent delegates directly. Executive authority rested in the national committee (the *comité confédéral national*), which delegated week-to-week operations to an administrative commission. Two facets of pre-First World War CGT organization are important for our immediate purposes. (1) The national committee, representing both industrial and departmental federations, was capable of coordinating strike activity across industries and municipalities, of alerting locals to pressing problems and of marshaling support for collective actions from the affiliates. (2) The CGT saw as its purpose in life not parliamentary activity of any sort but the promotion of industrial conflict, in which it was expressly assisted by a confederal commission on strikes.

Before the First World War roughly half of all organized workers in France were affiliated with this CGT bureaucracy.[9] But we must be absolutely clear on the reality behind this rather imposing word. The CGT itself had very little authority; it could not direct or compel anyone to do anything; nor did it have more than a pittance of resources to allocate. Unlike the situation that was to arise after the Second World War, the old CGT emphasized local autonomy and decentralization, the rights of the individual *syndicat* coming before the prerogatives of the constituent federations. The CGT was much more like someone standing on a table shouting exhortations during a bar-room brawl than a general directing his armies across the field of battle. But even this anarchic arrangement would suffice to coordinate strike movements at times when locals were prepared to be coordinated, which is to say, when unionists across France sensed that a political crisis was brewing at the center.

Centralization progressed further within the CGT after 1918. The July 1919 congress of the CGT decided to abolish the autonomy of the two sections (industrial federations and *unions départementales*), and to establish one overarching national confederal committee which in turn would elect the administrative commission. The thirty members of this commission would all be unionists of the Paris region.[10] Schism at the apex in 1921–2 meant that each of the confederations – the CGT and the CGTU – attempted to reconstitute for itself the hierarchy of industrial and territorial federations, so that two ordered pyramids sprang up with bureaucratic levels running precisely from bottom to top. The CFTC, a third confederation of Christian unionists established in 1919, was less centralized. Division meant that the ability of these three confederations to mount successful strike actions was seriously impaired, and most of the stations of the bureaucratic pyramid were manned only by dedicated volunteers, not by paid professional organizers. Yet the historic achievement of knitting together the myriad local unions remained unshaken by subsequent events.

Quite the opposite in fact, for after the First World War a far greater

percentage of local unions than before adhered to one of the central confederations. Before 1914 a substantial segment of the locals were not
affiliated with any non-local organization: after the war most joined with the
CGT, CGTU or CFTC.[11] This development meant that (a) the center's
control over the periphery would be enhanced simply because it had access
to greater numbers of people, and (b) greater numbers of people would
acquire the sense that actions they undertook out on the periphery would
have consequences for events at the center.

Political parties represented the third basis of nationwide working-class
organization. At the very beginning of the worker movement in the 1870s
no clear distinction was possible between labor unions and local political
groups; only later as the unions bridled at the rein of political parties and
insisted that parliamentary affairs be kept separate from 'corporate' affairs
could a rigid demarcation be made.[12] The first worker polical congress since
1848, held in Paris in 1876, was composed of representatives of *syndicats*,
largely from the Paris region. The delegates at the Marseille Congress of
1879, where a 'collectivist' majority of Guesdist Marxist socialists, anarchists
and 'possibilists' triumphed over the mutualists, came from *syndicats*. Only
in 1880 are we able to distinguish easily between corporate and political
organizations, for the organizational committee of this fourth national
worker congress refused to admit delegates from the Guesdist 'study circles,'
insisting that only worker unions could be validly represented. This refusal
touched off a schism, as the socialist collectivists went off to constitute
their own socialist Worker Party and the moderates stayed behind to hold
two more congresses before expiring.

Schism was the salient feature of the working-class political movement
during most of the great mobilization. In 1882 another rupture took place
as the Guesdist Marxists split from the anarchists (Possibilistes, Broussistes)
at the St-Etienne congress to form their own group. And in 1890 still another
schism occurred when this anarchist French Socialist Workers Federation
split at the Châtellerault congress between Broussist anarchists and Alle-
manist anarchists. How dreary is this tale of rupture and division. Moreover,
it is essentially unimportant to the story of strikes, so we needn't pursue these
sectarian ideologies in detail. The important points are that the militants at
all these congresses and splintering parties came largely from the working
classes, though less and less from labor unions and increasingly from political
action groups properly speaking, and that they were all socialists and
revolutionaries of one stripe or another, believing the working classes should
seize state power rather than pursuing bread-and-butter unionism through
collective bargaining. The official ideology of the CGT was *syndicalisme
révolutionnaire*, which differed from Marxism mainly in shunning efforts to
seize power via the legislature and in emphasizing decentralized democratic
organization. As is well known, revolutionary syndicalists preferred 'direct

action,' such as bringing the wheels of industry grinding to a halt through a general strike.[13] We agree with Yves Lequin that this ideological quibbling was of little interest to the rank and file.[14] Ideological differences account for almost none of the differences in either propensity to strike or the forms of strike action around this time.

The reconstitution of a single integrated working-class political organization began around the time of the Dreyfus Affair, when the Left felt itself threatened by a coup from the Right. In 1898 the anarchist Allemanists brought together a reconciliation committee (*comité d'entente*) incorporating all major socialist groups in France.[15] Life was blown into this committee the following year when it organized worker groups for the defense of the republic to protest the mistreatment of President Loubet at the Auteuil racetrack.

Socialist unity suffered a setback in the debates over 'ministerialism' of 1899–1900 (when Millerand joined the Waldeck-Rousseau cabinet). Then in 1902 another step toward integration: at the Lyon Congress of all socialist groups the independents and anarchists (Broussists, some Allemanists) merged in the French Socialist Party. Later that year at Ivry the Marxist wing of the socialist movement – Guesde and Vaillant – merged to form the Socialist Party of France (*Parti socialiste de France*). The 1904 Congress of the International at Amsterdam, impatient with the continuing fragmentation of the French movement, commanded the formation of a single socialist party in France. This was then accomplished at a special unification congress in Paris in April 1905. The new party was to be called the SFIO: *Parti socialiste, Section française de l'Internationale ouvrière*. Its basic administrative component was to be the departmental federation, all of which by the end of 1905 had together enrolled 36,000 members. (By 1914 the SFIO numbered 73,000 dues-paying members.) The working-class political movement was now unified and centralized, just as the shop-floor movement had unified itself three years earlier at the CGT's 1902 congress.[16]

The later schism between Socialists and Communists, much as it may have damaged the worker movement in other respects, did not impair the bureaucratic centralization accomplished in 1905; indeed Bolshevization of the CGTU enhanced the control of the center over the periphery of the movement, for Leninist views of the 1920s about elitist cadres able to command absolutely subordinate militants are familiar. The only trouble was that there were two centers instead of one.

The task of this section has been to demonstrate two things:
(1) that 1880–1914 was the period of the great mobilization of the working classes for participation in national politics; the mobilization was accomplished through the formation of centralized, bureaucratically integrated political and corporate organizations;
(2) that an awareness of competition for political power permeated these organizations from their very inception, as it was the parties which launched

the trade union movement, and the trade unions which sent delegates to the initial party congresses. When the CGT explicitly denied 'political' ambitions in the Charter of Amiens in 1906 it was saying that shop-floor organizations should not enmesh themselves in the legislative arena or organize to seize the center; it was not in any sense declaring the national polity out of bounds, nor saying that a fundamental transformation of power relationships in society was not a corporate objective.[17]

7   Unions and strikes

Here is a good place to examine carefully two central assumptions on which our argument rests: (1) that industrial technology is somehow important in the form and frequency of worker organization, and (2) that worker organization somehow matters in the form and frequency of strikes. We have thus far traced the trajectory of the French strike movement over the last hundred and fifty years; we have sketched in the principal way stations in working-class associational history since the July Monarchy; and we have summarized ideas other scholars have offered on the evolution of workplace character and scale. But we have not yet brought these independent little narratives together, showing what relationships existed among them. In this chapter we present a typology of industrial technologies, and associate each with a certain form of industrial conflict.

The reader is reminded that most statements about events since 1935 will be speculative, for the solid evidence on both union membership and strike activity ceases in the mid-1930s. The centerpoint of our analysis, therefore, will be two periods: (1) 1910–14, when our coding of the strike data was especially detailed and the sources themselves unusually rich, and (2) 1915–35, when industrial unionism blossomed in its classic form, leaving in the minds of most observers the impression this is the way things always had been and would continue to be.

The great mobilization of the worker movement had essentially nothing to do with technological change, for all kinds of industries and trades, whether artisanal or proletarian, acquired national organizations at roughly the same point in time. Where industrial technology matters is in the form that local unions take on, and in their relationship to their national headquarters. Fig. 7.1 illustrates the argument. Associated with *artisanal* technology are local organizations with little formal structure but with widespread solidarity among the practitioners of the craft. The *semi-skilled* technology of mass production means that local organizations will flicker ephemerally, command the allegiance of only a few dedicated ideologues and move to action only at the behest of a highly centralized national headquarters. Workers in the *science sector* resemble those of the artisanal sector in having widespread shop-floor attachment to strong, semi-autonomous local organizations, yet enjoy the advantages of a national headquarters for large-scale coordinated actions.[1]

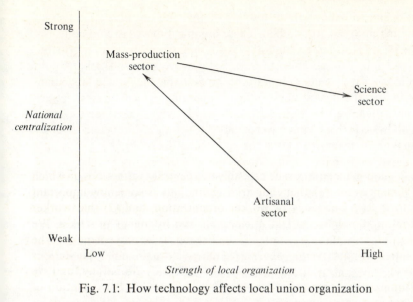

Fig. 7.1: How technology affects local union organization

Organization and technology: the artisanal sector

Scholars have devoted so much attention to the patterns of worker organization arising after 1884 that they often have lost sight of the rich associational life existing before then. If the history of working-class organizations becomes a search for the origins of the CGT, one will find little remarkable before the Paris Commune, save the tired old Utopian socialists trotted out in the standard accounts. If the history of worker organization becomes a search for institutions or folkways embedded in popular life that make possible large-scale mobilizations, we shall have to go back to the beginning of the nineteenth century, or even before.

The workers of nineteenth-century France who took part in strikes, were, as we have seen, skilled professionals. And any occupation requiring skills that can be learned neither on the job nor from books will have an organizational apparatus of apprenticeships, corporate work rules and such, and an intellectual apparatus of pride in one's work, artistic creativity and professional autonomy. The organizational exigencies of such crafts combined in the nineteenth century with the mentalities of their practitioners to create a certain pattern of association we have labelled artisanal. These organizations incorporated a high percentage of the craft's members, for they both crystallized a sense of occupational community and were successful in defending commonly understood interests: protecting the domain of craft autonomy from the inroads of employer authority, keeping down the influx of apprentices and maintaining high standards of quality. They therefore preserved the craftsman's material position and reinforced what he would like to believe about his own talents and usefulness, and about his place in the world around him. These organizations were commonly not centralized, and disdained binding ties running from locals all across the nation to some guiding hand in Paris. This is because the political and economic pressure points of importance to craftsmen lay in the immediate locality, not in the distant center stage. Accordingly, local craftsmen were not easily galvanized by non-local, nationwide issues. Yet their informal organization was strong, and a web spun by traveling workers tied together individual crafts from one end of the country to the other.[2]

Peculiar to artisanal organizations in nineteenth-century France, though not to all such associations in all times and places, was a bureaucratic informality and lack of complex institutional structure. So sketchy were the paraphernalia of written rules, treasuries and membership cards that we must often look twice to be sure any organization existed at all. This heavy bias toward informality was partly the result of anti-union legislation, for at no point before 1884 did the government permit the construction of nation-wide worker organizations with bureaucratic hierarchies stretching to a center point. In many cases therefore skilled organizations existed in the minds of the members alone: patterned ways of interacting with other members of the same trade, informal gatherings and commonly understood values and responses to threats.

Of course we cannot know, save by indirection, what went on in the minds of provincial stonecutters and copper moulders. But we can find out about the shadowy formal organizations they put together from such sources as *APO* and Aguet.

– Co-operative producers' societies. These were numerically the least important of the traditional forms of craft association. Although they had flourished earlier, by 1895 only 174 still existed, with 4,700 worker members and an additional 6,800 employees.[3] At their origin, of course, was the craftsman's hostility to the entrepreneur's exploitation of the skilled labor of others. The ebb and flow of cooperative sentiments has been an interesting tide in intellectual history, but never a matter of importance to popular worker life.

– Mutual aid societies (*sociétés professionnelles de secours mutuels*). Mutualism was a common form of association among nineteenth-century craftsmen. The ostensible purpose of these societies was the accumulation of rainy-day funds: collecting dues from the members to guard against sickness, accident and unemployment. Yet simultaneously they served the interests of *défense professionnelle*, although often in secret. In 1895 around 2,300 such mutualist societies existed, having 394,000 members. Although present within all industries, the greatest concentration outside of agriculture was in transport–commerce (300 societies and 143,000 members).[4]

We may take as typical of many of these early societies the mutualist organizations of the Parisian copper founders and moulders. In the Napoleonic years there existed in that trade only a few shards of the former *compagnonnage Quatre-Corps*, which was, like most *compagnonnages* by then, a historical relic of no practical importance.[5] The year 1821 saw the the foundation of the mutualist Society of Copper Founders with 86 members. It was open only to founders of age 21–40, had monthly dues of two francs and would sustain sick members and old. A rival organization sprang up in 1833 when, in the course of a labor dispute brought about by an employer–founder's efforts to suppress a *cabale* among his workers, five or six hundred journeymen decided to form an auxiliary fund (*bourse auxiliare*) to succor the jobless. As the idea was elaborated over the months, it became a mutualist unemployment fund to conceal 'a true resistance fund for the protection of professional interests,' providing for shop-floor delegations and such. The government struck out many of these provisions before approving the unemployment fund's statutes.

Both these societies 'vegetated' during the forties, and by the early fifties only a hundred or so workers were willing to continue paying dues. Yet their influence upon other members of the profession must have been substantial, for we find the president of the newly unified Mutual Aid Society directing the agitation against coal dust in copper foundries. It was directly out of this campaign that the five-month general strike of 1855 grew, in which 1,700 of the 2,000 members of the craft participated at one time or another. The president of the society continued in the sixties to organize the founders to various collective tasks, such as sending a delegate to the London Exposition of 1862 and mounting a large strike in 1864.

A successful 1872 strike, supported by the mutualist credit association of the Lyon founders, moved the Parisian founders to resume the threads of their own mutualist organization, snipped by the 1870 war. In September of 1872 they established the Society of Mutual Solidarity of Copper Founders. Two months later a new strike erupted, and membership in the society shot up from 650 on 9 November to 940 on 16 November. By the spring of 1873 the society had enrolled 1,360 of the 1,800 members of the trade. This part of the story ends as in 1874 the society transformed itself into a labor union (*chambre syndicale*).[6]

Similar stories may be told for similar crafts in cities all over the country. Many of the stories would begin later than the 1820s, say in 1848 or even in 1870. Yet in almost all there would be tell of mutualist societies providing an organizational basis for strike activity, concealing under innocuous self-help labels militant ambitions. They provided places and occasions to meet, and their leaders were able to mobilize resources because they were admired by fellow craftsmen. Most of their stories are interrupted by abrupt discontinuities, dissolutions, reconstitutions, yet throughout all of this the habits and routines of collective action were forming in the mentalities of the workers. We shall bring evidence on this point when in the next chapter we discuss interoccupational differences in strike activity.

– Labor unions (*syndicats ouvriers*). Before 1880 what were fundamentally labor unions were often called societies of occupational defense (*sociétés de défense professionnelle*) or societies of resistance (*sociétés de résistance*), and unlike later unions they did on occasion provide self-help services as well as organize strikes. The artisanal labor unions differed from later proletarian unions in not being rigidly encadred in sprawling federations, in having high membership participation and in shying away from militant class-conscious ideologies. By 1885, on the threshold of the great mobilization, there were approximately as many labor unions (2,352) and unionists (443,300) as mutual-aid societies (2,349) and members (393,000).

The joiners of Marseille constituted a typical artisanal labor union. Their craft had a long tradition of *compagnonnage* organization, and was one of the rare instances where *compagnonnage* allegiance continued important throughout the nineteenth century. The journeymen joiners had staged a big strike for pay increases in 1792. After 1844 mutualist societies took hold in the craft, organizing several strikes. Then in July 1873, a hundred joiners established the Joiners' Trade Union of Marseille, among whose statutes were the following provisions:

> Article 3 The union is to be composed . . . of sections of 20 members.
> Article 4 Each section will elect one member who will be part of the union council.
> Article 8 The union will intervene as much as possible in the discussions and conflicts which may arise between employers and workers. It will send delegates to contact the employers' union, and will exert all its efforts towards conciliation.

Several years later the Marseille joiners began to tie themselves into the lattice of local and national organization, participating in the third socialist workers' congress in Marseille in 1879, and adhering to the Marseille Federation of Workers Unions in 1881. At the beginning of 1882 the union had 500 members, and in the course of a long strike from May to July 300 new members enrolled, so that the union included 800 of the 1,000 Marseille joiners.[7]

The Marseille joiners were entirely unremarkable, a familiar kind of early craft union comprising, or sympathetically regarded by, most of the members of a skilled occupation in a given locality. It was merely one further step in the long organizational evolution of a traditional local craft. Its purpose was to represent local worker interests through face-to-face bargaining with local employers. Its structure was elementary and its ties with unions elsewhere casual. The Marseille joiners would have recognized little in common with the Billancourt auto assemblers.

The concept of artisanal technology says that we should find the same basic patterns of union structure at most points in time, as long as the thread of technological continuity holds. All occupations participated in the building of nationwide organizations from 1880–1914, but technological differences meant that federations of craft workers would differ in important ways from federations of proletarians. They had a less ponderous bureaucratic structure at the top, for example. The federal seat of the draftsmen's union hopped about from city to city between that organization's founding in 1905 and its final settlement in Paris in 1921. The federal 'bureaucracy' could scarcely have been more than a briefcase of papers. The National Federation of Glassblowers folded in 1898, eight years after its initial foundation; reconstituted in 1902, only in 1904 did it acquire a permanent secretary.[8] The printers, although distinguished by a massive bureaucracy at the top, have become famous as an international union for the democratic decision-making process prevailing below.[9]

If technology is to turn out the critical variable, it must also be established that the few semi-skilled and unskilled workers in the period we have characterized as 'artisanal' organized along patterns different from craft workers. Which is to say that they organized themselves scarcely at all. Jean-Paul Courtheoux pointed out a startling lack of class consciousness and organizational capacity among the textile workers of the Nord, who managed to form their first union only in the 1890s.[10]

Not only were the unskilled workers not unionized in these years, they sometimes found themselves siding with the employer against the skilled organized workers. We have, for example, the events at the bottle factory of Labégude (Ardèche) in 1892. The factory's workforce was composed of two elements, skilled glass blowers, all of outside origin, and their laboring unskilled auxiliaries, all local boys. The locals were willing to accept conditions of employment inferior to those of the outsiders and resented the outsiders' presence. 'From that fact the antagonism between the two groups of workers inevitably arose,' according to the *SG*. The crunch came when the skilled outsiders established a union which the locals refused to join. The employer capitalized upon this animus by precipitating a strike and then dismissing all the striking unionists, that is, the skilled outsiders. The locals had opposed the stoppage and so welcomed these dismissals; new outsiders replaced the old.[11] Once the provincial jealousies have been scraped away, we have fundamentally a division between artisans and laborers: the former, first with informal and then with formal organization, were able to command high pay and working conditions to their liking; the latter were unorganized, undemanding and largely the creatures of the employer.[12] That is how technology affects organization.

Organization and technology: the proletarian sector

In the twentieth century the chief modes of industrial organization changed, as specialization of production and subdivision of labor antiquated many traditional skills; and the scale of enterprise increased, commensurate with the demands of new machines and work routines. It was these changes that evoked the proletarian worker, and his singular pattern of unionism.

At this point we ask the reader to follow a somewhat speculative train of thought, to accept a series of assertions about proletarian factory life that are impossible to pin down exactly with empirical data. These are assertions that the industrial sociology of other times and countries suggests to be true, and that the few precious studies of French industrial life confirm, such as Friedmann's *Industrial Society*, Touraine's *Usines Renault*, and Collinet's *Esprit du syndicalisme*.[13] Both varieties of information converge on the three probable consequences of machine-tending and specialization for the mentality and the situation of workers:

1. The irrefutable logic of assembly-line production demands the rationalization of the shop floor, which means there is one right, efficient way to do everything. That way is best determined by management and its efficiency experts. The worker, therefore, becomes the creature of the machine, powerless to set his own schedules because he must attend to the schedules the assembly line sets. This powerlessness is of interest to our argument because it means the worker is essentially unable to influence the organization or control of his workshop world. Key decisions in his working life pass entirely into the hands of others. The situation of the craftworker is of course quite different, for skilled artisanal production grants to the individual producer large realms of autonomy over raw materials, mode of production and end product, to say nothing of giving him freedom to take toilet breaks as he chooses, eat his lunch at his workbench (or a leisurely dinner at home), take Monday off and take similar liberties.

2. The machine-tender has no sense of professional community, no awareness of place in an occupational tradition with standards, values and a unified world view to uphold. He derives, therefore, little emotional gratification in associating with his fellow workers, for there is no question of organizing to preserve or reinforce a collective way of life. His only motive in joining formal shop-floor associations is instrumental: to advance his material welfare or to further his political representation.

3. The machine-tender is a man without occupational skills, and whatever expertise he requires to operate his machine may be learned on the job. This means he is easily replaceable. Employers who are firmly against

Consequence of mass production :

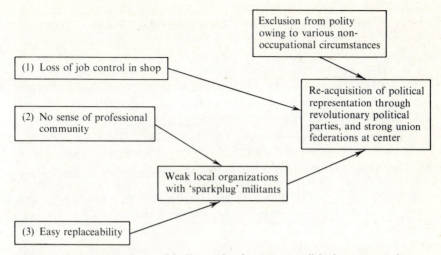

Fig. 7.2: The impact of assembly-line technology upon political representation

the unionization of their shops will be able to fire union militants if such men are a dime a dozen in the labor market.

These three aspects of the semi-skilled workers' position give rise to a distinctive pattern of unionization in mass-production industries: weak local organizations run by sparkplug militants combined with strong politicized central bureaucracies. The model above (fig. 7.2) suggests just how it works.

Proletarian unionism is composed of two related but independent elements: at the local level weak union organization run by sparkplug militants; at the national level revolutionary political parties and strong industrial federations. Why are shop- and community-level *syndicats* of mass-production workers so underdeveloped and ephemeral? The absence of a sense of professional community accompanying assembly-line production leads to indifference to what were once essentially professional (corporate) organizations; and the ease with which employers can replace union members makes affiliation a real danger to the worker's livelihood. Only dedicated ideologues can be found to serve as militants within the plants, which fact exaggerates the already explicit political cast of such local organizations.[14]

Why are proletarian unions so bureaucratized and centralized at the top, and so preoccupied with 'non-corporate' matters? Workers experience the lack of job control as a political problem, having to do with the access to and control over power, and so they seek out political remedies. They demand that their interests be represented at the national level, so that by manipulating the levers at the center they can recoup some local political losses, and assuage themselves through legislation on wages, hours, social insurance and the like for the loss of that which is non-recoupable, namely an artisanal organization of work. Tough, determined industrial federations are required for this task, as are avowedly revolutionary political parties.

This worker preoccupation with politics at the center has in France another, non-occupational source, the exclusion from political power the less skilled workers endured until the middle third of the twentieth century. Even though the best-organized of the skilled craftsmen had, via the Socialist party, acquired some voice in the polity around 1914, it would take until 1936 before the semi-skilled proletarians finally gained representation. And even after the Popular Front proletarian influence has been tenuous and inter-mittent. Given a political system that operates best when the various gladiators in the arena of power are constantly cheered on by their backers in the stands, this deprivation of representation has elicited a use of the strike that is thoroughly 'non-rational' in economic terms. Here is not the place to go into that, but we have represented it in the model.

What evidence is there that this model is right? Our argument predicts two features of local union life on which data are available: (1) proletarian unions are unstable, subject to wild membership fluctuations depending on the level of employer antipathy to unions and on events in the national polity; (2) proletarian unions organize only a small percentage of the workers in an industry because of the indifference of most of the workforce to shopfloor *syndicats*. Artisanal locals, on the other hand, should exhibit neither of these characteristics to a comparable degree.

The 'union explosion' of the Popular Front is a test of the idea that assembly-line technology creates local union instability, for the years 1914–35 saw the advancement of mass-production techniques in many industries. And in fact we noted in Chapter 5 that those workers most prone to explosive unionization after June 1936 were the underorganized pro-letarians in the large plants of the northeast. The CGT and CGTU had been weakly implanted in these sectors of mechanical construction and chem-icals, a thin scattering of militants trying to arouse class consciousness. Only in June 1936, after political victories had generated a critical mass of enthusiasm and employer hostility had been neutralized by the force of events, did these workers rush to take out formal membership. Chemicals and metals, two proletarian sectors, had coefficients of increase well ahead of leather and printing, two traditionally artisanal sectors. Two years later the falling off began, as the workers who had flooded in during the summer of 1936 lapsed into indifference in the fall of 1938, especially so after the failure of the November general strike. The outflow was heavier in metals and textiles than in printing.[15]

Point two: we learned in the last chapter that proletarian sectors had lower rates of unionization than did artisanal sectors. Printing–paper's rate was 9 percent unionized in 1884–97 and 11 percent in 1921–35; glass blowing's rate was 11 percent in 1884–97 (dropping to 6 percent in 1921–35 because of the dequalification in glassmaking brought about by technological change). Metals, on the other hand, had rates of 4 and 3 percent for the two periods. But anomalies make the pattern imperfect; textiles (7 percent) had a higher unionization rate than leather–hides (4 percent) in 1921–35. Ideally one would have unionization figures by specific occupation in order to assess the impact of technology upon levels of unionization, and while we have plenty of guesses from other authors that craftworkers are more highly unionized, firm quantitative data are seldom available.[16]

To complete this characterization of mass-production unionism we should look at the federal structures of several proletarian manufacturing unions. It is a commonplace of the literature on industrial relations that the textile workers' and metalworkers' federations had traditions of revolutionary socialist involvement in national politics going back to their inceptions. Guesdist militants put together the textile federation, according to Collinet the first bureaucratized federation in France.[17] The revolutionary ambitions of the Metalworkers' Federation are also familiar. Craft federations, on the other hand, belonged to the reformist tradition of cooperation with the government after 1919 and of decentralized anarcho-syndicalism before that time; here the printers and miners come immediately to mind.

We take a single example, the metalworkers, to highlight the characteristics of a mass-production federation. Metalworking was once an artisanal category par excellence, incorporating skilled mechanics, metalsmiths, coppersmiths and tinsmiths with long traditions of corporate professional life. In the 1880s and 1890s these artisans established several craft federations: in 1883 the Federation of Metal Moulders and the French Federation of Metallurgical Workers, in 1893 the National Federation of Copper and in 1899 the Federation of Mechanics. Their membership was composed overwhelmingly of craftsmen, not of semi-skilled proletarians. Then the explosive growth of the automobile industry in the 1900s forced a shift to industrial unionism, downgrading craft skills and bringing large numbers of 'specialized workers' (*ouvriers specialisés* or O.S.s) into formerly skilled metalworking shops. In 1909 the copper federation was dissolved, and the three craft metals federations merged into the industrial Federation of Metalworkers. It was highly centralized: local unions for different industries and crafts, directed by a single departmental metals union itself responsible to the national. In the 1920s this centralization became even more pronounced, for in each municipality there was to be but a single metals *syndicat*, divided if necessary into dependent sections. Thus in places such as the Paris region overtowering bureaucratic giants grew up: around 1919 the Unitary Metalworkers' Union of the Seine had 25,000 members, in 1921 only 5,000, but in 1936 230,000.[18]

There has been a lot of breast-beating about how the Communist Party's control over the CGT ruined the French union movement.[19] The argument is that once local unions became creatures of a doctrinaire political movement, their ability to gain bread-and-butter concessions, and in general to organize efficiently, was lost. These complaints confuse causes with consequences. It is true that postwar workers in manufacturing have been 'excessively' politicized, underunionized and ineffective in strikes. It is not true that this is the fault of the postwar PCF. We are dealing here with a trend in proletarian manufacturing that goes back to around 1900, a consequence of a new technology of production.[20] Workers in mass-production manufacturing have always acted with one eye for national politics, reasonably sensing where their offensive should take place; they have always been apathetic to local unions, permitting themselves now and then to be persuaded to collective local action by professional militants acting as sparkplugs; and their strikes have always been ineffective because the balance of power in industrial relations has lain so much on the employer's side. As we saw in Chapter 3, the innovations in strike activity since the Second World War have had little to do with changes in local union structure.

Organization and technology: white-collar work and the science sector

Two problems curtail our treatment of the science sector; one is that we are too close to it in history, for as we write this the high-technology industries are only about twenty years old, and insufficient time has elapsed to permit a proper perspective; the second is a complete lack of statistics on either the workforce, union membership or strike activity of the science sector, defined as such. To the extent that such data are reported at all in contemporary France, they are reported with conventional industrial categories, such as 'chemicals' and 'transformation of metals'; yet each of these grand aggregates harbors within it workers of all kinds, running from artisanal to high-technology. We wish it clearly understood, therefore, that what we say about the science sector is informed guesswork, buttressed by the opinions of other scholars and by the shards of available data, but essentially speculation about what one should find from a close look at the relationships between automation and union organization in the 1960s or 70s.

In postwar France the leading sectors of the economy are those dependent upon the technology of modern science, such as electronics and petrochemicals. These industries require a certain kind of worker, a man with substantial formal education, perhaps a technical degree, able to accept responsibility and to solve autonomously difficult technical problems; he differs from a traditional craftsman in not possessing specific technical skills acquired through long years of training within a craft community; rather, like a semi-skilled proletarian, he is trained on the job. Yet like an artisan but unlike a machine-tender, the autonomous, responsible nature of his work plus his previous education lead him to see himself as a professional person, entitled to independent latitude in decision-making and performing tasks requiring imagination and creativity. The technology of the science sector, though on the face of it as different as night is from day from the artisanal sector, brings together a workforce with essentially artisanal mentalities.

The 'professionals' of the science sector also have union organizations similar to those of traditional craftsmen, solidly implanted at the local or shop level and incorporating a high proportion of the workforce. Unlike machine-tenders, science professionals use their unions to reinforce their sense of occupational community and solidarity, and to wrest concessions from employers in realistic face-to-face bargaining. Unlike craft shops, however, the enterprises in which these professionals work are likely to be sprawling giants whose seats of power lie in some government ministry or corporate boardroom far away from the research laboratory in question. Therefore unions in the science sector must be plugged into centralized federations which can represent them in Paris. Science-sector unions appeared in the 1960s to be the vanguard of the worker movement. Michel Crozier, for instance, reports: 'The employees who operate data-processing equipment are usually the most aggressive and union-oriented segment of the [white-collar] labor force.'[21]

Let us take an example: Serge Mallet's description of the workers in the Caltex oil refinery at Ambès outside of Bordeaux. The men who operate the cracking and reforming equipment are far from the sullen proletarians of the *bagnes industriels*. They have enormous responsibility and derive considerable satisfaction from their work. Mallet describes the work:

> As operator or maintenance man, the worker is master of his job. He fulfills a task, within the framework of which he is the only judge of his decisions. Alone, or almost alone, at his post, he takes full responsibility for his work.
>
> No one is permitted to intervene arbitrarily in his task; the supervisors are quickly called to order when they infringe upon this strict division of responsibilities.[22]

Much the same might have been written of a master moulder in the 1840s.

The local unions at Caltex incorporated most of the workers, and were listened to respectfully by management. The unions controlled hiring. Even though the majority union was CGT, local adherents were far more attuned to local problems than to national ones. The key to power lay in the shop, not in the legislature:

> All the CGT militants admit that it is impossible, save at the cost of dissolution, to whip up support with the general slogans of the union organization. [The workers] are tied to the life of the refinery. In any case, their struggle takes place within the interior of the refinery. One could almost say that they consider their relations with their *patron* as a 'family affair' – considering of course that this impersonal family has no affective qualities.[23]

This sense of integration into the enterprise did not apparently diminish the militancy of the workers, for the union aggressively sought concessions from management. In 1957 a short but highly successful strike took place.

Perhaps the notion of new industrial forms can be broadened a bit to include not only the science sector but white-collar clerical workers as well. One runs the risk, of course, that in stretching a category it will be pulled out of recognition. White-collar clerical work utilizes no productive technology at all, and so strictly speaking should not fit into a taxonomy based on the worker's relationship to the tools of production. Yet there are notable similarities between the science sector and the office. The employees of both have considerable formal education, and for that reason alone demand some autonomy and scope for creativity. And much (though certainly not all) white-collar work demands responsibility, imaginativeness and some technical expertise from the employee; witness the posts of salesman, book-keeper, bank or insurance clerk and draftsman – all having unions in France.

White-collar clerical unions also resemble science-sector unions: high membership ratios, indifference to strutting and fretting upon the stage of national politics and a sense that local non-salary issues matter. Among six Parisian insurance companies, in 1957, for example, three were 20 percent organized, one 40 percent, one 50 percent and one 60 percent.[24] In the 1960s clerical workers belonged largely to the two confederations which stressed most decentralization and local autonomy: the FO and the CFDT–CFTC. White-collar proletarians seem to have been attached to the CGT (a common affiliation for department store clerks, for example), but middle levels within the clerical sector allied with either FO (government service unions), with CFTC–CFDT (banks, insurance companies) or with the CGC.

In this section we have tried to show how technology affects worker organization, both by shaping the mentalities of the workers and by structuring the industrial environment in which they work. But we do not want to overstate our case. Such influences as political ideology and legal *statut* of the workers also play a role; it would be implausible to explain differences in strike activity or organizational coherence between metalworkers and civil servants in terms of technological differences alone; that the former follow the Communist Party by and large, while the latter are reconciled to the existing political order is important to know. That the former have a private employer who looks down at their workbenches from his peephole high above, while the latter are part of a government bureaucracy is important to know. So are many other variable circumstances. Yet if we have to say what matters most over the years or across industries, we would say technology.

The effects of unions on strike activity

First, we turn to the role of worker organization in strikes, depicted between 1830 and 1934 in fig. 7.3. A substantial percentage of strikes early in the July Monarchy were mounted by some kind of formal organization, though more often by mutual aid societies and the like than by societies of resistance or labor unions. With 1835, however, a trough commenced that lasted roughly until the legalization of the strike in the early 1860s. (The high 1850–4 figure may be unrepresentative, based on a total of only eight strikes.) An upward surge of organization then took place in the 1860s and continued until the *belle époque*, interrupted by a real but temporary decline only in 1875–9 and an apparent decline in 1895–9. By 1910 the vast majority of all strikes saw the participation in some form of a labor union.[25] A trend during the 1920s and early 30s is not discernible.

A second method of noting the presence of union representation suggests as well that a major increase in union involvement in strikes took place from the prewar to the interwar periods. In order to make comparisons to the interwar period, when only 'remarks' data were available, we coded for 1895–9 and 1910–14 mentions of union activity made in the 'remarks' column of *SG*, as well as entries in the column 'Was a labor union present?' In 1895–9 unions were remarked upon in 2.1 percent of all strikes, in 1910–14 2.5 percent, but in 1915–35 in an impressive 8.5 percent. These figures catch only the tip of the iceberg, but nonetheless suggest a substantial increase in union representation. (The 1915–35 figure included *conventions collectives*.) This 'remarks' procedure is imperfect because the statisticians' decision to make special note of union involvement must have been haphazard. Yet imperfect as these data are, they do index the *direction* of change in the control over strikes by worker organization. Even though unionization rates were falling in the interwar years, the grip of the union movement upon the strike was hardening.

Exact statistics for the period after the Second World War are not to be had. Yet an inspection of the conflicts enumerated in the *RFT*, or in any given run of newspapers, turns up rarely a strike in which a union is not

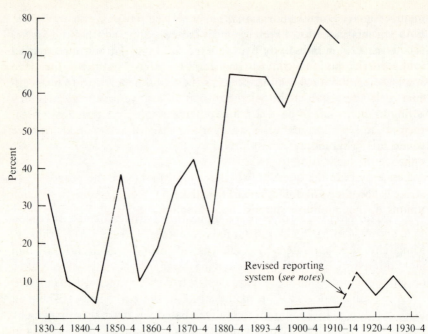

NOTES

1830–84: Source of data the coding of individual strikes. The forties are covered in the time blocks 1840–4 and 1845–7; sufficient data were not to be found for the 1848–54 period.

1893–1914: Source of data the statistics in the preface of yearly *SG*. The statistics include only *syndicats ouvriers*, yet by this time virtually all worker organizations which would have anything to do with strikes had transformed themselves into *syndicats*.

The special line for 1895–9, 1910–14 and 1915–35 represents the percent of strikes in which unions or collective agreements were mentioned in the 'remarks' column of the *SG*.

Fig. 7.3: The percent of strikes with worker organization, 1830–1934

somehow involved. The message of fig. 7.3, then, is that in the years 1860–1935 unions consolidated their grip upon strike activity.

Do unions increase the strike propensity of the workforce? In France the rule seems to hold that the more intense the unionization, the higher the strike rate. During all periods of rising unionization the incidence of disputes also climbed. The years 1884–1914, the epoch of initial union mobilization, corresponded to the first great efflorescence of conflict. The strike rate rose steadily during these years, as did the level of worker organization. The period 1915–35 was one of stagnation for both the strike rate and for union membership in manufacturing, the most strike-prone sector of the economy. Whatever increases in the number of strik*ers* took place were probably attributable to changing union structures, specifically to bureaucratization, rather than to an increase in the sheer incidence of conflict. And within this period the great moves from year to year in union membership and conflict have a rough synchronization: both rise in 1919–20, both fall in 1921–2 and so forth (see Chapter 4). The period 1945–68 was a second time of massive union implantation, and also a second period of long-term increase in strike activity. Just as levels of conflict in the 1960s were vastly higher than in either the 1890s or 1920s, so were rates of unionization. It is, therefore, clear that the secular rise in strike activity is in part owing to worker adherence to formal organizations, though several other factors must be considered to account for the character of conflict and to explain why French unions, as opposed to those in other countries, enhance the inclination to strike.

Less easy than the question whether unions influence the propensity to strike is how they affect the *form* of the strike. To put things briefly, French unions do not mobilize support by calling out all the workers in a given shop, but instead by persuading a portion of the workforce in a large number of different shops to join a strike. A network of individual militants will be spread throughout the establishments of a given city, controlled by the unionists in the Bourse du travail or by a departmental union of their particular industrial federation. The city is thus the basic unit of union action. When a strike is decided upon, these 'sparkplugs' (*noyaux* is the French militant's term) exhort their fellow workers to follow the union's call to action; some will walk out, some not, but these organizational efforts will have been taking place through the entire city.

What is the statistical evidence for these assertions about French mobilization techniques? Let us see how the characteristics of strikes in which unions were involved differ from those without unions.

– The presence of a union does *not* affect the proportion of a factory's workforce to join in the strike (number of strikers/workers in affected establishments). In 1910–14 the median plant participation rate where unions were involved was 69 strikers/100 workers; where no unions were involved, 70 strikers/100. Thus unions make no difference in mobilizing support for a strike at the level of the individual plant.

– On the other hand, unions were vastly effective in bringing out simultaneously some fraction of the workers of many separate establishments. We see this most impressively in the scope of strikes (number of establishments per strike).[26]

Average number of establishments per strike (medians in parentheses)

	1910–14	1915–35
Union present	10.2 (2.1)	23.2 (4.9)
No union present	3.2 (1.4)	8.3 (1.7)

The same goes for the number of participants in a typical dispute. Union-led strikes were much larger than non-union ones, mainly because unions called forth a greater number of establishments.

Average number of workers per strike (medians in parentheses)

	1910–14	1915–35
Union present	243 (56)	722 (156)
No union present	65 (46)	366 (78)

– In the preceding section we noted the apparent interwar paradox of local unions weaker than ever before plugged into central federations more bureaucratic and powerful than ever before. The emergence of this singular federal structure appears in statistics on grievances. Before the war unions organized strikes around pay issues perhaps half the time, and devoted the other half to such shop-floor grievances as demands for recognition, hiring and firing and the like. Strikes involving unions were more likely to be over shop-floor issues than strikes without unions (which aimed disproportionately at pay increases). Interwar bureaucratization and politicization modified this slightly. Union-led strikes in 1915–35 tended to be more for such issues as pay and hours than did non-union strikes, because, as we have observed already, centralized bureaucratic worker organizations think first to their own stability. Aware of the organizational damage that can result to them from failed strikes and fanatical employer resistance, they pick issues they can win on which will attract large numbers of workers in many different establishments. Before the war unions were more localized affairs, just in the process of building their central bureaucracies, and were unusually occupied with questions of implantation. A second reason for the shift is that the worker movement before the First World War made a last-ditch struggle against the loss of job control, in which skilled trades participated with vehemence. Therefore strikes protesting changes in work rules, and strikes over job control issues as well, occurred often. After the war this struggle against mechanization and rationalization was abandoned as hopeless, and the federations tried to direct workers toward higher wages.

Percent of strikes over pay issues[a]

	1910–14 %	1915–35 %
Union present	56.2	89.6
No union present	70.3	83.7

[a] 'Complex causes,' most of which concern pay matters, have been included in 'pay issues.' In the 1910–14 data the denominator is the total number of grievances, not the total number of strikes, because some strikes had more than one stated demand.

– In discussing the size of establishment in which unions are likely to be found we must sharply distinguish between the prewar and interwar periods, for things reversed themselves from the first era to the second. In 1915–35 unionized factories tended to be *smaller* by a good deal than non-unionized factories (keep in mind that we have no independent data on unionization by firm size, and are able to discuss only the size of those establishments that went on strike), which shows the deunionization of large mass-production establishments in the interwar years, the causes of which we have just examined. Median establishment size was significantly higher before the war for unionized than for non-unionized strikes. After the war the median size of unionized establishments *fell*, while that of non-unionized establishments rose.

Median size of establishments on strike

	1910–14	1915–35
Union present	54	43
No union present	46	77

– Once unions had succeeded in bringing out the workers, they were able to keep them mobilized until either the government intervened or the employer made it apparent that he would not relent however long his workers stayed out. Spontaneous and informal patterns of mobilization meant that the strikers would retain solidarity for a day or two at most, and then collapse, drifting back to work. The statistics on strike durations are dramatic.

Median duration of strikes

	1910–14 (days)	1915–35 (days)
Union present	6.6	9.4
No union present	3.1	5.6

These figures point to a central role for unions in the conduct of strikes. While the question of union involvement in the unleashing (*déclenchement*) of a dispute may be moot, some arguing for spontaneity hypotheses, others for organizational ones, there is absolutely no doubt that unions were required for the prosecution of a strike, however begun.

– Finally, what success did unions in strikes bring to the workers? Before the war, they made a moderate difference, thereafter an enormous one. This is not surprising, for workers may be persuaded to abandon part of their resources in time and money to the union organization only if they feel some chance of successful action will thereby result. And in fact union membership did improve their chances of success. The much higher percentage of union successes in the face of a generally falling success rate after the war mirrors from yet another facet the growing bureaucratization and centralization of the movement. The great federations, with the sophistication in bargaining and the large numbers of participants their engagement brought, made the workers more effective against the employers. Knowing this, we begin to appreciate how destabilizing assembly-line technology turned out to be at the plant level. For if organization increased the possibilities of successful action and heightened material returns, we may be able to explain why workers in 1915–35 did not flood into the unions in terms of the disaffiliating tendencies of technology.

Percent of strikes failing[a]

	1910–14 %	1915–35 %
Union present	44.9	11.2
No union present	50.2	42.8

[a] Includes strikes ending with more than $\frac{2}{3}$ of the workers replaced.

These data cause us to disagree fundamentally with Peter Stearns's conclusion that formal unions were relatively unimportant in triggering and shaping French strikes. Stearns argues that strikes erupted independently of, and often in opposition to union leadership; nor, he suggests, were unions important in either stiffening the workers' will to resist or in expanding the scope of the strike; rather, paradoxically, unions made the strike spontaneous and localized. We find this a false paradox, and challenge his belief that formal organization was irrelevant to the reality of French industrial conflict.

To rehearse for the reader the most elementary statistics, a direct positive relationship existed in 1910–14 between union participation and strike duration: whereas 21 percent of all strikes lasted but a day or less, only 18 percent of those with unions did so; whereas 11 percent of all strikes lasted a month or more, 14 percent of those with unions did so. And as for the argument that unions made strikes more localized, in 1915–35 only 2.8 percent of all strikes extended to several communes, yet 4.8 percent of those with unions did so. Michelle Perrot has found that unions were unusually well represented in strikes with prenegotiation, and in strikes involving street demonstrations. Etc. The facts, then, are directly contrary to Stearns's assertions.[27]

At the end of the chapter let's return for a moment to our starting question: why in France unionization increased the propensity to strike. The answer is that not all union movements bring with them higher strike rates, but only movements involving unions of a certain sort. The critical variable bearing on the strike rate is thus not whether unions are present at all, but what kind of unions they are, and what mission they assign themselves. Unions which imagine themselves as having a political mission will use the strike as a means of political action, and therefore strike often. Unions which imagine themselves with a wage-improvement mission will strike only when all else fails, and so strike seldom.

French unions and strikes were much like American ones before the 1930s, and the same push of unionization intensified industrial conflict on both sides of the Atlantic. Both countries, after all, had adopted approximately similar styles of industrial technology, and so one would scarcely expect a marked divergence in worker organization and attitudes. But let us, in conclusion, anticipate the argument of Chapter 12 on international differences. After the 1930s a North American pattern of strikes and unionism developed, sharply different from the French. This variety of unionism reduced strikes, rather than accelerating them.

Why? The difference is in politics and plant unionism. Extensive union implantation in North America after the Depression has reduced strike activity because the unions acquired substantial job control for the workers, and because the unions ceded to political parties the task of safeguarding working-class political interests. North American unions therefore set themselves the assignment of bread-and-butter material gains. In France unions continued virtually powerless at the shop level, so material gains for the workers had to be sought through political action at the center. Because French political parties continued to reject ideological compromise as a price for political success, French workers continued to rely upon the *syndicat* for representation at the center of power. With unions thus locked into the daily ebb and flow of political life, a high strike rate was inevitable. The strike became ever more a probe in the hands of an impatient contender for power, used continuously to test and try other contenders in an ongoing struggle. If the shoving and jostling abate, or if other more direct probes are discovered, the nature of the strike changes and its frequency declines. Both happened in North America. But in France no such changes have occurred, which means that the strike rate is a function of the workers' ability to organize themselves. The more organization you get, the more strikes.

8   Industrialization and strikes

If struggles for power set the rhythms and themes of French strike activity, the struggles nevertheless took place within forms established by industrialization. They involved men whose lives and whose aspirations depended on industrialization.[1] Our book's special task is to trace the impact of industrialization on the character and intensity of those struggles. By 'industrialization' we mean the movement of production toward specialized formal organizations and away from individual entrepreneurs, communities, kin groups and households, toward manufactured goods and services and away from agriculture. Out of that massive complex of changes, we will single out three sorts of transformation which are empirically isolable, plausibly related to struggles for power and often proposed as causes of industrial conflict:

1. The transformation of productive technology through mechanization. One straightforward sense of the term is the replacement of human skill and effort by machine. Much of the work on Europe assumes mechanization to be the very core of 'industrialization.'

2. The concentration of the workforce in large industrial establishments. Increases in the scale of enterprise are almost inextricably related to shifts in industrial technology; in practice we will have difficulty keeping the two separate. Yet analytically they are distinct, for technology affects the worker's relationship to his tools, and the scale of industrial life both modifies his relationship to his fellow workers and alters the authority patterns of the shop floor. How did increases in scale shift the organizational foundations and objectives of collective action?

3. The concentration of the labor force within mining and manufacturing, at the principal cost of agriculture. This migration of the employed population from the fields and forests first to cottage industry, then to factories, is relevant when talk turns to the 'dislocation' and 'uprooting' of the labor force – to breakdown as an origin of conflict and collective action.

In order to give a clearer sense of the impact of these changes on the pattern of industrial conflict, we attempt two things in this chapter: (1) to describe changes over the years in the industrial distribution of strikes, including some attention to specific occupations as well as to broad industrial categories; (2) to sort out the different ways in which the three features of industrialization just enumerated shaped the pattern of strike activity.

Long-term changes in strikes by industrial sector

To get a sense of the grand sweep of industrialization and conflict, let us begin with changes in the industrial composition of the national strike aggregates and in strike propensity over the last century and a half. The two matters are quite distinct; the former is a question of what industries contributed the greatest absolute numbers of strikes to France's totals, the latter of what industries have the highest propensity to strike, regardless of their absolute volume of conflict. Yet both intertwine, and only if they are joined together may the grand movements by industry be discerned.

First, a word about the data. From 1830 to 1935 allocating conflict by sector is straightforward, for we know how many strikes took place within each industry. And between 1890 and 1935 strike rates by industry may be easily computed because reliable labor-force data became available with the census of 1886. A problem arises after 1946, however, because only the number of man-days lost by industry is known. (Data cease between 1936 and 1945.) Man-days, of course, is highly sensitive to duration, and because some industries have longer strikes than others, the industrial rank order of

Table 8.1: *The share of strikes by industrial sector, 1830–1960, as percentages of the period's total (absolute number of strikes in parentheses)*

	Strikes				Man-days lost	
	1830–47	1850–89	1890–1914	1915–35	1915–32	1950–60
	(%) (No.)	(%) (No.)	(%) (No.)	(%) (No.)	(%)	(%)
Agriculture–fish–forest	1(3)	—(1)	4(823)	3(482)	—	—
Mining	3(10)	12(42)	3(679)	2(354)	9	10
Quarrying	3(8)	—	2(392)	2(286)	1	
Food industries	3(8)	2(9)	3(567)	4(626)	1	1
Chemicals	1(3)	1(2)	2(497)	3(546)	3	5
Printing–paper	8(26)	6(21)	3(629)	3(545)	2	1
Leather–hides	3(8)	13(48)	5(989)	5(868)	5	1
Textiles	35(107)	21(75)	24(4,720)	18(2,958)	29	5
Smelting	1(2)	—(1)	1(264)	3(507)	6	4
Metalworking	6(20)	23(82)	12(2,278)	17(2,885)	12	35
Wood industries	15(45)	11(41)	7(1,448)	8(1,346)	3	1
Building materials– ceramics	6(18)	6(20)	4(843)	5(862)	4	1
Construction	16(49)	4(15)	19(3,675)	15(2,444)	8	10
Transport	1(3)	1(4)	9(1,762)	10(1,643)	18	17
Tertiary	—	—	1(220)	2(307)	?	8
Total	101(308)	100(361)	99(19,782)	100(16,659)	101	99

man-days lost may differ from the rank order of strikes. Also, the comparison of changes over time, especially from 1915–35 to 1950–60, is endangered by the forced switch to man-days because strike durations may have changed unevenly among the various industries. The relevant data are presented in table 8.1.

How were strikes allocated by industry during the July Monarchy? In 1830–47 strike activity was dominated by the classical sectors of the traditional economy. Of the 308 strikes mentioned in Aguet which we have been able to identify by industry and place, fully 35 percent were in the textile industry, and the bulk of them among tailors. Crafts within the wood industries contributed a further 15 percent of the total, as did construction trades. The last notable sector was printing, with 8 percent of the aggregate. All other sectors had only token levels of conflict – fewer than eight strikes during the entire period.

Things were to change little during 1850–89. *APO* data may not give a true picture, for the source paid undue attention to strikes in politically sensitive sectors, and we therefore suspect that metalworking's share of 23 percent and mining's 12 percent of the national total are unduly inflated. If these possibly exaggerated figures are discounted, the composition of the strike movement remained little changed. With 21 percent of all strikes, textiles continued powerful, and woodworking and leather goods, both mainstays of the traditional sector, also registered substantial contributions.[2]

During 1890–1914 a decisive turn in the industrial distribution of strikes occurred. The modern sectors all scored heavy increases in their representation, outdistancing by far the traditional sectors. Printing, textiles and wood were considerably down from their July Monarchy shares, and the contributions of metalworking, construction and especially transport shot up dramatically. Strike rates in all sectors, both traditional and modern, were climbing during this time, but the shares of such leading sectors as metalworking grew most rapidly, both because their propensities to strike and their strikable populations were rising faster than those of the traditional sectors.

The modern sector continued to strengthen its grip upon the movement in 1915–35. The traditional sectors of printing and textiles lost ever more ground, while the new industries of metal production, metalworking, chemicals and transportation further increased their relative contribution.

Finally, the post-Second World War era witnessed the sag into virtual insignificance of many classical industries. Printing, leather goods, woodworking, textiles, building materials and ceramics all experienced drastic decreases in their contributions. Within the modern sector, however, metalworking, the bellwether of industrial advance, nearly trebled its share of man-days lost from 1915–32 levels. And the tertiary sectors similarly experienced impressive growth. The reader is reminded that these changes in man-days may mirror partly differential changes in strike durations by industry, for some inconsistency is evident between the industrial rank order of man-

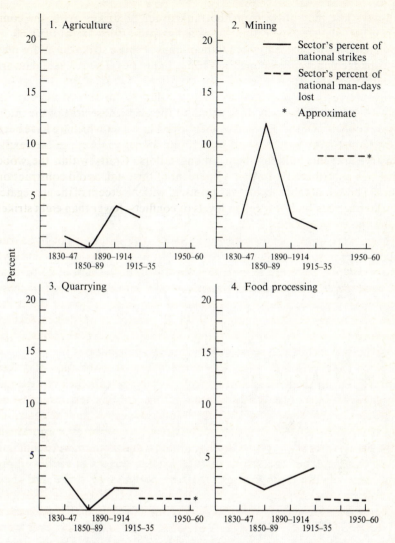

Fig. 8.1: The share of strikes by industrial sector, 1830–1960

days and of strikes in 1915–35. Yet even after this distortion is taken into the bargain, the dominance of metalworking, and the growing quiescence within the established small-shop sectors is indisputable. It is a nice irony that in 1950–60 the metalworking sector, with its great auto assembly plants and electrical equipment firms, had exactly the same percentage of the nation's man-days lost (35 percent) as the textile industry had of strikes in 1830–47.

Fig. 8.1 helps us draw these developments together in a pattern. (The raw

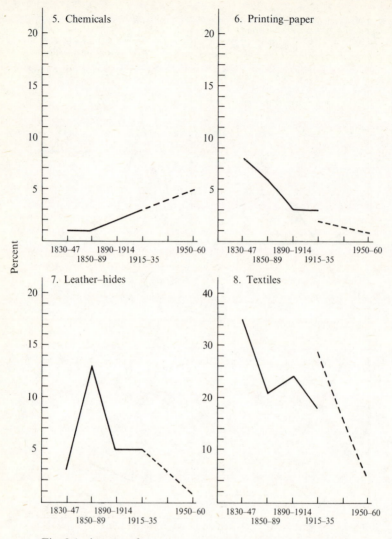

Fig. 8.1 (*continued*)

data were presented in table 8.1.) The classical sectors of the artisanal economy all began with high strike shares, and then declined over the years. All their graph lines run in a distinctive pattern from upper left to lower right. The proletarian industries of the modern sector, on the other hand, began in insignificance in 1830–47, and then climbed to predominance. Their graph lines run from lower left to upper right.

What all this talk of percentage contributions means is that over the very long haul the strike movement has kept pace with industrial modernization.

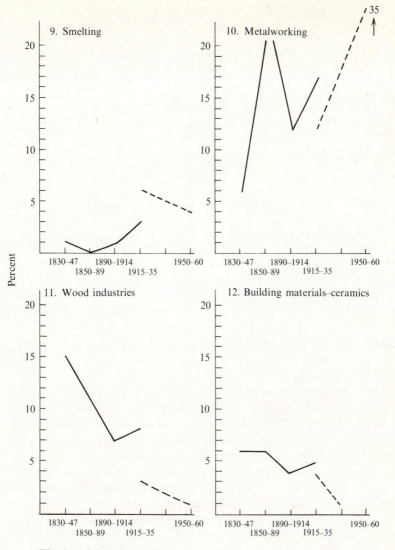

Fig. 8.1 (*continued*)

Seen in terms of decades, the leading sectors of the economy turn out to dominate the strike movement. This is true for two reasons, one banal, one of some interest.

If the leading sectors have the largest shares of strikes, it is partly because they have the most workers. The labor forces of public utilities (water, gas, electricity) and of banking have soared over the postwar years, and so if these sectors experienced in 1950–60 substantial conflict, it was partly because they were enrolling a large workforce available for conflict. Simi-

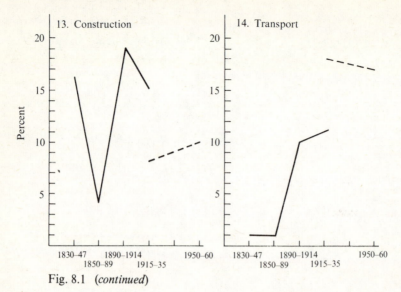

Fig. 8.1 (*continued*)

larly, the active population of the metalworking and transport sectors has climbed almost without interruption since the beginning of the nineteenth century, whereas the workforces of wood and textiles have gone down notably from their nineteenth-century levels. So a change in the composition of the strike movement mirrors partly a change in the composition of the active population.

A more intriguing proposition is that the decline in strike shares of the old artisanal industries reflects a maturation process. This maturity may be within the system of industrial relations alone, so that decade-long continuity in an industry's technology and industrial organization modulates conflict: most contentious non-wage issues are resolved, and only the give-and-take of collective wage bargaining determines the intensity of strikes.[3] On the other hand, this 'maturity' may come from changes outside the shop, from events occurring far beyond the technical matrix of industrial relations. We wish at least to raise the possibility that the decline of strikes in the 'classic' industries of France may reflect the political demobilization of their workforces, for as craftsmen acquired membership in the polity, via the the Socialist and Radical parties, they could afford to dispense with such forms of political struggle as strikes, which they once, as former challengers to the powerful, had found so useful.

Who had the highest strike rates? Information on propensity permits greater clarity about the forces at work upon various industries. Table 8.2 presents the basic series, contrasting strike rates for 1890–1914 and 1915–35, and man-days-lost rates for 1915–32 and 1950–60. First, how do the industries align in terms of their strike propensity at any given point in time? Second, what important shifts in propensity take place over time?

Table 8.2: *Strike rates by industrial sector, 1890–1935, and man-days-lost rates, 1950–60*

	Strikes per 100,000 active population		Man-days lost per 100,000 active population	
	1890–1914	1915–35	1915–32	1950–60
Agriculture–fish–forest	0.4	0.3		
Mining	19	5	151,000 ⎫	111,000
Quarrying	30	22	40,000 ⎭	
Food industries	5	6	10,000	6,000
Chemicals	24	10	54,000	62,000
Printing–paper	16	11	37,000	15,000
Leather–hides	13	14	77,000	13,000
Textiles–garments	8	7	72,000	27,000 textiles
				2,000 garments
Smelting	14	17	220,000	70,000
Metalworking	12	10	46,000	88,000
Wood industries	8	9	19,000	6,000
Building materials–ceramics	23	21	91,000	20,000
Construction	24	15	50,000	31,000
Transport proper	9	8	14,000[a]	86,000
National total/100,000 non-agricultural labor force	7	6	37,000	39,000

[a] Includes tertiary sector man-days lost.

It is disappointing, yet expected, that no pattern emerges in the clustering of industrial strike propensities before the Second World War. Neither industrial organization nor technology nor style of work nor any other familiar variable lets us make sense of the rank ordering of strike propensities. Different kinds of sectors intermix at all levels of the scale, and 'modern' metalworking, smelting and transportation congregate in the middle ranges during 1890–1914 and 1915–35.

More interesting by far is the change over time in strike propensities. While no meaningful shifts occurred in strike propensity from prewar to interwar periods, an interesting trend developed in post-Second World War man-days-lost rates (assuming that differential changes in duration by industry were small enough to make such rate changes trustworthy at all). In 1950–60 the rates of the proletarian industrial sectors flocked together at the upper ranges of the scale: mining, metalworking, transport, smelting and chemicals all had man-days-lost rates of more than 60/100 workers. These industries constitute the entirety of what we have been considering, on the basis of independent criteria of technology and semi-skilled workforces, the modern proletarian sector. The established traditional industries, on the other hand, clustered together in 1950–60 at the *bottom* of the scale: construction, textiles, building materials, leather goods, wood-working, food industries and garments all having a yearly average of less than 30 man-days lost per 100 workers.

Apparently some systematic sorting process was at work, for the newer modern industries all soared to the top in the postwar years, while the established traditional ones fell to the bottom, leaving the middle ranges of the man-days-lost scale vacant. Mining is the only ambiguous case in this scheme, for while it employs a proletarianized workforce, it by no means is a recently arisen sector, nor are its workers semi-skilled machine tenders in the same sense that auto assemblers are. Aside from mining, the sorting principle of 'new proletarian' versus 'established traditional' worked re-markably well after the Second World War, while failing before then as a dividing line. This new cleavage may well have been a function of new differentials in levels of political mobilization.

The level of strikes by occupation

Such aggregate industrial sectors as metalworking and chemicals encom-passed occupations whose technology and organization diverged as vastly as their styles of strike activity. There is, therefore, little point in contrast-ing the strikes of the metalworking sector to those of the textile sector, for within each were to be found occupations ranging from the hoary artisanal to the modern technological. Only the availability of time-series labor-force data by grand sector forced us to remain in the preceding section among these distorting aggregates. In this section we break down the composition of each grand sector into its constituent occupational parts, seeing exactly which crafts and industries were going on strike. In order to further convey the diversity sheltered by each sector we present strike rates by occupation, computed with the 1906 census as the labor-force denominator. (Compar-able labor-force data for other years are lacking, so we cannot calculate occupation-specific rates of conflict over time.)[4]

The conclusion of this section will be that industrial growth had quite different effects upon different occupations. Some trades escaped unscathed from mechanization, the subdivision of labor and the increasing scale of plant size. Even in the 1920s these occupations retained a firm awareness of their historic professional identities (with commensurate consequences for their collective action). Other established crafts were hollowed out by indus-trialization, so that the form remained in job titles evoking craftsmanlike functions, but the substance had evaporated in the sweatshop or at the machine bench. Still further jobs were created afresh by industrialization, and the workers in them called newly from the farm or from the ranks of the unskilled. These occupations lacked all professional identity or inherited tradition of organization, which meant the new proletarians would have patterns of collective action different from those of either the surviving or the perishing craftsmen. We survey first the traditional sectors whose occupations on strike in the 1920s were substantially the same as in the 1890s, passing then to the modern sectors where important transformations in the strikers' composition did take place.

Leather and hides

Within the leather goods industry a small group of crafts supplied a majority of the strikes; their contributions changed little over the years, relative to one another. In 1910–14, to take a point in time, shoe factory workers staged 38 percent of the sector's strikes, followed at some remove by tawers with 9 percent, saddlers with 8 percent, small-shop cobblers (*cordonniers*) with 7 percent and curriers with 6 percent.

These 1910–14 figures were not greatly different from those of the July Monarchy, when shoemakers[5] had two-thirds of the sector's strikes, and tanners–tawers–curriers the remaining third. During 1830–47 the numerous specialties later to surface in the strike movement were quiescent, and the harness-makers, furriers and *maroquiniers* experienced virtually no conflict. The shares of strikes of these principal trades did not change in relationship to one another during the Third Republic. What happened after 1935 is impossible to say.

Thus the leather–hides sector changed over time only in that some small fringe crafts became activated during the great mobilization after 1890. The classic artisanal groups held their share of strikes against the encroachment of the shoe factories and it would be entirely inexact to think of conflict within shoemaking and leather preparation as shifting from craft shop to factory. Although the average size of establishment within the leather–hides sector as a whole rose somewhat over time, the average size of *struck* establishment declined between 1895–9 and 1900–4, and again

Table 8.3: *Average size of struck establishment in the leather–hides sector, 1895–1934*

Period	Workers
1895–9	118
1900–4	40
1905–9	45
1910–14	58
1915–19	61
1920–4	53
1925–9	49
1930–4	118

NOTE
The craft labor forces of strikes in these industrial plants have not been used in 1895–9 or 1910–14.

SOURCE: Coding of *SG* data.

from 1915–19 to 1925–9, as table 8.3 shows. Clearly, then, any argument accounting for the rise of militancy in shoemaking and related trades in terms of 'industrialization' would fall flat over the fact that separate skilled trades retained a distinct identity in industrial warfare, and held their own in the general increase of strike propensity.

Nor may a uniformity be found cross-sectionally between strike propensity and industrial concentration. In 1910–14 industrial shoe factory workers and artisanal saddlers shared low strike rates; equally craft-based tawers, on the other hand, experienced a middling strike propensity:

	Median number of workers in establishments on strike, 1910–14	Strike rate per 100,000 workers, 1910–14
Shoe factory workers	105	25
Tawers	46	48
Saddlers	31	25

Whatever 'industrialization' meant to the leather–hides crafts, therefore, it did not necessarily mean loss of professional identity, or a new access of militancy.

Printing–paper

As a rule, half of the strikes in the printing–paper sector were waged by typographers, or by *ouvriers d'imprimerie* most of whom were typographers. Of the 153 strikes in this sector during 1910–14, 55 percent were among typographers, 14 percent among paper workers and the remainder spread out among lithographers and miscellaneous trades. Fine distinctions within this sector are especially risky, because so often typographers and lithographers, allied with other printing workers, would strike together. The essential point in 1910–14 is that four-fifths of the disputes within this sector occurred in printing shops, the rest within the paper industry.

This disproportion had not always existed. Paper workers experienced just about as many strikes as did printers during the July Monarchy. Militancy became thereafter more intense within printing than within paper and carton making, so that a decided imbalance was evident between the relative shares of the two in 1910–14. (The workforces of both grew fairly steadily.) Only in the 1950s was this reversed, as printing militancy plunged downwards.

Printing is famous as a craft that retained its artisanal integrity under the pressures of expanding plant size and mechanization. An increase in the average size of establishments on strike corresponded roughly to an increase in the scale of enterprise in printing in the interwar years. And Sales has documented the printers' struggle with the composing machine.[6] Yet in the 1950s the printers emerged with high unionization rates, solidary plant-level organization and an unprecedented degree of job control. Whatever in the 1950s caused the sag in printing's strike propensity, it was not the artisan giving up the ghost to the machine.

Woodworking industry

The four classic woodworking crafts composed a substantial majority of wood industry strikes. In 1910–14 joiners (*menuisiers*) in both building and furniture-making contributed 30 percent of the sector's strikes; behind them followed building carpenters (*charpentiers*) with 16 percent, cabinetmakers (*ébenistes*) with 8 percent and coachworkers (*ouvriers en voitures*) with 7 percent of all disputes in the sector. The remaining strikes were distributed across a large number of small crafts such as button-makers, sawyers, woodcarvers, coopers and the like.

Carpenters had had the lion's share of woodworking strikes during the July Monarchy, trailed by the joiners and then distantly by the cabinetmakers. By 1910–14 things were reversed, joinery contributing more strikes than carpentry. In the 1920s about the same proportion of workers calling themselves *ébenistes, menuisiers* and other hallowed craft titles went on strike as during the 1890s. So despite a contracting labor force and some increases in the scale of enterprise, artisanal strikes continued strong in the wood sector. Whatever impact mechanization had made upon woodworking, the labor force retained some notion of craft identification.

Building materials

Building materials was a very mixed bag, for few uniformities of skill, technology or organization existed within the sector. Of the 211 strikes in building materials in 1910–14, 14 percent came from glassmakers, 10 percent from marblecutters, and the remainder from a range of building products that included plaster, cement, clay pipe, tile, earthenware and ceramics, and bricks.

Virtually none of these industries save the porcelain workers (who in 1910–14 had a mere 8 percent of the sector's strikes) had gone out during the July Monarchy. The glassworkers had generated a burst of conflict around the turn of the century, then lapsed into passivity only to revive in the 1920s. A strike movement among the cement workers got going only around 1905. Otherwise no changes worthy of remark occurred in the composition of building materials strikes.

A further index of the disparity of the sector is the range of strike propensities among its component industries. In 1910–14 the marblecutters and polishers scored a yearly average of 92 strikes/100,000, the potters 72, but the porcelain workers only 25 and the tilemakers 15. Obviously little justifies holding these diverse groups together in the same aggregate.

Construction trades

Two construction trades totally overshadowed all others in strike volume:
the navvies (*terrassiers*) and the masons. Of the 1,489 construction strikes
between 1910 and 1914, 39 percent occurred among navvies, 31 percent
among masons. A number of other trades shared the remaining 30 percent
of construction's strikes: *ouvriers du bâtiment* (without further specification)
4 percent, roofers 4 percent and so on down through painters, stonecutters,
bricklayers, cement workers and others.

It had always been thus, for in the July Monarchy the navvies and masons
supplied easily the predominant share of construction strikes, and only
stonecutters and roofers had even token representations among the other
building trades. In the 1920s the overriding share of these two great occupations was diminished, as the representation of each sank by 10 percent or
so owing to a growing number of strikes among *ouvriers du bâtiment* and
cement workers. These shifts reflect both the spread of industrial unionism
and of technological innovation within construction. No solid information
exists on post-Second World War developments, but one might expect to
see craft insularity further diminished by the spread of industrywide union
organization (hence *ouvriers du bâtiment*) among construction workers.

How irritating to have to admit less than omniscience on our subject, yet
we can discover no pattern among the strike propensities of the constituent
construction trades. Different skill levels and degrees of historic tradition
are present at all ranges of the strike scale: the two classic construction jobs
(*maçons* and *terrassiers*) finding themselves at opposite ends, just as the two
rock hewers (*granitiers* and *tailleurs de pierre*) are also at opposite ends. We
have, in short, no explanation of the pattern of strike propensity within
construction. Table 8.4 is evidence of defeat.

Food industry

An early predominance of bakers within food industry strikes gave way to
dispersal among a great variety of products and trades. The spread of strike

Table 8.4: *Strike rates among the construction
trades, 1910–14*

	Strikes per 100,000 workers
Cement workers	262
Navvies	214
Stonecutters	193
Plasterers	85
Roofers	83
Brickmakers	68
Masons	53
Granite workers	35
Painters	30

activity to the newer factories and product categories meant a steady diminution of the bakers' share of strikes, which in the July Monarchy constituted the entire food industries sector. By 1910–14 the bakers had only a fifth of all disputes in the food industry. The 1920s and 30s registered few bakers' strikes relative to other parts of the food industry: in 1926, for example, only 6 bakers' strikes, yet 3 disputes among cookiemakers, 2 among fish salting factories, 1 among margarine workers, 5 among sugar refineries and so forth. Thus over time militancy had flown into the factory production of food products, and both in relative and absolute terms away from the core trade of baking.

None of the food industries was very strike prone, compared to other sectors. And in 1910–14 the bakers, with a yearly average rate of 13 strikes/100,000 workers, ranked close to the bottom of the sixty-two occupations for which such rates may be computed.

Garment industry

Garments and textiles occupy a point where the shading from changeless artisanal to mechanized factory industrial production leaps at the eye. Both industries had roots stretching far back into France's industrial history. Both were transformed by technological innovation and the subdivision of labor, yet in ways quite different from other modern proletarian sectors.

Time was when the garment industry led the entire strike movement. During the July Monarchy the tailors had more strikes (30) than any other occupation in any sector. But no other occupation within garments, except the hatters (*chapeliers*) had more than token strike levels at that time. By 1910–14 the picture had changed. The garment industry as a whole, of course, had after 1848 been outpaced by many other sectors, and a dozen or so occupations regularly accumulated more strikes than the tailors. Within the garment industry itself the hatters had pulled even with the tailors in numbers of strikes, and a proletarian industrial category – *confection des vêtements* or *ouvriers en confection* also registered in 1910–14 almost as many strikes as the tailors (33, as opposed to 36).

After 1910–14 the proportion of tailors' strikes within garments declined, both because the tailors themselves struck less, and because non-artisanal garment occupations were striking more: launderers and laundresses and *confection des vêtements* especially. Garment strikes were manifestly shedding their artisanal character as the labor force became proletarianized. Between 1906 and 1936 the garment industry drifted towards concentration in large shops, at the same time losing workers. The agony of the hatters and tailors in the loft system has been often chronicled, and oppressive conditions among laundresses and seamstresses many times recounted. The job labels remained those of the July Monarchy, but those wearing them were new men (and women).

Textile production

The textile industry properly speaking means cloth production, for in 1910–14 some 40 percent of all textile strikes were in spinning mills, and 33 percent in weaving mills. The small remainder was spread among dyers (10 percent), stockingers, finishers and lesser occupations.

An imprecision in the sources which Aguet used prevents us from saying how much this pattern had altered since the July Monarchy. Certainly the percentage of artisanal textile strikes had fallen to insignificance. By 1890 the industry was for the most part organized in big establishments which employed a semi-skilled labor force. The combined portion of spinning and weaving strikes, relative to other parts of the sector, did not change definitively during 1890–1935, oscillating between a half and three-quarters of the total. Nor were trends to be noted among lesser industries within the sector.

The three textile occupations for which strike rates could be computed fell within the middling class of intensity in 1910–14 (50–100 strikes/100,000 workers): wool twisting at 70, dyeing at 84 and spinning at 109 (just marginally outside the range). All three functions take place within large plants, indeed enormous ones in the case of wool twisting, whose average *struck* establishment size in 1910–14 was 680 workers (median size 528). Why such mills were likely to experience higher strike rates than, say, tawing shops, is a subject discussed in the last section of this chapter.

In a spectrum from craft artisanal to proletarian industrial, weaving-mill workers were as far from leather tawers (where we began) as it is possible to get, and yet remain more 'artisanal' than auto assemblers. Some faint sparks of artisanal tradition may have glowed within the early twentieth-century weaver's breast – certainly none did within the *métallo*'s. And textile workers differ from autoworkers also in having encountered mechanized production a half century previously. Yet the similarities of technology and plant size were sufficiently powerful to override these marginal differences, and we shall discover that spinning-mill workers and large-shop metal-workers strike in like ways.

Chemicals

The sprawling chemicals sector defies efforts to find unity and centrality among the occupations on strike. What the plant produced identified the strikers, and a limitless variety of chemical products marched through the pages of the *SG*. Yet some were more frequent than others. In 1910–14 a seventh of chemicals strikes were in gasworks (*usines à gaz*), another seventh in vegetable oil refineries; in addition small clusters of strikes took place in petroleum refining, fertilizer production and similar processes.

How had this distribution changed over time? In the traditional economy there was no chemical sector to speak of, aside from an occasional strike among the *gaziers* perhaps (Paris, 1847) or the soapboilers (Marseille, 1833).

A chemical industry proper arose only with modern technology. (Not until 1896 did the *SG* differentiate a chemicals industry from the paper–printing sector.) Chemicals was born a heavy-industrial proletarian sector, rather than experiencing a transformation from artisanal to industrial. Its workers were semi-skilled or unskilled, possessing no artisanal traditions. Except for matchworkers and tobacco workers in the public sector, they were poorly organized. The factories they worked in were big (workers were concentrated within large plants to a much higher degree than in most sectors), and grew larger from 1906 until the early twenties, when some tapering off began. Though the absolute volume of strikes within chemicals increased considerably over the years, the sector's occupational constitution did not change importantly before 1935. To be sure, the *SG* used with increasing frequency the category 'chemical products' in reporting, yet that may be a statistician's artifact rather than a sign of industrial modernization. Also, strikes of matchworkers and tobacco workers, which took up notable posts in the early *SG* listings, became ever less frequent. Yet in general the same kinds of workers in the same sorts of establishments seem to have been striking late in the 1890s and early in the 1930s.

Metalworking

Our principal archetype of the transformation from small-shop artisanal to factory industrial is metalworking. The rise of great electrical equipment and automobile plants where small locksmith and tinsmith shops once stood rivets the imagination. Yet strike data suggest that this image is incomplete, for many small firms were not supplanted by the giant automakers, and many of the workers who moved into the factories were craftsmen, and continued to execute polyvalent artisanal tasks.

The period 1910–14, midpoint in the process of industrial modernization, provides a convenient starting place. Table 8.5 gives the percentage share of strikes among crafts and industries within metalworking. A handful of familiar names constituted a vast majority of all strikes in the sector: *mécaniciens–constructeurs* (machine-builders at one time, semi-skilled machine-tenders at another) had with 27 percent the largest single share. Moulding and foundry workers came next, together having 18 percent of the total. Then much more distantly behind followed metalsmiths (*serruriers*) and iron structural workers (*charpentiers en fer*). All other occupations within metalworking had only minuscule percentages of the total, though in absolute numbers some of the less important crafts still had substantial strike activity.

What changes occurred over the years? Metalsmiths and foundry workers had accounted for most of the few metals strikes during the July Monarchy, other standard crafts, such as the nailmakers, shoeing smiths and coppersmiths each for two or three. Several classic metals trades such as machine-builders and tinsmiths seem to have mounted a rich organizational life, at least in the big cities, yet had few strikes. At all events, the strike movement

Table 8.5: *Strike rates and shares within the metalworking sector, 1910–14*

	Number of strikes	Percent of strikes within metalworking (%)	Rate of strikes per 100,000 workers[a]	Median size of struck establishment (Workers)
Metal-polishers (*polisseurs sur métaux*)	16	2	400	46
Metal-turners (*tourneurs sur métaux*)	10	1	250	96
Metalsmiths (*serruriers*)	34	5	189	13
Iron structural workers (*charpentiers en fer*)	32	5	118	80
Gunsmiths (*armuriers*)	15	2	94	40
Coppersmiths (*chaudronniers*)	29	4	55	190
Electricians (*électriciens*)	12	2	39	136
Artmetal and large-scale ironworkers (*ferronniers*)	14	2	14	103
Foundry workers (*fonderies*)	50	7	25[b]	107
Forge workers (*forgerons*)	11	2	8	267
Shoeing smiths (*maréchaux-ferrants*)	26	4	14	2
Leadworkers and plumbers (*plombiers*)[c]	27	4	51	20
Tinsmiths (*ferblantiers*)	30	4	—	32
Mécaniciens–constructeurs	183	27	—	209
Moulders (*mouleurs*)	76	11	—	63
Other metalworking crafts and industries	120	18	—	—
Total metalworking	685	100	25.6[d]	80

[a]   The labor-force denominator is the actual number of *ouvriers* employed in *établissements*. Isolated workers, *chefs* and employees, and the unemployed are excluded.
[b]   This rate is probably deflated because so many *fonderie* strikes took place in connection with *mouleurs*. Labor force for *mouleurs* was not available.
[c]   After the First World War this occupation was classed with the construction sector.
[d]   The labor-force data for this calculation are as described in note *a*, and include both workers in *métaux ordinaires* and *métaux fins*. All strikes within metalworking constitute the numerator, not just those listed by occupation in the table.

within metals during the first half (or even two-thirds) of the nineteenth century was exclusively among skilled craftsmen, not among semi-skilled or unskilled workers doing standardized, routinized jobs.

Yet during the 1890s a new category of striker emerged: the *mécanicien–constructeur*, with 9 percent of all metals strikes in 1890–4 and 22 percent in 1895–9, as table 8.6 shows. These workers increased their share of sector totals to a highpoint of 35 percent in 1915–19 (mainly because of the 1919 strike wave), leveling off then at a third of all metals strikes in the 1920s. We must assume that their strike propensity climbed upwards as well, though existing labor-force data do not cast themselves as a ready denominator.

Table 8.6: *Share of* méchaniciens–constructeurs *in metalworking strikes, 1890–1929*[a]

	Strikes among *mécaniciens– constructeurs*	Strikes in *travail des métaux*	%
1890–4	21	224	9.4
1895–9	80	368	21.7
1900–4	86	415	20.7
1905–9	136	586	23.0
1910–14	180	685	26.3
1890–1914	503	2,278	22.1
1915–19	201	575	35.0
1920–4	297	838	35.4
1925–9	301	938	32.0
1915–1929	799	2,351	34.0

[a] The category *mécaniciens–constructeurs* becomes unreliable after 1926 as product categories are used increasingly to describe occupations. We felt able to ensure comparability through 1929.

SOURCE: Hand tabulations from yearly *SG*.

Metal structural workers (*charpentiers en fer* – in reality a construction, not a metalworking, craft) also increased their share of the total during these years.

In the face of this advance the strike share of tinsmiths and coppersmiths declined, though what happened to their strike rates is not known owing to a lack of occupational labor-force data. The measure 'share of strikes' thus leaves unanswered some important questions.

The most interesting question, however, is how had the reality behind these occupational titles transformed itself over the years?[7] To be a *chaud-ronnier* in 1910 was probably quite different than in 1832, for we know that the mean size of coppersmithing establishments on strike in 1910–14 was 460 workers (median 190). We do not know how large the plants were in which coppersmiths worked during the July Monarchy, or exactly what tasks these workers executed, but almost certainly things had become different by the *belle époque*.

Mécaniciens–constructeurs are a prime example of an occupation transformed by industrial advance. Before the advent of assembly-line production, machine-building was, although not a traditional guild craft, an exacting, skilled profession, calling for many-sided competence and substantial training. The assembly line made *mécaniciens–constructeurs* into machine-tenders, drillpress operators and wheel-nut screwers-on. The *SG* retained the customary occupational title for those who worked in large engineering plants that fabricated machinery. Yet the men themselves had become proletarian *métallos*.

Information on plant size hints at the transformation of much of the sector from skilled labor to machine-tending. Between 1906 and 1926 the percentage of the employed population in metalworking establishments larger than 100 increased from 39 to 51 percent, and that in small establishments decreased from 42 to 28 percent, a rate of concentration more rapid than in any other sector. Clearly, the industrial realities behind some occupational labels in metalworking were being hollowed out.

Yet not all metals crafts underwent the skill dequalification and professional degradation of the *mécaniciens–constructeurs*, if size of plant is any guide to skill level. The establishments of striking metalsmiths (*serruriers*) remained tiny, as did those of tinsmiths and armorers. Presumably the technology in such enterprises remained pretty much as before. All this is uncharted ground, and any conclusions about the social effects of industrialization drawn from such strike data must be chancy. The interim conclusion seems safe, however, that industrialization within metalworking had highly differential effects upon traditional workers. In some industries and trades, most notably the machine-builders, mechanization and a rise in the scale of industrial organization brought with them disaster for the artisan. The move from small shop to dark satanic mill was for these men a historic fact. Yet other occupations which had been traditionally well organized and militant seem to have been scarcely at all affected by 'industrialization.' Their shops remained small, and their members retained established habits of militancy. The upshot of all this is that considerable differentiation is necessary before the concept of 'industrialization' will permit us to understand anything about strikes.

Transport–warehousing

The sector where unskilled, proletarianized workers were most common was transportation. More than any other industry, transport had been called into existence by industrialization, and the threads hung slack that bound together the transport workers of the early twentieth and those of the early nineteenth century. Indeed, if the *APO* survey is to be trusted, the traditional transport sector was entirely unorganized, or at least it left no residue of associations and traditions for the new workers of the late nineteenth century to seize upon.[8]

Dockers staged about half of transport's strikes. In 1910–14 their exact share was 42 percent (249 of 597 strikes), followed very distantly by carters with 15 percent, seamen with 9 percent and tramways, coachmen and furniture removers with several percent apiece. The 1910 railway strike confused the counting in this period, for it was simultaneously a single great dispute and a large number of separate walkouts, depending on how one draws the boundaries of a strike. Yet rail strikes were highly infrequent, and any attempt to gain a 'normal' picture of disputes in transport need scarcely consider them.

Little change over time took place in the occupational composition of transport strikes. They hardly existed before 1890. And by the 1930s approximately the same occupations were going out in the same proportions as around the turn of the century. A decline in the share of carters' strikes must be noted, for the wagon-hauling of goods was a dying trade. As for the stevedores (*dockers – débardeurs – déchargeurs – ouvriers de port*), seamen and truckers, their relative proportions remained more or less steady, and one may assume that their strike propensities rose with the climb in transport's general strike rate.

We have been able to calculate the strike rates of a few occupations within transport for 1910–14.

Carters	1,300 strikes/100,000 workers
Coachmen	226
Furniture removers	117
Tramways	54
Seamen	47

The rates tell us nothing about change over time, of course. But, as an aside, they indicate that the occupations most interleaved with the surrounding economic and social order had the highest strike rates. Seafarers, presumably the most isolated occupation, had the lowest rate of conflict. The importance of this small finding will be demonstrated when, three chapters from now, we turn to the Kerr–Siegel 'isolation' hypothesis.

Tertiary

The most radical discontinuity with traditional patterns of organization and conflict has been strikes in the services sector. The growth of the tertiary labor force at the cost of manufacturing and agriculture, and the efflorescence in white-collar strikes in the 1950s and 60s – not just in France but all over the Atlantic community – gives white-collar strikes an importance quite disproportionate to their numerical significance. Who, precisely, has gone on strike in the tertiary sector?

Before the Popular Front, services strikes were an uninteresting grab bag. The slow upward crawl of the tertiary's percentage of the total strike movement was owing to hairdressers and musicians, theater employees and various types of workers devoted to the removal of fecal material. Of interest, of course, was the first civil servants' strike in 1899 among the mailmen; it heralded several subsequent prewar walkouts in the PTT. Another harbinger of things to come was a strike of telephonists in 1908, all of whom were dismissed. Finally there was a steady drumbeat of strikes of *employés de commerce*, especially within the big Parisian department stores, starting in 1905.

The first genuine white-collar strikes in the critical office sector of banks– insurance companies–corporations took place in 1917. There followed a wave of such disputes in 1919–20, capped by a major banking strike in 1925. Between 1926 and 1935 the office employees fell again silent, to revive in

1936. Aside from the proletarian store clerks, no white-collar group commenced a sustained campaign of strike activity before the Popular Front. There is in the years before 1936 no trend whatsoever to militancy among teachers, civil servants, bureaucrats, white-collar employees, 'free' professionals or other similar groups. Such disputes as did occur within these ranks were isolated and sporadic in the extreme, like the occasional eruptions among PTT workers. The tertiary sector remained a residual category, populated mainly by strikes of musicians and *vidangeurs*.

The further increase in the tertiary's share of national totals since the Second World War seems due (though aggregate reporting categories and the use of man-days lost frustrate exact measurement) to banking–insurance and to public utilities. Before the war public utilities–gas, water, electricity– were classed partly within the chemicals sector, partly among the residual of transport and 'XI *bis*.' After the war these utilities were given a special grouping of their own. Before the war such disputes totaled to little more than a handful; in 1950–60 they amounted to 4 percent of all man-days lost in France. After the Second World War commerce and the 'free' professions constituted an additional 3.7 percent of all man-days lost, which is probably higher by a good deal than their interwar or prewar share of man-days. One final change is a decline in the representation of retail clerks among the strikers, probably reflecting a drop in retail militancy. Table 8.7 gives the exact figures for tertiary sector strikes in 1950–60, to the extent that precision is possible with official statistics. But the government's refusal to report strikes among civil servants means that the data are incomplete, and there is a real danger that the tertiary's contributions to national strike totals has been understated.[9]

Two broader issues are brought to mind by this survey of occupations on strike. One involves merely the restatement of a vexing question: are changes in the structure of the economy behind the great postwar increase in strike activity? We suspect that the answer is in part yes. But our occupational data do not give access to the kind of structural change we consider strategic,

Table 8.7: *Distribution of man-days lost within the tertiary sector, 1950–60*

	man-days lost (thousands)	% of total man-days lost in tertiary
Commerce in foodstuffs	76	2.5
Non-food retailing	126	4.1
Banks–insurance	548	17.8
Entertainment	60	2.0
Health services	36	1.2
Free professions	636	20.7
Water–gas–electricity	1,591	51.8
Total	3,073	100.1

SOURCE: Annual totals in *RFT*.

the rise of the science sector within manufacturing. We have argued that a shift to automated production and the formation of a new stratum of skilled professionals within manufacturing probably altered the form of strike activity. This technological transformation has some thin roots in the 1920s and 30s, but on the whole is a postwar development. Yet our strike data prevent us from tracing science-sector strikes, (a) because the critical sectors are identified in the *SG* by product type (e.g., *produits chimiques*, *mécaniciens–constructeurs*, *aéroplanes*), without indication of the kind of workers on strike; and (b) because fine-grained occupational classifications are abandoned entirely in postwar strike reporting. Thus we have the strong suspicion that new types of workers, such as the highly trained, well educated skilled workers in the employ of the 'technobureaucrats,' have played a key role in the transformation of the strike, perhaps only by providing models to other groups within the labor force, perhaps by weighing heavily in the numerical balance. But we are unable to ground this argument with quantitative data.

Secondly, we may now make some important distinctions about the impact of industrialization upon the labor force. Our strike data show that workers in some sectors of the economy were not subjected to the loss of professional identity and downgrading of artisanal skill commonly thought to follow from factory industrialization. We have specified these occupations and sectors precisely in the above pages, and need not review them here. Other jobs and trades, however, were radically transformed by mechanization, and by changes in the nature of industrial organization. The great metalworking section is a prime example, though shoemakers and hatters, among other crafts, come also to mind. Still other industries and trades were the creatures of factory industrialization, having been unknown and unneeded in the traditional economy. Here transport and chemicals may be mentioned.

Thus factory industrialization had three kinds of outcomes for the occupational structure: (1) the preservation of some traditional crafts by creating a new demand for their services and products; (2) the hollowing out of other traditional crafts through technological change; (3) the creation of entirely new, hitherto nonexistent occupations. A different mode of worker organization and collective action accompanied each end product of industrialization. In the preceding chapter we showed how each outcome had a singular type of organization; in the following section we demonstrate how each had a unique pattern of strike activity.

The character of strikes by occupation

Here is another good place for checking hypotheses. To remind the reader, we have thus far mounted two separate but connected arguments about the relationship among organization, technology and strike activity. In Chapter 7 we suggested that artisanal workers tend to form one kind of organization,

semi-skilled proletarians another. The former are embedded in a rich associational life and act collectively to defend prerogatives of job control
against employer challenges. The latter are organized, if at all, only loosely
by politicized sparkplug militants who lead their followers toward bread-
and-butter issues in shop-floor action, and towards radical *revendications*
in national political action.

Then (to further remind the reader of the argument's unfolding), we
claimed in the preceding section that industrialization affected craft labor
in different ways: technological change meant the hollowing out of some
crafts, a desperate but failed struggle for job control resulting in the artisan's
proletarianization. Other established crafts, however, escaped this fate,
either because technological change did not threaten their particular function, or because they managed to blunt its worst thrusts by retaining, in
one way or another, control over the job site. Still other occupations, some
skilled, some not, were called into existence by industrial growth; indeed
the major vertebrae of the modern economy were largely unheard of before
1850, at a time when the strike movement among artisanal groups was already under way, and their professional associations flourishing.

Both kinds of arguments converge to 'predict' the characteristics of a
craft's strikes at any given point in the process of industrialization. We need
know merely the antiquity of an occupation's organizational life, and the
extent to which mechanization and plant-size increases have endangered its
corporate solidarity. A more modest formulation might be that certain
aspects of conflict and worker cohesiveness within a craft around the turn of
the century appear to be dependent, first, on the presence of established corporate traditions and control within the craft, and second, on the extent to
which that craft has survived the dequalification that mechanization en-
tailed, escaping the dissolution of its professional identity that the subdivision of labor and the aggregation of the workforce into large industrial
plants brought with them.

We might expect to encounter during the *belle époque* – to somewhat
arbitrarily take a point midway in France's industrial transformation – three
different types of crafts and jobs, each with a distinctive pattern of conflict:

1. The craft survivors of industrialization. High levels of union involvement
   mark the disputes of such trades as printers and metalsmiths, a sign of
   organizational tradition. And because such workers are well organized
   their strikes tend to be long, for the strikers are able to hold out in an
   economic endurance contest, rather than folding quickly because solidarity crumbles or because the dispute was initially intended as only a
   symbolic protest. Craft workers who have met industrialization successfully need also pay little attention to shop organization issues, for the
   obvious reason that they already are running things pretty much to suit
   themselves, and instead concentrate on wages-and-hours issues. The
   reader will remember that this 'economism' characterized most disputes

in the July Monarchy, a time when craftsmen were virtually the only strikers. Finally, an absence of rancor should characterize the craft survivors' disputes with their employers, for both parties are agreed on the rules of the game; employer authority is not being challenged, nor worker control threatened. So the issues lack the emotionality running through strikes among the threatened crafts.

2. The threatened crafts. By 'threatened' we mean a prospective loss of job control and professional solidarity from mechanization and more generally from employer inroads upon traditional worker prerogatives. Like the craft survivors, such threatened crafts as hatters and moulders have behind them venerable guild and corporate traditions; unlike the successful crafts, however, they are losing the struggle with the capitalist employer, who tries to arrange shop-floor authority, technology and work patterns to serve the profitability of his firm. Such craft workers will be highly unionized, and like their above mentioned colleagues, will also engage in lengthy disputes. Yet unlike the successful artisans, these men will strike often over job control questions, and great bitterness will run through their conflicts, as evidenced by high rates of striker dismissals.

3. The new occupations. Recently arisen in consequence of industrial advance, the new industries and occupations lack entirely the historic traditions and habits of collective action that hold artisans together. Moreover, these workers face technologies and plants that are inherently disaggregating: machine-tending and large firm size are commonly, and rightly, thought in industrial sociology to inhibit small-group cohesion. We would expect strikes in chemical plants to be short, for two reasons: (a) because the solidarity born of sparkplug unionism is short-lived; the participants in a collective dispute quickly fall apart and drift back to work; (b) because the purpose of the dispute is to make a political protest, rather than to force the employer to concessions by outlasting him; and so such symbolic protests need not last long. A similar logic says that the new workers will be relatively unconcerned about job control issues, because they experience no loss of established powers and perquisites, and, what is more, see the hopelessness of advancing such demands. Finally, strikes within new occupations are distinguished by no especial acerbity on the shop floor, for the expectations of both workers and employers are that only bread-and-butter demands are legitimate (or advisable).[10] Thus, if the argument presented in these pages is correct,

(1) The strikes of craft workers who successfuly crossed the bar of industrialization will be:
– long
– well organized
– for bread-and-butter issues

–unemotional (in the visceral sense of threatened loss of authority and influence)

(2) The strikes of craft workers who ran aground on the bar will be:
–equally long
–equally well organized but
–for job control issues and, and therefore,
–embittered

(3) The strikes of new workers in both skilled and unskilled occupations of recent origin will be:
–short
–poorly organized
–for bread-and-butter issues
–unemotional

The period 1910–14 is one for which we have unusually fine information. Occupational differences in strikes during this five-year interval largely bear out these above-mentioned expectations. It would be appropriate to mute somewhat the ring of confidence in our 'predictions' because the assignment of various occupations to each of these three categories poses considerable difficulties. How do we know if an occupation possessed firmly established traditions, if it rode well the crest of industrialization or if its professional identity was hollowed out by rationalizing entrepreneurs?

The present paucity of monographic work in the area of occupational history makes answers to these questions highly speculative. The fact of the matter is that we know very little about what it was like to be a *serrurier* in 1920, or what vicissitudes over time the metalsmith's craft underwent. Nor is much known about any of the other major occupations in either the traditional or the modern economy; the dockers, the machine-builders, the masons, the shoe factory workers – all are blank spaces to date. Some work has been done here and there on isolated groups, such as the hatters or the railway engineers. But even the broad outlines of most occupational history still lie in darkness.

A few tentative guidelines have served us in taxonomizing. If a craft was mentioned in the *APO* survey as having had organizational experience before 1848, we considered it 'traditional.' And if, in 1910–14 the median size of its struck establishments was below seventy-five workers (or thereabouts) we considered it to have remained largely artisanal. Determining whether a craft had 'successfully' coped with industrialization posed more severe problems. It is general knowledge, for example, that the construction industry underwent before the First World War very little mechanization or organizational change. So in drawing on this variety of 'general knowledge' we could make some assignments. More precisely, if a craft managed to maintain its initial share of the sector's total strike activity, we considered it to have dealt on favorable terms with industrialization. Conversely, if a craft's share diminished greatly, that meant (to our way of thinking) that either its strike propensity was diminishing (a diminution that often accompanies organizational dissolution), or that its labor force was shrinking. Either occurrence points to a devastating encounter with industrial modernization. All this is to say that our categorization of 'craft survivors,' 'defensive crafts' and 'new occupations' is a hesitant one, subject to revision both by ourselves and other scholars as more exact information on occupational history becomes known.

Let us take several industrial sectors, and break down some of the occupations within each in terms of our three ideal types. The argument works with pleasing accuracy for some, less well for others; yet nowhere save in the construction industry does it fail to make some sense of an otherwise confusing, disorderly mass of facts about strikes.

Metalworking

Table 8.8 gives essential information on the strikes of four occupational groups within metalworking.

Table 8.8: *Some characteristics of strikes in metalworking, 1910–14*

	Metalsmiths (*serruriers*)	Moulders (*mouleurs*)	Small-shop *mécaniciens– constructeurs*
Number of strikers	34	90	140
Median duration (days)	7.2	9.6	6.1
% union present	88	89	85
Median strikers/100 workers in struck establishments	88	69	76
% worker organization issues	11	51	42
% strikes with workers fired	12	18	9.3
Median size of struck establishment	13	63	136

	Large-plant *mécaniciens– constructeurs*	Electricians	Metalworking total
Number of strikes	37	12	672
Median duration (days)	5.5	6.7	6.7
% union present	97	75	82
Median strikers/100 workers in struck establishment	30	35	67
% worker organization issues	28	47	37
% strikes with workers fired	0[a]	17	13
Median size of struck establishment	1,243	136	80

[a] The explanation for the absence of massive dismissals among strikers from large plants is, to some extent, obvious: with so many workers on strike, an employer would have to be Draconian indeed to fire two-thirds or more of them. Large-scale firings among smaller workforces, on the other hand, would be both politically and economically more feasible. This explanation partly accounts for the fact that 9 percent of strikes among small-shop *mécaniciens* ended in dismissal, whereas none did among large-shop *mécaniciens*.

SOURCE: Coding of *SG*.

–The metalsmiths (*serruriers*) exemplify a craft to have survived industrialization. Their median establishment size (establishments on strike, that is) in 1910–14 was only thirteen workers, and the trade managed to keep up its share of strikes within the sector as a whole from 1890 to 1935.

–Moulders and machine-builders were traditional occupations in serious trouble. New casting techniques were altering the moulders' *métier*, and the transformation of machine-building has been discussed above. Because in large establishments the term *mécanicien* seems merely to have been official jargon for 'machine-tender,' whereas in small establishments a *mécanicien* was probably a genuinely skilled machine-builder, we have considered *mécaniciens* in big plants to illustrate new, semi-skilled workers, and those in small plants to illustrate a traditional trade in trouble.

–Electricians were also new workers, yet skilled, as opposed to the semiskilled machine-tenders. Like the machine-tenders, however, the electricians were without benefit of an associational tradition.

How do the strikes of each differ in 1910–14? As expected, metalsmiths, moulders and small-shop *mécaniciens* had long disputes, electricians and large-shop machine-assemblers short ones (within the context of the sector; compared to dockers, electricians would appear to have struck interminably).

The artisanal workers were best-organized, for metalsmiths and moulders had high percentages of union participation in strikes; electricians low percentages; both varieties of *mécaniciens* had very high rates of union participation, and an astonishing 97 percent of all large-shop *mécaniciens*' strikes saw union engagement. After the First World War a deunionization process commenced among these big-plant workers, and in 1915–35 small-shop *mécaniciens* scored the highest union involvement rates.

The successful artisanal trades had the highest solidarity, the threatened ones the next highest, and the new trades the lowest – which is exactly as the argument says it should be. At the median, 88 percent of the metalsmiths joined strikes in progress in their establishments, 69 percent of the moulders, and 76 percent of the (presumably) artisanal *mécaniciens*. Yet only 30 percent of the large-shop *mécaniciens* and a very low 35 percent of the electricians went out when strikes took place in their establishments.

The struggle over job control was sharper in the threatened artisanal than in the successful artisanal trades. Only 11 percent of the metalsmiths' grievances concerned worker organization, whereas 51 percent of the moulders', and 42 percent of the small-shop *mécaniciens*' did so.[11] (The electricians, perhaps as a skilled trade, were also upset about job control questions, for 47 percent of their grievances aimed at such matters, whereas only 28 percent of the proletarian large-shop *mécaniciens'* grievances concerned job control.) The relative 'bitterness' of these disputes, as measured by the percentage of strikers fired, went in the predicted direction for the *mécaniciens* but not for the electricians.

The news from metalworking, therefore, is that the old artisanal trades were well organized and solidary, the new jobs that industrialization had called to life much less so. What men struck for reflected their varying perceptions of occupational community, and how long their strikes lasted showed possibly how effective their organization was, possibly on the other hand the extent to which they conceived of their strikes as an 'economic' action (as opposed to a political one) at all.

Textile production

The argument works perfectly for textiles in 1910–14, as the new industrial jobs go in the direction of sparkplug unionism for economic demands, the established artisanal ones cling bitterly to job control and occupational identity. The three test cases are:

– Ribbon weavers (*rubaniers*) and cloth printers (*imprimeurs sur étoffes*), both established artisanal occupations subject increasingly to mechanization and shop-floor reorganization. Both represent 'threatened' trades.

– Spinning mills exemplify, on the other hand, a new industry employing a semi-skilled workforce. Large spinning establishments had, of course, been around since the dawn of the industrial revolution, but few traditions of conflict seem to have been transmitted from one generation of factory spinners to the next.[12]

Table 8.9: *Some characteristics of strikes in textile production, 1910–14*

	Ribbon weavers (*rubaniers*)	Cloth printers (*imprimeurs sur étoffes*)	Spinning-mill workers (*ouvriers en filatures*)	Total textile production
Number of strikes	7	14	362	946
Median duration (days)	7.2	9.3	5.8	6.0
% union present	100	79	78	76
Median strikers/100 workers in struck establishments	52	68	51	60
% worker organization issues	71	29	22	24
% strikes with workers fired	14	14	3	3
Median size of struck establishment	117	77	228	173

SOURCE: Coding of *SG*.

Ribbon weavers and cloth printers were, as one would have expected, well organized, cotton spinners slightly less so (table 8.9). Median plant participation rates of both the trades were above (in one case marginally, in the other significantly) those of the industrial spinners. And both skilled trades had longer strikes than did the spinners. The struggle for job control burned considerably more fiercely in the ribbon-weaving and cloth-printing shops than in the spinning mills, for 71 percent of all ribbon weavers' grievances were over such matters, 29 percent of the cloth printers', but only 22 percent of the spinning workers'. And a much higher percentage of skilled strikes ended with the strikers' dismissal than did spinning mill strikes. Thus the hypothesis fits very neatly to textile production.

Leather–hides
The notion of differential consequences of industrialization permits us, similarly, to sort out occupational strike differences within leather and hides.

– Shoe factory workers (*ouvriers en chaussures*). Let us take factory shoe-making as an example of skilled craftsmen in trouble. Trained workers from a number of different crafts found employment in these factories, a measure of artisanal competence being required even on the industrial factory floor to cut and stitch together shoes. Coming from a craft tradition, these men were not really 'new' workers, but seem rather to have thought of themselves as artisans in duress.[13]

– Small-shop shoemakers and repairers (*cordonniers*), on the other hand, may count as craft survivors of industrialization, skilled workers who held their own against mechanization and female labor. The small shoe-makers maintained throughout their modest percentage of the sector's strikes, and in 1910–14 worked in little establishments (median size of struck firm, 15 workers).

The shoe factory workers were, in formal terms, better organized than the cobblers (90 percent of all strikes with unions versus 81 percent; see table 8.10). Yet the latter evidenced more solidarity in strikes, with a plant participation rate 83 percent at the median, as opposed to the shoe factories' 70 percent. Whatever the cause, small shoemakers had longer strikes (19 days at the median) than did the shoe factory workers (6 days). Most interestingly, the shoe factory workers were much more agitated about job control than the small shoemakers (35 percent of all grievances over worker organization matters compared to 10 percent for the small shoemakers). And shoe factory owners and managers were much more likely to fire insurgent strikers than were master–entrepreneur cobblers (8 percent of shoe factory strikes ended in firings; none of the cobblers' strikes did so).

Table 8.10: *Some characteristics of strikes in leather and hides, 1910–14*

	Shoe factory workers (*ouvriers en chaussures*)	Cobblers (*cordonniers*)	Leather–hides total
Number of strikes	83	16	216
Median duration (days)	6.2	19.1	8.3
% union present	90	81	86
Median strikers/100 workers in struck establishments	70	83	83
% worker organization issues	35	10	26
% strikes with workers fired	8	0	9
Median size of struck establishment	105	15	51

SOURCE: Coding of *SG*.

The comparison within leather–hides remains essentially incomplete, for we could not find a 'new' occupation with meaningful strike activity. Yet by and large the former artisans in the shoe factories and the small-shop shoe repairers and craftsmen behaved as they were supposed to.

The garment industry

An uncertainty about the exact course of events in the garment industry prevents hard-and-fast classifications for 1910–14, yet the following tentative judgments seem plausible:

– The tailors were threatened artisans, facing proletarianization in the sweatshops (median size of struck establishment, 17 workers).

– The hatters were likewise fundamentally artisanal, menaced by an inrush of female labor and by new felt-making processes[14] (median establishment size, 43 workers).

– The garment workers (*ouvriers en confection*) and related trades (*chemisières* etc.) were the true proletarians of the garment industry, with an unskilled, heavily female labor force and with no classic tradition of professional community to draw upon. In 1910–14 women were the majority in about half the trade's strikes. We consider the trade a 'new' one.

The advanced proletarianization of the artisanal trades by 1910–14 blurs the edges of what we have discovered in other sectors to be a neat pattern. Yet the outlines of differing strike profiles remain.

The two craft groups were more highly unionized than the garment

Table 8.11: *Some characteristics of strikes in the garment industry, 1910–14*

	Tailors (*tailleurs*)	Hatters (*chapeliers*)	Garment workers and allied trades (*ouvriers en confection*)	Garment industry total
Number of strikes	36	32	33	148
Median duration (days)	7.8	10.9	5.3	6.6
% union present	100	91	82	82
Median strikers/100 workers in struck establishments	57	82	63	68
% worker organization issues	18	34	41	30
% strikes with workers fired	19	22	15	19
Median size of struck establishment	17	43	118	39

SOURCE: Coding of *SG*.

workers, as table 8.11 reveals. This more thoroughgoing organization probably caused the crafts to have considerably longer strikes than the proletariat of garments and, among the hatters at least, produced high plant participation rates (strikers/100 workers employed in struck establishments).

It is an anomaly that the *ouvriers en confection* were more upset about job control issues than either skilled trade, for our argument would have predicted the reverse. Yet the two skilled occupations evidenced higher striker dismissal rates than did the garment proletariat, pointing to more heated clashes over authority issues among the skilled than the unskilled workers.

Other sectors

Two sectors – chemicals and transport – had arisen so recently in time that by 1910–14 they had not had opportunity to form organizational traditions, or to integrate their workforces within solidary professional communities. It is gratifying that strikes in these sectors show the characteristics that our model calls for in newly arisen occupations.

Table 8.12 presents the results for two segments of the transport sector – dockers and tramway workers. Although unions were heavily involved in these disputes, they appeared to have little real efficacy in mobilizing the workers. Plant participation rates were but middling in 1910–14, and worker organization issues of secondary importance (compared at least to the bulk such matters assumed within some of the declining crafts we have reviewed above). Most important, strikes in both occupations were extremely short. To be sure, such brevity may mirror as much the pressures the community placed upon these strategically situated workers for settlement as the strikers' inability to hold out. Yet somewhere in these 'quickie' strikes lay

Table 8.12: *Some characteristics of strikes: other industries, 1910–14*

	Dockers	Tramways	Transport total	Chemicals total	Semi-skilled manufacturing (*ouvriers en* . . .)
Number of strikes	249	35	660	157	339
Median duration (days)	2.4	3.3	3.1	3.4	4.3
% union present	86	86	81	56	54
Median strikers/ 100 workers in struck establishments	70	66	70	65	66
% worker organization issues	25	24	23	28	25
% strikes with workers fired	5	0	9	9	9
Median size of struck establishment	73	209	52	144	87

SOURCE: Coding of *SG*.

an element of symbolic political protest – a hallmark of new proletarian conflicts that was absent in most varieties of artisanal strike. Few strikers were fired in the transport sector, a further characteristic of strikes of new occupations, where authority questions were much less likely to embitter shop-floor relations. (The workers had no authority over anything, pure and simple, and furthermore did not expect to acquire any.)

Strikes in chemicals, another new sector, took on during 1910–14 much the cast of transport disputes: very brief, low plant participation rates, small degree of unionization. As our argument calls for, they had a middling proportion of grievances devoted to worker organization questions, and a low percent of strikes ending disastrously with the strikers out of jobs.

Finally, to demonstrate the singularity of strikes within newly arisen manufacturing occupations, let us lump together all strikes whose perpetrators are identified as *ouvriers en* . . ., *ouvriers du* . . . or some counterpart formulation indicating laborers who themselves possess no trained artisanal competence, but rather make their living by tending machines or performing other varieties of semi-skilled labor. (*Fonderies* and *confections* have been excluded from this category.)

Those workers whom the *SG* is able to identify only in terms of the goods they produced participated in the most underorganized, ineffectual strikes of all (339 in number):

– only 54 percent of strikes with union involvement;

– a low 66 percent of the affected workers participating in the typical strike;

–Median duration of only 4.3 days (compared to durations of craft strikes almost invariably above 7 days);

–25 percent of the grievances over worker organization issues, the same level as in transport or chemicals;

–Median plant size (of struck plants): 87 workers, which means that this ineffectuality is not necessarily the result of working in a large plant.

There is one major piece of bad news for the case we wish to make. Not one of our hypotheses about declining artisanry or proletarian workers of recent origin applies to the construction and building materials industry. Perhaps the institution of citywide bargaining within construction, or the curious location of tile and brick factories in outlying places, intervenes in some unanticipated way between the exigencies of technology, organization and the pattern of strikes. It is superfluous to present construction industry data here. Suffice it to say that we make no claims to having clarified disputes in that sector.

The larger message to emerge from this occupation-by-occupation comparison is that contemporary observers erred who expected great solidarity from modern industrial workers, and hoped from them in vain especially intense fury against oppressing employers. It was the craftworkers, men involved in a basically premechanization technology and in premodern modes of industrial organization, who were most solidary in their collective action. And it was the craftworkers threatened by industrialization whose animosity against their employers was most intense.

To review, craftworkers were moved more by formal worker unions to strike, or at least guided more by the union in the course of the dispute itself, than industrial workers. A higher percentage of craftworkers than industrial workers would turn out in the affected establishments. Craft strikers were customarily more concerned about questions of apprenticeship, hiring–firing prerogatives, being respectfully addressed, and similar 'job control' matters than industrial workers (who accepted with glum resignation the authoritarian work rules and overweening power of the employer). And craftworkers – both those who coped successfully with industrialization and those who went under – were more likely to be fired from their jobs in the bitter recrimination of a small-shop, artisanal conflict.

We do not wish to be understood as saying that proletarians were 'disorganized,' cursed with the disaffiliation and disaggregation that some scholars believe accompany rapid industrial advance. We prefer instead to argue, as we did in the last chapter and shall again in the next, that new proletarian industrial workers found the urban neighborhood the friendliest setting for their burgeoning associational endeavors. They went to the Bourse du travail, and later the neighborhood cells of the PCF, rather than attempting collective action at the shop-floor level against individual employers. In fact, they saw quite accurately that their best chances lay in action against the state itself.

How establishment size matters

This book reinforces the need for a reexamination of the conventional wisdom on large-scale enterprise and worker militancy. In previous sections we suggested *en passant* that big plants might sooner cripple than stimulate worker 'class-consciousness' and willingness to engage in collective action. And we hinted that the most furious forum of conflict might well be the small shop, not the industrial colossus. Richard F. Hamilton has raised this issue for the French working classes in the 1950s, concluding that the most alienated, antagonistic workers are those in small shops in provincial towns. And Geoffrey K. Ingham has recently argued for England that large-scale enterprise encourages individualistic behavior from workers, who find themselves more interested in personal economic gains through intensive labor at good piece rates than in group solidarity against an oppressive employer class.[15] In this section we address squarely the question of how big plants affect worker militancy

A straightforward answer comes in two parts: (1) large plants greatly boost the *propensity* to strike; (2) such plants, on the other hand, enervate worker solidarity and organizational capacity. Large plants, in other words, promote frequent strikes, but ensure that such strikes, once off the ground, will be poorly organized and relatively unsuccessful.

Table 8.13 presents strike propensities for various kinds of enterprises in 1915–35, expressed as the number of strikes per 100,000 establishments of a given size and strikers per 100,000 workers. It is immediately clear that strike

Table 8.13: *Strike and striker rates for various sizes of industrial establishments, 1915–35*

Establishment size	Average annual number of strikes per 100,000 establishments	Average annual number of strikers per 100,000 workers
1–10 workers	4	300
11–20	184	2,212
21–100	872	2,238
+100	2,800	6,856

NOTES
Data on establishment size were taken from the 1921 census, which provided information on both the numbers of establishments of various sizes, and the numbers of workers employed in them. The category +100 was the top of the scale, and so we have been forced to use it, instead of our customary +500 workers, as the threshold of truly large firms.
Agriculture and transport are excluded.

intensity is a smooth function of establishment size, for the rates ascend at an even pace as establishment size rises. The same is true for striker rates, save that the middle range flattens out.

In every industry except food in 1915–35 strike propensity rose steadily with establishment size: the larger the establishment, the higher the strike rate. (Food's establishment-specific strike rate peaks at the size class 21–100, presumably the work of all those militant small-shop bakers' helpers.) The same linearity prevailed at the departmental level. In every department except the Loire-Atlantique and the Yonne, the largest establishments had the highest strike rates, the smallest, the lowest, with smooth gradations in between. The fact that almost nowhere did local territorial or industrial peculiarities override this steady relationship suggests the powerful impact of scale of enterprise upon willingness to stop work in protest.

A correlational analysis at the level of the department–industry (data for each industry within each department) complements our view of the impact of establishment size upon strike propensity. Fairly strong correlations, as such things go, emerge between the distribution of large establishments and the distribution of strikes in the early twenties, and again in the early thirties. If we correlate the number of strikes in each department–industry unit with the number of large ($+100$ workers) establishments, and then partial for the total non-agricultural labor force to eliminate spurious 'scale' effects, we get the following first-order correlations:[16]

> Strikes in 1920–4 correlated with number of large establishments in 1921, $r = .30$
>
> Strikes in 1929–32 correlated with number of large establishments in 1931, $r = .31$

The stability of the association of the two different time periods inspires confidence, and confirms what the study of establishment-specific strike rates has already suggested about the interrelationship between the two variables.

But what bearing does establishment size have upon how *well* workers strike, as opposed to how often they do so? Here the large establishments fare poorly. Table 8.14 helps us review the differing characteristics of strikes in large versus small establishments, and their relative change over time. ('Large' means more than 500 workers; 'small' means all smaller establishments.)

A dramatic shift in formal organization occurred between the prewar and interwar years. Before the First World War, large plants had significantly higher levels of union involvement than small plants. (As we saw in the preceding section, once skill level is controlled for, this relationship would probably reverse itself, even before the First World War.) It was probably the skilled workers in the big factories who were responsible for

Table 8.14: *Differences in strike characteristics by establishment size*
(large = +500 workers; small = −500 workers)

	1895–9	1910–14	1915–35
% of strikes with union involvement[a]			
Large	64 (0.4)	84 (2)	(5)
Small	54 (2)	74 (2)	(9)
Duration (days)			
Large	5.2	4.6	4.7
Small	4.9	5.6	6.2
Median strikers/100 workers in struck establishment[b]			
Large	18 (55)	10 (42)	21
Small	47 (71)	57 (73)	67
% of grievances on worker organization issues			
Large	25	28	18
Small	18	23	10
% of strikes ending with at least ⅔ of strikers replaced			
Large	6	4	3
Small	13	10	5
% of strikes ending in failure (*échec* + replaced)			
Large	42	52	51
Small	45	46	38

[a] In parentheses is the percent of strikes mentioned in the *SG* 'remarks' column.

[b] The plant participation rates in parentheses include in the denominator the labor force of the specific craft on strike, whenever a craft strike occurred within a large industrial plant. In such cases, the workforce of the plant as a whole is excluded from the denominator. After 1919 *SG* discontinued reports of the number of workers in the craft actually on strike, whenever there were craft strikes within factories.

the high unionization levels of such places in, say, the 1910–14 period. After the war, however, the large plants deunionize and the small ones increase their unionization rates, so that things are exactly turned about: in 1915–35 strikes in small shops witnessed higher levels of union participation than did strikes in big plants. Previous discussions of occupational versus communal strike waves, and interindustry changes in formal unionization have prepared us for this finding. Here it is nailed down.

Yet once the question of formal union participation in strikes is placed aside, by every other index of solidarity and 'tension,' small shops staged more solidary, more effective strikes than large ones, at all periods of our study.

–Duration. Table 8.14 shows further that small-shop strikes lasted longer than large factory strikes. And in fact the duration of disputes in big plants dropped somewhat over the years, whereas the duration of small-shop disputes *rose*, so that in 1915–35 strikes in large plants lasted 4.7 days at the median, those in small firms 6.2 days. One might take this as further evidence of a turn of heavy industrial proletarian workers away from endurance encounters with employers and towards symbolic political protest strikes.

– Plant participation rates (strikers/100 workers in struck establishments). Small shops scored considerably higher on this index of worker solidarity than did large factories. Clearly proletarians in the dark satanic mill did not think of themselves at all as a 'homogeneous mass,' else they would have acted more in unison.

– Percent of grievances on worker organization issues. Here we must confess to puzzlement, for contrary to our expectations, large-shop workers evidenced more concern about job control issues, hiring–firing questions and the like than did small-shop workers.[17] If the analysis of the preceding part holds true, the precise big-factory workers making these demands were artisans drawn into factories who found plant managers threatening cherished privileges and perquisites at every turn. Genuine proletarians within the big plants were probably less concerned about such questions. Yet we have no sure way of verifying this suspicion.

– Percentage of strikes ending with strikers replaced. At any point in time strikers in small shops were about twice as likely to be fired from their jobs as those in large plants. The dismissal rate for both sizes of firms declined steadily from 1895–9 to 1915–35, yet the relative relationship stayed constant. What does this result mean? To some extent, the difference in rates reflects merely the political and economic difficulties a large-plant manager would face in firing large numbers of strikers: the prefect would presumably complain, and replacing so many workers would be troublesome. Yet even after this element has been discounted, we believe the differences in dismissal rates reflect genuine differences in the acerbity of conflict. Workers in large plants were less likely to see themselves as directly challenging or opposing the management of the firm, and more likely to think of their dispute as a symbolic gesture aimed at impressing political authorities within the community or national polity as a whole. Small-shop strikers, on the other hand, probably imagined themselves more to be confronting the master–entrepreneur of the shop, an employer who was likely to respond venomously to this assault upon his authority by firing the insurgents.

– Percentage of strikes ending in failure (*échec* proper plus fired). Although in 1895–9 large-plant strikes fared slightly better than small ones in outcome, thereafter the small firms' strikes saw happier conclusions. Especially in 1915–35 only 38 percent of small-shop strikes ended in failure, while 51 percent of large-shop strikes did so. One might argue that this 1915–35 result is further evidence of the weakness of the worker movement in large-scale, mechanized industry between the wars, therewith further enlightenment about the sources of the Popular Front. We have here something of a chicken–egg problem: were the workers indifferent to serious shop-floor action because they saw their strikes as basically political posturing, or were they forced to politics in 1936 as a result of failed but seriously intentioned shop-floor actions? We prefer to emphasize the former alternative, although there is truth in the latter, and to see the strikes of the 1920s as a continuation and elaboration of a thrust to political action long inherent in the worker movement.

The large plant was thus ill suited as a place of collective action or enduring association; the small shop, with its emotional rivalries and natural benefits to worker cohesiveness, was a much superior incubator of solidarity.[18] Yet while we understand the linkages between establishment size and strike *character*, we are still uncertain about exactly how the large scale of enterprise produces a high *propensity* to strike. Our data permit us to go little beyond the received wisdom on wildcat strikes: the sudden eruption of angry resentment on the part of workers without authority or influence.[19] This received wisdom probably has a kernel of truth to it, for big-plant strikes had all the qualities imputed to wildcat strikes to a greater extent than did small-plant strikes: they were more frequent, shorter and less well organized.

This popular conception of the wildcat strike may be slightly modified, however, by a conclusion of a foregoing chapter on strike waves. Even though the sullen proletarians who suddenly throw down their tools and stamp off the job floor are without the benefit of preplanning or formal union leadership, they will likely find themselves in an area where traditions of conflict and group action are of long standing. In all probability such strikes will not take place in big plants recently arisen in areas where no such traditions are to be found. Thus it must not be forgotten that the influence the large plant itself exerts upon collective action may be intertwined with the influence of the locality in which the plant is situated.

To say that large establishments help, at any given point in time, to promote high strike frequencies is not at all the same thing as saying that an increase over time in industrial concentration produces an immediate increase in the strike rate. In Chapter 10 we shall propose a counterpart argument for urbanization: although residence in a large city promotes strike activity, living in a rapidly *growing* city, or better yet, moving to such a city, does not; indeed sudden increases in population *impede* strikes. While rising establishment size does not necessarily hinder militancy, it does not in the short run stimulate it either.

The likely course of industrial concentration in France during the nine-

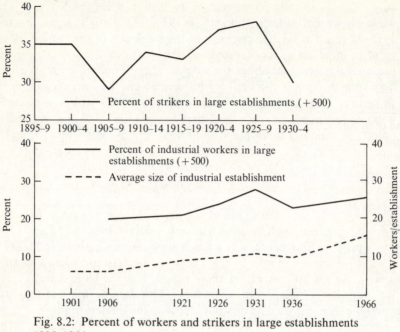

Fig. 8.2: Percent of workers and strikers in large establishments
1895–1966

NOTES

1901–6
Data are from Statistique générale de la France, *Résultats statistiques du recensement générale de la population* ... 4 Mars 1906 (Paris: Imprimerie nationale, 1910), vol. 1, part 2, pp. 117–24. Establishments with 1 or more *salarié* are included, as are industrial sectors 3 (*industries extractives*), 4 (*industrie*), and 9B (*services publics industriels*).

1921–36
Information is from R. C. Marchand, 'La Concentration du personnel dans les entreprises en France entre les deux guerres,' *Bulletin de la statistique générale de la France* (Jan.–March 1945), pp. 77–100, esp. pp. 95–8. The data are for establishments with one or more employees and concern *ensemble des industries* only, excluding *transport, commerce–banques* and *professions liberales*.

1966
Data are from the *Annuaire statistique*, 1969, pp. 646–7. We have taken as 'industrial' nomenclature codes 06–67. Data concern *salariés* in establishments with more than one employee. As far as we know, the 1901–6, 1921–36 and 1966 data are comparable.

teenth century was towards powerful increase; in the twentieth century, however, the rate at which workers were agglomerated into large plants slowed, for as fig. 8.2 demonstrates, little change took place in the percentage of the workforce in large establishments between 1906 and 1921; then between 1921 and 1931 a swift acceleration occurred in the pace of concentration; the Depression saw a falling off in the scale of enterprise; then since the Second World War industrial concentration has resumed a slow march upwards.

The concentration of the strike movement within large establishments has followed a roughly similar course. In the July Monarchy most disputes – though the exact proportion must remain indeterminate – occurred in small shops. Yet by 1895–9, when data first become available (fig. 8.2), already 35 percent of all strikers found themselves employed in big factories. This percentage underwent the same 1905–29 rise that industrial concentration experienced, and both the concentration of strikes and of industry diminished during the Depression. The sudden dip of striker concentration during 1905–9 is probably attributable to the sudden involvement of many hitherto unengaged small establishments in strike activity, an activation that seems to have radiated from the strike wave of 1906, which carried the message of militancy more powerfully than ever before to the industrial hinterland. Yet the roughly parallel movement between the percentage of strikers in large plants and the growth of such plants themselves is not at all evidence that an increase in the scale of enterprise accelerated the strike *rate*.

It is true that, cross-sectionally, large establishments tend to produce high strike frequency and short duration – both hallmarks of post-1945 strikes. May we therefore argue that increases in the scale of enterprise have been the main cause of the transformation of strike activity? A correlational analysis says that rising establishment size was neither responsible for decreasing the duration of strikes, nor for increasing their frequency. First, let us take the relationship between change over time in industrial concentration and the change in strike activity. Information on establishment sizes at the department–industry level exists for 1921 and 1931. Did a change in the number of large establishments in each industry within each department tend to produce a corresponding change in the number of strikes at that level? The answer (after partialing for changes in the non-agricultural labor force) is no. A first-order correlation of 0.03 exists between the two variables, which is so low as to be not worth considering. The absence of a correlation says that in those industries where establishment size did increase, strike activity did not necessarily move either up or down; the same for industries where industrial concentration diminished. In other words: no relationship. Would the same lack of association appear after the Second World War, or before the First World War? Aggregate census data give us no way of knowing. The more general question remains open whether changes in strike propensity are related to changes in the scale of enterprise.

The same lack of a relationship prevails for changes in establishment size and changes in duration between 1921 and 1931 at the department–industry level. Duration did not decline in those areas and industries where concentration advanced during the twenties, which suggests that changes in industrial structure were not responsible for whatever foreshadowing of the dramatic post-Second World War decrease in strike duration occurred in the 1920s.

In addition to the two dimensions of 'industrialization' we have already explored – changes in industrial organization and technology (skilled versus semi-skilled), and changes in the scale of enterprise (large factory versus small shop) – there exists a third: the sheer growth of the workforce in mining and manufacturing. Did the social changes and dislocations that accompanied the massive movement into industry somehow stimulate conflict? Was the process of labor-force growth itself, through some mechanism of dislocation or marginality stemming from the act of migration, important in elevating strike rates? The answer, essentially, is no.

The question may be answered through correlations of change over time. What we have done, in a lengthy correlational analysis that shall not be reproduced here because it is so boring, is to see if a change from one census year to the next in the number of workers in each industry within each department (excluding agriculture, transport and the tertiary sector) produced a corresponding change in the strike rate. We took a number of different time periods, observing for each of them (1896–1906, 1896–1911, 1906–11, 1921–6, 1921–31, 1926–31 and 1896–1926) the strike activity surrounding the first and the last year in the period. Was there evidence of a department–industry-level correlation between changes in the size of the labor force and changes in the frequency of the strikes? For no period did we discover any but the most uninteresting relationships. Moreover, the signs on most of these low correlations were negative, indicating that if the two variables moved in association at all, it was inversely.

In this chapter we have examined the impact of industrialization upon strike activity from several different aspects. Perhaps three points need be emphasized in conclusion.

First, industrialization quite obviously affects the strike by transforming the working-class population from which strikes are drawn. Old occupations go under as their products and services are no longer required or are incorporated under new titles in factories. New occupations arise, unknown in the traditional economy yet great sites of strike activity in the modern. Still other occupations are transmuted, so that the same job titles remain, but the strikers bearing them are workers with very different kinds of skills who labor in modern factories and belong to newly arisen organizations. All this has long been known, and indeed is just a matter of common sense. Yet often forgotten amidst the standard application of common sense to working-class history is that a number of important occupations survive industrialization unscathed, and it is these occupations that constitute the organizational backbone for the working classes in the first stages of their political mobilization.

Second, industrialization transforms the nature of strike activity by creating a new organizational base, and by fixing the eyes of the strikers upon new, explicitly political, objectives. A constant thread in the argument has been how the unions and solidarity patterns of proletarian industrial workers differ from those of traditional artisanal workers, and how semi-skilled machine-assemblers appear to have quite different purposes in mind as they go on strike than do craftsmen. These organizational and ambitional differences show up in such basic characteristics of conflict as union representation, duration, plant-level solidarity and the form of bargaining with the employer.

Third, however industrialization accelerates strike frequencies, it does *not* appear to do so by creating instability, dislocation or marginality within a workforce subject to swift industrial advance. In the next three chapters we shall look more carefully at a set of arguments that predict alienation and hostility towards the surrounding social order among workers who have been wrenched from their peasant or artisanal roots and thrust suddenly in large clumps into the dark satanic mill. We have been unable to detect any correlation at all between the rate of *change* in the size of the labor force or in the number of large establishments – two reasonable proxies for industrialization – and the incidence of strike activity, a proxy for 'hostility' and 'alienation' that many social disorganization theorists have themselves adopted.

It thus appears that industrial growth increases strike activity through two complementary mechanisms: (1) by concentrating masses of workers within the same municipality, indeed within the same enterprise, for as we saw large plants have high strike rates, and we shall shortly discover that large cities do so as well; (2) by changing the very nature of organization itself, making of worker associations politicized, bureaucratized giants whose legs span the nation-state and whose actions are tied closely to the central political arena; the 'sparkplug' locals of these militant organizations strike often – though not well – because they are laced into an ongoing struggle for power. So the answer to the question whether industrialization stimulates strikes is no, not unless it first grips and modifies the capacity of the workers to organize themselves.

9   Territorial differences in strike activity

If the immediate organizational conditions of work and of workers explain differences among industries in the extent and form of conflict, and if those conditions change unevenly throughout the country as a whole, we should find important variations from place to place in the level of industrial conflict. If the differences among industries we have already identified are the *only* factors at work, of course, the map of industrial conflict will represent nothing but the varying industrial mixes of different cities and regions. But we have already encountered some reasons for thinking that the locality itself makes a difference: the clustering of strikes in different industries in the same city at the same time, the exceptional contribution of already active centers of industrial conflict to strike waves, the unevenness of unionization, the influence of the Bourse du travail and other more scattered pieces of evidence. We need to get the geographic pattern straight, and then scrutinize some of its possible explanations.

In this chapter and the next we will emphasize the descriptive part of the job. Here we will work on the distribution of strikes by department and region, with no more than passing proposals for explanations of the patterns that turn up. In the following chapter we will close in on the individual city, again spending most of our effort on describing the geography of strikes accurately. Two chapters hence we will finally take a systematic look at possible explanations of the geographic patterns – our own and other people's.

The distribution of strikes by territory

Most strikes took place within a small number of communities and departments, especially, as one would expect, in those having the largest numbers of industrial workers and manufacturing plants. In this section we look at the localities contributing the largest bulk of strikes and strikers. Our procedure will be to sketch briefly the principal changes over time in the territorial distribution of strikes, and then to examine the components of strike activity in the major regions of conflict during a single span of time.

As a start, we shower the reader with maps. Seven basic maps make clear

236

the principal components in the national aggregates of conflict, and their geographical change over the years:

Map 9.1: Distribution of strikes by department, 1830–47
Map 9.2: Distribution of strikes by department, 1890–1914
Map 9.3: Distribution of strikes by department, 1915–35
Map 9.4: Distribution of strikes by region, 1915–35
Map 9.5: Distribution of strikes by region, 1960–4
Map 9.6: Distribution of strikers by department, 1890–1914
Map 9.7: Distribution of strikers by department, 1915–35

What may be learned about shifts in the sheer volume of strike activity over the decades from these maps?

The period 1830–47 (map 9.1) is the point of departure. The strike movement surfaced first in seven clearly delineated regions: the Nord, upper and lower Normandy, upper Alsace, Brittany and the west, the area around Lyon, the Mediterranean coast southwest from Marseille and the Paris region. In between these narrow concentrations, wide expanses of territory were virtually untouched by conflict during the July Monarchy: the northeast and southwest provinces (save Marseille), and eastern Brittany. So at its outset the movement was territorially confined, an affair of a few people in a few places.

By 1890–1914 a substantial territorial dispersion of strikes had taken place and many more departments made sizable contributions to the national totals than during the July Monarchy. Yet, except for Normandy, the regions we noted in 1830–47 maintained their traditional identity. By 1914 the departments of Nord, Pas-de-Calais, Somme and Seine-Maritime had come to constitute a clearly delineated cluster, while strike activity in lower Normandy had faded. In the east the rump of an Alsace–Lorraine region continued to exist in Vosges and Meurthe-et-Moselle. The Breton region had by 1914 extended itself west to Brest. The Lyon region had expanded to embrace Grenoble and Roanne. The Mediterranean region had grown southwest to the Aude. And the grip of Paris had reached west to the Seine-et-Oise, where the first links in the Red Belt were being forged. Thus eighty years after the July Monarchy we encounter growth and expansion of conflict, but little fundamental change.

Again in 1915–35 we see this six-part regional structure, now unnecessary to reiterate. Normandy, the seventh region in 1830–47, had by this time faded from view. Since 1890–1914 some modifications in the scope of each region had occurred, to be sure, such as a lessening of the west's contribution, and an augmenting of the northeast's share by the return of the lost provinces and by a new access of militancy in the Aube. Yet no substantial alterations appeared during these years.

Limited postwar time series and the use of the region as the unit of reporting make it difficult to determine whether these patterns persisted after the Second World War. Maps 9.4 and 9.5 suggest that they did. Of the six northeastern provinces in the bottom third of the scale 1915–35, five continued in that humble position after the war. (Only Champagne had ascended into the middle third of the scale.) Of the four provinces of central France to rank in the bottom third during 1915–35, three remained there after the war. (Only the Center had climbed to a middling position.) The apparent decline of strike activity in Languedoc may be an artifact, for the government ceased to record agricultural strikes in the 1950s. What other changes? The years 1960–4 saw vigorous strike activity in the Midi-Pyrénées, probably among the new Toulousain industries, though present data make it impossible to say. And the western heavy industrial provinces of Pays de la Loire and Haute Normandie slid from top to middling positions. The highly aggregated postwar figures doubtless conceal numerous small-scale shifts, yet department-level data might also leave such movements unrecorded. All in all, maps 9.1 to 9.7 reveal few dramatic changes in the territorial composition of French strike activity over the last century and a half.

It is worth reflecting for a moment why this is so. The last century and a half have witnessed stunning overturns in the structure of industry, the ongoing rise and decline of entire industrial sectors over wide reaches of territory. Yet the geographical components of conflict remain essentially familiar, the six regions with centerpoints of Paris, Nantes, Lyon, Marseille etc. This suggests that traditions of industrial conflict themselves represent a force of enormous momentum in shaping the collective action of a working-class population. If people strike in a place, it is partly because their fathers and grandfathers also struck, or because they find themselves in a community with firmly rooted conflictual institutions and with collective mentalities of ancient pedigree. If people strike, it is not solely because they are boilermakers or machine-assemblers or masons, though the structure of their jobs may limit or shape the exact forms their collective action assumes. It is also because they are enmatrixed in a certain kind of community with certain acquired habits of joint action.

Let us examine the territorial components of the strike movement more closely during a single slice of time, pinning down for each of the six regions the communes and industrial sectors contributing the most strikes and strikers to the national totals. The years 1915–35 will serve as the period of observation, because before 1915 the striker movement had not yet spread to its fullest extension and because after 1935 suitable data for a cross-sectional analysis are lacking.

How geographically concentrated was the strike movement? All together, 1915–35 saw strikes occur in some 2,854 different communes. Yet one-third of all strikes (5,200 of 15,500) took place in just fifteen communes. And nearly one-half of all participants in strikes (47 percent, or 2,496,000 strikers out of 5,333,000 strikers identifiable by commune in all France) found them-

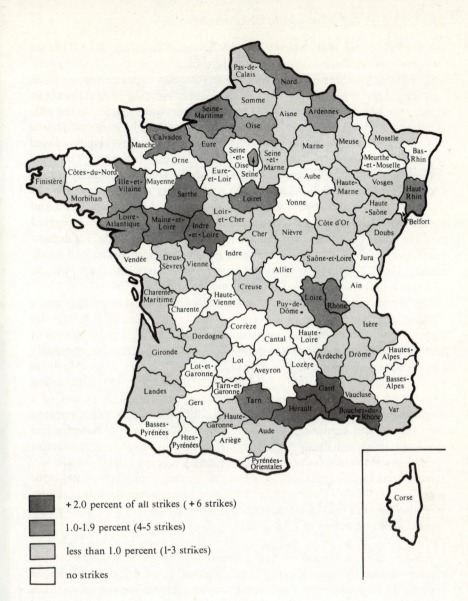

Map 9.1: Distribution of strikes by department, 1830–47

+ 2.0 percent of all strikes (+ 6 strikes)

1.0-1.9 percent (4-5 strikes)

less than 1.0 percent (1-3 strikes)

no strikes

Corse

Map 9.2: Distribution of strikes by department, 1890–1914

Map 9.3: Distribution of strikes by department, 1915–35

NORD

HAUTE
NORMANDIE

PICARDIE

BASSE
NORMANDIE

ALSACE

BRETAGNE

RÉGION
PARISIENNE

LORRAINE

CHAMPAGNE

PAYS DE LA LOIRE

CENTRE

FRANCHE-
COMPTÉ

BOURGOGNE

LIMOUSIN

POITOU-
CHARENTES

RHÔNE-ALPES

AUVERGNE

AQUITAINE

PROVENCE-
CÔTE D'AZUR

LANGUEDOC

MIDI-PYRÉNÉES

CORSE

+5 percent of all strikes

3.0 - 4.9

less than 3.0

Map 9.4: Distribution of strikes by region, 1915–35

+5 percent of all strikes

3.0 - 4.9

less than 3.0

NORD

HAUTE
NORMANDIE

PICARDIE

BASSE
NORMANDIE

ALSACE

RÉGION
PARISIENNE

LORRAINE

BRETAGNE

CHAMPAGNE

FRANCHE-
COMPTÉ

PAYS DE LA LOIRE

CENTRE

BOURGOGNE

POITOU-
CHARENTES

LIMOUSIN

RHÔNE-ALPES

AUVERGNE

AQUITAINE

PROVENCE-
CÔTE D'AZUR

LANGUEDOC

MIDI-PYRÉNÉES

CORSE

Map 9.5: Distribution of strikes by region, 1960–4

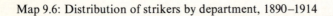

Map 9.6: Distribution of strikers by department, 1890–1914

Map 9.7: Distribution of strikers by department, 1915–35

+ 2.0 percent of all strikers

1.0-1.9

less than 1.0

selves in these fifteen cities. These figures point to a high degree of territorial concentration.

Five of those fifteen communes were in the department of the Nord: Lille, Roubaix, Dunkerque, Halluin and Tourcoing together represented 6 percent of all strikes in France and 10 percent of all strikers. Two of the fifteen were in the Seine-Maritime: le Havre and Rouen, piling up smaller shares of the national total. A further seven communes within the top fifteen were located away from the industrial northwest: Marseille in the Bouches-du-Rhône, Bordeaux in the Gironde, Nantes in the Loire-Atlantique, St-Etienne in the Loire, Limoges in the Haute-Vienne and Strasbourg in the Bas-Rhin. The preponderant share among the fifteen was held, of course, by Paris. The City of Light alone (not counting its Seine suburbs) contributed 14 percent of all strikes and 19 percent of all strikers in 1915–35.

How had concentration among communes changed over the years? It was the period 1848 to 1914 that witnessed most dispersion of strike activity to hitherto passive communes. By the end of the First World War just about all the municipalities that were going to experience militancy had already done so. From post-1895 commune-level data we can see the opening up of ever more places to strike activity. In 1895–9 some 749 different communes had strikes, a number which almost doubled to 1,497 by 1910–14. But by 1925–9 a decline had taken place, so that only 1,319 different municipalities experienced strikes. Thus there was no additional territorial diffusion after the First World War, and indeed by the late twenties an ebbing of militancy from some hinterland places.

The *concentration* of strikes in communes, as opposed to the sheer number of communes experiencing strikes, changed little over the period of which we coded commune-level data. To be sure, by 1910–14 a slightly larger share of the nation's total strike activity took place within a slightly smaller number of municipalities than in 1895–9. The territorial concentration of strik*ers* was in 1925–9 a bit less than in 1910–14, though that of strikes was the same. None of these movements are dramatic, and we are not prepared to offer explanations of this alternation of dispersal and accumulation. Whatever concentration of conflict did take place in the prewar period was probably the result of Paris's steady gains on the total. The inequality curves on which these conclusions rest are insufficiently interesting to warrant space here.[1]

Let us review the principal industries and municipalities involved in strikes, using as a departure point department-level data. A look at map 9.3 will introduce the reader to the distribution of conflict. The black-colored departments are those with 2 percent or more of the national total of strikes in 1915–35, those gray-colored had between 1 and 2 percent, and those left blank less than 1 percent of all strikes. Map 9.7 is the same thing for strikers in 1915–35. These black-colored departments had 55 percent of all strikes in 1915–35, and the gray departments a further 17 percent. Thus the territories we single out for special mention in the following pages represented a total of 72 percent of the strike movement. And the black and gray departments in map 9.7 had together 78 percent of all strikers in 1915–35 (the black ones 65 percent of all strikers, the gray 13 percent).

A. Northern France. As map 9.3 demonstrates, the four departments of the Nord, Pas-de-Calais, Somme and Seine-Maritime had in 1915–35 a massive concentration of disputes. What cities and sectors figured most prominently in this region?

In Flanders and Artois we are talking essentially about textiles and mining. Textile strikers added up to 60 percent of the Nord's total, and coalminers to 85 percent of the Pas-de-Calais's total strikers in 1915–35. So numerous were the industrial workers of the Nord that even industries of lesser importance in that department's strike aggregate had, in absolute terms, large numbers of strikes and participants. Strikes in Nord's food industries, for example, while only 2 percent of the department's total, represented 12 percent of all food strikes in France. Similar ratios prevailed for Nord's chemicals, mining and metal production industries.

Unlike many other departments, however, Nord strikes were spread amongst small industrial towns. Lille itself had only 14 percent of the Nord's strikes, and 21 percent of its strikers. Among other communities to figure prominently were Roubaix, Tourcoing, Halluin and Armentières, all spinning and weaving towns around Lille. Compared to these, the other mining, metalworking and textile centers in the Nord (save transportation industries in Dunkerque) pale into insignificance, yet in absolute terms had considerable levels of conflict; la Gorgue, Denain, Hautmont, Comines, Douai, Wattrelos, Jeumont – the list would ultimately encompass 23 industrial towns in the Nord each of which had at least 16 strikes between 1919 and 1935, an average of one a year. Only 116 towns in France had 16 or more strikes in that period. Only 12 towns in the whole country had in fact one strike every year between 1919 and 1935, and four of them – Lille, Tourcoing, Roubaix and Halluin – were in the Nord.

The Somme knew mainly textile strikes, centered more in Amiens (27 percent of all Somme strikers) than in any other place.

The Seine-Maritime was a long-standing locus of worker militancy. In bulk terms the construction, textile and transportation industries accumulated three-quarters of all strikes in the department. (The highly strike-prone transport sector, its big battalions in docking and shipping, had 43 percent of all participants.) Most of this conflict occurred in le Havre and Rouen.

B. Eastern France. The important thing about the east and northeast is the relative absence of conflict. In the years 1915–35 only the Aube, a few Vosgian textile centers and the Alsace contributed notably to national aggregates of strike activity. Lorraine, Burgundy and the Franche-Comté had little impact upon nationwide figures as a whole.

Almost all the strikers and most of the disputes in the Aube were in Troyes, and the vast majority of these in textiles. Indeed 86 percent of all disputants in the Aube between 1915 and 1935 were textile workers, mainly stockingers. The city presented a great center of militancy in an otherwise pacific Champagne countryside.

Strikes in the Vosges also centered in the textile sector, specifically in cotton weaving and spinning. Disputes were spread among small mill towns, such as Remiremont, St-Dié and Epinal, in all likelihood encouraged by and coordinated with the larger worker centers of the Haut-Rhin.

Mulhouse contributed almost half of the Haut-Rhin's strikes and strikers, who came predominantly in textiles and transportation. Haut-Rhin cotton workers were part of a larger band of textile plants stretching from Belfort into northern Alsace. As the principal militants in eastern France, these Alsatian mill workers demand further study, yet we lose track of them statistically before 1919.

In Bas-Rhin industrial conflict centered in Strasbourg (roughly half of the department's strikes and strikers there). Disputes were primarily to be found, in equal proportions, in wood, metalworking, textiles and construction. All four of these eastern departments fell into the 1–2 percent category during 1915–35, and thus were relatively unimportant in national aggregates.

C. Brittany. Like so many characteristics of Breton life, the massive strike movement of that province has been largely ignored. Yet the cities stretching from Brest to Nantes contributed a significant percentage of France's total strike activity. Of the Breton departments, only the Côtes-du-Nord experienced little conflict.

Brest in Finistère had a quarter of the department's strikes and over half of the strikers, lesser shares going to Douarnenez and Quimper. The most militant sectors were shipbuilding and mechanical construction in Brest, and the construction and wood industries within the entire department. The same distribution among metalworking, construction, woodworking, and additionally the transport sector, prevailed in neighboring Morbihan, with the port of Lorient easily dominating the department. (Three-quarters of Morbihan's strikers were in Lorient.) The leather and shoe industry was the single largest component of strike activity in Ille-et-Vilaine, with construction, woodworking and building materials following close behind. Construction strikes predominated in the departmental capital at Rennes, shoe-working conflicts in Fougères.

Finally in Brittany were the great industrial and commercial cities of St-Nazaire and Nantes in the Loire-Atlantique. Here shipbuilding and metalworking plants supplied the largest groups of strikers and strikes, trailed at some remove by docking, construction and woodworking.

Two features stand out about the Breton region. One is the absence of textile strikes, an important component of regional totals everywhere else save Paris (because Brittany had no textile industry to speak of). The second is the extreme concentration of Breton strikes in a handful of important ports and capitals, such as Brest, Rennes and St-Nazaire. Small towns were left largely untouched by the movement.

D. The Lyon region. The cities from Grenoble to Roanne, with Lyon and St-Etienne at midpoints on the line, constituted a fourth distinct region of conflict in 1915–35.

Grenoble and Vienne had together around half of the participants of the Isère, and a third of the disputes. Other strikes in that department were distributed among rural industrial communities. The textile industry provided half of the department's strikers, followed by metalworking, and then construction a distant third.

Across the Rhône River lay Lyon, ranking third among French cities in the sheer bulk of disputes and dominating strike activity in the Rhône department (80 percent of all strikers). Although the city had a sprinkling of stoppages in every sector, most strikers came in fact from the garment and textile industries, and from the construction trades. We have encountered these workers throughout our text, their first appearances the 1831 and 1834 uprisings and the 1833 strike wave. Here we see them as a major component of the national French aggregates.

The Loire department was the third contributor in the Lyon region. The great proletarian center of St-Etienne, with its smelting, metalworking and mining industries, represented around half of the department's strikers; the lesser industrial center of Roanne to the northeast had another fifth, and the small worker towns ringing St-Etienne, such as le Chambon-Feugerolles and St-Chamond, supplied the remainder. Strikers in the Loire came largely from the coalmining and textile (especially the ribbon weaving) industries, with a third each of the total, then from smelting and metalworking.

Among the regions of France, the Lyon region is probably most akin to the north, both in its industrial admixture, and in the graded distribution of strike activity from semi-rural mill town to giant metropolis.

E. The Mediterranean coast. Cities from Narbonne to Marseille represented the fifth important contribution to national totals of industrial conflict. To take them from east to west:

Strikes in the Bouches-du-Rhône were, essentially, those of Marseille. The great port had more conflict than any city save Paris. A quarter of the city's strikes came in transport: tramways, dockers, sailors; a further quarter came in the general construction sector: mostly the building trades, followed by building materials and woodworking. The remainder of the strikes and strikers were distributed among the other sectors, with, surprisingly, food industries ahead of the lot, a reflection of the militancy of café waiters and bakers.

Nîmes and Alès together had about half the strikes in the Gard, the remainder distributed throughout the countryside in agriculture or centered in small mining towns. Fourteen percent of strikes and 11 percent of the Gard's strikers in 1915–35 were within the agricultural sector, specifically among vineyard laborers (*ouvriers agricoles et viticoles* in *SG* parlance). The other important sectors were mining (43 percent of all strikers) and textile workers (17 percent of total strikers).

Vineyard strikes distinguished the Hérault (half of all strikers) with woodworking, construction and transportation following distantly behind. Sète, Montpellier and Béziers had roughly half of the disputes and participants, the others spread among smaller settlements, as is customary with agricultural conflicts.

To an even greater extent were the vineyard workers responsible for disputes in the Aude: 93 percent of all strikers there between 1919–35 were in agriculture, and 67 percent of all strikes. No single town had even as much as a quarter of the department's strikes, again evidence of the territorial diffusion of stoppages in agriculture.

To sum up, aside from the numerous and heterogeneous disputes of the city of Marseille, agricultural strikes constituted the principal contribution of the Midi to national aggregates. This characteristic united France's Mediterranean coast with much of Italy.

F. The Paris region. The reach of Parisian militancy extended beyond the boundaries of the department of the Seine. Let us take first strikes in the worker suburbs of the Seine-et-Oise, where metalworking and construction predominated, *terrassiers* figuring prominently among the building trades and large mechanical construction plants among metals establishments. Strike activity was highly diffused among small suburban towns, for the largest concentration was in Argenteuil, with only 11 percent of the department's strikes (13 percent of the Seine-et-Oise's strikers in 1915–35).

Within the department of the Seine we must distinguish between Paris and its industrial suburbs. The city had 66 percent of the department's total disputes, and 79 percent of the participants; the latter figure is substantially higher than the former because the average strike within the urban core tended to be larger than the typical strike in the less dense suburbs. Table 9.1 shows which suburbs contributed most to total strike activity in the Seine. The reader should not let the small percentage contributions of Seine suburbs imply that in absolute terms these outlying communities of the Red Belt had few conflicts. Each of the 10 Seine towns on table 9.1 had more than 40 strikes over the 1915–35 period, a volume of conflict experienced by only 43 other municipalities in France.

Although every sector save agriculture and mining experienced some conflict in the Seine, in absolute terms metalworking had the largest amount: 31 percent of the department's total strikes in 1915–35 (and 37 percent of the strikers). Construction and transport followed from a great distance behind. No other industry contributed even 10 percent of the total. Yet it should be kept in mind that even sectors with a small contribution to the

Table 9.1: *The distribution of strikes and strikers within the department of the Seine, 1915–35*

	% of strikes within Seine	% of strikers within Seine
Paris	65.8	78.7
Levallois-Perret	2.7	1.6
Boulogne-Billancourt	2.4	5.3
St-Denis	2.3	1.7
St-Ouen	2.1	1.2
Ivry	2.1	1.5
Montreuil	1.5	0.3
Courbevoie	1.5	0.6
Gennevilliers	1.2	0.9
Issy	1.2	0.8
Others	17.2	7.4
Total	100.0	100.0

Seine's aggregate represented gigantic proportions of the nationwide total of strikes and strikers within a given industry. Food workers in the Seine had only 4 percent of aggregate strike activity in that department, yet 40 percent of all food strikes in France; printing strikers 4 percent of the Seine yet 49 percent of all printers on strike in France, and so on. Almost a quarter of France's strikes (21 percent exactly) and strikers (24 percent) were registered in the Seine department in 1915–35. This great bulk means that one should always check Paris first to understand shifts in the composition of national aggregate levels of conflict.

Much of the increase in French strike levels from 1885 to 1935 was in fact due to the Paris region, for the three departments Seine, Seine-et-Oise and Seine-et-Marne expanded their share of national totals from 9 percent of all strikes in 1885–9 to 37 percent in 1930–4, and of strikers from 6 to 26 percent. The quiescence of the provinces during the July Monarchy inflated the 1830–47 Parisian contribution; and the post-Second World War provincial effervescence depressed Paris's 1960–4 share to a fifth of the total, which happens also to have been its 1830–47 contribution. Table 9.2 presents these figures, giving in yet a different way a message often presented in these pages: strike activity was a form of working-class mobilization for action at the center of political power, and the most intensive mobilization took place right at the center, the city of Paris.

Let us struggle to regain an overview after this lengthy recitation of place names and percentages.[2] What general points emerge from our survey of the principal industries within the main regions?

1. A handful of industrial sectors alone need be considered when the overall level of strike activity in any given region is broken down into its constituent parts. Such sectors as chemicals, printing, food, smelting and

Table 9.2: *The Paris region's share of the nation's strikes, 1830–1964*

	% of all strikes	Strike rate/ 100,000 total active population	% of all strikers	Striker rate/ 100,000 total active population
1830–47	23.2	—	—	—
1885–9	9.1	0.7	5.9	100
1890–4	10.0	1.8	5.6	300
1895–9	13.2	2.7	17.5	600
1900–4	8.2	2.3	6.5	400
1905–9	19.8	7.9	26.2	2,000
1910–14	18.5	7.3	28.2	1,600
1915–19	16.4	3.8	31.9	3,600
1920–4	20.2	6.5	17.2	2,000
1925–9	27.7	8.1	27.3	1,600
1930–4	36.6	4.9	26.3	900
1960–4	20.8	10.3	—	—

NOTES
The Paris region includes the departments Seine, Seine-et-Oise and Seine-et-Marne. Multi-department strikes have been excluded from the national totals in calculating these percentages.

agriculture almost never supplied important numbers of strikers in the cities making a firm impress upon national totals. Metalworking, textiles, construction and transportation – the big four – simply overshadowed all other sectors because they employed so many strike-prone workers. And in a few exceptional communities mining played a major role.

2. A handful of cities and regions alone need be considered when national totals of strike activity are broken down into their component parts. Single dominant cities account for most of the heavily marked areas on map 9.1: Brest, Nantes–St-Nazaire, Rouen, le Havre, Lyon, Limoges, Bordeaux, Marseille and of course Paris and its suburbs. Only in the cotton mills of Alsace and the Nord, and in the agricultural strikes of the Midi, did a notable dispersion of conflict beyond the big city contribute importantly to the absolute numbers of strikes and strikers.

3. Nevertheless, the effects of region and of industry are not simply additive; neither one reduces to the other; they interact.

Region versus industry

Let us dwell a bit longer on this third point. How much of the apparent variation in conflict by region reduces to differences in the industrial composition of each region, hence to variation by industry? Some, but not all. If the major determinants of strike activity were the characteristics of a certain kind of industry, one would expect all the workers in that industry, regardless of location, to have high strike propensities. Conversely, if the principal determinant of strike activity were regional mentalities or traditions, one

Table 9.3: *Strikers per 100,000 labor force per year by region and industry, 1915–35*

Region	Agriculture	Mining	Food	Chemicals	Printing and paper	Leather	Textiles	Metal production	Metal working	Construction	Transport	Mean
Alsace	20	1,347	120	207	69	209	2,605	519	902	915	4,876	1,072
Aquitaine	466	19	222	338	112	595	214	561	1,372	1,351	1,710	633
Auvergne	0	316	219	132	12	31	455	339	284	713	81	235
Burgundy	13	143	15	36	51	47	134	534	626	576	103	208
Brittany	161	172	330	288	112	608	191	164	2,271	1,290	843	585
Center	58	27	43	366	92	178	606	0	436	811	118	249
Champagne	94	156	156	22	61	58	2,877	442	995	1,457	226	595
Corsica	16	9	8	4	0	2	3	0	0	42	109	18
Provence	214	325	1,161	1,546	113	416	1,109	919	1,487	4,179	5,389	1,533
Franche-Comté	0	229	10	18	67	1	1,263	675	2,621	589	101	507
Languedoc	4,610	1,431	230	132	33	105	626	358	137	649	786	828
Limousin	0	144	19	1	136	1,200	304	22	40	1,182	91	285
Lorraine	4	5,090	25	74	64	283	1,952	1,772	589	817	32	974
Midi-Pyrénées	0	685	98	204	17	1,684	1,572	401	323	770	126	535
Nord	160	9,484	277	485	520	89	25,048	3,046	2,364	5,844	3,475	4,618
Upper Normandy	50	0	82	342	93	159	4,310	1,562	1,129	1,084	4,358	1,198
Lower Normandy	0	57	8	78	10	15	419	192	286	270	146	135
Paris	342	260	2,512	5,266	2,518	2,446	5,347	357	23,584	11,274	10,437	5,850
Loire	152	607	247	125	146	356	1,075	964	1,962	1,248	1,254	740
Picardy	35	12	35	35	37	103	2,717	818	785	968	155	519
Charente	65	35	19	106	60	18	41	44	209	326	347	116
Rhône-Alpes	2	3,076	267	387	626	1,687	9,359	3,292	2,985	5,673	1,289	2,604
Mean	294	1,074	278	464	225	468	2,829	772	2,064	1,911	1,639	1,093

would expect all the industries in a region with a high strike rate to have high strike rates, regardless of what the industries were and regardless of how high their customary conflict levels were. If both industry and region mattered, but independently of each other, one would expect to find approximately the same rank order of regions within each industry, and the same rank order of industries within each region. If, finally, region and industry interacted with each other, one would expect to find some combinations of the two producing far greater reduction or swelling of strike activity than their average individual effects would lead us to predict.

Table 9.3 contains some essential information on these matters. It cross-tabulates the average yearly number of strikers per 100,000 labor force by industry and region for 1915–35. A cavernous table like this one is hard to find one's way around in. But once our eyes are adapted to the dark and the layout of the space becomes familiar, we can locate some distinct regularities. Obviously there are strikeless and strikeful regions: no matter what the industry, Corsica has few strikers; Paris and the north run above the national mean in almost every industry. It is less clear from the table that there are regular differences among industries, although the food industries can generally be counted on to produce few strikers regardless of region, and construction ordinarily runs above the regional mean. An analysis of variance for the data in the table produces the results shown in the small table.

Source of variation	Degrees of freedom	Sum of squares[a]	Mean square[a]
Industry	10	3.63	0.36
Region	21	10.48	0.50
Industry × region	210	23.12	0.11
Within cells	4,840	134.44	0.03

[a] In billions.

Thus the F-ratio for interaction is 3.96 (P < 0.01). If we compare the effects of industry and of region with those of the interaction between them, we again get 'significant' F-ratios. Region apparently has a stronger effect than industry. But the high level of interaction makes the meaning of these tests unsure. The prudent interpretation of the findings is that some industries – mining is the clearest case, with its exceptional rates of strikers in Languedoc, Lorraine and the north – are peculiarly sensitive to the overall level of militancy of workers in their region.

The pattern, nevertheless, lasted quite some time. Stepping backwards, we can perform the same sort of analysis for comparable data from 1890–1914.

Source of variation	Degrees of freedom	Sum of squares[a]	Mean square[a]
Industry	10	1,772.53	177.25
Region	21	3,665.00	174.52
Industry × region	210	11,693.70	55.68
Within cells	5,808	39,382.30	6.78

[a] In millions.

This time the F-ratio for interaction is 8.21, higher than in the later period. The measured effects of industry and region are approximately equal, and still 'significant' by conventional statistical tests. Again the great responsiveness of the miners in a few critical regions like Languedoc and the north to the general level of militancy in their regions stands out as an example of the interaction of region and industry.

In conclusion, region, industry and the interaction between the two of them all affect the propensity to strike. These findings are all the more interesting in view of the relative constancy in the scale of enterprise across regions. On the basis of information on the distribution of various sizes of industrial establishments in each industry within each department, Pierre George concluded that 'the dimensions of firms correspond closely to a certain balance for each type of manufacturing, much more than to any regional pattern.'[3] It therefore seems unlikely that subtle regional variations in the scale of firms in different industries account for the industry–region interactions. Perhaps a finer analysis treating smaller areas and taking into account such important matters as wage levels or modernity of the industrial plant would completely erase the effect of area. We doubt it, and believe instead that if there are more strikers in the Nord than in Poitou, it is partly because the Nord has many coalminers and metalworkers, Poitou few. But it is partly also because for historic reasons the folkways and traditions of Flemish workers are just different from those of Poitevin workers; presumably the workers of the Nord would still strike differently from the workers of Poitou even if the industrial compositions of the two regions were identical.

Changes in regional strike propensity

Useful enough in highlighting the components of national aggregates, absolute numbers of strikes and strikers are inadequate for a study of changes over time in the strike activity of various territories. If strike levels in the Champagne, for example, decline over the years, is it because Champagne workers have become less militant, or is it because the economic contraction of Champagne industry has reduced the population of workers available for industrial conflict? Clearly, to study strikes from one period to another among the various territories, rates must be employed.

All this sounds like an introduction to a department-by-department study of strike propensities. But it is not. We shall not repeat for strike rates the kind of areal analysis presented above, for two reasons:

1. The reader will be able to convince himself that the more refined measure of strike rates does not change the general picture presented by strike shares among the departments. In map 9.9 of strike rates by department the same six regions we noted above reemerge, and the shadings and variations the rate adds to the six rough-hewn images are not worth puzzling over in a work of this scope. Strike rates show the north, Alsace and eastern Lorraine, the Breton triangle bounded by Fougères, Brest and Nantes, the Lyon area, the Mediterranean coast, and the Paris region – which were the six basic regions of strike activity noted above – to have notable intensities of strike activity. Save a few scattered outliers, such as Limoges in the Haute-Vienne, Bordeaux in the Gironde, the Ardennes and the Nièvre, high strike frequencies were confined in 1915–35 to those six regions. Hence further discussion of regional distributions as such becomes superfluous.

2. In Chapter 11 we shall explore systematically the structural sources of territorial variation in strike intensity, as in various statistical analyses we attempt to specify the independent variables – such as unionization, level of mechanization, presence of a historic tradition of conflict and the like – which cause some areas to have high strike frequencies, other areas low ones, all the while taking account of the distribution of the worker population available for participation in strikes. A discussion of regional differences in relative strike levels would inevitably assume an *ad hoc* quality, for at this point it is inconvenient to demonstrate methodically with quantitative data that the explanation adduced for some region's singularity is in fact the correct explanation. So in this section we concentrate upon changes over time, ignoring the reasons for differentials in intensity in any single period.

Once again, a shower of maps:

> Map 9.8: Total strike rate by department, 1890–1914
> Map 9.9: Total strike rate by department, 1915–35
> Map 9.10: Total striker rate by department, 1890–1914
> Map 9.11: Total striker rate by department, 1915–35
> Map 9.12: Strike rate per 100,000 non-agricultural labor force by department, 1915–35

One prefatory remark upon the measurement of intensity is required. Our standard measure of intensity is the number of strikes or strikers per 100,000 total active population, including agriculture. We normally bring agricultural strikes into the rate's numerator, and agricultural workers into the denominator, because of the great number of such strikes. (The strike rate of the Aude sinks to insignificance, for example, if agricultural strikes are removed.) Yet differences in the relative size of the agricultural population from one region to the next may conceal, or enhance, territorial differences in the real propensity of non-agricultural workers to strike. If Finistère has a lower strike rate than the Aube, for example, might that not be because Finistère has a larger rural population (which is to most intents and purposes non-strikable) than the Aube?

A comparison of maps 9.9 and 9.12 shows what practical distorting effect the inclusion of the agricultural population has upon regional patterns. There are three cases where the presence of the agricultural labor force conceals a high strike propensity of the industrial and service labor force. The true proportions of the Breton strike rate are submerged in the peasant population of the Finistère, Morbihan, Ille-et-Villaine and Loire-Atlantique. Map 9.12 shows only the Côtes-du-Nord of the Breton departments as lacking in substantial industrial conflict. The Savoyard peasant population obscures high strike rates in Haute-Savoie, Savoie, and Hautes- and Basses-Alpes. And when the rustics are omitted from the rate denominator, high strike levels turn up on the Limousin (Creuse, Corrèze and neighboring departments). Aside from these three clusters of departments, the total and non-agricultural strike rates give substantially the same picture.

What major shifts in the territorial distribution of strike propensity occurred between 1890 and 1935? Because conflict rates in virtually every industry in every department changed from one year or period to the next, we must resolve to concentrate only on the main trends in departmental aggregates. We shall consider as having changed notably any department to either enter or leave the top three classes of strike intensity (2.0 strikes/100,000 active population and up) between 1890–1914 and 1915–35. We take up the six regions of strike activity one after the other.

A. Northern France. The Pas-de-Calais experienced a major decline in strike propensity from 1890–1914 to 1915–35, its strike rate plunging from 4.1 to 2.3/100,000, its striker rate sliding modestly from 2,700 to 2,100/100,000. Two things happened: (1) the Pas-de-Calais's coalmining strike rate sank from 7.0 to 1.0, the striker rate from 15,200 to 6,900/100,000. In the prewar period 85 percent of the Pas-de-Calais's strikers were in coalmining, and so industrial peace in that industry would greatly depress the department's overall rates. (2) The strike rates of many other industries in the Pas-de-Calais dropped also between the two periods, yet their strik*er* rates did not; participation rates in transportation, metalworking and smelting even rose over this time, indicating that the size of the average strike in these sectors was growing, and that labor-force militancy itself was on the wane nowhere save in coalmining.

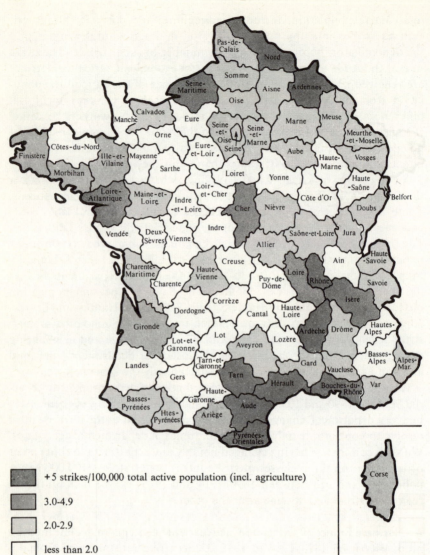

Map 9.8: Total strike rate by department, 1890–1914

+5 strikes/100,000 total active population (incl. agriculture)

3.0-4.9

2.0-2.9

less than 2.0

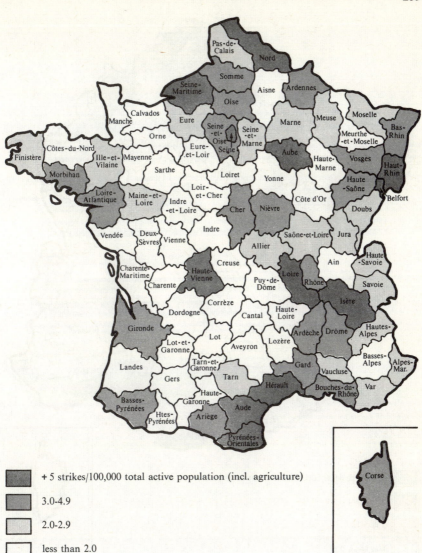

Map 9.9: Total strike rate by department, 1915–35

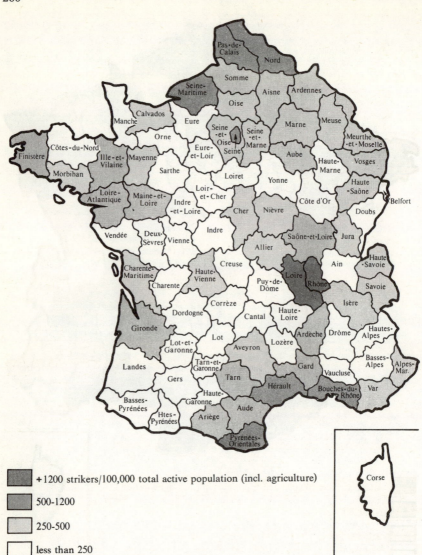

+1200 strikers/100,000 total active population (incl. agriculture)

500-1200

250-500

less than 250

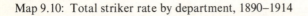

Map 9.10: Total striker rate by department, 1890–1914

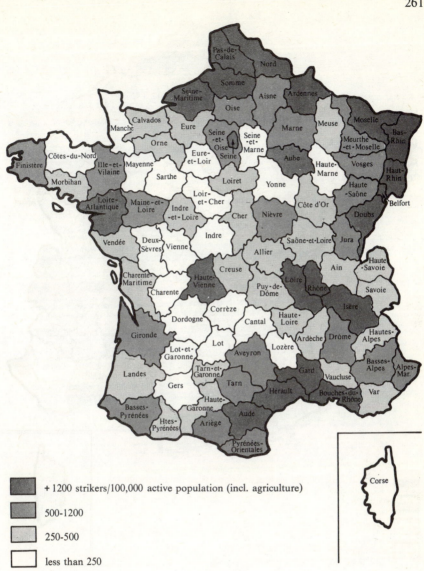

Map 9.11: Total striker rate by department, 1915–35

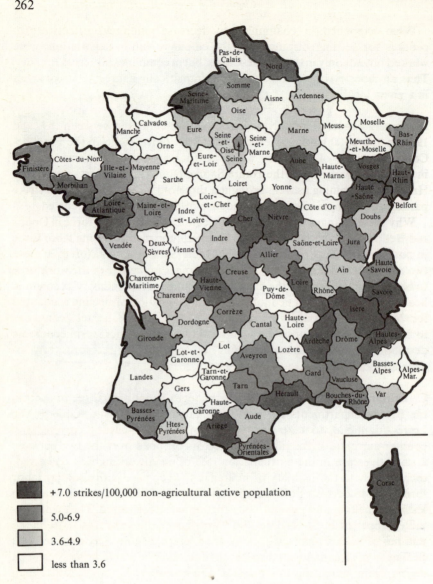

+7.0 strikes/100,000 non-agricultural active population

5.0-6.9

3.6-4.9

less than 3.6

Map 9.12: Non-agricultural strike rate by department, 1915–35

What happened in coalmining to decrease militancy? Effective procedures for settling disputes and for employer–union negotiations were worked out not only in the Pas-de-Calais, but in coalmines all across France.[4] Thus an industrywide change affected dramatically aggregate strike levels in a given locality.

B. Eastern France. The only changes worth mentioning between 1890 and 1935 in the patchwork patterns of eastern France came in the Franche-Comté. A surge of militancy within textiles, metalworking and smelting in all three departments – the Haute-Saône, Doubs and Belfort – and within Haute-Saône mining as well, brought a threefold increase in regional strike participation. Some rise in the incidence of disputes as well occurred.

Why these changes took place is unclear. The textile labor force in Doubs and Belfort declined between 1906 and 1926; the metalworking labor force in both departments rose; and in the Haute-Saône the workforces in these two sectors remained stable. Assuming changes in the size of the workforce to be a rough indicator of the direction of change of that industry's economic health, may we say that economic growth, stagnation or decline accounted for this across-the-board rise in militancy? The lesson of Chapter 4 continues to hold true that a consistent relationship between short-term economic development and strike activity does not exist. But the real forces responsible are obscure.

C. Brittany. A number of diverging changes in individual sectors within the Breton departments left net strike and striker intensity stable. In the Loire-Atlantique, to take an example of the cross-cutting currents and counter-currents, strike rates in all sectors dropped over the two periods; a small decrease in the participation rate of metalworking was registered, owing solely to the inability of militancy to keep pace with a soaring labor force, not to declining absolute levels of conflict; and sizable increases in leather, smelting and general construction were registered. Thus what actually happened in St-Nazaire and Nantes over this time was a rise in the number of workers participating in the average dispute, accompanied by a decline in the frequency of disputes themselves. The whole process came, it seems, from increasing unionization and *revendicative* action, rather than from stagnation and backsliding within the worker movement. In the next chapter we shall place this pattern of falling strike and rising striker rates in a broader context. The immediate point is that one must be very circumspect in interpreting these statistics.

D. The Lyon area. From Montceau-les-Mines in northern Saône-et-Loire to Romans in southern Drôme separate tales of rise and fall for the worker movement were to be told. The most startling change was the shattering of militancy in the Schneider empire, for the miners and smelters of

Montceau and le Creusot never recovered the momentum they lost in the failed strikes of 1900–1 (see Chapter 5). Striker rates in the Saône-et-Loire as a whole fell from 920 per 100,000 in 1890–1914 to 260 in 1915–35, and that department's mining striker rate from 12,300 to 900.

A drop in the Rhône department's strike rate (7.4/100,000 in 1890–1914 to 4.7 in 1915–35) must be contrasted with an increase in participation in every Lyon industry except metalworking: as in Nantes–St-Nazaire, Lyon workers struck somewhat less frequently in the 1920s and early 30s, but much more massively. The Rhône's participation rate from prewar to interwar climbed from 1,200 to 2,300 strikers/100,000 active population.

Finally, in the Drôme the striker rate shot up nearly four-fold from 1890–1914 to 1915–35 (240 to 890/100,000), a result of exploding militancy within the leather industry in Romans, and in other communities too.

E. The Mediterranean coast. As in Lyon and Nantes, the principal changes to occur in Mediterranean cities over the long haul were a decrease in the outbreak of separate conflicts, and a simultaneous increase in the number of participants in those strikes that did occur. In the Alpes-Maritime (which means mainly Nice), Bouches-du-Rhône, Vaucluse, Gard and Aude strike rates went down, striker rates up. Only in the Var (where strikes were in small towns) and in the Pyrénées-Orientales (where agricultural striker rates sank for some local reason) did departmental levels of conflict, as measured by both strike and striker rates, subside.

F. The Paris region. Participation in strikes almost doubled in the department of the Seine between 1890–1914 and 1915–35, as the striker rate climbed from 1,200 to 2,200; the strike rate rose less swiftly, from 4.9 to 6.2/100,000 active population. In course here was a process we have noted for other metropolitan regions, striker rates soaring across the board in the face of a declining or stagnant incidence of conflict, a sign that workers were coordinating and linking together disputes that otherwise would have erupted isolated from one another. Table 9.4 shows how each industrial sector within the Seine changed over this period.

Thus in no Parisian industry except construction was there a real decline in militancy. But some industries within the Seine conformed to the pattern of falling outbursts of strikes coupled with rising participation, while in other sectors both indicators of militancy shot upwards. The net effect of these ebbs and floods was, as in all big cities, an important elevation of participation in strikes, and only a modest rise in the frequency of disputes themselves.

What overall patterns emerge from this regional survey? What systematic sources of variation lay behind that portion of the flux in strike propensity we have been able to single out with our maps? Three kinds of change have become apparent in our review of the six regions:

Table 9.4: *Strike and striker rates by industry in the department of the Seine, 1890–1914 and 1915–35*

	1890–1914		1915–35	
	Strike rate/ 100,000 active population	Striker rate/ 100,000 active population	Strike rate/ 100,000 active population	Striker rate/ 100,000 active population
Food industries	6.2	1,100	9.3	3,700
Chemicals	8.5	3,200	5.2	6,800
Printing	6.9	1,200	8.9	2,900
Leather–hides	21.0	1,500	21.5	4,000
Garments–textiles[a]	1.5	200	4.1	1,700
Metalworking	13.5	2,500	14.2	6,000
Wood industries	10.4	3,000	15.3	2,000
Building materials	19.6	1,900	30.3	3,800
Construction	31.6	10,500	24.6	6,100
Transport-residual[b]	1.1	400	1.2	700
Seine total	4.9	1,200	6.2	2,200

Industries with few strikes are omitted from the list of sectors, yet included in the Seine totals.
[a] Mainly strikes in the garment industry.

[b] Labor-force denominator includes entire tertiary sector; most disputes in numerator are within transportation proper, however. The rates are thus vastly deflated.

First, in some departments the vicissitudes of a single massive industry dragged overall rates of conflict about. The Seine-et-Oise's higher striker rates in the interwar years, for example, stemmed largely from more combativeness in metalworking. Or the drop in the Pas-de-Calais striker rate was the consequence of passivity in coalmining. Thus to 'explain' a change in the conflict levels of these departments we need merely cite the experience of its dominant industrial sector. A wider view of such industrial trends was the task of preceding chapters, and we need dwell no longer on the matter here.

Second, in other departments overall rates changed because of an across-the-board increase or decrease in the militancy of all local industries. The burden of explanation in this instance lies not on the national experience of a single dominant industry, but upon shifts in some local or regional circumstance, such as a greater willingness of local employers to bargain collectively, higher levels of unionization within the area as a whole (moving across all the area's industries) or a regionwide economic crisis. The experience of the Franche-Comté exemplifies this kind of explanatory challenge, for regional frequencies there rose not because developments taking place within one or two strategic industries all over France chanced to reverberate in the east with special resonance, but because some feature of local mentalities or local conditions common to workers in most industries became different. We cannot here present explanations of this variety of regional change, because such explanations require a detailed knowledge of local circumstances in dozens of different areas. Not only would such an accounting take many chapters to present, it would need to rest on a timbering of local monographs that have not yet been written.

Last, a third variety of regional change had at its origin a systematic shift in social structure and social organization, and that is the kind of territorial movement we are best able to get a purchase on. A number of departments experienced a scissors-variety of change in militancy we have several times noted: a decrease or stagnation in strike rates coupled with a sharp increase in strik*er* rates over the years. We argue that this common pattern of change surfaced chiefly in large cities during the 1920s, though why it happened remains a puzzle.

The study of regions dissolves rapidly into the study of particular communes. A very small number of communes produce the great bulk of all strike activity. Many of the peculiarities which appear in the regional comparisons turn out not to be regional in any broad sense, but rather the special features of one place like Lille or Marseille. We had better turn more deliberately to the influence of particular cities and of cities in general.

10 Cities, urbanization and strikes

It is clear from the preceding chapter that the city is a major source of territorial variation in conflict. Our task now will be to show exactly what difference urbanity makes. We have throughout this book emphasized the big city as the modern locus of conflict, the place where contenders for political power come to engage one another. In this chapter we first point out the singular evolution of urban strikes. Secondly we demonstrate differences between the character of conflict in big cities and small towns. Finally, we attempt to explain strike variation from city to city with multivariate analyses of unionization, population growth and the like. These three analytic perspectives converge upon the same findings: the city makes a very substantial difference in strikes.

Localizing the areal effect

Let us first try to localize the scissors effect – stable or declining frequencies of strikes, rising numbers of strikers – by comparing highly urbanized and little-urbanized departments. (We may as well, however, restrict our attention to areas which have more than a negligible amount of industrial conflict; let us consider only those departments producing at least 1 percent of France's strikes from 1890 to 1914.) If the scissors effect of 1915–35 was indeed a big-city phenomenon, urban departments should have rising striker rates but falling strike rates from 1890–1914 to 1915–35. Less-urban departments should not evidence the divergent movement of rates. Table 10.1 shows this prediction coming true. The six most-urban departments – Bouches-du-Rhône (Marseille), Hérault (Béziers etc.), Nord (Lille and surrounding industrial towns), Rhône (Lyon), Seine (Paris) and Seine-Maritime (le Havre, Rouen) all had *falling* strike rates and rising rates for strikers from 1890–1914 to 1915–35. The Seine is a slight exception; its strike rate went up rather than down. But its striker rate climbed much faster. Equally interesting, five of the six least-urban departments failed to show the scissors pattern. (It appeared, however, in the Ille-et-Vilaine.) Both indices of strike activity in these rural departments declined together or didn't move at all. Thus it appears that the wider worker participation in strikes of the 1920s, combined with a lesser eruption of separate outbursts, was indeed a big-city phenomenon.

Table 10.1: *How urbanity is associated with the scissors movement of strike and striker rates, 1890–1914 to 1915–35*

The 6 least-urban departments

Department	Measure	1890–1914	1915–35
Ardèche	strike rate	5.1	3.8
	striker rate	500	400
Finistère	strike rate	3.0	2.6
	striker rate	800	700
Ille-et-Vilaine	strike rate	3.2	2.9
	striker rate	500	700
Isère	strike rate	5.2	5.7
	striker rate	900	1,500
Maine-et-Loire	strike rate	2.7	2.4
	striker rate	900	700
Morbihan	strike rate	3.0	3.1
	striker rate	400	400
All France	strike rate	4.0	
	striker rate	800	

The 6 most-urban departments

Department	Measure	1890–1914	1915–35
Bouches-du-Rhône	strike rate	8.1	4.8
	striker rate	2,800	3,100
Hérault	strike rate	7.0	6.3
	striker rate	1,400	1,600
Nord	strike rate	17.8	10.9
	striker rate	2,600	4,400
Rhône	strike rate	7.4	4.7
	striker rate	1,200	2,300
Seine	strike rate	4.9	6.2
	striker rate	1,200	2,200
Seine-Maritime	strike rate	6.8	5.9
	striker rate	1,300	2,700
All France	strike rate		3.7
	striker rate	1,400	1,400

NOTES
The six least-urban departments were selected from among those departments with a substantial amount of strike activity (a share of France's total strikes in 1890–1914 greater than 1 percent), not from among all departments. The six most-urban departments were similarly chosen. The urban–rural ratios are for the year 1911.
Strike and striker rates are per 100,000 active population.

To put things another way, part of the kaleidoscopic movement in the coloration of the maps came from changes in strike size: strikes in big cities grew much larger than did strikes in small towns over the two long time blocks. This shift in size partly explains the decline in separate outbreaks of conflict in highly urban departments; what formerly would have been separate small strikes owing to a lack of coordination were now a single great dispute. In table 10.2 we verify the fact that rapid increases in the mean number of strikers per strike characterized urban departments but not rural ones. The average strike size in *no* pastoral department increased as much as in *any* urban department except Hérault.

When the size of the average dispute changes, several different mechanisms may be at work, and understanding why the change occurred will be possible only if we can identify the exact one. An increase in the size of strikes may be the result of three different factors: (*a*) an increase in the size of the average establishment on strike; (*b*) an increase in the average number of establishments per strike; (*c*) an increase in the percentage of workers within the struck establishments actually joining the strike – the plant participation rate.

No clear trend emerges over time in the size of the typical establishment on strike (factor *a*). In some departments, both very urban and less so, the median size of the struck establishment rose over the long haul, in others it declined. What happened where was more a function of changing industrial structures than of the diffusion of militancy, and departments at

Table 10.2: *Mean number of strikers per strike for the most-urban and the least-urban departments, 1890–1914 and 1915–35*

	1890–1914	1915–35	Index $\frac{1915-1935}{1890-1914} \times 100$
The 6 most-urban departments			
Bouches-du-Rhône	352	659	187
Hérault	207	254	123
Nord	149	406	272
Rhône	165	493	299
Seine	249	372	149
Seine-Maritime	191	462	242
The 6 least-urban departments			
Ardèche	105	138	131
Finistère	255	279	109
Ille-et-Vilaine	170	236	139
Isère	178	257	144
Maine-et-Loire	331	271	82
Morbihan	125	123	98
All France	214	382	178

Table 10.3: *Mean strikers/100 workers employed in struck establishments (plant participation rate), for the most-urban and the least-urban departments*

	1890–1914	1915–35	Index
The six most-urban departments			
Bouches-du-Rhône	55	76	136
Hérault	84	81	96
Nord	35	56	160
Rhône	68	74	109
Seine	59	42	71
Seine-Maritime	56	62	111
The 6 least-urban departments			
Ardèche	69	77	112
Finistère	78	70	90
Ille-et-Vilaine	68	27	40
Isère	60	66	110
Maine-et-Loire	60	52	87
Morbihan	50	44	88
All France	51	55	108

NOTE
'Special' workforces in craft strikes within industrial plants have not been used in the denominators of these calculations.

all levels of urbanity were equally subject to increases in the scale of enterprise.

Factor (*c*) is a more promising explanation of the increase in average strike size. Plant participation rates (the number of strikers/100 workers employed in the struck establishments) were rising more rapidly in highly urban departments than in less-urban ones. In four of the six departments, plant participation rose between 1890–1914 and 1915–35; in only two of the non-urban departments did it go up. Table 10.3 presents these figures.

What about factor (*b*), which we call 'scope': the average number of establishments per strike? In some urban departments, such as Bouches-du-Rhône and Hérault, the scope of strikes dropped; in other urban departments – for example Nord and Rhône – it as much as doubled. The same story, though the percentages of decline were sharper and the pace of the increase less, is told for the least-urban departments. Thus department-level data dismiss the importance of the number of establishments per strike as a mechanism in the rising size of strikes.

Commune-level data tell a slightly different story, however. When we take as the unit of analysis not the department but the municipality itself, larger towns experience an increase in the number of establishments per strike, smaller communities do not. Table 10.4 gives the essential information.

Table 10.4: *Mean number of establishments per strike by size of town*

	1895–9	1910–14	1915–35
Towns larger than 20,000[a]	7.9	10.6	13.4
Towns smaller than than 20,000	3.3	6.1	5.1

[a]Population in 1911.

The critical information in this table is the decline in establishments per strike in small towns from 1910–14 to 1915–35. Department-level data obscured this news because two of the six departments saw declines in the scope of their strikes in 1915–35 owing to enormous increases in establishments per strike in 1900–9. Once we get away from the six selected departments, and look at all large cities versus all small ones, the importance of mechanism (*b*) appears with clarity.

The analysis of areal changes in strike propensity has thus led us to an important finding: in the 1920s, living and working in a large metropolitan center predisposed workers in many different establishments to join together, and moved workers in the same establishment as well to link up in strikes. This predisposition to collective action on a local basis did not exist to a comparable degree in any kind of community before the First World War. The predisposition lessened in smaller towns after the war, but rose in the larger places. The scissors movement – declining number of strikes, increasing numbers of strikers and establishments – is surely related to the increase in the communal coordination of strike activity between 1895–9 and 1925–9 which we uncovered in Chapter 7. We speculated at that point that a strengthening of territorial (as opposed to industrial) ties among striking establishments arose from more effective Bourses du travail, from Communist Party residential cells and from a likely but quite undocumented cementing of sociability in working-class neighborhoods during the interwar period. Such speculations suggest themselves again at this point; yet only detailed monographic research will establish the precise mechanism of the change.

How the city matters

In assaying the impact of the city upon strike activity we must rigorously distinguish between the effects of urban *growth* and the effects of an urban *setting*. A bagful of theories on the migration of workers from countryside to city illuminate the consequences of drawing peasants into an industrial labor force. And a less well defined corpus of ideas explains the impact of urban life upon patterns of cooperation, organization and militancy. The former question concerns essentially the consequences of the move *to* a city, the latter the consequences of living *in* a city.

Ever since the 1840s the percentage of the French population living in cities had been on the rise, and the share of the largest cities (those above 50,000 population) had risen fastest of all. Many of the migrants pushing into these urban places were industrial workers. As we have pointed out, the last quarter of the nineteenth century, when this urban expansion was most rapid, witnessed as well the great mobilization of the working classes for political action. Is there a relationship between these two grand phenomena, so closely united in timing and pacing? The answer is no and yes, depending on whether the move to the city itself is under discussion, or whether the subject is the nature of the urban setting and the kinds of events going on there. Let us take up these matters in turn.

Patrick de Laubier, in a challenging article, has made a case for the move *to* the city as an accelerator of working-class militancy.[1] He comes to the tie between urbanization and conflict by asking what circumstances determine whether union ideology will be revolutionary or reformist. Workers who have recently migrated to a city, he hypothesizes, will not for a long time become integrated into the wider urban social order. The unions they join therefore become surrogate communities, providing the workers with values and attitudes different from those of the surrounding dominant social order, with friendship ties, networks of communication and other components of 'integration.' Because these unions are called upon to take the part of the downtrodden and miserable against an oppressive larger society, they advance revolutionary ideologies, advocating the overthrow of the economic system which has exploited their members and of the social organism which has excluded them. De Laubier expects, therefore, a strong positive correlation between urban migration and revolutionary unionism. Because these new migrants are difficult to organize, the membership of these unions will be unstable, representing only a minority of the workforce. He does not take up the subject of strikes, but one might fairly extend his model to anticipate a close relationship between the inflow of peasant recruits to the labor force and militancy.

De Laubier, of course, is not the first scholar to have postulated such a relationship. An idea familiar to many revolutionary socialists is the revolt of the wretched of the earth, the industrial worker torn freshly from his rural roots, filled with bitterness and fury against his harsh new industrial environment.[2] De Laubier's service is rather in applying these ideas to the French experience.

To the extent that this line of argument foresees a connection between migration, dislocation and the appearance of organized conflict, we think it wrong. In our view, the motors of militancy are set in motion not by the marginal, the unintegrated and the recently arrived, but by workers who belong to firmly established networks of long standing at the core of urban industrial society. We would therefore expect the move to the city to *impede* worker capacities for collective action and to stifle militancy simply because recently arrived migrants, however hostile and sullen they may feel towards 'bourgeois society,' have great difficulty in forming effective organizations.

We may support our case, and cast doubt on the 'unintegrated militant' argument, by observing statistically the relationship between urban growth and strike activity. As an indicator of urban migration let us take the percentage change in the population of each of the 128 cities larger than 20,000 by 1911. (The populations of virtually all increased to some extent.) Then with correlation coefficients we can see what impact the growth of each of these cities has upon militancy and proletarian solidarity within that city. In order to make sure these correlations measure regular relationships rather than artifacts of some particular constellation of circumstances at some particular point in time, we compare the urban population change of two different periods (1872–1911 and 1896–1911) to the strike activity of two different blocks of time (1910–14 and 1915–35). The results of the two sets of analyses, given in table 10.5, are much the same.

It is clear that urban growth impedes solidarity and reduces the ability to act together.[3] Negative correlations turn up for both periods between the number of establishments per strike, the median plant participation rate (median number of strikers per 100 workers in the struck establishment) and the urban population change. And urban growth increases the percentage of strikes ending in failure.

Rising urban population appears, however, to increase levels of unionization, to go by the positive association between the percentage of strikes in which unions were involved during 1910–14, and the rate of urban population change over the preceding thirty years. Yet a negative correlation for 1915–35 commands wariness: the cities which had grown most rapidly before the First World War were least likely to see extensive union participation in strikes *after* the war. Possibly this reversal is an artifact, owing to inadequacies in our 1915–35 union participation data. Possibly, on the other hand, this reversal means that in high-growth cities workers made radical by the war tended to seek out alternative forms of political action.

Correlations for both 1910–14 and 1915–35 make clear that urban growth does reduce militancy: there are negative relationships between the percent of urban population change and the change in strike and striker rates. Thus as people pour into cities, the incidence of conflict falls off.[4]

The substantial positive correlation between urban growth and establishment size suggests that two mechanisms may be operating in expanding cities to impede solidarity and militancy. One is the newness of much of the industrial population themselves: workers only recently arrived in the city were unpersuaded to divert resources of time and energy from individual to collective ends. The second is the disaggregating impact upon joint

Table 10.5: *Zero-order correlations between urban population change and strike activity in 1910–14 and 1915–35*

	Correlations between % population change in 128 communes from 1872 to 1911 and characteristics of strikes in 1910–14	Correlations between % population change in 131 communes from 1896 to 1911 and characteristics of strikes in 1915–35
Mean establishments/strike	−0.25	−0.17
Median size of struck establishments	0.24	0.29
Median plant participation (strikers/100 workers in struck establishments)	−0.23	−0.18
Mean strike size (number of strikers/strike)	0.24	−0.02
Median duration	−0.08	−0.07
% of strikes ending in failure	0.11	0.27
Strike rate (number of strikes/100,000 total urban population) in 1911	−0.14	−0.10
Striker rate (number of strikers/100,000 total urban population) in 1920s	−0.04	−0.13
Absolute number of strikes	−0.09	−0.04
Absolute number of strikers	−0.04	−0.05
% of strikes with unions	0.23	−0.34

NOTES

1910–14
Three of the 131 cities with a population of more than 20,000 in 1911 had no strikes between 1910–14, and so were not included in the analysis. Strike and striker rates were computed on the basis of the city's 1921 population. The denominator of median plant participation, which is to say the number of workers in the struck establishments, includes only the plant workforce of the single craft on strike, whenever single crafts strike within large industrial establishments. The denominator in this calculation for 1915–35 includes the labor force of the entire plant. This discrepancy makes little difference, for the two correlations are very close.

1915–35
The four cities in Alsace–Lorraine larger than 20,000 in 1921 were omitted from the file. Rates were calculated from an average of the city's total population in 1921, 1926, 1931 and 1936.

action that large industrial establishments have. In the last chapter we saw that workers in large plants have a much harder time in organizing and acting collectively than workers in small shops. And if an increase in the scale of enterprise drew workers into the city by offering them jobs within the leading industrial sectors, employment in these establishments, as well as newness to the setting itself, would hinder cohesiveness among the workforce. So both circumstances converge to limit militancy in the short run. The long run is another matter.

When we look away from change within the city to the impact of the urban setting over the long haul, the big city appears a place of militancy and solidarity. It is certain that the sheer intensity of conflict in the big city was higher than in smaller communities. It is certain that the big city, more than the small town, aided the mobilization of workers for strike activity. And it is likely (though not sure) that the setting of urbanity exacerbated the bitterness of industrial conflicts because the city was a central place of political conflict. These assertions may be documented in several ways.

The relative frequency of strikes was higher in big cities than in small towns. Table 10.6 gives strike and striker rates by size of place for the years 1910–14. The relationship between intensity of strike activity and size of the arena in which it unfolds is almost linear: the larger the community, the higher the rate of conflict. Certainly cities of population above 100,000 have stronger rates than smaller cities. (This effect is more visible for stri*ker* than for strike rates.)

Map 10.1 conveys the diversity behind these aggregate figures by giving strike rates in 1910–14 for each city over 20,000 population. The map highlights four features of differentials in strike activity.

— Paris and Marseille, the greatest of the cities, fared poorly relative to other urban centers in 1910–14. Only the massive conflict in the arrondissement of Lille (a yearly average of 90.2 strikes/100,000 industrial workers) pulled strike rates within cities of 200,000 or more population up to the top of table 10.6. Thus, while it remains true that larger cities (+100,000) had higher strike rates than smaller cities, it is not true that the largest urban centers had the highest rates.

— High strike rates characterized the seaports. Strike activity rimming the coast of France from le Havre to Toulon was not merely the work of maritime occupations, but of all the diverse industries that found themselves in these port cities. Location in a port seemed to pull up the conflict levels of the non-transportation industries as well. We would argue that the variety of life within a port, as within a metropolis, stimulated militancy among the local workforce. Whatever characteristics of urbanity promoted strike activity were surely most pronounced in a bustling seaport, as men, goods and ideas converged from all over France, and from international sources too. The knots of far-flung organizational networks would be tied in the crossroads of the port; and the inhabitants would be exposed sooner and more systematically than the residents of any other kind of community save the metropolis itself to all the diverse

Map includes only communes with a population
of more than 20,000 in 1911; cities having fewer
than 10 strikes total, 1910-14, are excluded

* Roubaix and Tourcoing are included in Lille arrondissement

x   1-12 strikes/100,000 industrial workers

•   13-20

o   21-30

O   over 30

Map 10.1: Yearly average strike rate, 1910–14

Table 10.6: *Strike and striker rates by size of place, 1910–14*

Population of chief city of arrondissement in 1911 (number of communes in parentheses)	Strike rate/100,000 industrial and transport workers	Striker rate/100,000 industrial and transport workers
+200,000	24.2	4,400
100,000–200,000 (9)	25.2	3,800
75,000–100,000 (9)	21.8	3,200
50,000–75,000 (9)	15.1	2,400
30,000–50,000 (23)	20.9	2,600
20,000–30,000 (37)	16.0	1,800

NOTES

The labor-force denominator in these rates is the industrial active population, including transport workers, in 1906. Agriculture and the tertiary labor-force save transport are excluded.

Rates by city size class were computed in a two-step procedure: (1) the arrondissements were sorted into size categories on the basis of the total population of their chief commune (the commune after which each was named) in 1911; (2) strike and striker rates were then computed for each size class using the 1906 labor-force data as the rate denominator and the 1910–14 strike activity as numerator. In these calculations, the strikes of all communes in the arrondissement (not just of the central commune) were included in the numerator, in so far as the smaller outlying communes could be matched to arrondissements.

The 94 arrondissements in this set represent all those whose central places had a population larger than 20,000 in 1911. Population data on smaller communes were not available to us.

The arrondissement of Lille includes both the labor force and strikes of Roubaix, Tourcoing and smaller surrounding communities.

ideas about working-class representation in politics that were abroad in the land.

— Map 10.1 mirrors a regional effect of some kind, for strike-prone cities clustered together around the Mediterranean littoral, in eastern Brittany, around Lyon and of course in the Nord.[5] (It is such clusters of militant towns that compose the six regions of conflict identified in the previous chapter.) Thus residence itself within a given region, or near a militant city, would stimulate local workers to a higher strike propensity than workers in a similar-size town of similar industrial composition outside that region, or beyond the bourn of that turbulent city. It was probably historic tradition that shaped the identities of recurring constellations of social and economic conditions.[6]

— Finally, as the eye sweeps inland away from the ports and strike-prone regions on the rim, it encounters vast blank spaces on the map. The small, isolated industrial centers in the hinterland were remarkably uncombative compared to the great cities and ports. Except for Limoges in all the in-land reaches of the west and southwest passivity prevailed among the industrial workers. The same is true for Burgundy and Champagne, save for a couple of textile towns.

A lack of labor-force data simply does not permit us to say much about strike rates in places smaller than 20,000 people. Such towns had as large a share of aggregate strike activity as did towns over 20,000. Of the 16,000-odd strikes in 1915–35, for example, large towns had 8,900 (or 54 percent) and small towns 7,600 (or 46 percent). The distribution. of participants in strikes was similarly equal until the First World War, but in 1915–35 the big-city share of strikers rose to 66 percent.

If the relationship between strike intensity and size of place holds as steady for small places as for large, we may gather than these villages and burghs were not very strike-prone. For even though in the aggregate such places had many strikes, there were many such places; indeed, many little towns with industrial workers had no strikes at all. On the whole it is unlikely that small towns with industrial workers had anything beyond meager strike intensities.

How about size-of-place differences in worker mobilization, as opposed to sheer strike intensities? Table 10.6 shows that big cities have higher strik*er* rates than smaller towns (yet still above 20,000 population), a partial indication of superior metropolitan mobilization. To examine exactly how worker support for a given strike develops, let us break the concept of mobilization down into its three component parts, and examine size-of-place differences for each part.

The reader will recall these three constituent elements as (*a*) the typical size of the establishment on strike; (*b*) the average number of establishments per strike, sometimes called the scope of the strike, and (*c*) the percent of workers within the affected establishment actually joining in the strike, occasionally termed the plant participation rate.

Many more establishments participated in the average strike in the big city than in the small town, as was demonstrated in table 10.4. This is factor (*b*). And it was this expanded scope that made the average number of participants in a big-city strike almost twice as great as in a small-town strike during the 1915–35 period. Big cities scored much less well than small towns on the other two contributing elements to aggregate strike size: plant participation and the size of the struck plant, as is shown in table 10.7. The size of the median establishment on strike (factor *a*) was greater in towns than in cities, and the customary percentage of the workforce in a struck establishment to walk out (factor *c*) was smaller in cities than in towns. The three largest cities, however, had quite high plant participation rates; see table 11.2, p. 292.

Why did more establishments participate in big-city strikes? To some extent, the answer is obvious. There are more establishments available for conflict in a large city than in a small town. In Paris, for example, the shops of dozens and dozens of machine-builders can simultaneously parti-

Table 10.7: *Some characteristics of strike activity by size of place*

	1895–9	1910–14	1915–35
	Mean number of strikers per strike		
Big cities (+20,000 population)	167	181	404
Small towns (−20,000 population)	188	217	238
	Median number of strikers per 100 workers employed in struck establishments[a]		
Big cities	67	68	56
Small towns	73	71	62
	Mean number of strikers per 100 workers employed in struck establishments		
Big cities	65	66	52
Small towns	77	53	59
	Median number of workers employed in struck establishments		
Big cities	71	54	69
Small towns	81	52	78
	% of strikes with unions present[b]		
Big cities	67.8 (2.7)	87.4 (2.7)	(8.9)
Small towns	40.0 (1.4)	61.6 (2.3)	(8.1)
	% of grievances over worker organization matters		
Big cities	18.5	25.8	12.1
Small towns	18.5	21.8	10.1
	% of strikes ending in success for the workers		
Big cities	21.2	17.5	21.2
Small towns	23.6	18.5	22.1
	% of strikes ending with the strikers replaced[c]		
Big cities	17.1	12.0	6.7
Small towns	7.4	6.3	3.1
	Median duration of strikes (days)		
Big cities	4.8	5.7	5.5
Small towns	4.9	5.2	6.4

[a] The denominator of this calculation changed slightly after 1915. For details see notes to fig. 3.6, p. 63.
[b] The figures in parentheses represent the percent of strikes in which allusions to unions were made in the remarks column of *SG*. These are the only data on union participation available for 1915–35, and so note was taken of this information in 1895–9 and 1910–14 as well to provide a basis for comparison over time.
[c] At least ⅔ of the strikers replaced.

cipate in a given strike action, whereas in Dijon only a few such establishments will be available. Hence no surprise that the scope of Parisian metalworking strikes is larger than the Dijonais. The multivariate analysis in the next section confirms the banality of the relationship, saying that if more establishments per strike turn up in big cities, it was just because such cities had more establishments. The following analysis also rules out the possibility that it was the consistently higher percentage of strikes with union involvement in big cities that made for high ratios of establishment per strike. And yet . . . in the metropolises of France extraordinary numbers of establishments participated in the average strike; but in other large cities, where many shops were also available (though perhaps not in such superfluity as in Paris) considerably smaller establishment/strike ratios turn up. Perhaps there *was* something about the tempo of life in Paris and Marseille, some quality of moving and working in these bustling *Weltstädte*, that persuaded workers in many establishments to move and struggle together.

The third principal way strikes in big cities differed from small towns was their high acerbity. This may be measured in several ways. Strikes over 'worker organization' questions – likely to arouse impassioned discord – became more common in cities than in towns after 1899, as table 10.7 shows. Big-city strikes were a little less likely to end in success than were small-town strikes. And, the most interesting indicator of all, big-city strikes were much more likely to end with the strikers being replaced. Although the percentage of strikes in which the workers were fired declined steadily everywhere, such disastrous strikes remained consistently twice as frequent in big cities as in small towns. Here again, as with the findings on establishments per strike, we may be dealing with a relatively banal explanation: if more workers are fired for striking in big cities, it may not be because social tensions are more acute there than elsewhere, but rather because the labor pool from which the employer can make replacements is larger; so the employer can better afford to fire strikers in the big city than in the small town. Yet we shall shortly contrast the three largest cities in France with slightly smaller urban centers in which industrial manpower was also abundant; these findings will show that the largest cities have much higher rates of striker dismissals than other communities with labor supply in equal plenitude. The differentials in acerbity thus appear genuine.

Multivariate analysis of variation among communes

Cutting the pie into two halves, and then checking for differences between the halves, does not permit us to say if these factors stand in a constant *linear* relationship. Just because there are more unions on the big-city half of the pie than the small-town half does not mean that a constant, predictable association exists between urbanity and unionization. We turn now to a procedure we used much earlier in the book – path analysis – in order to lay bare the exact relationships among multiestablishment strikes, city size and unionization. The path diagrams in fig. 10.1 permit us to observe these variables simultaneously in their relations with one another.

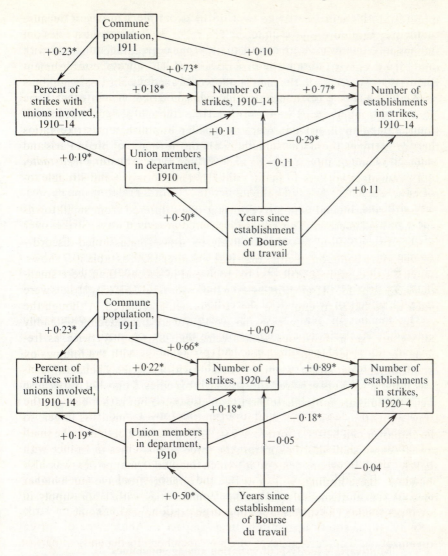

* Coefficient at least two times standard error

Fig. 10.1: Path analysis: strike activity in communes of +20,000 population in 1910–14 and 1920–4

The first diagram deals with variation in strike activity from 1910 through 1914 among the 128 communes with populations of 20,000 or more. The second diagram treats the same variables over a period ten years later, from 1920 through 1924; in this case, however, the explanatory variables still refer to the earlier period. So the two tests are not quite equivalent. Some of the variables, furthermore, refer to the department in which the commune was located rather than to the commune itself. Since these few communes accounted for the great bulk of the urban population, union members and strike activity during these periods (and had always done so up to then), that weakness of our data is not terribly serious.

We find a strong relationship (standardized regression coefficient +0.73 in 1910–14, +0.66 in 1920–4) between the number of strikes and the commune's population in 1911. When we make allowance for the strong, and hardly surprising, relationship between the number of strikes and the number of establishments involved in strikes, there remains only a weak, unreliable relationship (+0.10, +0.07) between city size and number of establishments.[7] Although the moderate zero-order relationship between city size and the number of establishments *per strike* is consistent with these refinements, it appears that the increase in the number of establishments with size of city is not much greater than the increase in the sheer number of strikes. When we substitute the recent rates of growth of these cities for the population in 1911 (as we have in other analyses not reported here) we discover trivial or negative effects on strike activity. We are dealing with effects of scale, not of disruption.

The number of years since the establishment of Bourses du travail enters the analysis as an indication of the age of local working-class organizations. Old organizations had presumably been working longer to produce the sort of socialization we have said was crucial to militancy. (In order to capture that cumulative effect, we express the variable in commune-years: if at the time-point of the analysis three separate communes in the department had Bourses du travail, and they had been in existence respectively 25, 16 and 2 years, we calculate $25 + 16 + 2 = 43$ commune-years.) What we find is weak, unreliable and mainly negative direct effects of the variable on the number of strikes and the number of establishments in strikes, and a substantial *positive* relationship to the unionization of the department, as measured by number of union members. The effect of long organizational experience on strike activity, then, shows up entirely in its impact on the degree of current organization. The current level of union membership depends in part on the sheer length of time that organizers have been working.

According to our analysis, the department's unionization has a moderate positive effect on the level of strike activity, coupled with a moderate negative effect on the number of establishments in strikes. (Other analyses we are not reporting here make it fairly clear that the negative relationship is due to the fact that areas with only a few large employers – and therefore a smaller number of establishments which *could* strike – tend to be more heavily unionized than those with many small employers.) All together, the lower sections of the diagrams make the case for a significant effect of local working-class organization on the level of strike activity.

We have brought the percentage of union-organized strikes, 1910–14, into the analysis as a representation of the overall vigor of the unions which existed in the area. (We have some misgivings about the direction of the arrow connecting union involvement with the number of strikes because of the mathematical and logical interdependence of the two measures.) If the equation of vigor with union involvement is correct, the analysis shows an unsurprising increase in vigor with the number of union members, a more interesting moderate association between city size and union vigor, and another moderate tendency for the number of strikes to rise with the vigor of local unions. Again we come round the circle from organization to strike activity.

One clear message emerges from our analysis: the city helped to transform the nature of industrial conflict. As time passed, the bulk of strikes became concentrated in the greatest city, Paris, the hub of French social and political life. And at any given point in time the metropolis was more conducive to effective organization and intense conflict than either the small town or the isolated cluster of industry.[8]

We submit that there are two reasons behind the city's superiority as a site for militancy: (1) Organization in large, dense places is easier than in small, diffuse, homogeneous places. The ties which bind and criss-cross urban society hold its members more firmly in associations than do the ties in other kinds of places. This is not news to sociologists, but somehow the message has been blurred as it reaches students of industrial conflict. (2) Collective actions within the city echo more resoundingly in the halls of political power than do similar efforts from more remote locations. The awareness among individual groups of urban workers that their activities might weigh in the grand scale of political contest surely spurred them to intensify their militancy and to band to-gether more firmly. If the strike was, as we have claimed, a means of mobilizing workers for political action, the most suitable locus for strike activity would be under the noses of the politicians and adminis-trators.

11 The interplay of organization, location and industrial conflict

A review of the argument

By now, the reader who wants to account for the differences among groups of workers in the intensity of industrial conflict may well be seeing a blur. We have first clubbed him with argument after argument, then buried him in descriptive statistics. The treatment has no doubt left him gasping and groggy. We have no master theory which accounts for all the variation. We have offered a superabundance of hypotheses and a shortage of rules for choosing among them.

In fact, we have tried to do three partly contradictory things at once: (1) to provide a quantitative description of French strike activity sufficiently ample for other students of industrial conflict to draw on in their own work and to evaluate our interpretations by means of the data; (2) to call attention to the recurrent patterns in the data – even those we can't explain – especially where they bear on questions already widely debated or frequently misunderstood; (3) to verify and develop our own ideas concerning the central importance of organizational processes in the generation of industrial conflict. So let us now abandon the description and *ad hoc* interpretation in favor of a last pursuit of the central argument.

Several broad assertions have recurred through the discussion so far, and have borne up well against repeated assaults by evidence. The first is that the scale and intensity of strike activity in a setting depend closely on the prior organization of the workers in the setting, on the availability of a structure which identifies, accumulates and communicates grievances on the one hand, and facilitates collective action on the other. Although that sort of conclusion is self-evident from several points of view, it contradicts two widely held interpretations of industrial conflict: (1) the reading of the level of strike activity as an index of worker 'discontent'; (2) the attribution of a large weight to momentary impulse or accidents of local leadership. To be sure, we have presented precious little evidence concerning the day-to-day dynamics of individual strikes and the week-to-week waxing of conflict within particular workplaces. Our evidence has taken the form of general correspondences between unionization and strike activity, demonstrations that strike waves tend to draw disproportionately from those industries which already have high propensities to strike in ordinary years, materials showing

284

the great concentration of strike activity in a relatively small number of intensely organized metropolitan centers and so on.

A second recurrent assertion has combatted the idea of strikes as direct responses to dislocation and deprivation. We have not denied that workers had real grievances, that wage cuts often incited walkouts, that craftsmen resisted dequalification by various forms of concerted action or that the appearance of new industries made a difference to the qualities of industrial conflict. Our time-series analysis, in fact, led us to modify our original argument by conceding that economic downturns tend to stimulate strike activity in the short run. But we have argued that in general dislocation and severe deprivation tend to *reduce* the propensity of workers to strike – except in the important case where they touch groups which already have a high degree of solidarity and internal organization. Our reasoning is threefold: (1) dislocation and deprivation fix the attention of workers on survival from day to day, leaving them little disposed to risky collective action; (2) dislocation and deprivation reduce the resources available for any sort of collective action; (3) for a number of different reasons (well known to the nineteenth-century employers who preferred docile recent migrants over the tough old hands, just so long as the work didn't require a very high level of skill or experience) dislocation and deprivation generally go along with an unfavorable bargaining position for workers.

To support this line of argument, we have pointed to the tendency of French strike activity to rise in times of prosperity, to the generally lower levels of strike activity in fast-growing cities, to the fact that the average strike brings out lower proportions of the whole workforce in large plants than in small ones (despite the fact that large plants have strikes more frequently) and to other evidence of that kind.

Third, we have asserted that struggles for power among groups of workers, employers, local authorities and segments of the national government strongly influenced the rhythm, distribution and character of French industrial conflict throughout its history, despite the fact that the bulk of the explicit grievances in strikes had to do with wages and hours. We have argued, furthermore, that over the century after 1850 strikes became increasingly oriented to the *national* political position of labor; we claim to have detected a particularly strong shift in that direction some time between the Popular Front and the end of the Second World War. Here the evidence has been flimsier than in the case of the first two assertions, for we have had to reason mainly from information about strikes themselves rather than about the wielding of power in general. Still, our analyses of year-to-year covariation of political conflicts and strikes, of the character of governmental intervention and mediation in strikes and of the political timing of strike waves all appear to move in the same direction.

Our fourth persistent argument has rested on the distinction among three types of industrial organization: (a) the type depending on the interaction of well defined crafts, (b) the type characterized by semi-skilled workers, machine-tending and bureaucratic control, (c) the type applying complicated technologies and requiring high levels of formal training of its personnel. The schema goes something like this:

		Professional solidarity	
		Low	*High*
Scale and bureau-cratization of workplace, labor organization	Low	NONE	Craftsmen
	High	Factory proletarians	Skilled professionals in science sector

(The big NONE for the low–low category means we expect no significant labor organization or strike activity where producing units are small, informal and staffed by heterogeneous and/or unskilled workers.) With due recognition of the incompleteness and overlap of these categories, we have called attention to the implications for industrial conflict of the general historical shift from artisanal to proletarian to professional as dominant sectors of the labor force. We have claimed that each produces a characteristically different form of worker organization, and consequently a different pattern of industrial conflict. In the chief period under observation – from the 1890s to the 1960s – we see the shifts from artisanal to proletarian exemplified in the increasing size and frequency of the strike, its increasing orientation to national politics and a number of other features. Only in the 1960s do we begin to see traits which one might reasonably attribute to the increasing prominence of the science sector.

Even if true, our four broad assertions leave at least one serious open question behind them, and suggest as well the need for some statistical wrapping-up. The remaining question is whether 'isolated masses' of workers have some special propensity to industrial conflict. Such a notion does not follow easily from the line of argument we have been presenting. Indeed, it tends to contradict our argument. We need to pay attention to it precisely because some of the most plausible alternatives to our argument crystallize around the idea of strikes as the protests of homogeneous, deprived and proletarianized workers separated from the rest of the world and aware of their separation. Although Marx's stress on the development of communication, proletarian organization and class consciousness as the basis of collective action jibes with our argument, his expectation that these processes would thrive on the homogenization and isolation of the working class does not. The non-Marxist reasoning represented in the famous analysis of strike propensity by Clark Kerr and Abraham Siegel likewise emphasizes isolation and homogeneity; in that analysis isolated, homogeneous masses of workers are supposed to be more combative because they have distinctive common codes, because outward and upward mobility are difficult for them and because they are especially likely to unite in hostility to a distant employer.

Then a final tying-together may be in order. Thus far in this book we have lined up such forces as the growth of unions, technological innovation and the nature of big-city life, asserting that a shift in each at some point in time gave industrial conflict a further push towards 'nationalization.' The reader may wish to witness these enormous historical forces in *simultaneous* movement as they nudge the strike away from localized shop-floor protest towards national political bargaining.

The completion of these tasks will permit us to draw together the implications of a variety of arguments made separately at different points in the book, by two means: (a) a few more of the relatively simple tabulations of strike rates by locality, time and industry that have done so much of the earlier work of the book, (b) some compact multivariate analyses which likewise treat variation in strike propensity among groups of workers in different times and places as the object to be explained, but examine a whole set of explanatory variables simultaneously in order to identify their relationships to each other and their joint effects on strike activity. We begin with the Kerr–Siegel hypothesis and close with a more general attempt to deal simultaneously with the major determinants of a department's strike activity.

The Kerr–Siegel 'isolation' hypothesis and France's experience

In 1954 Clark Kerr and Abraham Siegel published what was to become the standard interpretation of interindustry differences in strike propensity.[1] The notion of isolation was the centerpoint of their argument: industries which were isolated would show higher strike propensities than industries whose workers were integrated into the rest of society. The authors had in mind primarily territorial isolation: the remoteness of a mining town or logging camp from bustling centers of urban activity. Yet they incorporated into their argument the concept of 'social' isolation, so as to include stevedores and seamen in the range of explained phenomena.

The argument had two refinements and an alternative. In addition to being geographically isolated, the workforce of the strike-prone industry was to compose a homogeneous mass – hence the famous 'isolated mass,' a body of workers not riven by skill or wage differentials and alert to a commonality of condition. Second, the isolated mass was to be 'capable of cohesion' – be together in territorial proximity for collective action – which would rule out such dispersed working populations as agricultural workers, isolated though they might be.

Sensing difficulties in this argument, the authors advanced in the same article an alternative hypothesis for interindustry strike differentials: the character of the job and the worker. This was a truly 'industrial' explanation, for it adduced structural differences among industries as the strategic variable. Industries involving hard, dirty work seemed to attract 'tough, inconstant, combative and virile workers,' who apparently took part in strikes as a way of expressing their manliness, or perhaps just because hard men did bold deeds. Industries with easy, pleasant job tasks, on the other hand, attracted a 'more submissive type of man who will abhor strikes. Certainly the bull of the woods and the mousy bank clerk are different types of people and can be expected to act differently' (p. 195). Fortunately, Kerr and Siegel saw even greater difficulties with this explanation of industrial psychodynamics and made of it a distinctly minor aside to their main 'isolated mass' case.[2]

Exactly what properties of 'isolation' produced a high strike propensity? Kerr and Siegel appeared to single out at least three. Geographical apartness created a sense of common condition, for one thing. Workers saw they were all in the same boat; they all had the same grievances; and they shared in general a mutual world of values and beliefs: 'These communities have their own codes, myths, heroes, and social standards' (p. 191).

Secondly, geographical isolation trapped the worker in his present job, making upward or outward mobility difficult and therewith channeling his individual grievances into collective protest. Kerr and Siegel explained:

> Protest is less likely to take the form of moving to another industry and more the character of the mass walkout ... It is the mass grievance which leads to 'class' action. The individual grievance can be more readily absorbed and managed by society. Industrial tranquility depends on keeping grievances dispersed so that they may be handled one at a time. Proponents of social unrest are most successful in those places where, and at those times when, grievances are most highly concentrated [p. 192].

Thus when the unhappy worker is permitted to take another job in a different industry within the community, or to advance himself through promotion, his discontent will be neutralized; but the aggregation of individual unhappiness produces mass unhappiness, and therewith protest and revolt.

Thirdly, according to Kerr and Siegel, isolation causes protest by making employer authority remote and impersonal, an object of hatred and rebellion rather than of respect and veneration. ('The worker is as detached from the employer as from the community at large' [p. 192]). Absentee mine-owners and lumber barons excite worker fury; resident owners of small shops attract loyalty and sympathy.

Industries which are not isolated in this manner have, Kerr and Siegel suggest, quite different characteristics. Integration within a large diverse community brings a modulation of militancy; 'neutrals' are present who adjudicate conflict; exposure to heterogeneity itself in some way seems to moderate worker anger; and of course escape from unpopular jobs is possible owing to the presence of alternative sources of employment within the community. Finally, 'community' pressures for industrial peace assert themselves (somehow).

As evidence for these assertions Kerr and Siegel took strike propensities by industry for a number of different countries. Using some rather rough techniques for sorting and computing, they found that mining and the maritime–waterfront sectors had, as the most 'isolated' industries, the highest strike propensities. They found that railroading, agriculture, trade and the like, as the least 'isolated,' had lowest strike propensities. They were unable to make much sense of the intermediate ranges of the scale.

Now embedded within this structure are some useful insights. The authors noted, for example, a tendency for strikes within many industries to resemble political revolts rather than bread-and-butter jockeying for economic advantage. They also saw the labor unions within these militant sectors (places) as integrating the worker into a subsociety of the oppressed, and representing him to a larger, oppressing outside society. To be sure, other writers before Kerr and Siegel – one thinks especially of Marx – have theorized along these lines; yet no one previously had applied the wisdom of political sociology to systematic data on interindustry differences in strike activity.

It is important to note that the Kerr–Siegel logic was in fact suited to account for territorial, not industrial, differences in strike activity. The only important 'industrial' strut in their argument is the assertion that the homogeneity of skill elicits high strike intensity, whereas occupational stratification calms protest. All their other assertions concern the militancy-producing effects of living and working in a certain kind of *place* rather than a certain kind of industry, a place where the employers are away, where the workers are not made mild by exposure to diversity, where employees can avoid that 'trapped feeling' by changing jobs easily.

The authors claimed, to be sure, that their case applied to industries 'socially' as well as territorially isolated. Yet this is not to be taken seriously. Most occupations are 'socially' isolated, if by that is meant a sense of corporate community or segregated places of work – and so the observation is trivial. To illustrate the radicalizing effects of 'social' isolation within a heterogeneous urban setting, they cited strike-prone seamen and stevedores. Yet as a factual matter, these occupations are surely no more 'isolated' than any of a score of other urban jobs having low strike propensities. The notion of 'social' segregation, therefore, does not provide an escape hatch: if the isolation hypothesis is substantially correct, it must explain *territorial* differentials in strike propensity.

We believe that Kerr–Siegel 'isolated mass' argument to be largely wrong. It is based on a misreading of the data it claims to explain; moreover, it collapses when called upon to make sense of the French experience.

Let us divide French industrial towns in a way that will permit the testing of the argument. The 1906 census published information on the industrial composition of each arrondissement in the country. The arrondissement is the equivalent of the North American county, and arrondissemental data provide the nearest available proxy for municipal-level data. We assume that the industrial mix of an arrondissement reflects roughly the industrial composition of its principal center, the town after which it is customarily named. These 1906 data permit the classification of arrondissements into three principal types:

1. Mono-industrial. If a single blue-collar sector predominates over all others within the arrondissement's non-agricultural labor force, that arrondissement will be considered mono-industrial. Such places should represent perfect test cases for the Kerr–Siegel argument, for here if anywhere is to be found the isolated mass, a population composed mainly of manufacturing workers or miners within a single sector. Here above all workers should feel themselves 'trapped,' as Kerr and Siegel hypothesize, unable to escape or to shift jobs to a different sector. Here above all militancy and solidarity should be at their peak.

2. Poly-industrial. If a mix of industries prevails within a place, rather than a single dominant sector, we shall consider that arrondissement poly-industrial. Such towns differ from mono-industrial communes in not being single-industry, 'company' towns. The isolated mass is to be found in them, but it is a heterogeneous mass.

3. Metropolitan. We classify the three largest cities in France – Paris, Lyon and Marseille – as metropolises in order to have a clear antithesis to the isolated mass. In the great cities one finds an infinite variety of occupations, a dazzling heterogeneity of people and diversity of experience. The worker can change jobs easily. And here, if anywhere, one would expect to find the 'neutrals' who mediate conflict, the associations of 'people with quite different working experiences,' the small-shop employers whose nearness to the workforce allays hostility, and the community pressures for peaceful conduct that Kerr and Siegel consider characteristic of 'the integrated individual and the integrated group.' If these conditions for industrial passivity are not found in the big city, they will be found nowhere.

If the Kerr–Siegel hypothesis has any explanatory power at all, it will discover the intensity of conflict, or the elements of proletarian solidarity, to be highest in mono-industrial towns, middling in poly-industrial communities, and lowest in metropolises. Unfortunately for the hypothesis, things turn out largely the opposite.

Evidence from territorial differentials in the rate of conflict is the first piece of bad news. Once the upward pull upon mono-industrial arrondissements of the conurbation Lille–Roubaix–Tourcoing has been discounted, conflict appears more intense in the metropolitan centers than among the isolated mass (table 11.1). Lille–Roubaix–Tourcoing is a case difficult to classify because the city of Lille was both the fifth largest city in France in 1911 and a mono-industrial commune by virtue of the tremendous concentration of spinning and weaving mills there. If we include Lille in the mono-industrial ranks, the apparent strike rate of the 'isolated mass' soars far above that of the three metropolises. If we remove Lille (and its adjacent suburbs Roubaix and Tourcoing), the strike rate of mono-industrial arrondissements sags considerably below that of Paris, Marseille and Lyon. It is especially noteworthy that each of the three cities Paris–Marseille–Lyon had higher strik*er* rates than *any* isolated mass arrondissement.

Most of the mono-industrial arrondissements were textile centers, and so one might dismiss their lackluster performance as owing to a general lack of militancy within textiles (even though Kerr and Siegel consider textiles an isolated mass industry). Yet the poly-industrial arrondissements, where a genuine diversity of industries prevails, were even more docile. When the arrondissements of the Nord and Seine-Maritime are removed from the 'industrial' ranks, the isolated mass turns out to be not in the least prone to strike activity.

Yet Kerr and Siegel have a possible way out (one we create for them, only to close it off). Perhaps the isolated mass strikes rarely and not in large numbers. But when these workers do go out, the Kerr–Siegel hypothesis might be extended to predict great proletarian *solidarity* for them, high cohesiveness and resolution in conflict. In other words, if the isolated mass strikes not often but well, the Kerr–Siegel argument will retain some grip on life.

In fact, compared to metropolitan workers, the labor force in the isolated mass evidences an organizational incapacity and an inclination to irresoluteness in disputes. Let us compare in table 11.2 the two kinds of communities with our familiar indicators of solidarity.

– Metropolitan centers registered in 1910–14 more union involvement in strikes than either mono- or poly-industrial arrondissements. And in 1915–35 the cities Paris, Marseille and Lyon continued to have union participation rates higher than those of mono-industrial towns, while being surpassed by poly-industrial communities.

– Participation in strikes within single plants was marginally higher in the three big cities than in mono-industrial communes, both during 1910–14 and 1915–35. If the Kerr–Siegel argument were correct, the relationship would be exactly reversed, the isolated mass showing greatest solidarity.

– Finally, the scope of metropolitan strikes was broader than of strikes in either sort of industrial commune. A single dispute would typically stretch

Table 11.1: *Strike and striker rates for metropolitan centers versus the 'isolated mass,' 1910–14*

	Rates of strikes and strikers in 1910–14 per 100,000 industrial workers, as recorded in the 1906 census	
	Strikes	Strikers
Metropolis	16	4,600
Poly-industrial	17	1,900
(Poly-industrial minus		
Nord and Seine-Maritime)	(14)	(1,300)
Mono-industrial	27	1,300
(Mono-industrial minus Lille)	(12)	(1,200)
(Mono-industrial minus Nord		
and Seine-Maritime)	(12)	(2,000)

Table 11.2: *Characteristics of strike activity in metropolitan centers and poly-industrial and mono-industrial towns*

	1910–14	1915–35
	% of strikes with union involvement[a]	
Metropolitan	93.2 (4.2)	(8.8)
Poly-industrial	83.4 (1.1)	(9.5)
Mono-industrial	87.3 (0.0)	(6.7)
	Median strikers/100 workers in struck establishments	
Metropolitan	67	60
Poly-industrial	68	53
Mono-industrial	62	53
	Mean number of establishments per strike	
Metropolitan	18.7	24.3
Poly-industrial	4.4	7.9
Mono-industrial	3.1	7.9
	Median workforce in struck establishments	
Metropolitan	46	57
Poly-industrial	61	80
Mono-industrial	107	100
	% of strikes with strikers replaced	
Metropolitan	21.9	11.5
Poly-industrial	8.6	4.2
Mono-industrial	5.0	2.5
	% of grievances over worker organization issues	
Metropolitan	32.9	11.3
Poly-industrial	26.0	15.8
Mono-industrial	21.8	12.5

[a] Figures in parentheses represent percent of strikes in which allusion to unions was made in the remarks column of *SG*. On this index see pp. 187–8.

NOTES TO TABLE 11.1
Metropolis includes Paris, Lyon and Marseille.

Poly-industrial includes 29 arrondissements, mono-industrial 17 arrondissements. The mono-industrial arrondissement of Lille incorporates Roubaix and Tourcoing.

The 1906 arrondissemental labor-force data exclude agriculture and all tertiary occupations except transportation. The rates have been divided by five to make them yearly averages.

Our exact procedures for sorting the arrondissements into categories were as follows:

The arrondissement would be considered 'industrial' if blue-collar industries (mining, food industries, chemicals, printing–paper, leather–hides, textiles, smelting, metalworking, general construction or transportation) composed more than 40 percent of its total active population (including agriculture).

The arrondissement would be considered 'mono-industrial' if one of the above industries had more than 50 percent of the industrial workforce, and if there were no other industry with more than 15 percent of the workforce. The town would also be thought mono-industrial if a single industry had more than 60 percent of the workforce, and the next largest industry had less than 20 percent.

The arrondissement would be considered 'poly-industrial' if more than one of the above industries had between 15 and 50 percent (or 20 and 60 percent) of the industrial population.

On the basis of these principles, 17 arrondissements came into the 'mono-industrial' category in 1906: Amiens (Somme), Béthune (Pas-de-Calais), Cambrai (Nord), Doullens (Somme), Epinal (Vosges), Lille (Nord), Mézières (Ardennes), Montbéliard (Doubs), Nogent-sur-Seine (Aube), Remiremont (Vosges), Roanne (Loire), Rouen (Seine-Maritime), St-Dié (Vosges), St-Quentin (Aisne), la Tour-du-Pin (Isère), Troyes (Aube) and Yssingeaux (Haute-Loire).

Lyon should actually have been classed as a mono-industrial city because its textile–garment industry represented 51 percent of its arrondissemental labor force; yet we put Lyon in the metropolis category because of its great size and general heterogeneity.

These principles further dictated that the following 29 arrondissements be classed 'poly-industrial': Alès (Gard), Autun (Saône-et-Loire), Avesnes-sur-Helpe (Nord), Avignon (Vaucluse), Bar-le-Duc (Meuse), Beauvais (Oise), Boulogne-sur-Mer (Pas-de-Calais), Briey (Meurthe-et-Moselle), Clermont (Oise), Corbeil (Seine-et-Oise), Douai (Nord), Grenoble (Isère), le Havre (Seine-Maritime), Lunéville (Meurthe-et-Moselle), Nancy (Meurthe-et-Moselle), Nantua (Ain), Mirecourt (Vosges), Pontoise (Seine-et-Oise), Reims (Marne), Rocroi (Ardennes), Sceaux (Seine), Sedan (Ardennes), Senlis (Oise), St-Claude (Jura), St-Etienne (Loire), Valenciennes (Nord), Versailles (Seine-et-Oise), Vervins (Aisne) and Wassy (Haute-Marne).

The sprawling arrondissement of St-Denis should properly have been made poly-industrial. Yet because of its proximity to Paris, and the mono-industrial nature of many of its constituent parts, we omitted it entirely as a mixed case.

In all calculations involving the matching of strike data to arrondissemental labor force, we have allocated Roubaix, Tourcoing and other outlying communes of Lille to the Lille arrondissement. The census of arrondissemental labor force had, in fact, separate lines for Roubaix and Tourcoing, even though they were not arrondissements. Yet Roubaix and Tourcoing contributed only half of those strikes which took place within Lille arrondissement though which were outside the city of Lille proper in 1910–14. It therefore seemed best to aggregate all strikes within the Lille arrondissement so as to be confident the labor force would match the population producing the strikes.

Strikes in Lille arrondissement, 1910–14

Lille	126
Roubaix	186
Tourcoing	175
Other communes in Lille arrondissement	289
Total strikes in Lille arrondissement	776

to twice or three times as many establishments in metropolitan centers as among the isolated mass. During 1915–35, 22 establishments were enmeshed in the average strike in Paris, 26 in Marseille and 39 in Lyon. At this same time, by way of contrast the typical dispute was limited to 2 establishments in Roubaix and Tourcoing, 4 in le Havre and 7 in St-Etienne, to take examples of places where a sizable number of establishments are available to participate simultaneously in strikes, but don't.

If our indices of 'social' animosity are to be trusted, metropolitan strikes aroused more hard feelings, with their small shops and resident employers (believed by Kerr and Siegel to ameliorate conflict), than did strikes in industrial communities with their large mills and plants.[3] The median size of struck establishments in industrial arrondissements of either poly- or mono-variety were substantially higher than in the metropolitan centers.

– In 1910–14 Paris, Marseille and Lyon saw a higher percentage of grievances involving worker organization questions – normally the most sensitive issues in industrial relations – than did either poly- or mono-industrial towns. In the 1920s this relationship was upset, doubtless as part of the still unclarified changes taking place within the metropolis during the interwar years.

– The risk that a striker would not be rehired was four times as great in a metropolis as in a company town. The commonplace firing of militants is definitely not the employer response to militancy one would expect to encounter among the 'integrated individual and the integrated group,' if Kerr and Siegel are correct.

Let us rest our case here. The French experience points directly away from explanations of territorial differences in strike activity that invoke marginality, peripheralness and isolation. Our study of the geographical dimension of conflict indicates rather the strategic role of the central place and of exposure to diversity in eliciting militant organization. The French cities with the highest intensities of conflict and the most efficient mobilization of participants were places where a riot of experiences and of possibilities for association crowded in upon the working man. They were places where people could meet easily, communicate swiftly and above all be confident of attracting the attention of the powerful in their public demonstrations and protests. They were the loci of extensive working-class organization.

French strikers were not, by and large, marginal workers on the periphery of social life. Kerr and Siegel's label 'inconstant' does not apply to most of them. They were bearers of the core traditions of working-class protest, skilled craft workers in the hearts of classic urban centers.[4] Genuine proletarians were only able to overcome the sizable obstacles to organization set by homogeneity of rank, lack of skill and large size of enterprise by drawing upon the resources of the metropolis. It is a nice irony of the French experience that precisely the structures which Kerr and Siegel saw as producing 'integration' were those making for conflict.

Pinning down the differences among departments

If we are right, we should be able to show that the variables we stressed in earlier discussions actually provide a plausible statistical account of area-to-area differences in strike activity. The path diagrams at the end of the previous chapter make the case for differences among communes. But most of the areal tabulations in this book are at the level of the department. Let us look again at variation among departments.

In this last analysis, we take the total strike activity in a department over a substantial block of years as the object to be explained, and attempt to specify the simultaneous effects of a number of departmental characteristics on that strike activity. The analysis breaks into two parts. The first concentrates on the explanation of the sheer number of strikes in the department without regard to the size, shape or other characteristics of those strikes. The second deals mainly with the relationship among different characteristics of the strikes occurring within a department. In both cases the analysis begins with simple correlation coefficients covering several sets of years, and then moves rapidly to path diagrams representing the most important relationships (and non-relationships) revealed by the correlations.

We have computed (in tables too bulky to present here) correlations among a number of characteristics of departments, including the extent of their strike activity, in three substantially different five-year periods: 1910 to 1914 (a time of high militancy and mass strike activity in modern industry, including the famous railroad strike crushed by Briand in 1910), 1920 to 1924 (covering the last part of the strike wave of 1919–20 and a few relatively quiet years), 1925 to 1929 (except for the flurry of 1926, a time of moderate industrial conflict). Table 11.3 sums up the relationships over the years from 1915 through 1935, the longest span for which we have comparable data. We have not analyzed 1915–19 or 1930–4 separately because we lack appropriate baseline data for some of the background variables – especially unionization, mechanization and plant size.

The first feature of these data to strike the eye is their remarkable similarity. Some of the similarity, to be sure, comes from the repetition of precisely the same variables from one period to the next. But the set of strikes under consideration in each case is quite different, yet the data representing measures of strike activity display approximately the same relationships for all three periods. The principal exception is the relationship of strike activity to urban growth, which is moderate to strong in 1910–14 and 1925–9 but practically nonexistent in 1920–4 and over the long period 1915–35. That

Table 11.3: *Zero-order correlations of selected characteristics of departments, 1915–35*

	1.	2.	3.	4.	5.	6.	7.	8.	9.	10.	11.	12.	13.	14.	15.
1.	1.00														
2.	0.79	1.00													
3.	0.03	0.16	1.00												
4.	0.04	0.14	0.86	1.00											
5.	0.11	0.05	0.64	0.57	1.00										
6.	0.04	0.10	0.84	0.77	0.46	1.00									
7.	−0.04	0.19	0.46	0.46	0.20	0.38	1.00								
8.	−0.04	0.12	0.77	0.74	0.45	0.66	0.55	1.00							
9.	0.03	0.14	0.84	0.78	0.64	0.61	0.42	0.73	1.00						
10.	0.00	0.14	0.83	0.80	0.61	0.58	0.50	0.82	0.94	1.00					
11.	0.10	0.16	0.72	0.70	0.67	0.48	0.23	0.61	0.89	0.87	1.00				
12.	0.05	0.12	0.71	0.65	0.63	0.49	0.24	0.58	0.85	0.81	0.86	1.00			
13.	−0.02	0.11	0.78	0.68	0.62	0.59	0.46	0.64	0.89	0.83	0.75	0.78	1.00		
14.	0.04	0.14	0.84	0.77	0.66	0.61	0.40	0.72	0.99	0.93	0.90	0.85	0.86	1.00	
15.	0.00	0.11	0.87	0.78	0.69	0.65	0.44	0.70	0.95	0.88	0.82	0.78	0.88	0.95	1.00

1. % urban growth, 1911–21
2. % urban growth, 1906–21
3. Industrial labor force, 1921
4. Number of union members, 1920
5. Number of years since establishment of of Bourse du travail, 1910
6. Number of steam engines in department, 1911
7. Mean size of industrial establishments, 1921
8. Workers in establishments larger than 100, 1921
9. Number of strikes, 1915–35
10. Number of strikers, 1915–35
11. Number of struck establishments, 1915–35
12. Number of strikes with unions involved, 1915–35
13. Number of defensive strikes, 1915–35
14. Number of offensive strikes, 1915–35
15. Number of strikes failing, 1915–35

NOTES

All strike data come from our own coding of *SG*.

Information on the distribution of a department's population by commune size ('urbanization') is taken from official census reports in the *Statistique générale de la France*.

Information on the distribution of steam engines comes from periodic volumes of the *Statistique de l'industrie minérale de la France*.

'Commune-years' of Bourse du travail existence' was computed by aggregating the number of years by 1911 that each Bourse du travail in the department had survived. Because the Bourse was a municipal rather than a departmental institution, we had to find some way of representing Bourse implantation for a department-level analysis. One solution would have been to take the number of years since the first Bourse in the department was established, on the assumption that labor militancy arrived everywhere in the department shortly after this initial foundation. We rejected this course because in fact many worker communities in hinterland departments were quite isolated from one another, and to assume that they all marched to the same beat would be unjustified. A second solution would have been to compute an average Bourse du travail existence for the department, by adding up the years each Bourse had existed, then dividing by the total number of Bourses. We rejected this course because it gave insufficient weight to departments with many Bourses. The third technique – which we in fact adopted – was simply to add up the number of years each Bourse in the department had existed by 1911, thus deriving the total 'commune-years' of Bourse implantation. This technique risks underweighting large urban agglomerations which have but a single Bourse, such as Marseille. But we selected this third procedure because most regions of heavy worker concentration have, in fact, a number of Bourses du travail.

pattern we will have to examine carefully (also, because it reverses the negative correlations between urbanization and strikes we found in the last chapter at the level of the municipality). Otherwise, similar numbers show up in all the data: strong associations of strike activity with the size of the industrial labor force, the number of union members, the total number of years that individual Bourses du travail had existed, the number of steam engines installed in the department (our crude measure of the presence of highly mechanized industry) and the number of workers in establishments employing more than 100 persons. Some of these are obviously no more than matters of scale: more workers, more strikes. The path analysis will sort them out. Still, the stability of these associations over a variety of periods provides assurance that they are more than coincidence.

The correlation matrices also identify a cluster of variables one might call 'industrialism.' The size of the industrial labor force, the number of union members, the total commune-years of Bourse du travail presence, the number of steam engines and the number of workers in large establishments tend to vary together. It is their persistent association with each other and with the level of strike activity, in fact, which accounts for the stability of the general pattern of correlations.

The correlations, finally, give us some faint indications of associations among large-scale industry, unionization, 'offensive' strikes (strikes, that is, in which workers demanded new advantages, especially shorter hours and higher wages, rather than resisting speedups, wage cuts and the like) and success in strike activity. Some of these zero-order coefficients are hard to interpret because we have used absolute numbers rather than rates. The correlations therefore include strong scale effects: more defensive strikes and large totals of strikes obviously run together. We have used absolute numbers in order to avoid the serious logical difficulties presented by correlations of rates (since high coefficients can result as easily from covariation of the rates' denominators as from covariation of their numerators) and to obtain a distinct measure of the effects of scale themselves. The path analyses will again dispel that obscurity. In any case, the pattern of coefficients consistently indicates a stronger association of the various measures of scale with offensive action than with defensive action.

To see whether our earlier explanations of strike activity hold up, however, we must examine a number of the relationships simultaneously. A new set of path diagrams, two per correlation matrix, opens the way. In each case, the first diagram sorts out the most important relationships (and non-relationships) behind the total number of strikes in a department during a particular time period. The second relates a number of characteristics of the strikes to each other.

The first diagram for 1910–14 brings out some interesting connections (fig. 11.1). During that period, departments which had large industrial labor forces, departments which were more heavily mechanized and departments which had long experience in labor organization, as represented by the

A. *Determinants of total number of strikes*

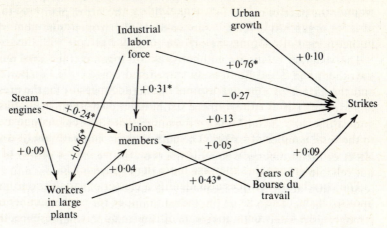

B. *Characteristics of strikes*

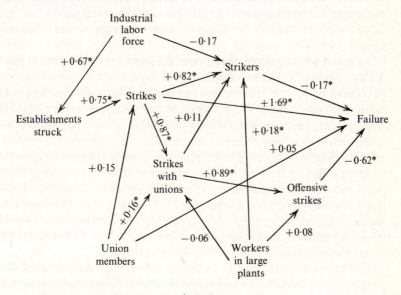

* Coefficient at least two times its standard error

Fig. 11.1: Path analysis at departmental level, 1910–14

commune-years of Bourse du travail presence, also tended to have more union members; once these factors were taken into account, the sheer size of plants did not significantly affect unionization. Mechanization displayed a moderate but unreliable relationship to the number of strikes. The only strong, reliable relationship with the number of strikes in a department during 1910–14 was the rather obvious one: size of industrial labor force. Neither the pace of recent urban growth nor the size of plants nor the extent of labor organization reliably predicted the department's number of strikes in that period of militancy before the First World War.

The diagram relating characteristics of strikes in the same period, on the other hand, does offer some evidence of an impact of the scale of industry and the extent of unionization on the kinds of strikes that occurred in a department. Let us disregard the strong coefficients representing effects of scale alone, like the 0.87 linking the number of strikes with unions involved to the total number of strikes. The path analysis shows us a small, unreliable effect of the number of union members on the frequency of strikes, a small but reliable effect on the number of strikes involving unions and no direct relationship at all to the frequency of success or failure in strikes. There appears, however, to be an important indirect effect: offensive strikes were strongly associated with strikes involving unions; where offensive strikes were frequent, failures were relatively infrequent. Another indirect path is equally interesting: although size of plant had no significant effect on the offensive or defensive character of a department's strikes, larger plants did mean more strikers (even after allowance for the total size of the industrial labor force), and failures were less frequent where the number of strikers was larger.

As one might expect from the correlation matrices, the path diagrams for 1920–4 (fig. 11.2) greatly resemble those for ten years earlier. In general, the relationships for the later period come out in the same direction but somewhat stronger. Among the determinants of the total number of strikes in a department, the biggest exception is the shift away from a direct positive effect of the maturity of union organization (as represented by commune-years of Bourse du travail presence) on the number of union members toward a direct effect of that maturity on the number of strikes; surely the CGT's mass recruitment of members in the newer industries immediately after the First World War played a major part in that shift. Annie Kriegel's work on postwar unionization suggests as much. In our own analysis, so do the increased relationships between union membership in 1920 and (a) the total size of the industrial labor force and (b) the number of workers in large plants. Nevertheless, during 1920–4 we find the older organized centers (again, as represented by the longevity of the Bourse du travail) especially prominent in strike activity, another negative relationship of strikes to mechanization, and only slightly increased relationships of the number of strikes to unionization or the scale of industrial plants.

During that same five-year span 1920–4, the few significant shifts in the relationships among characteristics of strikes reflect the changing nature of unionization. A weakening of the relationship between offensive strikes and union involvement in strikes accompanies a strengthening of the impact of large plants on both the number of strikers and the number of offensive strikes. We see the pattern we have called 'sparkplug unionism' in

A. *Determinants of total number of strikes*

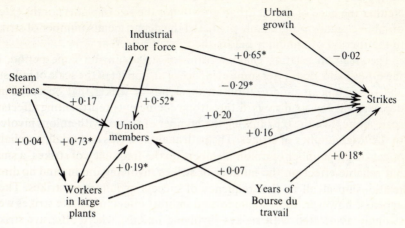

B. *Characteristics of strikes*

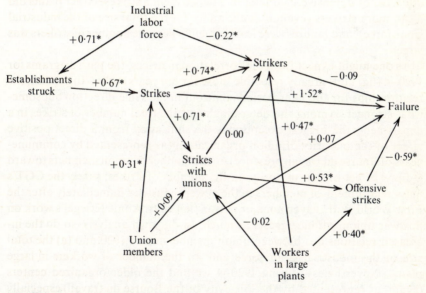

* Coefficient at least two times its standard error

Fig. 11.2: Path analysis at departmental level, 1920–4

formation: the presence of an organized nucleus sparks strike activity, but the formal and informal structures of workplaces play important independent parts in determining how far and how well that activity goes.

The diagrams for 1925–9 (fig. 11.3) are so similar to those for 1920–4 that they hardly merit separate discussion. The apparent slight weakening of the effects of plant size and of unionization in the later period may well result

A. Determinants of total number of strikes

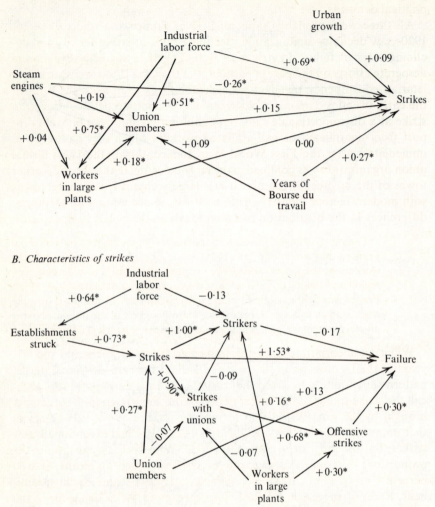

B. Characteristics of strikes

Coefficient at least two times its standard error

Fig. 11.3: Path analysis at departmental level, 1925–9

from the fact that in both the 1920–4 and 1925–9 analyses our plant size and unionization data for departments come from the beginning of the decade. There was only one significant change in the pattern. That one boded ill for the workers: in 1925–9 a *positive* relationship emerged between failure and offensive strikes. It is as if the unions involved in strikes (whose presence still predicted strongly to offensive rather than defensive actions) were miscalculating or losing their strength. Or, perhaps, as if the offensive wage strikes were becoming increasingly a cover for inherently ungrantable political demands.

All three were probably happening. Over France as a whole, the later 1920s saw declining unionization, declining rates of strike activity and declining rates of failure in strikes as well. Together this helps explain the desperate efforts on the part in particular of the CGTU to reactivate a proletarian constituency that had been demobilizing itself since the furor of the early twenties. Unions in older centers of labor strength continued to strike at a disproportionate rate, but could not count on the buoyant support from unaffiliated or half-affiliated workers which they had received immediately after the First World War. Indeed, during the 1920s formal union organization was confined to the large cities and to the historic worker towns of the nineteenth century; it was largely absent from worker towns with modern factory industry. Antoine Prost, in accounting for territorial differences in the distribution of union locals on the eve of 1936, explains:

> The most strongly unionized population is in fact that of old industrial France, that which one calls today static France. On the other side the workers of the most working-class regions, the Nord, Lorraine, the Lyon region and the lower Seine estuary, were scarcely unionized at all: dynamic France was behind static France ... The unionism which appears on these maps is thus, to a very large extent, a prolongation of the unionism of the nineteenth century, that which could be termed 'historical unionism.'[5]

When we incorporate both the immediate postwar years and the first years of the Depression in the pair of diagrams for 1915–35 (fig. 11.4), the pattern shifts quite a bit from that of 1920–9 alone. Perhaps we should recall the strike trends of the longer period. After the trough in strike activity brought by the First World War arrived the strike wave of 1919–20; from that point on, strike activity declined to 1935; 1927 had exceptionally few strikes, but the great drop came after 1930. With very few exceptions, the proportions of strikes that were offensive ran very high – typically 70 to 80 percent – up to 1930, after which defensive strikes became equally prominent. Rates of success and failure fluctuated more. After rising during the teens, successes hovered around 20 percent of all strikes in the 1920s; after 1926 or 1927, their overall frequency declined, but also varied more from year to year. Outright failure rose rapidly with the strike wave of 1919–20, reaching more than half of all strikes in the wave's second year. The frequency of failure declined only slowly from 1920 to 1929, then rose sharply after 1929. So in treating 1915–35 as a bloc, we are compounding rather different kinds of periods.

As we might expect, the broadening of the time period produces less change in our understanding of the determinants of the level of strike activity than in our sense of the relationships among characteristics of strikes. We still find that the department's mechanization and the scale of

A. *Determinants of total number of strikes*

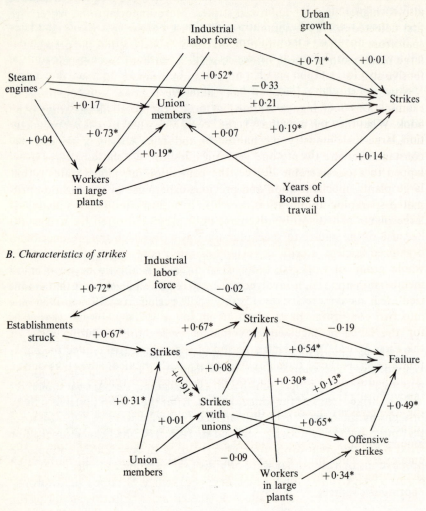

B. *Characteristics of strikes*

* Coefficient at least two times its standard error

Fig. 11.4: Path analysis at departmental level, 1915–35

its plant predicted the level of unionization; the union membership, plant size and maturity of labor organization contributed positively to the number of strikes while the direct effect of mechanization on strike activity is negative, and so on. Over the long period, the direct positive effect of large plant size on the number of strikes, and the direct negative effect of mechanization on that same number, came out stronger than in our observations of the 1920s alone. From 1915 to 1935, we discover a weak but reliable tendency for higher union membership to lead not only to more frequent strikes but also to higher rates of failure in strikes. More important, the pattern we first detected in 1925–9 actually gains in clarity when we observe the whole span from 1915 to 1935: union involvement in strikes and the presence of large plants both promote offensive strikes; but both the frequency of offensive strikes and the extent of unionization promote failure.

Now we should remember that these are regional comparisons, no. examinations of change over time like those we reported much earlier in the book. What they tell us is that (1) the geographic patterns of labor organization, large-scale industry, mechanization and strike activity remained fairly constant over the twenty-one years in question; (2) those patterns overlapped to a considerable degree; the contention our model states is that large plants, mechanization and previous experience in organization promoted sparkplug unionization, which in turn promoted strike activity; (3) large plants and union involvement both promoted offensive strikes; (4) because of the nature of sparkplug unionism (in which the presence of an organized nucleus is critical, yet unions rarely control an entire strike or a whole group of workers), there is no direct relationship between union membership and union involvement in strikes, despite the fact that unionized areas have more strikes; (5) the whole period from 1910 to 1935 falls into two contrasting parts, the time up to the 1920s (with due allowance for the labor–management–government *modus vivendi* during most of the First World War) being a period of expanding, strike-filled organization among workers; during that first period, the tactical advantage once a strike had begun went to the workers in established centers of labor militancy; during the decade up to 1936 (and especially during the first years of the Depression), however, those same workers persisted in striking for higher wages and better working conditions while strikes were declining among workers elsewhere, and the tactical advantage was shifting to the employers. The militant, experienced workers began to fail more often than in the past. That was the immediate background of the Popular Front's enormous conflicts.

12 French strikes in international perspective

There are two good reasons for comparing French strikes to those of other countries. One is that international comparisons help us put to rest an old bogey who, despite resolute attempts to keep him underground, haunts at the window from time to time: 'national character' as an explanation of collective action. A second more positive purpose is to squint at the political content of strikes through one final prism: explaining changes in conflict patterns among nation-states on the basis of changes in the political representation of their working classes. After all, it is quite possible that the 'political action' hypothesis we have elaborated for France does not transfer easily to strikes elsewhere in the West. One might argue that national uniqueness inevitably frustrates international comparisons: no other country has had the same history as France, and so nowhere else will explanations be valid that adequately account for France. Or one might object, at a more practical level, that while common denominators do indeed exist among the strikes of western countries, we have not successfully identified the most important ones because our immersion in the intricacies of French history has obscured our overview.

Thus an agenda for international comparisons is presented. In the first half of this chapter we attempt to show how trends in French strikes reflect universal trends, movements running parallel in all western states during the last hundred years. Our argument will be that in the first half of the twentieth century the working classes in all western countries mobilized themselves for political action, with varying degrees of effectiveness and within disparate constellations of national politics; this mobilization generated everywhere a great wave of strike activity, observing the essential similarity of patterns of conflict among countries with similar modes of worker representation in the central polity. Here our emphasis will be on the resemblance of disputes from one country to another, seen over long periods of time. The treatment of both secular change and cross-sections at a given point in time converges in the Great Depression and immediate post-Second World War period, when the fundamental identity of strikes among nations gave way to three distinctive patterns of conflict.

Secular changes in strikes among nations

As we noted in Chapter 3, the French strike has changed over the years by becoming ever more frequent, shorter in duration and larger in size. The rise in strike incidence began in the 1880s, while the fall in duration and the increase in size took place only after the Second World War. In previous chapters we have suggested that the climb in the sheer number of conflicts resulted from improvements in worker ability to organize, and that the great brevity and size of postwar strikes resulted from the use of the strike as a vehicle for political protest. Now we must ask ourselves whether these trends and explanations are unique to France, or whether they characterize strikes all over western society.

Aggregate dispute data are available since around the turn of the century for all western countries in which free collective bargaining prevailed between workers and management. These data permit us to plot changes in the incidence, duration and size of industrial conflict over the last seventy years. To measure frequency we take the number of strikes per 100,000 non-agricultural active population; to measure duration we take a weighted average, dividing the total number of man-days lost in a given year or five-year period by the number of strikers; finally, to measure strike size, we divide the number of strikers by the number of strikes. Such data do not, of course, supply the analytic flexibility of our own enumerations of French strikes, and we know little of size of establishments on strike, number of establishments involved in the typical conflict and so forth. And information on cause and outcome is not available in a standardized form for long periods of time. Yet these three indicators delineate the essential dimensions of a strike.

These aggregate data show that the transformation of the strike in France was part and parcel of a larger reshaping of conflict occurring throughout Europe and North America. In virtually all countries for which data are available three great changes occurred, parallel to the changes in the French strike:

— All western countries experienced a secular increase in the *rate* of conflict during the last quarter of the nineteenth century and the first quarter of the twentieth, followed by a large-scale decline during the 1920s and the Depression. In the French case we have called this distinctive, mountain-like rise and fall the great mobilization of the working classes.

— All western countries experienced a secular decrease in the *duration* of conflict starting around the Great Depression, and continuing after the Second World War.

— Most western countries experienced an increase in *participation* in strikes, so that postwar numbers of strikers per strike would be vastly higher than prewar or interwar numbers.

Let us look at each of these massive secular shifts in detail, comparing and contrasting the case of France with other European and with North American countries.

Size of strike

In France, the reader will recall, an important increase in the number of strikers per strike began just after the Second World War. Whereas in 1900–29 an average of 300 workers had participated in the typical strike, in 1946–67 this figure increased almost fourfold to 1,100. And in 1946–9, to single out the period of most widespread participation, the typical strike encompassed 2,500 workers.

Other western nations too have seen this secular increase in strike size, sometimes beginning during the Great Depression, sometimes beginning in the agitated period just after the Second World War. Fig. 12.1 shows the development of strikers per strike in major western industrial countries during the twentieth century. In every case save Britain, the graph line swings up definitively during the 1935–45 period. In some countries such as the United States and Sweden the increase is undramatic, carrying postwar strike sizes scarcely above their interwar levels. In others, such as Finland, Italy, Belgium and the Netherlands the rise is as sweeping as in France, with a trebling or quadrupling of strikers per strike. Thus the secular course of strike participation during the twentieth century has been a directionless up-and-down in the 1900–35 period, and an upward trend during the years from 1935 to 1968.

What common denominator may we associate with this nearly universal increase? The precise mechanisms responsible for swelling postwar participation in the typical French strike were an increase in plant size, placing more workers within hearing distance of a strike call in a given factory, and an increase in plant participation rates, which meant that a higher percentage of the workers in the affected establishment would join in the strike. The former mechanism comes from a structural change in the economy, namely an increase in the scale of enterprise. The precise source of the latter mechanism – higher plant participation rates – is still unclarified in the absence of detailed strike data for France. Yet it appears likely that this improvement in worker mobilization is tied in some manner to the explicit politicization of the French strike.

Similarly, part of the international rise in strike size doubtless stemmed from a postwar increase in the scale of enterprise. Yet in many countries

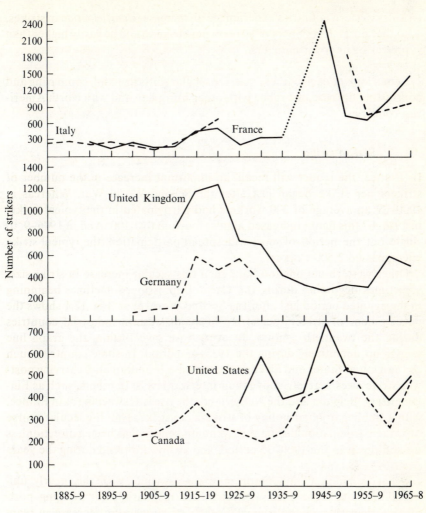

Fig. 12.1: Strikers per strike by country, 1890–1968

the upturn began during the Depression, when as yet no increments in industrial concentration had occurred – quite the opposite in fact, for many western nations experienced an industrial deconcentration in the thirties. Perhaps we do not exceed the bounds of permissible inference in suggesting that the upturn in strike size in the 1930s, both in France and in other nations, reflected rising plant participation rates, which in turn mirrored labor's outrage at the Depression and its accompanying resolve to capture control of the government in order to make national economic policies more responsive to popular needs.

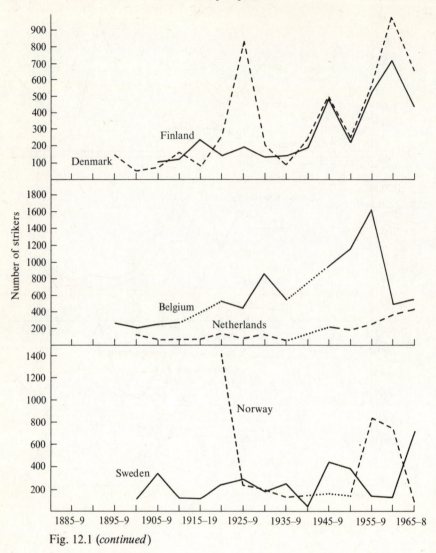

Fig. 12.1 (*continued*)

Duration of strike

As we have seen, the duration of strikes in France fluctuated trendlessly from the 1890s until the 1930s. The measure used customarily in this book, median duration, evidenced a profound stability from one five-year period to the next, changing scarcely at all. The measure of duration we use for international comparison, weighted average man-days lost per striker, is subject to greater variability from one period to the next because it is highly vulnerable to the influence of giant general strikes. What picture does this index give? Man-days lost per striker in France showed no trend

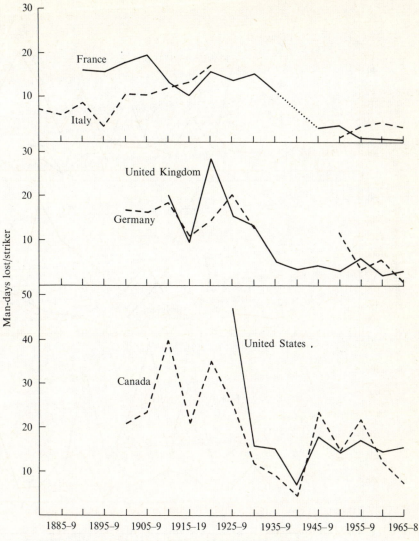

Fig. 12.2: Duration of strike by country, 1890–1968

before 1935, moving up and down in grand oscillations. Then after 1946 the duration of French strikes plunged downwards. Between 1900 and 1929 the customary strike lasted 15 days in France (15 man-days lost per striker); between 1946 and 1967 the average strike lasted barely 3 days, indeed only 1 day in 1965–7. Possibly the slide began during the Popular Front period 1936–9, although an absence of information on total man-days lost then makes it impossible to say. At all events increasing brevity characterized postwar strikes.

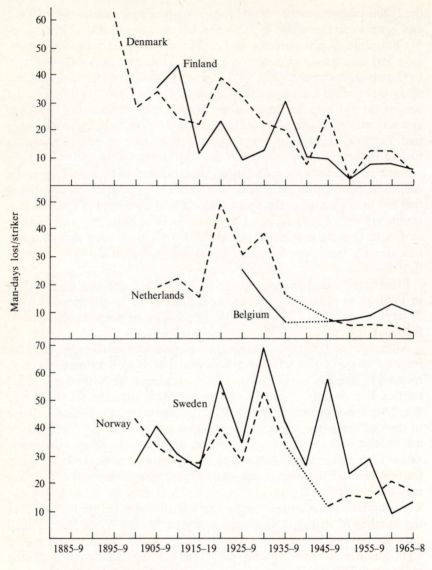

Fig. 12.2 (*continued*)

To what extent did other industrial countries recapitulate this fall in strike duration? Everywhere strikes became dramatically shorter. In most countries the decline took place either during the Depression or just after the Second World War. As may be seen from fig. 12.2, the plunge in strike duration commenced in Belgium, Canada, the United Kingdom (and possibly the United States, though data are not available before 1927) during the 1920s; in the Netherlands and Finland strikes grew shorter in the 1930s; and in Italy and Denmark, as in France, duration dropped after free collective bargaining was restored in the postwar period. A sharp decline in man-days lost per striker occurred in Germany between 1925 and 1929 and 1930 and 1932; then between 1950 and 1968 the Federal Republic of Germany experienced a dramatic shortening of strikes. The exact timing of the decline therefore varied from country to country, and the hiatus of fascism and war robbed the duration drop of a symmetry it might otherwise have had. Yet the decreases are close enough in time – ranging from late twenties to late forties – to make clear that we are dealing with a unitary process.

Some of the declines in duration, though substantial, do not suggest a radical transformation in the strike. In Norway, for example, the few strikes that did take place after the Second World War continued at a respectable length (15 man-days/striker, as opposed to 34 in 1903–29). And postwar strikes in Canada continued at a middling duration, even though down considerably from previous levels (28 man-days lost/striker in 1901–29, 17 in 1945–68).

Elsewhere the decline was astonishing. In Italy duration sank from 14 days in 1900–23 to 3 days in 1950–68; in Britain strike length dropped from 27 days in 1911–29 to 3 days in 1945–68; and in the Netherlands duration fell from 32 days in 1904–29 to 6 days in 1945–68.

Although the timing is not exact, some coincidence exists between the increase in strike size and the fall in duration. Both developments commenced in Belgium in the twenties, in Finland and the Netherlands in the thirties, and in Italy, France and Denmark just after the Second World War. Not too much should be made of this simultaneity in timing, because of the thirteen western nations for which we have collected statistics, there are at least two anomalies: in Britain strike size declined over the years, rather than rising, and in Norway the duration decline began in the early thirties, the size increase in the early fifties (though the Nazi occupation may have distorted a parallel movement). And data are missing for some key countries: for man-days lost in the United States before 1927, and for the number of strikes in Germany after the Second World War; and all data are missing, or misleading, for Franco's Spain. Yet in the remaining eight countries the parallelism holds between falling strike length and rising strike size. This parallelism suggests to us that the two developments are integrally related, betokening a transformation of the strike to which we shortly return.

Frequency of strike

Long-term changes in the strike rate show a smooth unity between 1900 and 1930 (or thereabouts), then divide after the Second World War into three distinctive patterns. Before the Great Depression all countries experienced

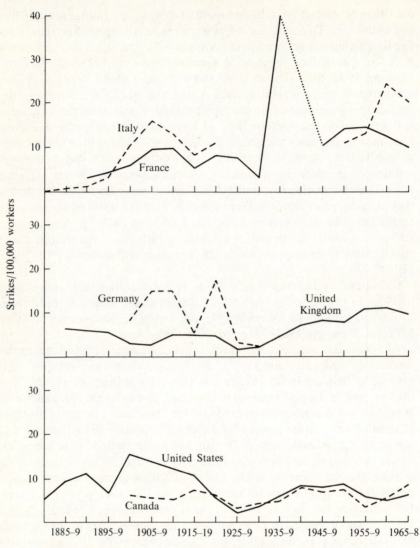

Fig. 12.3: Strike rates by country, 1890–1968

the same parabolic movement of strikes from relative infrequency, to commonality, back to infrequency. The Depression and the war marked, however, an important hinge, and in the postwar period strike rates in western nations have taken quite discrepant courses.

The reader will recall that French strike rates experienced this parabolic movement. Strike rates in France climbed steadily from around 1885 to 1914, then peaked in 1919–20, to decline through the 1920s and into the Depression. After the Second World War the intensity of French strike

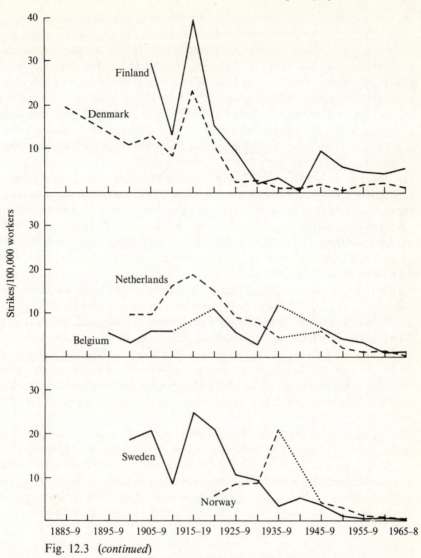

Fig. 12.3 (*continued*)

activity skyrocketed far above previous levels, so that France became, next to Italy, the most strike-prone nation in the western world.

Almost every other western nation followed the first part of the French experience, of rising strikes during the first two decades of the century, then a sharp decline into the 1920s and the Depression. Fig. 12.3 reveals an unmistakable mountain-like course in strikes from low to high to low again between the time strike data first became available in these countries until the 1920s and Depression, with the years just after the First World War representing the peak of the mountain. Only Denmark, Canada and the

United Kingdom appear exceptions to this rule, for there strike activity seems to have begun at a high level, without a long, gradual acceleration, then to have declined or remained steady until the *belle époque*. Elsewhere, in Germany, the Netherlands, Sweden, Finland, the United States, France and Italy strikes start at a low level of frequency, become ever more common until the Great War, decline between 1914 and 1918 (in the countries at war), crest climactically between 1918 and around 1921 and then slide downwards through the twenties into the grand trough of the Depression.

After the Depression and the Second World War strike frequencies diverged into three patterns:

(1) Upsurge to unprecedented heights in the 1950s and 60s. This happened to French, Italian and British strikes. Strikes became far more common in these countries during the postwar era than ever before, so that the Italian yearly average strike rate in 1950–68 was 18 strikes/100,000 non-agricultural workers, up from 12 in 1900–23. The British strike rate rose from 4/100,000 in 1900–29 to 10 in 1945–68. And the French strike rate increased from 8 in 1900–29 to 13 in 1946–67.

(2) Decline to token levels. Other lands witnessed the 'withering away' of industrial conflict, in Ross and Hartman's often-quoted phrase. In Belgium, the Netherlands, the three Scandinavian states of Denmark, Norway and Sweden and in Germany strikes became a rarity in the average worker's experience. All these nations experienced a yearly average of fewer than 3 strikes per 100,000 workers between 1945 and 1968. Swedish strike intensity sank lowest of all, so that between 1946 and 1968 only 648 strikes took place in that country, making for a rate of 1 strike for every 100,000 workers.

(3) Fluctuation at middling levels. Only in North America has postwar strike activity returned to precisely the heights of the prewar period. In the 1950s and 60s the American and Canadian strike rates oscillated in the singular pattern of business unionism within a narrow range of an in-between level. In 1900–29 the average annual American strike rate was 7/100,000; in 1945–68 it was 6. In 1901–29 the Canadian strike rate was 5/100,000; in 1945–68, 5 again.

An infinite variety of circumstances bore upon the strike rate in each of these countries, and many of the factors making for more or fewer strikes from one year to the next arose within the specific context of singular historical situations – that goes practically without saying. Yet the uniformity and simultaneity in the movement of strikes hints at the presence of at least a few underlying regularities. If the experience of France is any guide, this much may be said in interpretation:

— The secular increase in strike rates from the 1880s to the 1918–21 strike wave reflects the initial mobilization of the working classes. As a means of *pression ouvrière* for political representation, workers of these western countries undertook collective action in strikes. The strike permitted worker elites (a) to mobilize rank-and-file support by preaching the gospel of labor militancy, therewith building their organizations, and (b) to commit these organizational resources in a political struggle with other contenders to the polity.

— The downturn of conflict in the 1920s and 30s reflects not so much the accomplishment of these objectives, or a shift in labor's political strategies, as the economic miasma of the interwar years. Hard times in the 1920s struck especially industries which before the war had been highly strike-prone, as for example coal and steel in Britain. Worker organization and militancy are difficult to sustain over long periods of business depression, though short economic crises have in most of Europe the opposite effect – and the high unemployment of the late twenties and thirties inhibited job-site protest.

— The post-1945 dissolution of these uniformities in the trend indicates a new international differential in the politics of labor. The relationship of industrial workers to the polity in countries with exalted postwar conflict rates had become vastly different from countries where strike activity withered away. Where the strike rate soared, revolutionary unionism acquired new organizational resources in a drive for political representation. Where the strike rate fell, workers had been accepted into the polity, and now needed no longer use strikes as a means of pressing political demands. Where the strike rate fluctuated, as in North America, labor had discarded the industrial work stoppage as a means of political action, turning instead to political parties.

Thus a study of trends yields some valuable information; the closeness in the movement over time shows that, whatever influences were at work to make the absolute level of strikes in one country different from another, the changes from decade to decade in the social and political structures in which strikes were embedded proceeded across nations in the same direction, and with approximately similar timing and pacing. However this variety of analysis leaves open the question why, at any given point in time, the strikes of France resemble or diverge from the strikes of other countries. International differences in strike activity continue to perplex scholars, even with the important work of Arthur Ross and Paul Hartman to build upon, and we cannot here aspire to a complete explanation of them.[1] This book is, after all, mainly about France. Yet we may better sort out the singularity, and the commonality, of the French experience by seeing briefly how the three principal structural features of French strikes – frequency, size and duration – appear in other industrial countries.

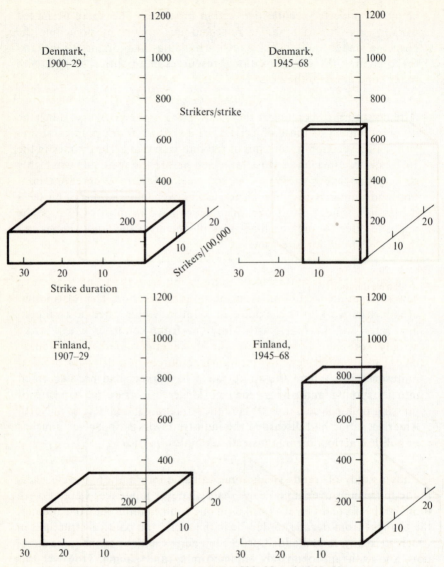

Fig. 12.4: The shape of strikes by country, 1900–29 and 1945–68

International differences in the level of strike activity

To study international differences in strikes, we return to the building blocks of three-dimensional figures we used in Chapter 3. Variations in these shapes from one country to another, or from one period to the next, give us a convenient way of drawing together variations in the structure of strikes.[2]

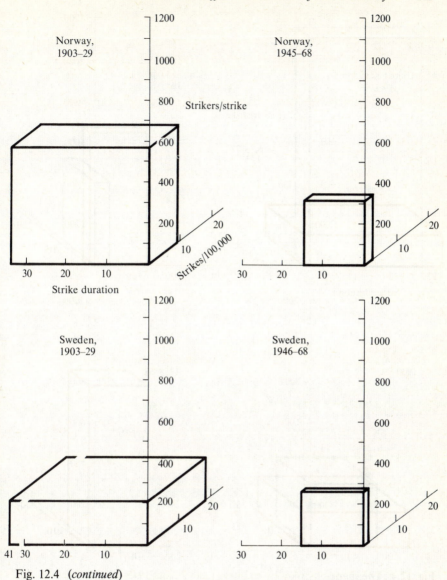

Fig. 12.4 (*continued*)

Let us begin with the years from 1900, when data first become available, until 1929, when the Depression and Second World War precipitated the series of changes enumerated above. Fig. 12.4 gives the shapes of strikes for thirteen western states during the first third of the century. How closely do French strikes resemble those of other industrial lands?

The resemblance among strikes of the 1900–29 period is startling

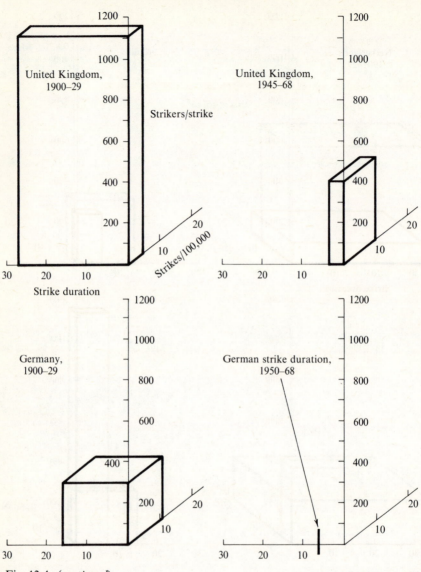

Fig. 12.4 (*continued*)

among the countries of western Europe. France, Germany, Belgium, Italy and Spain all have three-dimensional boxes quite similar in height, breadth and width. During these years the chief features of industrial conflict in these countries were much alike:

–Strikes in France, Germany and Italy had almost exactly the same dura-

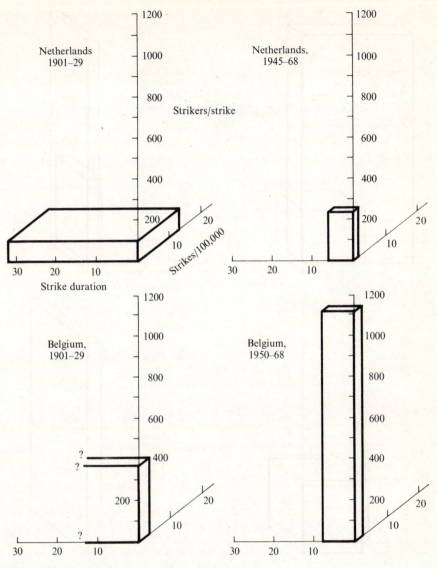

Fig. 12.4 (*continued*)

tion: 15 man-days lost per striker. Those in Spain (23 days) were somewhat longer. Belgian data are missing.

– Strikes in France, Germany and Italy had almost exactly the same size: 300 strikers per strike as a yearly average, 1900–29. Strikes in Belgium and Spain were only slightly larger (400 strikers/strike).

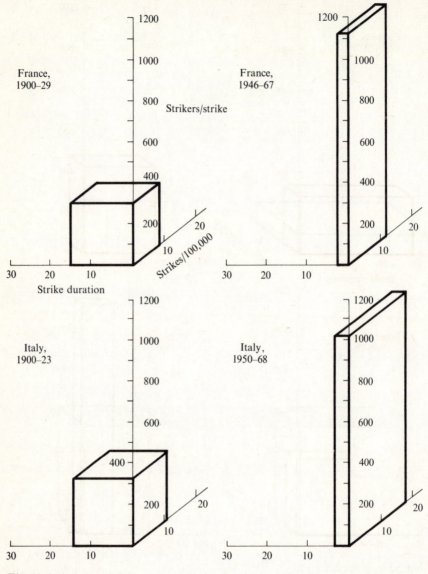

Fig. 12.4 (*continued*)

−Strike rates in these five countries ranged between 6 and 12 conflicts per 100,000 workers as a yearly average. In view of the dispersion later introduced into the distribution of conflict rates, this spread is not a wide one.

When these three dimensions are considered together, a distinctive west European strike shape emerges for the period 1900–29; symmetrical cubes

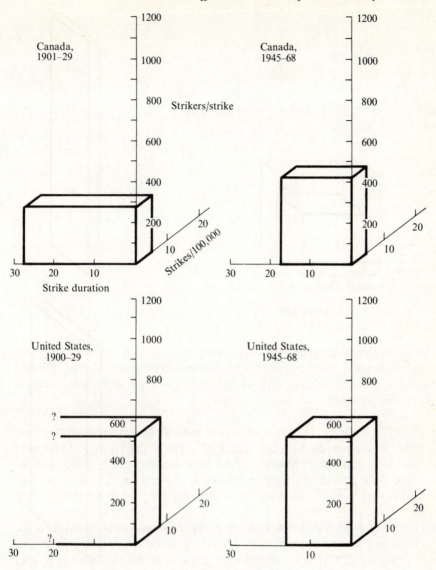

Fig. 12.4 (*continued*)

of smallish size, signifying durations in the 10–20 day range, participation scores in the 300–400 strikers/strike range and rates per 100,000 workers in the 6–12 range. In fig. 12.4 these five countries appear as square hatboxes, nestled against the rectilinear grid.

Another distinctive, though not distantly removed, international pattern was to be found in northern Europe, where strikes in 1900–29 were long,

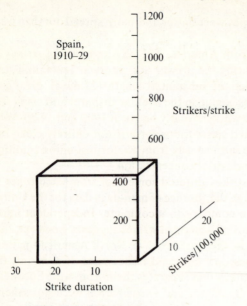

Fig. 12.4 (*continued*)

frequent and small, giving the appearance in fig. 12.4 of a thickish book laid flat on the table. This shape distinguishes the Netherlands, Sweden, Finland and Denmark. (Norway, with its exceptionally high strike size, diverges from this pattern.)

–North European strikes lasted on the average several times longer than west European: 26 days in Finland, 32 in the Netherlands, 34 in Norway and Denmark, 41 in Sweden. These long struggles testify that Scandinavian strikes were much more endurance contests, pitting together well organized workers and employers, than was the case in western Europe.

– North European strikes were somewhat smaller than west European ones, involving fewer strikers per strike. The largest strikes of northern Europe – in Sweden (210 strikers/strike) – were still about 80 participants smaller than the smallest strikes in western Europe (Germany 290 strikers/strike).

–North European strikes tended to be, though were not invariably, more frequent than west European. In 1900–29 west European strike frequencies ranged downwards from Italy's 12 strikes/100,000; during that period north European frequencies climbed upwards from Norway's 9 to Finland's 16 strikes/100,000 workers and Sweden's 18.

Thus before the Second World War Scandinavian and Dutch strikes were characteristically drawn-out affairs, involving relatively few workers but erupting often. Their shapes were flatter and more spread out than west European strike shapes.

This leaves Britain and North America. The physiognomy of strikes in Britain was quite singular during the prewar and interwar years: long, tall and narrow, denoting conflicts of substantial length (27 days), great size (a whopping 1,100 workers engaging in the average dispute) and small frequency (4 strikes per 100,000 workers yearly between 1900 and 1929). Why Britain's strike profile assumed this curious form is not entirely clear, but one may assume that it came in some way from a reformist union tradition within the context of great industrial concentration.[3]

Canadian and American strikes differed somewhat from each other in shape during 1900–29, although the absence of man-days data for the United States before 1927 makes the comparison incomplete. Independent information on the actual duration of American strikes suggests, however, that they were quite long,[4] and so the outlines of a North American pattern emerge: exceptional durations, low sizes and frequencies. It is mainly the length of North American strikes that separates them from west European disputes, for divergences in frequency and participation were not salient.

In the years 1900–29 we have, therefore, identified three distinct international patterns of strike activity, and the one maverick case of Britain. The west European pattern combined a middling frequency with short duration and great size; the north European pattern meant long, commonplace but small disputes; and North American strikes were, like north European, long, but like west European, of middling frequency and substantial size.

Yet compared to the variety we encounter in 1945–68, the most remarkable feature of western strikes in the 1900–29 period was their essential similarity. Seen in the light of later divergences, the disputes of the countries during the first third of the century were much more alike one another than unalike. Stressing this resemblance provides us with a convenient escape from having to account for these international differences, of course. And we dodge this task in part because we really have no good ideas about why in 1900–29 west and north European strikes split so clearly along regional lines. But in fact international differences during 1900–29 were not as pronounced as during 1945–68, for in the latter period the nature of strike activity in some countries had undergone a radical transformation, whereas in the former period a common thread continued to hold together the disputes of the western world. In 1900–29 work stoppages – except for strike waves – were undertaken by localized groups of workers and aimed at shop-floor objectives. Thereafter, things were different.

In the 1945–68 period strikes in several western countries had entirely changed their form and function; in others, established patterns of action continued. The reader must bear in mind that in those countries where the transformation of the strike took place, the roots of change lay in the 1930s and the Great Depression, in fascist regimes and the warfare state, not necessarily in postwar events as such. Only in the postwar years do suitable data become available, and for that reason only do we emphasize 1945–68, rather than, say, 1935–68.

Fig. 12.4 tells at a glance where the transformation occurred. Most obviously, the shape of strikes changed according to prewar pattern, so that most of the members of the west European pattern experienced one kind of transformation, all the members of the north European pattern underwent another and both members of the North American pattern were subject to little change. Let us revisit these countries, pattern by pattern.

– The postwar west European pattern. This cell is now populated by just two main cases and a marginal one: France, Italy and perhaps Britain. For among the nations of western Europe only France and Italy acquired the configuration of worker representation in national politics that leads to the following distinctive pattern: a tall, narrow profile, signifying great size and brevity, but with the great depth that goes with high strike frequencies.

The historical record for both France and Italy since 1945, and the entire analysis of France in previous chapters of this book, leaves little doubt that this new pattern comes from the determination of newly organized, politically impotent working classes to participate in national politics through protest strikes. French strikes – and surely this applies to postwar Italian as well – became after the Popular Front short, large and frequent because the workers had decided to use the strike as a means of symbolic action upon the stage of national politics.[5] What changed was not the French and Italian workers' relationship to the polity, but their determination to advance collective interests, and concomitantly their levels of organization, so that they were after 1945 both better able and more resolved to undertake collective political protest. In postwar France strikes became, in effect, political demonstrations, waged to impress those in power of the vigor and justice of the working-class case for a greater share of the national product and a louder voice within the chancelleries and chambers. Before the war, strikes had been 'political' as well – but in a different manner, designed to compel the intervention of the government in the arena of local labor relations, or to mobilize support for worker organizations whose purpose were political. After the war strikes had become immediate vehicles of agitation over power. Such disputes are frequent because they blend with mechanisms of ongoing, routine political action; they are short because only a brief stoppage is required to make a symbolic point, and they are large, embracing many workers in many different shops, because politicized unions are able to interest a wide sweep of workers in limited commitments of time and energy for collective enterprises.

Britain is an ambiguous case. Like France and Italy, its strikes are frequent and brief, but unlike strikes in the two continental nations,

British strikes are quite small. And over the years they have grown smaller, rather than following the almost universal pattern of increase in size. Moreover, since the Second World War British workers have had firm, boisterous representation within the central government; the Labour Party has been in office for several extended periods, and some measure of income redistribution has proceeded. Britain's postwar experience with wildcat 'quickie' strikes has manifestly not been of a piece with militancy in France and Italy, even though the strike shapes assume a certain superficial similarity. It cannot be the task of this book to offer an accounting of British strike evolution, except insofar as Britain's strikes shed light upon France's. And they do to this extent: British wildcat strikes seem to indicate a turn to shop-floor protest over plant-level authority relationships, job control issues and worker organization problems in general. Although seemingly over wages and hours, the wildcats are fundamentally localized protests over the local distribution of power.[6]

It may be that Britain provides an alternative to the Scandinavian answer to the question: what happens to strikes after the workers have won political representation? Rather than abandoning extra-parliamentary collective action, as has been the case in northern Europe, British workers have turned to shop-floor issues and away from national political ones. These strikes are without formal union support, and so both end quickly and are limited in scope. They arise out of day-to-day shop-floor authority relationships, and so are commonplace. It is thus the fact of Labour's success in Britain, and the socialist failure to control governments in France and Italy, that makes an apparently similar pattern of strike activity fundamentally different.

The prewar west European pattern had three other members: Spain, Germany and Belgium. What happened to them after the Second World War? Spain is obvious; free collective bargaining disappeared under Franco, and therewith Spain vanished from the list of countries with which France may be usefully compared. Belgium, like Britain, is an ambiguous case for which we have no ready answer; Belgian strikes have been, like French and Italian, large and short, but surprisingly infrequent. Their size and brevity suggest a continuing role for political protest. Perhaps the instability of Belgian worker representation within the central polity accounts for this pattern, because ping-pong–like, the Belgian socialists have several times bounced in and out of the government since the Second World War. One such bounce, the Socialist–Catholic coalition of 1961, was precipitated by the December 1960–January 1961 general strike, which in turn had been touched off by a political crisis over the Congo and over the government's controversial austerity program. But this instability of cabinet participation aside for a moment, the Belgian unions have found solid representation at many lower levels of bureaucracy and government, to say nothing of the increased willingness of the employers to conduct centralized negotiations.[7] So perhaps the substance of political power has moderated Belgian militancy, while not robbing strikes, when they do occur, of their core of political action.

Germany, the last nation in the prewar west European group, appears to have joined the north European pattern.

– The postwar north European pattern. Here too the strike has been transformed since the Second World War, but in a direction entirely different from western Europe. In Scandinavia, the Netherlands and Germany the working classes all entered the polity between the threshold of the Great Depression and the immediate postwar period. The Norwegian Labor Party began to govern in 1935; in Sweden the socialists took power definitively in 1933, after some fits and starts at governance in the early twenties; in Denmark labor became a more or less permanent member of governing coalitions in 1929; in the Netherlands labor participated in a government for the first time in 1939, and dominated governments from 1948 to 1959; Dutch worker interests were safeguarded in the 1960s through the labor wings of the other political parties; in Finland the Social Democrats coalesced to govern with the Agrarians just after the Second World War; and in Germany, although a formal Social Democrat victory remained in the wings until 1969, elaborate constitutional arrangements have since the war given the workers an important voice at every political level from the running of the plant to the governance of the *Länder*.[8]

This access to political power, we argue, resulted in a radical alteration of industrial conflict. At least two specific consequences flowed from the fact that the Labor parties in these countries either joined or dominated coalition government:

(1) With their hands on the levers of power, the worker parties could insist that the state intervene in industrial conflict on behalf of their constituencies, establishing formal arrangements for grievance settlement, wage advance and the like. With the state an active partner sympathetic to the workers in industrial relations, the strike became largely superfluous in settling shop-floor disputes and arranging for standard-of-living increases. The government undertook of its own initiative to do these things.

(2) Membership in the polity meant that the working classes needed no longer take to the streets to make political points. They could negotiate and jostle other members of the polity using parliamentary suasion rather than public demonstrations and threats of force, which are, after all, the political tools of challengers hitherto *ex*cluded from the charmed circle. So the need for strikes as symbolic political demonstrations also vanished.

Political power for workers meant the diminution of strike frequencies to virtual insignificance in north European countries, which is the most important feature of the shift in conflict there. In the preceding section we commented on the extremely low level to which Scandinavian strike rates had fallen, from the highest prewar levels in western countries. The upshot of this plunge was that in all of northern Europe save Finland strikes ceased in the 1950s and 60s to be of any practical importance in collective bargaining. Germany did not in the postwar era report the number of strikes to the ILO, but the testimony of observers, together with the very low German strik*er* rate, permits the conclusion that the Federal Republic of Germany had a negligible strike rate as well.

Patterns of duration and strike size in northern Europe were somewhat less uniform. Strikes in Scandinavia proper stretched to considerable durations after 1945, which is the second distinguishing feature of the postwar north from the west of Europe. Strike durations in Sweden, Denmark, Finland and Norway ranged from 13 to 15 days in 1945–68; those in Germany and the Netherlands, however, were only 5–6 days. Because all these durations were longer than France's, Italy's and Britain's, and shorter than the United States's and Canada's, we are further justified in asserting the unity of a north European pattern. The meaning of these long durations is that once strikes do break out in Scandinavia (although that happens seldom), they are endurance contests to the end. Northern Europe has seen wide variability in strike size, with tall profiles for Denmark and Finland, low ones for Sweden, Norway and the Netherlands. German data do not permit the computation of strikers/strike.

– Finally, the postwar era saw a distinctive North American pattern emerge, for strike shapes in the United States and Canada look much like each other, and like the boxes of no other country. The exact shape was a large cube, indicating durations of around 15 days, sizes in the vicinity of 500 strikers/strike, and frequencies on the order of 5–6 strikes/100,000 workers. Nowhere else in the postwar world were even remotely similar shapes to be encountered. We associate this cubist pattern with business unionism, where the strike has a fundamental role to play within the collective bargaining process – the *ultima ratio* which brings the parties to the table – yet has few political functions.

Postwar North American strikes differ not markedly from prewar shapes; yet we suggest that the role of the strike on this side of the Atlantic did undergo an important transformation. A small but persistent strand in the literature of North American labor history maintains, in contradiction to the dominant doctrine of 'economism,' that before the Depression collective action was as much political as economic, intended equally to build political organizations and press political demands and to elevate the standard of living by pressuring individual employers.[9] Our interpretation of the upswing of strike rates during 1900–20 – the American counterpart of the working-class mobilization we noted in France – reflects from another mirror this political action viewpoint.

Then during the Depression the North American working classes succeeded to political power. The 1930s meant in the United States the worker entry to the polity, as part of a coalition of farmers and ethnic groups. But strike activity did not wither away in the United States, as it did in northern Europe after a similar entry. Why? The answer to this question suggests some of the ways in which historic tradition and national character and custom have made France, and Europe, so different from the United States. In Europe, control of the government meant simply weighting government intervention in shop-floor conflicts on the side of the working classes, and making of a haphazard, occasional process a routine procedure. The result was that long-established habits of state supervision would now benefit the new coalition of contenders, instead of the old, displaced coalition. In the United States no such traditions existed. And although American labor tried hard during the late thirties to obviate the strike through government intervention in labor relations, the weight of historic traditions of non-intervention, plus the indifference or opposition of other members of the polity, doomed these efforts to failure. Finally, American labor reconciled itself to a watertight division between job action, where the mechanisms of free collective bargaining were to function unobstructed by government intervention, and political action, which was to be executed through interest-coalition political parties.[10] The political parties did not do badly by the working classes, and so strikes in postwar United States and Canada became resolutely non-political. The North American case is important because it shows that admission to the polity need not automatically lead to the withering away of the strike; other variables, such as national tradition, interpose themselves. It is the diametrically diverging strike experience of northern Europe and western Europe that establishes the fundamental importance of politics in the taming of industrial conflict.

In conclusion we return to the subject of national character as a way of explaining why the strikes of one country differ from those of another. Perhaps the principal finding of this chapter is that the strikes of western Europe before the Depression were very much alike: they occurred with approximately the same frequency; they lasted about the same amount of time, and they involved fairly equal numbers of workers.[11] There are, of course, other dimensions of strike activity we cannot capture with these aggregate statistics, such as stated grievance and outcome. But let us for the moment assume that these three facets give windows in some way to the essential core of a labor dispute.

This startling similarity in strike shapes means that it is pointless to attach great importance to stereotypes of *individual* psychological characteristics in explaining *collective* action. The individualistic, volatile French worker, quick to explode in outbursts of fury, is a familiar figure in the literature.[12]

So is the well disciplined German familiar, reverent before employer and state authority and prone to membership in every organization from the singing club to the SPD. Perhaps these sketches of the personality traits that individuals of the nation are supposed to possess have some merit, and it may in fact be that Frenchmen, taken one by one, fly off the handle more easily in confronting authority than do individual Germans. The point here is that, right or wrong, these traits of national character are unimportant in explaining *collective* behavior, for the aggregate is more than the sum of its parts. A French crowd does not turn in revolt because Frenchmen as individuals are prone to defy authority; nor do French strikes break out because the rebelliousness of each worker somehow reaches a critical mass when workers congregate together.

We emphasize in this chapter, and throughout this book, how surrounding political, social and industrial structures call forth and transform collective action, quite independent of the psychologies of the individuals who join these unions and parties. In this chapter we have paid special attention to influential participation in a nation's political life. Yet other structural features must be considered as well in understanding international differences in organization and conflict, features we have only dimly recognized in the surrounding mist. And so our emphasis upon politics must not be understood as a single-factor explanation of such a complex subject as strike differences among nations. We have chosen this device, rather, to highlight the crucial importance that politics has had in shaping and changing strikes in France. If in doing so, some small increment of understanding of other nations' strikes is accomplished, all the better.

Appendix on data for international comparisons

Sources of data on strikes

1890–9. W. Woytinsky, *Die Welt in Zahlen*, II: *Die Arbeit* (Berlin: Rudolf Mosse, 1926), pp. 279–326.

1900–6. Arthur M. Ross and Paul T. Hartman, *Changing Patterns of Industrial Conflict*, pp. 194–9. Data for countries not covered in Ross–Hartman are taken from annual *Year Book* of the International Labour Office, and from Woytinsky's series.

1957–68. Annual *Year Book* of the International Labour Office.

Source of data on labor force

P. Bairoch, *The Working Population and its Structure* (New York: Gordon and Breach, 1968; International Historical Statistics, vol. 1), *passim*, reports periodic industrial censuses. Labor-force data are invariably the total active population of a country, from which the first line of the sectoral breakdown – agriculture, forestry, hunting and fishing – has been subtracted.

All data on France presented in this chapter are taken from the above-mentioned sources, not from our own records of French strike and labor-force data.

Belgium
Strike and striker data 1896–1913, 1919–39, 1950–68. Man-days lost data available after 1927. 1936 excluded from duration calculations.

Canada
All series 1901–68.

Denmark
All series 1897–1968.

Finland
All series 1907–68. 1950 omitted in calculating 1950–4 duration.

France
1890–1926 from *Annuaire statistique*, 1966, p. 120. 1939–45 and 1968 data never reported.

Germany
All series available for Deutsches Reich, 1900–32. Only strikers and man-days lost reported for Federal Republic, 1951–68.

Netherlands
Strikes and strikers series 1901–68, except gap in 1941–4; man-days series begins 1904.

Italy
All series 1878–1923, 1950–68. Man-days lost missing for 1904–6.

Norway
Strikers and man-days lost begin 1903, strike series in 1921. 1931 omitted from 1930–4 duration figure.

Spain
Strikes and strikers 1905–34 (our series incomplete for 1923–6); man-days lost 1910–34.

Sweden
All series 1903–68. 1945 omitted from strikers/strike and man-days lost/ striker calculations for postwar aggregate, but included in 1945–9 figures.

United Kingdom
Number of strikes only available for 1881–1910; Ireland included, and so Irish non-agricultural labor force has been added to Great Britain for 1881, 1891, 1901 and 1911 censuses. Series for strikes, strikers, man-days lost 1911–68 for Great Britain and Northern Ireland only. 1926 omitted

from 1925–9 duration calculations, but not from 1900–29 aggregate. 1888–1910 data from B. R. Mitchell and Phyllis Deane, *Abstract of British Historical Statistics* (Cambridge: University Press, 1962), p. 71.

United States

Strike series only 1881–1905; strikes and strikers available 1914 (1916)–68; man-days lost published after 1927. 1881–1905 strike data from John I. Griffin, *Strikes*, p. 207.

Table 12.1: *Strike characteristics for 13 western industrial countries, 1900–29 and 1945–68*

	Strike rate/ 100,000 workers	Strikers per strike	Man-days lost per striker
Belgium			
1901–29	6.4	400	—
1945(50)–68	2.6	1,100	7.6
Canada			
1901–29	5.3	280	27.5
1945–68	5.2	420	17.3
Denmark			
1900–29	11.5	140	33.8
1945–68	1.8	640	13.4
Finland			
1907—29	15.9	180	25.7
1945—68	6.0	780	13.4
France			
1900—29	7.8	300	15.1
1946—67	12.8	1,130	2.3
Germany			
1900—29	11.1	290	15.7
1951–68	—	—	5.4
Netherlands			
1901–29	13.0	100	32.0
1945–68	2.5	240	5.6
Italy			
1900–23	12.1	320	14.2
1950–68	18.1	1,030	3.3
Norway			
1903–29			33.9
1921–29	9.3	570	
1945–68	2.2	310	15.3
Spain			
1910–29	6.0	420	23.2
Sweden			
1903–29	18.0	210	40.8
1945(46)–68	1.3	260	13.5
United Kingdom			
1900–29	3.8		
1911–29		1,100	26.7
1945–68	9.9	400	3.4
United States			
1900–29	7.4		—
1916–29		530	
1945–68	6.4	540	16.1

International standards of strike reporting

The determination of French officialdom to record every single dispute, regardless of its minute size or length, creates some problems for the comparison of France to other countries. Several other western states, to be sure, adopt the French procedure of noting all stoppages without qualification. The Netherlands, Austria, Italy, Sweden and Switzerland come into this category. Yet other large industrial states record only disputes *above* a certain size and length, in some cases requiring that the strike go on for at least a single working shift (U.S., Norway), others stipulating that at least 10 man-days be lost (Canada, Australia); other states set higher thresholds such as 100 man-days lost, unless the strike is longer than a working day or involves more than 10 workers (Great Britain, Federal Republic of Germany). What is the consequence of such variations in reporting criteria?[13] Must we be cautious in attributing the relatively high French strike rates to a greater degree of worker militancy in France than in other countries? May we be dealing with a statistical artifact: France appears to have more strikes because she records disputes other lands ignore?

Fortunately the answer is no. Of the western industrial countries, only the United States has twin criteria of both size and duration in excluding disputes. Strikes are dropped from American statistics if either they last less than a full shift or if they involve fewer than 6 workers.[14] The other industrial lands stipulate that above a certain number of mandays lost a dispute will be recorded, even if it is exceptionally brief or exceptionally small. France has, to be sure, many brief stoppages: 16 percent of all strikes in 1915–35 lasted a working day or less. Yet most such quickies are strikes in which the workers lay down their tools one day and come back the following day, not strikes lasting less than a shift. (Only 3.6 percent of all French disputes in 1915–35 lasted less than a working day.) Thus they would have been recorded in U.S. labor statistics. And almost none of the short strikes involved fewer than 10 workers. (Only 140, or 0.9 percent, of the 15,454 French strikes in 1915–35 both involved fewer than 10 workers and lasted a full day or less.) What all this means is that French strike statistics are essentially comparable to those of other nations with higher reporting thresholds despite the fact that the French record all strikes, not just those above a certain size or duration.[15]

13 Conclusion

If we are right, who else is wrong? If our arguments linking strikes to changes in social structure and in political participation are correct, alternative arguments on the subject must be incomplete or misleading. If it is true, as we suggest, that organization is a precondition of large-scale collective action, then it cannot be true, as some other researchers argue, that most strikes are spontaneous outbursts of angry individuals. If it is correct that the strike movement in western Europe was launched to political ends, it cannot be accurate to say that most strikes aimed merely at higher wages and improved conditions.

We began this inquiry with a broad distinction among 'breakdown,' 'deprivation' and 'interest' theories linking collective action to industrialization, and extended the distinction to theories of industrial conflict. The three kinds of theories have hung over the book like heavy clouds: always there, but not always clearly outlined. We have recurrently worked to show the inadequacies of breakdown and deprivation theories, and concurrently worked to refine and verify an argument which stands squarely in the shadow cast by interest.

Yet something intriguing has happened to the categories. On searching diligently through the accumulated literature, we have not found any unadulterated version of the deprivation argument sufficiently specified to apply seriously to the explanation of strike activity in France. Nor have we found careful statements of the breakdown thesis to confront with the evidence we have accumulated. Deprivation and breakdown theories abound in general statements about industrialization, but they somehow disappear when the difficult business begins of generating specific inferences concerning the locus, form and intensity of strikes.

Even in compound theories, breakdown rarely figures very importantly. Among the many theorists we have called on in the course of this book, only Scott and Homans, de Laubier and perhaps Stearns have given us statements along that line which we could reasonably translate into expectations concerning our data. When we *have* tested whether fast-growing industries, migrant-filled cities and the like produce extensive strike activity, the results have been uniformly negative.

Deprivation appears more frequently as one of the factors in a compound theory, mainly either as a short-run trigger to industrial conflict or as a constant which can hardly account for variations over time, space and different types of structure. Only as the basic conditions of work themselves – timing, discipline, autonomy, skill requirements and so on – become defined as deprivations or satisfactions does this line of argument begin to yield plausible explanations of the big variations from time to time, place to place and industry to industry with which this book has been chiefly concerned. We have employed this special sort of deprivation argument ourselves in adopting the Touraine–Mallet scheme of artisanal, mass-production and science-sector industries; as we read the evidence, however, the deprivations intrinsic to different sorts of work settings do not spill over immediately into strikes, but shape the kind of organization for collective action which grows up among workers in those settings. We have also come across some indications that short-run economic deprivation stimulates strike activity under either of two conditions: (a) where the group affected is already well organized for collective action, and accustomed to using the strike for common ends, and (b) when it follows sustained economic improvement or well-being.

This last qualification may remind our readers of an explanation for collective action which has gained a good deal of currency in the last decade: the psychological account in terms of frustration–aggression, expectation–achievement or relative deprivation. (The three terms are not equivalent, but the accounts of collective action offered in their names have a lot in common.) Most authors who have put a serious effort into applying this line of argument to collective action have concentrated on violence and protest rather than on strikes; it tends to enter the discussion of industrial conflict sideways rather than head on. As a consequence, we have not had an opportunity to face its implications for our study directly so far. We will stage that confrontation in a moment.

In the course of our long discussion, we have also had to cut in two the broad category of 'interest' theories with which we began. The analysis of political interest which has emerged from the discussion differs significantly from the many available interpretations of strikes as the calculated pursuit of economic interests in a relatively narrow sense of the term. Since that disagreement, too, has only entered the previous discussion obliquely, we had better review the economic-interest interpretation of strike activity as well.

After all the sifting, three lumps of theory remain. The first we will call, for convenience, frustration–aggression theory. The second, economic interest. The third, political action. Let us sum up our reasons for thinking that the third is solid, and the first two ready to crumble.

Frustration and aggression

This group of arguments explains collective action as the immediate result of individual perceptions of deprivation, dislocation and injustice. When people sense they are being ill treated and denied some legitimate recourse – or indeed when they just feel bewildered by the rapid flux of events about them – they become frustrated. Such frustration generates hostility, and therewith aggressive sentiments. As the social changes causing this sense of deprivation accelerate, so does aggressiveness increase as well. Finally some critical mass of individual anger is reached, and a collective social explosion eventuates.

One famous variant is the 'relative deprivation' hypothesis, which claims that in economic growth the aspirations of a population climb more rapidly than the ability to satisfy those aspirations; the gap in the 'wants–gets' ratio widens intolerably; finally, all that frustration and aggression pour into the streets and violent protest takes place. Another variant is the 'J-curve hypothesis,' which says that violence is triggered at the moment when the ability of the economy to satisfy rising expectations turns suddenly and dramatically downwards, as in a depression. The hopelessness of one's ambitions becomes then infuriatingly apparent, and people become violent.[1]

The frustration–aggression hypothesis is commonly used to account for strikes, on the assumption that the step is smooth and easy from worker perceptions of deprivation and dislocation to collective group response. E. P. Kelsall, for example, characterizes wildcat walkouts as 'psychological' in nature: individual workers coalesce spontaneously as all perceive economic phenomena at an 'irrational' level. The fear of losing one's job, say, leads to frustration and anxiety, which vent themselves in a sudden, explosive work stoppage.[2]

Several researchers have newly put forth 'psychological' explanations of French strikes. Peter Stearns, for one, sees the spontaneous walkout as a safety valve for pent-up emotions. 'Many strikes occurred because workers felt so much frustration and hostility that these simply had to find an outlet.'[3] And Michelle Perrot offers an eloquent statement of the strike's expressive – as opposed to instrumental – functions:

> For rationality does not totally dominate the terrain of the strike. To the extent that it results from multiple, fragmented, isolated decisions it steals away from reason. Born roughly, suddenly and brutally in the rush of emotion, anger and desire, the strike retains in part the whiplash of the primitive wildcat walkout. This spontaneity, which weakens its instrumental consequences, guarantees its expressive richness. *La naïveté, même relative, vaut souvent mieux pour nous que le calcul qui masque et la discipline qui uniformise.*[4]

Frustration–aggression theorists consider a wide variety of social changes, both economic and non-economic, as potentially responsible for these collective outbursts of rage. Mechanization is thought an especial villain. Michel Collinet speaks of the sense of detachment, the depersonalization, the 'nomadic escapism' that accompanied assembly-line production. 'The moral and physical isolation is complete, and the worker is caught in the middle of a swarming hive, plunged into bitter thoughts about the fate of his family, thoughts which dim the *idée fixe* of unemployment.' In these circumstances wildcat strikes break out like bushfire through dry timber.[5] Other frustration–aggression writers indict social changes outside the world of the shop as responsible for worker alienation and frustration: the vortex of urban migration, the agony of professional dequalification and of skidding down the status ladder from craft to factory work, the remorseless logic of the marketplace.

We are ill advised to dismiss out of hand such psychological theories. Prudence is indicated, if only because many advocates of frustration-aggression hypotheses are distinguished scholars of French labor history, whose work commands attentiveness and respect. Yet we have grave reservations. Perhaps theories which go directly from individual states of mind to collective phenomena are not so much wrong as incomplete. We have argued in this book that the missing variable is organization. Individuals are not magically mobilized for participation in some group enterprise, regardless how angry, sullen, hostile or frustrated they may feel. Their aggression may be channeled to collective ends only through the coordinating, directing functions of an organization, be it formal or informal. The patterned, habitual interactions of a network of buddies may count as an organization. So may, of course, more highly elaborated structures such as mutual aid societies or labor unions. But organization there must be to focus on this individual unrest, otherwise the unhappy merely brood passively on the sidelines.

Where we really part company with the frustration–aggression hypothesis, however, is by asserting that individuals with cheery, satisfied states of mind stand just as much chance of being mobilized as do individuals with aggressive, resentful mentalities. The important thing is what group the individual is a member of, and whether that group is activating its members for participation in some collective task.

What specific findings from the record of France's strikes lead us so confidently to challenge and modify the folk wisdom of the frustration-aggression hypothesis? We have, for one thing, the various tabulations and regressions showing the importance of unionization in conflict. Multivariate analyses at the level of commune and department highlighted the importance of labor unions and Bourses du travail in strikes. Mechanization, a supposedly 'alienating' influence, turned out to be without any direct influence upon strikes in these statistical analyses, but of considerable importance in explaining variations in unionization, which shows nicely what we mean by organization as an intervening factor.

The unimportance of 'states of mind' also appeared clearly when we considered the difference between the strikes of established artisans and of rawly recruited factory proletarians. If it is true that the imputed anxiety, alienation and frustration of the factory system made a difference in the strike movement, one would expect to find conflicts among semi-skilled assemblers more bitter and harshly fought than those among small-shop craftsmen. But in fact the opposite is true. Several different indices demonstrated that the most acrimonious battles occurred within the traditional sector. Disputes among factory workers, on the other hand, were brief, over impersonal issues such as wages, and ended with all the strikers rehired (as opposed to the massive dismissals encountered among small-shop artisanal disputes). We argued that craftsmen had these bitter slugfests because they were better organized and more conscious that group prerogatives could be defended only through resolute group action. Factory proletarian strikes, by way of contrast, often (though not invariably) had lower rates of union representation. While it is true that factory workers struck more often than craftworkers, they certainly struck less well. It was probably the differences in organization between craft shop and assembly line, rather than variations in their mentalities, that were responsible for these differences in the structure of conflict.

Where states of mind do seem to matter is in the *kind* of organization they produce. If artisans had strong, effective unions it was partly because they shared a certain outlook upon life, possibly a certain mixture of psychological traits. May we indulge, for a moment, in a hypothetical reconstruction of the artisanal psychology? Craftsmen were probably anxious about job displacement through technological change, confident about their own self-worth and ability to cope, fulfilled (or whatever the opposite of the industrial psychologist's notion of alienated is) because of their creative involvement in the production process. These attitudes doubtless stimulated active participation in local associational life. Similarly, one might imagine that assembly-line workers drifted inconstantly in and out of their local unions because they felt isolated and estranged from the surrounding environment, reluctant to engage in any permanent commitment of resources and eager only to escape from the dreadful plant at closing time, get home and not think about the job until the next morning. Thus craftworkers built solid local unions with high participation rates, and semi-skilled workers put together fragile locals combined with oppressive national bureaucracies. We have called this latter pattern 'sparkplug unionism': massive indifference at the base, held together through a clutch of dedicated ideologues taking orders from on top, and subject to mercurial fluctuations in affiliation.

Meaninglessness, powerlessness: the dimensions of alienation rush to the scholar's pen as he describes the *ouvrier specialisé* in Puteaux or the weaver in Roubaix. How easy is conjuring with the wand of psychology! With what facility do we account for high strike rates in the Nord, low ones in the Maine-et-Loire – alienation! yes, and the happy peasant worker integrated in his farm and factory in Cholet. One could go on like this, spinning out the instant psychology. But such an exercise is pointless, because confirming data on comparative states of mind are completely lacking, and because we can quite satisfactorily account for the important kinds of variation with sociological variables, affording ourselves the luxury of keeping the psychological ones on the shelf.

We have, in short, three points to make about frustration–aggression explanations of strikes. One is that we don't believe the 'typical' striker was necessarily any more hostile or aggressive than any of his fellow citizens not on strike. Two is that regardless how 'angry' this typical striker was, he needed access to networks of association before his individual fury could be translated into joint action with numbers of other 'furious' workers. Three is that we think it unnecessary to invoke these explanations at all, when more trustworthy arguments, grounded on solid data, can explain why the strikes of one epoch, region or industry differed from those of another.

'National character' is the last refuge of the psychological explanation of conflict. If states of mind do matter, we should be able to spot their impact through international comparisons of strike activity, for the psychological profiles imputed to the workers of one country are quite different from those of another. Fiery French workers, like Frenchmen in general, are thought to anger at the drop of a hat, walking off the job in furious explosions of temperament to the accompaniment of much Gallic posturing and declamation.[6] Eternally contentious, these workers soon fall to squabbling among themselves and abandon whatever collective end to which they had so precariously coalesced. German workers, on the other hand, are commonly stereotyped as serious and phlegmatic, and even though the march lead into the sea they plod obediently along in Teutonic unity.

If such 'states of mind' help shape collective action, one might expect French strikes to be frequent, small and short, German ones to be infrequent, but once under way long and massive. In fact as we observed in Chapter 12, strikes in both countries have virtually identical profiles: equally frequent, of similar duration and of comparable size. If national character turns out to make no difference in such fundamental dimensions of conflict as these, can it be said to matter much at all?

Economic interest

This variety of general explanation assumes that the participants in industrial conflict mainly act to maximize their profits and to minimize their losses: that the workers will strike when erosion of their personal income threatens or when their employer can least accept a work stoppage, that employers will give in to a strike when business is flourishing but accept one when orders are slow, inventories high and profits less endangered. These kinds of logic are normally cast within two time frameworks, the short-term, which concentrates upon accounting for year-to-year variation in conflict in terms of the business cycle, and the long-term, which matches secular trends in strikes to trends in economic life. Let us look at each in turn.

First, year-to-year variation. Identifying a conventional wisdom in the existing literature on strikes and the business cycle is like trying to find portraits of the presidents in confetti on the sidewalk. There has been little uniformity in the selection of indicators of economic fluctuations, some writers concentrating on nominal wages, others on real wages, some on industrial production, others on employer profits. And inconsistency has similarly appeared in the indicators of strike activity chosen for study: some writers have taken aggregate composite measures of conflict, such as man-days lost, others have focused upon such single dimensions as the numbers of strikes or of strikers. Then too, the theoretical problems are forbidding in what is, at first glance, a straightforward question: are fluctuations in strikes related to fluctuations in the business cycle? May the model assume that workers perceive changes in real wages, or that they notice changes in nominal wages alone? How attuned are workers to employer profits, and do they demand more if they feel the employer can pay more? And what is the role of unions in converting worker perceptions of economic reality to collective action? Do unions encourage strikes? Discourage them? Different answers exist to almost all of these questions for different countries at different times. The entire business of annual variations is terribly difficult.

What contribution have we made to sorting all this out? Our claims must be modest indeed, for in Chapter 4 we discovered the relationships between the business and strike cycles to be unstable and elusive, after the effect of trend had been eliminated. Before the First World War strikes rose with real wages; thereafter the opposite was true: strikes declined as real wages rose. One of the few consistent relationships from year to year was between strikes and employer prosperity, so that when profits were flowing in workers would be more likely to walk out, either because as a matter of justice they wanted a larger share of the take, or because they thought the employer could less well accept a work halt, or because their own disposable incomes were going up, augmenting the resources they could give to collective action. Finally, we concluded that some tendency existed for a short-term economic crisis to spark a flurry of strikes.[7]

Second, secular trends, A standard view of the impact of long-term changes in worker and employer prosperity upon strikes is equally difficult to discover in the literature. Some writers feel that a long wave of prosperity will inhibit conflict, as the need to pay off installment purchases makes workers reluctant to risk pay interruptions. Others argue that upward trends in prosperity reduce 'discontent,' and therewith strikes. Our own trend analysis suggests that long-term increases in employer prosperity bring with them corresponding increases in worker well-being. Higher worker real wages then increase the resources available to unions, and in that way stimulate conflict; but there is in France little direct relationship between trends in worker prosperity and trends in conflict. Some of these findings are unstable, and it is possible that further analysis, especially of individual industries, will modify this tentative model. But for the time being French time-series data appear to cast doubt upon models that associate prosperity and conflict directly, and suggest rather that organization is an important intervening variable.

Economic interest arguments receive much apparent support from an analysis of worker demands, and students of France have always been struck by the high proportion of worker grievances over wages. On the face of it, this single statistic would appear to provide impressive confirmation for those who argue that the French strike movement was non-political and that the average worker was far more interested in fattening his pay envelope than in making revolution. Is this not evidence of 'economism' in strikes?

Not necessarily. The stated grievance and the real purpose in going out on strike are not always the same thing.[8] We believe that unions selected 'higher wages' as a convenient rallying cry, but that neither they, nor the workers who were thereby mobilized, were committing their own money and time merely for the sake of a few more francs a week. Indeed any model imputing economic rationality to the strikers would be confounded by the high failure rates, the absence of employer–worker negotiations, the brevity of the disputes, the yawning gaps in the ranks of the participants themselves. Surely fewer efforts could have been less conducive to getting results from individual employers than a typical French strike: a handful of workers would fall out for a few days, mill about in front of the factory gates, march back and forth with banners in the street, denounce the employer in public placards, then drift sullenly back to work. Was this exercise really for the sake of forcing the employer to pay higher wages?

Not really. Wage demands were a mobilizing device, not a real issue. Those who called the strike, at least, had objectives in mind quite different from the bread-and-butter variety. In the interwar years the union move-ment associated itself with pay grievances, and the CGTU avowed explicitly its intention of using wage hikes to mark time until the Revolution arrived. It is difficult to tell exactly what those who followed such strike calls thought they were doing. Did they believe they were contributing to a glowing to-morrow of socialism for the working classes, or merely insuring that inflation would not leave them behind? The followers, as opposed to the leaders, remain mute to the historian, but our figures on the lacking plant solidarity and ineffective outcome of a typical dispute suggest that if the participants had really gone on strike to win pay increases, they would have forged for themselves American-style unions that could have brought that happy result about.

Of course such 'economic' variables as employer profits and industrial production must be incorporated into any comprehensive model of conflict. But rather than being used as strategic master variables to explain why the whole business gets going in the first place, they should be relegated to less central, intervening positions. With the aid of time-series and cross-sectional multivariate analyses, we have demonstrated that the business cycle may affect employer readiness to make concessions, or worker perceptions of the risk of dismissal in striking. Thus the state of the economy helps to explain why one year sees a lot of strikes, another year fewer. But such relationships are not constant, and indeed display a disconcerting tendency to reverse themselves from one epoch to another. And such economic rationality arguments have little ability to account for the apparition of massive periodic strike waves. If we want to know why France hovered on the brink of revolution in 1936, or why the years after 1946 experienced a grand secular rise in disputes, we shall have to seek our master variables outside the state of the economy.

Political action

The main arguments of this book portray the strike as an instrument of working-class political action. Workers, when they strike, are merely extending into the streets their normal processes of political participation. This theory sees strikes not so much as real tests of economic strength as symbolic displays of political energy and resoluteness. And the people whom these displays are intended to impress are not individual employers against whom – for reasons of practical convenience – the strike is ostensibly directed, but the political authorities of the land, in the form of either the government itself or powerful members of the polity.

The strike may involve workers in political processes through several different avenues:

(1) By compelling government intervention in the dispute itself. We have argued that the true objective of many strikes was to force the government to step in, thereby strengthening working-class relays to the political center, as well as achieving the stated purpose for which the strike was launched. (Government intervention improved enormously the chances that the strike would end in a compromise, and equally decreased the likelihood of failure, or indeed of the strikers' dismissal.)

(2) By impressing upon public consciousness the force and vigor behind working-class demands. French strikes tended to be dramas staged in the forum of the street or the town square, and all the marching back and forth, the public meetings, the placards and demonstrations were designed to catch the eye of the political powers-that-be. If we keep in mind this true role of the strike as demonstration, many hitherto incomprehensible features suddenly become clear: the extreme brevity, the low participation among workers in the struck establishment, the large number of shops all across the city joining hands, the absence of negotiation with the individual employer, the high failure rates – all would defy comprehension if we assumed the strike's real purpose was to exact wage increases from the boss. But once

we realize that a walkout was meant as a public, symbolic display of strength, all these features fit into place: French strikes were short because a symbolic point can be quickly made; they failed often because the workers had not seriously intended to embark upon an economic endurance contest; only a fraction of the shop's workers would take part because many workers were out of sympathy with the particular brand of politics involved; many establishments joined together simultaneously because (a) citywide networks existed to orchestrate individual plants and (b) because all involved realized that the effectiveness of the demonstration of strength depended upon mobilizing as many workers as possible; finally, the employer himself refused to negotiate because he was reluctant to lend legitimacy to what was, after all, an insurgent political movement.

(3) By exerting pressure directly upon the political center through strike waves. As we noted in Chapter 5, since the 1890s great concentrations of conflict have surged up at critical junctures in France's political history. In particular, at precisely those points when the industrial working classes seemed to be making an entry to or an exit from the polity, giant waves of strikes have broken out. The first of these occurred in 1899, just around the time that Millerand, the first socialist minister in the Third Republic's history, took a portfolio in the Waldeck-Rousseau government. Another wave came in 1906, as the May elections returned to the Chamber of Deputies a substantial socialist contingent. A giant cycle of protest rolled through the years 1919–20, as the soldiers poured back from the front, determined to get a new political deal. The famous sitdown strikes of 1936 erupted just as the Blum government was taking office – France's first socialist-led ministry. And in 1947 a revolutionary outburst of conflict occurred as the Communist Party left the government, commencing its long Cold War vigil outside the charmed circle of power. Finally, factory and white-collar workers undertook in 1968 the longest, largest general strike in history as student unrest reopened the question of who were to be the constituent political groups of the Fifth Republic. In each of these instances the political spokesmen of the working classes were able to command a more attentive hearing, both in the corridors of power and on the curbstones, because of these great mobilizations of popular strength behind them.

It is not coincidental that strikes and violent disturbances have tended to peak in the same years, indeed to vary smoothly together over the last century. We have argued elsewhere that both varieties of collective action help serve the same instrumentality: smashing open the door of the polity to some contender hitherto excluded.[9] Waves of strikes and of disturbances do not blossom forth because wages are low, living costs high (although such economic factors might widen the networks which the contending organizations control); strikes and violence do not erupt because for some reason – structural or adventitious – those who participate in them suddenly feel 'alienated,' 'frustrated' or 'aggressive': perhaps some of the personnel are in fact angry, yet others will surely be of moderate disposition, at peace with themselves and with the world. We have argued in this book that major accumulations of strikes and disturbances eventuate when it becomes apparent to the working classes as a whole that a point of critical importance for their own interests is at hand in the nation's political life, *and* when the latticework of organization suffices to transform these individual perceptions of opportunity into collective action.

Phases of collective action in France

Throughout this book we have tried to introduce differentiation into the notion of 'working classes.' And the history of the strike may best be understood as the history of different groups of the labor force successively using industrial conflict to safeguard their own political as well as their shop-floor interests. When the modern French strike movement commenced in the 1830s, the principal participants were craftsmen. Almost certainly they had their eyes fixed upon the arena of *local* rather than of national politics, and they struck not so much to acquire for themselves a voice in the polity as to halt a further erosion of their existing political position. We have argued that they glimpsed in industrial capitalism a deadly threat to their control of shop-floor routines, to their self-administration of their corporate life, and to their established hold upon municipal politics. We have by no means proven this case, yet available published evidence, combined with our secondary analysis of Jean-Pierre Aguet's data, suggests that the political action hypothesis helps illuminate craft strikes in the middle third of the nineteenth century.

A new lurch in industrial advance later in the century brought with it a shift in the composition of the contenders, and in the nature of the arena in which they chose to agitate. The years 1880–1930 cohere as a second important phase of strike history. Factory industrialization and the mechanization of work routines stepped into high gear after the 1880s, creating the new political use of the strike that we have called 'the great mobilization of the working classes.' An occupation-by-occupation analysis showed that craftsmen in skilled occupations continued in the vanguard of the strike movement, but that militancy was seeping from artisans in more traditionally active sectors such as woodworking towards artisans in the construction and metalworking industries.

Another important difference between this second phase and the first was the locus of agitation. Strikes were no longer intended to impress observers within the local arena of municipal politics, as in the years before the Second Empire, but those at the center of national power itself. The great mobilization meant that local groups of workers all over France joined hands in order to concentrate more efficiently their efforts upon the apparatus of the central state. The years after 1880 witnessed the construction of national union and political party organizations with which went, hand in hand, a centralization of conflict itself. Paris acquired an ever higher percentage of strikes; urban disputes in general became larger and more imposing. And the coordination of conflict from one municipality to another improved. These trends suggest strongly to us that the strike was becoming an instrument in the working-class political struggle at the center of power.

The middle third of the twentieth century experienced a third major shift in composition of the strike movement and in the political objectives of the strikers. By the interwar period many of the traditional militants had achieved their objectives, and so had begun to demobilize themselves, or else had gone under and so were simply no longer around to take part. Many artisanal crafts had been extinguished by the logic of industrial advance; dying trades, further protest was for them pointless. Other artisanal groups managed, however, to come to terms with the industrialization process. Such trades as the printers had finally guaranteed their own workshop positions, and had as well acquired political representation through the Radical and Socialist parties. So they began to drop from the strikers' ranks.

A new breed of striker took over the movement in the interwar years, the assembly-line proletarian. Semi-skilled workers had premonished their coming importance during the strike wave of 1919–20. But during the 1920s as such the proletarians in the huge chemicals and metalworking plants remained relatively passive. It was in 1936 that these workers made definitive both their shop-floor militancy and their political ambitiousness; the two went together. The factory occupations marked the political mobilization of a vast, hitherto passive and unrepresented range of industrial workers. The merger of the CGT and CGTU, and the action coalition of PCF and SFIO, seem to have touched off vibrations in the associational networks of which these men were a part. Then the entry of the Popular Front into power in May of 1936 provided the signal for the activation of this major new political challenger.

After the Second World War these political networks emerged as before, and the industrial struggles of the late 1940s and 50s were played out against the backdrop of proletarian factory workers, represented by the CGT and contending for membership in the polity. The shift in the structure of the strike itself – higher frequency, greater size, shorter duration – which seemed to take place after the Second World War had in fact begun in the Popular Front with the definitive activation of the proletarian contender. Yet only in the years after 1946 did the consequences of this third shift become fully manifest in the strike statistics.

For the CGT this was where the story ended: industrial proletarian militancy. Official dogma predicted that sooner or later the 'workers' would be victorious, and that would be the end of circulation in polity membership; the class struggle would be over, and strikes become a dim recollection from the past.

But a fourth major shift in the relationship between industrial structure and political representation seems to be under way in France. In 1936 there was a strong hint of white-collar militancy: office clerks within the bureaucracies had participated substantially, and their more skilled co-workers who had responsible professional positions within leading 'science sector' industries appear also to have taken part, here and there. ('Professional,' the reader is reminded, means formally educated skilled workers, not 'free' professionals such as doctors and lawyers.) It was in the 1950s that science-sector militancy emerged in its own right as a force to be reckoned with, not the lumpenproletariat of the office world but the skilled professionals within the glistening glass cubes, the artisans of twentieth-century technology whom Alain Touraine has grasped so eloquently in their struggle against the 'techno-bureaucrats.' Is this a new contender mobilizing, demanding political representation in the same manner as its two predecessors, the artisans and assembly-line proletarians? Or are these new militants merely bread-and-butter unionists without more enduring political demands?

May 1968 seemed to provide a sort of answer. The skilled professionals turned out to be intensely political, but they wanted to manipulate the levers of power at the center in order to solve *local* shop-floor problems. Much of the science-sector labor force already had political representation in the conventional sense, for as members of fairly influential social classes they disposed of political parties to protect their property interests, to keep down their taxes etc. What did not exist for them was political leverage over the giant bureaucracies in both public and private sectors in which they worked. And such leverage could be obtained only via such central political forums as the ministries and the Chamber of Deputies. So in order to satisfy their needs for more job control and for a greater democratization of local decision-making they joined hands in the streets with students – who thought of themselves as a new political class hammering on the door of the polity for initial admission – and with the conventional factory workers, who were occupying and demonstrating in a manner which had become routine for them since 1936. Thus did a newly arisen contingent of workers use the strike as an instrument for obtaining new political demands.

This account of strike history over the last one hundred and fifty years suggests that there is a regular, intimate relationship between industrial structure, the organizational bases of working-class life, worker participation in politics and strike activity. Every new stratum of workers which economic modernization tosses to the surface will sooner or later demand participation in the nation's political life; and established groups will struggle against the eclipse of their present position of power by some upstart. Whether activation for this political struggle comes sooner or later depends on the challenger group's success in putting together an organizational launching pad. Some groups quickly got this collective basis for political agitation in place: the artisans working in factories in the 1890s and 1900s.

Other groups endured long lapses of time before their organizational fundaments would sustain a political take-off: the automobile-assemblers of the 1920s come at once to mind.

A number of structural factors conjoined to determine exactly when this launching pad would be ready, but one of these factors we have emphasized at some length is industrial technology. Some technologies, such as assembly-line production, are inherently disaggregating, and enormous momentum must be built up, either in the plant or in the *quartier*, before the isolated machine-tenders will be persuaded to surrender precious resources in time, money and energy to collective ventures. Other technologies stimulate small-group cohesiveness, and make necessary only a short run before the pole vault: the classic system of craft production, and possibly the new 'artisans' of the science sector.

All of these groups of workers used strikes to attain political objectives, just as they employed other forms of concerted action as well. That seems a constant, though the political ambitions of craftworkers on strike before 1850 are least well documented. What is variable in the relationship between labor-force transformation and the politics of conflict is the *locus* of protest. Some kinds of workers prefer collective action at the national level because the prospects are hopeless for successful negotiation with their employers (the semi-skilled proletarians). Other groups prefer national political action because the corporations which employ them are nationwide, and so closely intertwined with the central political system that only a change in national political decision-making can effect a change in corporate authority (civil servants, computer programmers). Sparkplug unions prefer to agitate on the center stage because their own bureaucratic structure makes mobilization of any kind possible only when it is conceived as nationwide in scope, and when the demands for which the workers will walk off are explicitly political. Guild-style unions tend to be averse to center-stage politics, seeing the vital interests of their members at the local level. Thus do various circumstances determine whether the site of agitation will be local or national.

Yet not only have the working classes which participated in strikes evolved over the years, the structure of industrial conflict itself has become transformed. The frequency of disputes, of course, has increased enormously. Then too, strikes have become much larger, involving many more workers on the average, and much shorter, lasting at the median only a day or two after the Second World War, as opposed to six days or so before the First World War. We tie these changes in *form* to the nationalization of the strike: to the industrial workers' use of the labor dispute to make a collective symbolic political statement at the center of power. And we link the surge in *frequency* to a tremendous increase in formal organizations within the modern worker community, measured in terms of unionization and membership in political parties.

Where we stand

How often is the first person plural used in these pages, suggesting that the only platform on which we stand is our data themselves. And how misleading is this impression! For if we have been able to reach grandly across the skies of theory, it is because we are standing on the shoulders of tall men. Many other scholars have speculated on the relationship between economic change and political and industrial protest, and we see ourselves firmly within a major intellectual tradition. Some of the arguments on which we have had to build are good ones; others are lacking in ability to make much sense of the real world. All stand in need of some modification, now that the French experience lies before us.

One seriously inadequate effort to explain conflict in terms of industrial change was presented by Clark Kerr and Abraham Siegel in 1954, the famous 'isolated mass' hypothesis. And if we have been able to do little else in this volume, we hope to have relegated to the domain of fantasy this homogeneous mass of militant workers, made hostile by their isolation from the surrounding society. As we tried to show in Chapter 10, the most militant, effective workers are precisely those in the middle of the heterogeneous, swirling metropolis, not the isolated proletarians on the territorial margins of the population or the social margins of the civic community. The city is an accelerator, not a brake of conflict. And the small shop is a place where collective rivalries burst swiftly into struggle. The large plant, by way of contrast, may see many disputes, but they will be lacking in solidarity and effectiveness.

And what about old Marx? How does his attempt to link economic change and political conflict fare in light of France's strike history? Not badly at all. We have rediscovered, to the accompaniment of loud self-congratulation, some of the truths about economics and militancy that Marx described so passionately a hundred years ago. So the factory proletarians used strikes to political ends? That will scarcely come as news to Marxist scholars. Marx recognized no significant distinctions among industrial relations, class relations and relations of power. In his view, 'Every movement in which the working class comes out as a *class* against the ruling classes and tries to coerce them by pressure from without is a political movement.'[10] The reader will find nothing in our text to contradict this, although we slide uneasily over the distinction Marx made between political movements as such and 'economic' movements.

What may be a little unsettling to Marxists, however, is the paramountcy we assign to craftworkers for virtually the entire period before the First World War. Marx realized of course that artisanal militancy would appear, indeed that an aristocracy of labor would lead the proletariat for a time. Yet we continue to find skilled workers in the forefront of protest long after mechanized factory production had become an ugly reality in France's industrial life. What may more seriously upset Marxist arguments is our speculation that a fourth major phase in the interrelationship between economic change and political protest is now afoot, in the form of disputes among office workers and science-sector professionals. These people are not exploited toilers at all, and attempts to explain away their militancy as that of a 'white-collar proletariat' are bound to miss an essential reality.

We asked at the beginning of this book whether such structural changes as urbanization and industrialization had regular and independent effects upon strike activity. The answer in the case of France turns out to be yes only if these grand transformations first alter the pattern of organization and the nature of the struggle for political power. Finding out whether this model holds true for other countries, which don't have France's historical inheritance, her singular folkways and her unique rules for playing the game in Paris, will surely represent the coming agenda for the political sociology of industrial conflict.

Sources and methods

Discovering strikes

Unlike Germany and England, where non-official sources of strike statistics exist alongside the official ones, in France the only source of data is the government. The official nature of our information on conflicts means, therefore, that we must pay some attention to how the government found out about strikes, and to what biases and inaccuracies may exist in the data as a result.

As early as 1830 tentative steps in the direction of central strike reporting had been taken, at least indirectly. Engaging in a *coalition ouvrière* was until 1864 a crime, and so the government in Paris kept loose track of strikes via pipelines of reporting for criminal activity: the judicial one, through the *procureurs généraux* and the *procureurs du roi*, and the administrative one, through the *gendarmerie*. Because strikes posed problems of law enforcement, the Ministry of Justice would collect reports at the end of one pipeline, and because they affected the maintenance of order, the Interior Ministry would stand attentively at the end of the other. In order to gather information for his book on strikes in the July Monarchy, Jean-Pierre Aguet – to whom we shall come in a minute – had to pore through the archives of both central agencies in order to compile a unified list of conflicts.

After 1860 the Ministry of Commerce made several efforts to poll the prefects for information on strikes[1]. But reporting remained haphazard, for as late as 1892, in order to collect a list of all strikes in 1890 and 1891, the *Office du travail* of the Commerce Ministry had to ask the *Direction de la sûreté générale*, the Ministry of Public Works, the Ministry of War, the Paris *Préfecture de police* and a number of departmental prefectures and town halls for lists of all conflicts known to them.[2]

In 1885 the Commerce Ministry made its first determined attempt to collect under one roof strike statistics, as in a circular it instructed the prefects to send in regularly an enumeration of strike activity in their departments.[3] Late in 1891 a special office was created within the Commerce Ministry to handle labor matters, the *Direction de l'Office du travail.* It took the final initiative in collecting strike data by demanding in 1892 rigorous and systematic reporting from prefects of all strikes in their jurisdictions. The prefects were provided with a printed blank form four pages long on which they were to note a wide variety of information about each conflict. The *Office du travail* (called the *Direction du travail* after 1899) would then collate these numerous reports streaming in from all over the country and publish each year both a list of individual strikes and tables giving aggregate characteristics of strike activity. Both documents appeared in the *Statistique des grèves*.

The system of strike reporting established in 1892 worked well for the next fifty-three years. From time to time, to be sure, the *Direction du travail* would reproach the prefects for not despatching reports of individual conflicts quickly enough,[4] or for rounding off the number of strikers to the nearest hundred or for some similar abuse.[5] But on the whole the system provided a reasonably fine mesh through which, according to our estimates, only one out of ten strikes escaped official notice.[6]

The last year to be covered in the *SG* was 1935. The strike wave of 1936 seems to have swamped the system, for the strikes of 1936–8 received only the most cursory treatment in the *Bulletin du ministère du travail*. Official silence on strikes marked 1939–45.

After the Second World War official gathering of strike data underwent a drastic change. Rather than continuing to make the prefects responsible for noting individual strikes, the Labor Ministry (established independent of the Commerce Ministry in 1906) shifted the task to the *Inspecteurs du travail*. Individual factory owners, *délégués du personnel*, unions and other interested parties were to report strikes directly to the *Inspecteurs du travail*, who would then send the *fiches de conflits* on to the statistical division of the Labor Ministry. The *fiches* themselves were greatly simplified from the detailed forms the old *Direction du travail* had demanded of the prefects, and required the respondent to give only the dates of the conflict. Two separate questionnaires were necessary if the strike lasted longer than forty-eight hours, one to register its beginning, the other its end. Information was solicited on the following: the numbers of strikers and of workers employed, the general subject matter of the dispute, a general area of grievance and its outcome.[7] The statistical division was to aid in the search for strikes by scanning independently the pages of *L'Humanité*, and by other means, and then to instruct the *Inspecteurs du travail* to contact the establishment on strike.

After the Second World War several government agencies circumvented the *Inspecteurs du travail* in reporting strikes, as for example the collieries, which sent word directly to the statistical division. More serious in affecting the reliability of the official statistics, however, was the refusal of the *Sécretariat d'état chargé de la fonction publique* to release for publication data on conflicts within the civil services. This was a serious omission because the *fonctionnaires* struck often and in large numbers.[8] On the whole we doubt that the completeness of the government's data on strikes was greater in the 1960s than in the 1890s. Certainly the information collected was much less extensive, and much less available to the public.

Defining strikes

We must understand exactly how the government defined a strike in order to compare France to other countries, where different criteria for delimiting may prevail, and in order to allow for changes in standards of measurement from one period to another within France. The French government has always viewed any collective work stoppage, regardless how short or how few workers were involved, as a strike. This policy was laid down in 1894 and has been followed ever since.[9] The strike is said to begin when the first workers lay down their tools, not when it is officially declared, and to end when the first workers go back on the job. Statisticians distinguished until the Second World War between strikes and lock-outs, but we combine the two in this study. The only practical differences between them is that in a strike the workers initiate the stoppage, in a lock-out the employers do so in response to some collective threat from the workers.

Only one kind of strike has *not* been regularly reported: massive, one-day (or less) political stoppages, such as 12 February 1934 or 24 September 1948. Government statisticians doubtless realized that the inclusion of these giant protests would have completely overshadowed the smaller 'normal' strikes, making annual strike series into an index of political demonstrations.

Reporting of the number of *strikers* has been inconsistent since the Second World War. Before the war, the government differentiated between the number of strikers as such, and the number of workers in the struck establishment indirectly affected by the strike, which is to say forced out of work yet not themselves on strike. Since the war the statistical division has lumped the two as the *effectifs en grève*. Another change in the consistency of official statistics is the 1954 decision to count but a single time strikers who have participated in several conflicts in the course of a year. Previously, of course, each time a worker went out he was counted separately as a striker in the aggregate statistics.[10] Finally, strikers in the civil services have been excluded from official statistics in the postwar period.

Large strikes, which reach out to involve a number of different establishments in various localities and industries, pose a problem of classification. How do we know when to say a conflict is one strike or several? The *Office du travail* offers a simple rule: if 'concerted action' is present, then strikes that break out simultaneously in a number of establishments should be counted as one. 'It is essentially this *concert général* which seems to us to constitute the unity of a strike, even when there is not complete concordance in the beginning and ending dates, nor in the causes or outcomes of the strike.'[11] The International Labour Office's definition of a strike incorporates this same element of central coordination: 'Disputes affecting several establishments should be considered as one case if they are organized or directed by one person or organization.'[12] Yet some ambiguity remains in the case of giant general strikes sweeping over wide regions and numerous industrial sectors. Simultaneity and commonality of purpose do not necessarily mean central direction. The 1936 sitdown strikes are a case in point. When faced with such major disturbances, the *Office du travail* customarily devoted a separate line in the publication to each industry within each municipality or department, giving these individual lines a common serial number. The labor statisticians adhered to these principles consistently before the Second World War. Since the war they have collapsed some regionwide and nationwide stoppages into a single strike, possibly because the hand of centralized union leadership has been so much more apparent since 1945.

Reporting strikes

Since 1890 the government has reliably and consistently collected strike data. The problem is the great unevenness and incompleteness the official services have often permitted themselves in making this information available to the public. Published strike data for some years extend into volume after volume of elaborate detail; data for others are almost unusable.

1830–47

Jean-Pierre Aguet combed the archives of the Interior and Justice Ministries in Paris to compile a record of all strikes in the July Monarchy. He was able to determine, for most of the 382 conflicts he uncovered, data on the industry, the location, the involvement of a worker organization, the duration, the stated grievance and the like. It is clear to Aguet that these 382 strikes represent only a fraction of the total amount of industrial conflict in the July Monarchy, for in those eighteen years the Justice Ministry noted 1,049 prosecutions for the crime of *coalition ouvrière*. In all likelihood judicial officials either failed to notice or regarded benignly many additional strikes. So Aguet has given us essentially a sampling of strikes, biased in the direction of the larger, politically sensitive conflicts which found their way into the central files. Nonetheless the Aguet data should reveal accurately the movement of strikes over time, and give information on basic structural characteristics of these early conflicts.[13]

1848–84

The new official interest in strikes during the 1880s led the Commerce Ministry to publish detailed statistics on both retrospective and current conflicts in the yearly *Statistique annuelle*. In the 1885 volume the ministry released tabular information on strike activity since 1874. In the 1889 volume similar information going back to 1852 appeared: tables giving the aggregate results, stated grievances and distribution by industry; the only year-by-year data were the number of strikes since 1852.[14] The Commerce Ministry assembled these historical data from prefectoral reports, but presumably the figures for the 1850s and 60s are quite incomplete.

A decade later the *Office du travail* of the Commerce Ministry launched a much more substantial historical inquiry into strikes and worker organization going back to 1800. Clerks went through official records, newspapers and other publications; they interviewed union officials, talked with aging militants in *hospices de vieillards* and in general evaluated every source of both verbal and written evidence they could think of in order to compile a record of past industrial relations, conflicts and worker organization. Among other uses, this marvelous source may serve as a chronicle of strikes. *Les Associations professionnelles ouvrières* (*APO*) mentions in some detail 363 strikes between 1830 and 1889. Those included have a notable bias towards Paris, which we know about because other sources covering part of the period, such as Aguet and the *Statistique annuelle*, demonstrate a heavier provincial contribution than *APO* shows. Like Aguet, the *APO* is neither a random sample of all the strikes nor an exhaustive enumeration of the prominent ones, and so must be handled with care.[15] In this study we use evidence from the *APO* in order to supplement our knowledge about the distribution of strikes by industry, or to calculate typical issues and outcomes, rather than to chart frequencies over time or territory.[16]

The industriousness of Michelle Perrot, however, has handed us and other scholars a marvelous short cut through this thicket of *APO* and *Statistique annuelle* reporting problems. For in her *thèse* she has assembled an exhaustive series on strikes, strikers and various characteristics of disputes in the years 1864–85(90). We rely upon her for our time series of strike frequency.

1885–9

In 1885 the Commerce Ministry began to publish the enumerations of strikes which are the heart of our data, supplying lists on the years until 1889 to the editors of the *Statistique annuelle*. There we may find data on the industry and occupation, the locality, the stated grievance, salaries, duration and outcome of each of 794 strikes gathered in the rather coarse official net.

1890–1935

The *Office du travail* brought out the remarkable *Statistique des grèves* for the first time in 1892, in that volume surveying the conflicts of 1890 and 1891.[17] The *SG* was to appear every year thereafter until 1939, chronicling in its final volume the strikes of 1933–5. (A single volume published in 1921 covered the war years 1915–18.) Perhaps the *Direction du travail* despaired of listing the thousands of strikes in June 1936, and so discontinued the *SG*. Perhaps, on the other hand, the *SG* was permitted to lapse because the nature of strike activity itself had shifted in 1936, becoming a political spear directed against the government; officialdom may have thought that the less known about such things, the better. It is disappointing, of course, that the publication stops at 1936, just on the verge of a major turning point in the worker movement. Yet let us count our blessings. The *SG* permits a detailed look at each of the 36,441 strikes to have occurred in mainland France and Corsica between 1890 and 1935. Strikes in the three 'lost' departments of Bas-Rhin, Haut-Rhin and Moselle are included after 1919.[18]

Over the years the *Direction du travail* reduced somewhat the amount of information given for each strike. The years from 1895 to around 1903 are the richest, owing to both the extensiveness of the enumerations and the discursive accounts of principal conflicts appended at the end of each volume. The numbered lists of strikes provide the obvious information: commune and department of the dispute, industrial sector and occupation involved, the numbers of strikers, of establishments and workers employed therein, the beginning and ending dates of the strike and its duration in days. But the *Direction du travail* also supplied information which permits us to go deeper than mere magnitudes and to specify the framework of organization and discontent within which the conflict unraveled. Two columns note the presence of employers' and workers' unions. Other columns give the workers' wages before and after the strike, likewise their hours of work. Others tell the stated grievances of the strikers, offering as many as four or five separately. Still others indicate whether the strike was a success, a compromise or a failure, and what outcome met both the strike in general and each particular demand. Another field of information specifies whether piece work or time was the basis of payment. Finally, a wide column entitled *modes de réglement des conflits et observations diverses* summarizes in a non-standard way the course of the dispute, indicating which government authorities intervened, whether the 1892 collective bargaining law applied, whether the unions supported the strikers financially, how the strike was settled and what fraction of the workforce was taken on again by the employers.

In addition to these uniform tabular data, a concluding section in each volume gives an extensive prose account of all disputes in which the official collective bargaining procedure was used, or which the officials in the *Direction du travail* thought worthy of public notice by virtue of their magnitude, political importance or some other feature. In this part of the volume are often reprinted the texts of collective agreements, letters from strikers, employers and government officials to one another, wage scales, factory internal regulations and other written material bearing on the conflict.

After 1903 the tabular enumeration of individual strikes continues unchanged but the loquaciousness of the little histories at the end is curtailed. Accounts of the course of events give way to formalized recitation of the legal collective bargaining steps trod in the strike, and the sheer volume of interesting miscellany is reduced.

The Great War changed strike reporting extensively. The first interwar volume was a poor cousin of the fat books opulent in detail of the prewar years. Whereas formerly two printed pages were required to give the various attributes of a single strike, the interwar volumes needed but a single page, dispensing with all the information on wages and hours, union activity, the breakdown of strikers by numbers of men, women and children, and squeezing the splendor of 'remarks' into a paltry space which normally revealed only if the collective bargaining law had been applied. The appended chronicles of individual strikes had been entirely abolished. We know reliably in the interwar years the number of strikes, but we know much less about each of them.

1936–8

From 1936 to 1966 we have only meager tables summarizing for each year the fundamental dimensions of industrial conflict. The enumerations that formerly made strike statistics such a useful indicator of the impact of social change upon working-class life cease entirely.

The *Bulletin du ministère du travail* (*BMT*), published monthly since its inception in 1894, is our only source of data for the years 1936–8, giving cross-classifications of strikes by department, industry, cause and duration. Because reports from some departments failed to reach the *BMT* in time for publication, the usefulness of its strike data is impaired.

1946–65

The quarterly *Revue française du travail* (*RFT*) replaced the *BMT* in 1946. Scarcely an improvement in strike reporting, the *RFT* supplied a few aggregate statistics for each year, a breakdown of man-days lost by industry and by region (not department), at irregular intervals, and some frequency distributions of duration, stated grievance and outcome. The principal conflicts were also mentioned from time to time. The *RFT* gave way to the *Revue française des affaires sociales* in 1966, when the Labor Ministry became the Social Welfare Ministry. The latter journal made no report of industrial conflict; and published inadequate strike figures thereafter were to be gleaned only from that ministry's monthly *Statistiques du travail et de la securité sociale*. Thus the disrepair of French strike reporting was complete. Precisely at the time when the strike movement became a force for political revolution, we find ourselves faced with a deafening official silence on the subject.

Coding and measuring strikes

It would be impossible to study these thousands and thousands of strikes without the techniques of quantitative analysis: preparing data on the different features of each strike for machine processing, and then using high-speed electronic computers to calculate frequencies, to cross-classify characteristics of strikes one against another and to find statistical relationships. Here we review the coding schemes employed for various kinds of strike information.

The *SG* furnished the vast bulk of our data. How much of the information it contained was transferred onto IBM cards? To exhaust completely the wealth of material published by the *Direction du travail* for each of 36,000 strikes would have required far more time and money than were at our disposal. In this imperfect world of limited budgets and scarce human resources one must be selective, coding not every single fact on every single page but selecting crucial variables for inclusion and leaving less essential items of information by the wayside. Yet for a restricted number of years we permitted ourselves some extravagance in data recording, so as not to ignore completely quantitative data on, for example, the collective bargaining process. To be precise, in coding the *SG* we divided the years into three groups:
(1) 1890–4, 1900–9. For these years we collected a bare minimum of information on the magnitude of each strike – number of strikers, duration and the like – and the industry and department in which it took place. A skilled keypuncher sat down with the source in front of her, putting the numerical information directly onto IBM cards with the codes of territories and industrial sectors written in the margin of the photocopy.
(2) 1895–9, 1910–14. In these years we took maximum notice of complexity. Trained coders noted almost all the standard items of information about each strike, writing down such variables as the commune and the stated grievance. In addition they recorded references in the 'remarks' column to how the strike was settled, what government authorities intervened and who of the parties showed greatest reluctance to participate in direct negotiations.

(3) 1915–35. We tried to strike a balance in the interwar years between the cursory measurement of strike dimensions and the exhaustive recording of the course of strike itself. Research assistants coded most of the standard information for each strike, but did not tarry long over the qualitative data mentioned in the remarks, noting mainly the presence of worker organization. Of course the scope of the information in the *SG* itself is greatly reduced from the prewar period.

To complete this recitation of data collection procedures, we tried to accumulate quantitative information on the massive changes operating upon working-class life and upon the structure of French industry and society. Owing to the assiduity of the *SG*, data on many indicators of change and upheaval exist in published tables. We have preserved on IBM cards information on such matters as the growth of cities, the diffusion of steam engines, the size of industrial establishments, the industrial composition of the larger cities and other related kinds of information. Most of these data come from the five-yearly censuses. Many published data are simultaneously cross-classified by department and industry, so that we may know the number of steam engines, for example, in each industry in each department for every census year between 1886 and 1911. (For a review of sources and methods, see the following articles in Jacob M. Price and Val R. Lorwin (eds.), *The Dimensions of the Past* [New Haven, Conn.: Yale University Press, 1972]: Louise A. Tilly, 'The Materials of the Quantitative History of France since 1789'; Louise A. Tilly and Charles Tilly, 'A Selected Bibliography of French Sources for Quantitative History since 1789'; and Charles Tilly 'Quantification in History, As Seen from France.')

Strikes are a little like wars, or like any other complex social phenomenon, in defying a single measurement of magnitude. We would have grave reservations about comparing a series of wars on the basis alone of the number of soldiers participating, for the 'size' of a war has other obvious dimensions than mere battalions engaged, such as loss of life, the length of time it endured, the percentage of the nation's population called to arms and so forth. So with strikes no single statistical series will serve us, for the magnitude of a strike is determined by several dissimilar factors which may vary independently from one conflict to another.[19]

How, then, may we compare the strikes in one period, industry or territory to those in another? The three classic strike series are the number of strikes themselves, the number of workers participating in them and the number of man-days of work lost due to them. Each series conveys a different impression of the elephant. Man-days in strikes is a useful summary of the total amount of strike activity; it corresponds to the volume of the strike solids we employ in Chapters 3 and 12. As the solids themselves indicate, however, man-days is simply a compound of the size, duration and frequency of strikes. In order to get at the shape and texture of industrial conflict, we have to treat these components separately. That is what we do throughout the book.

Our normal practice is to compare years, industries or whatever simultaneously on the basis of their numbers of strikes and strikers. But taking the number of strikes alone to measure magnitude is risky because the number of workers participating in each conflict may change greatly from industry to industry. The average number of workers in a dispute in printing, a small-shop industry, for example, will be fewer than in mining, where the scale of enterprise is enormous. So we grasp the elephant's size imperfectly if we assert that printing and mining had the same volume of conflict because each had three strikes in the same month. Vastly greater numbers of miners than printers went on strike. By the same logic, we should not rely on the number of strikers alone as the basic measure of size because the number of conflicts tells us something about the number of 'friction points' in an industry or municipality. The number of strikes, in other words, reveals the number of separate outbreaks of the phenomenon we have set out to study, and we must not lose sight of it by fixing upon merely one of its characteristics: the number of workers taking part.[20]

The measurement problem is not resolved if we limit ourselves to *absolute numbers*, for we will be unable to determine if differences in the number of strikes and strikers over territories are owing merely to the fact that one region has more industrial workers than another region, and therewith a greater potential pool of militants and friction points. When we make such comparisons, we are contrasting the relative frequency or intensity of the phenomenon, and so must compute a rate of strikes or strikers based on the potential population which might have been drawn into the conflict. Normally we compare years, industries or areas with the statistic: number of strikes or strikers per 100,000 workers in the labor force. Because many workers go on strike who are not in manufacturing proper, such as those in agriculture and in transportation, the labor-force denominator in these rate calculations is the total active population.[21]

Selected data on industrial conflict in France

Table 1: *Absolute numbers of strikes and strikers, 1830–1967*

		1830–64 Likely number of strikes, as measured by criminal prosecutions for *coalition*	Actual number of strikes given in sources
	1830	40	8
	1831	49	6
	1832	51	8
	1833	90	72
	1834	55	14
5-year average	1830–4	57	22
	1835	32	8
	1836	55	18
	1837	51	9
	1838	44	6
	1839	64	15
5-year average	1835–9	49	11
	1840	130	37
	1841	68	24
	1842	62	20
	1843	49	18
	1844	53	20
5-year average	1840–4	72	24
	1845	48	38
	1846	53	34
	1847	55	27
	1848	94	
	1849	65	3-year average 33
5-year average	1845–9	63	
			New series
	1850	45	
	1851	55	
	1852	86	1
	1853	109	4
	1854	68	2
5-year average	1850–4	73	3-year average 2
	1855	168	8
	1856	73	3
	1857	55	9
	1858	53	12
	1859	58	10
5-year average	1855–9	81	8
	1860	58	28
	1861	63	25
	1862	44	24
	1863	29	15
	1864	21	19
5-year average	1860–4	43	22

Table 1 (*continued*)

		1865–1967	Number of
		Number of strikes	strikers
	1865	58	27,600
	1866	52	14,000
	1867	76	32,100
	1868	58	20,300
	1869	72	40,600
5-year average	1865–9	63	26,900
	1870	116	88,200
	1871	52	14,100
	1872	151	21,100
	1873	44	4,900
	1874	58	7,800
5-year average	1870–4	84	27,200
	1875	101	16,600
	1876	102	21,200
	1877	55	12,900
	1878	73	38,500
	1879	88	54,400
5-year average	1875–9	84	28,700
	1880	190	110,400
	1881	209	68,000
	1882	271	65,500
	1883	181	42,000
	1884	112	33,900
5-year average	1880–4	193	64,000
	1885	123	20,800
	1886	195	35,300
	1887	194	38,100
	1888	188	51,500
	1889	199	89,100
5-year average	1885–9	180	47,000
	1890	389	119,400
	1891	313	108,900
	1892	268	45,900
	1893	634	172,500
	1894	397	54,400
5-year average	1890–4	400	100,200
	1895	409	46,000
	1896	486	49,700
	1897	366	68,500
	1898	386	81,300
	1899	771	177,300
5-year average	1895–9	484	84,500
	1900	890	215,700
	1901	541	110,800
	1902	571	212,400
	1903	642	120,300
	1904	1,087	269,900
5-year average	1900–4	746	185,800
	1905	849	175,900
	1906	1,354	437,800
	1907	1,313	197,500
	1908	1,109	123,800
	1909	1,067	177,000

		1865–1967 Number of strikes	Number of strikers
5-year average	1905–9	1,138	222,400
	1910	1,517	287,000
	1911	1,489	228,200
	1912	1,150	270,700
	1913	1,099	226,400
	1914	685	161,400
5-year average	1910–14	1,188	234,700
	1915	98	9,200
	1916	312	41,000
	1917	686	288,100
	1918	496	177,100
	1919	2,047	1,310,100
5-year average	1915–19	728	365,100
	1920	1,879	1,139,900
	1921	565	450,400
	1922	695	305,700
	1923	1,094	354,400
	1924	1,068	278,500
5-year average	1920–4	1,060	505,800
	1925	907	243,600
	1926	1,644	361,400
	1927	393	111,700
	1928	788	206,200
	1929	1,188	242,700
5-year average	1925–9	984	233,100
	1930	1,079	575,100
	1931	276	44,800
	1932	360	71,400
	1933	336	108,300
	1934	383	97,200
5-year average	1930–4	487	179,400
	1935	365	102,300
	1936	16,907	2,423,000
	1937	2,616	323,800
	1938	1,220	1,333,000
4-year average	1935–8	5,277	1,045,500
	1946	523	180,100
	1947	3,598	2,997,600
	1948	1,374	6,561,200
	1949	1,413	4,330,000
4-year average	1946–9	1,727	3,517,200
	1950	2,585	1,527,300
	1951	2,514	1,754,000
	1952	1,749	1,155,200
	1953	1,761	1,783,700
	1954	1,479	1,318,900
5-year average	1950–4	2,018	1,507,800
	1955	2,672	1,060,600
	1956	2,440	981,700
	1957	2,623	2,963,800
	1958	954	1,112,500
	1959	1,512	939,800
5-year average	1955–9	2,040	1,411,700
	1960	1,494	1,071,500

Table 1 (*continued*)

	1961	1,963	2,551,800
	1962	1,884	1,472,400
	1963	2,382	2,646,100
	1964	2,281	2,603,100
5-year average	1960–4	2,001	2,069,000
	1965	1,674	1,237,100
	1966	1,711	3,341,000
	1967	1,675	2,818,600
3-year average	1965–7	1,687	2,465,600

NOTES

1830–64 data on prosecutions for strikes (*coalitions poursuivies*) taken from *APO*, I, pp. 27, 40.

1830–47 data on number of strikes 'in source' taken from Aguet, p. 365

1852–64 data on number of strikes 'in source' taken from *Statistique annuelle*, 1889, p. 134. (Figures for 1854 and 1855 derived from our coding of *APO*.) Note: Michelle Perrot reported 110 strikes for 1864.

1865–89 data on number of strikes and strikers from Michelle Perrot, *Ouvriers en grève*, p. 61.

1890–1935 data on number of strikes and strikers from our coding of *SG*. Note: The official yearly totals are slightly at variance with ours because we exclude Algerian strikes, and because we sometimes count separately the components of those massive strikes which *SG* treats as single disputes.

1936–8 data on number of strikes and strikers from *Annuaire statistique*, 1966, p. 121.

1946–54 data on strikes from *Annuaire statistique*, 1966, p. 121.

1955–67 data on strikes and 1946–67 data on strikers from the International Labour Organization's *Year Book of Labour Statistics*, 1951–2, 1957, 1966, 1969.

1967 data on strikes and strikers from *Annuaire statistique*, 1967.

Table 2: *Strike and striker rates, 1885–1967*

	Number of strikes per 100,000 total active population	Number of strikes per 100,000 non-agricultural active population	Number of strikers per 100,000 total active population
1885–9	1.1	2.0	300
1890–4	2.2	4.0	600
1895–9	2.5	4.5	400
1900–4	3.7	6.5	900
1905–9	5.5	9.5	1,100
1910–14	5.7	9.6	1,100
1915–19	3.5	5.8	1,800
1920–4	4.9	8.0	2,200
1925–9	4.6	7.1	1,100
1930–4	2.3	2.8	800
1835–8	26.0	40.3	5,200
1946–9	8.5	12.7	11,400
1950–4	9.2	14.6	8,100
1955–9	10.7	14.2	7,400
1960–4	10.5	13.1	10,800
1965–7	8.6	10.4	12,500

Table 3: *Selected characteristics of strike activity, 1830–1935*

		Median duration (in days)	Median number of establishments per strike	Median plant participation rate (strikers/100 workers employed in struck establishment)	Median number of workers in establishments on strike
	1830–4	2.9 (15 strikes)			
	1835–9	1.8 (6 strikes)			
	1840–4	2.9 (12 strikes)			
	1845–7	6.3 (24 strikes)			
	1885	5.1			
	1886	6.2			
	1887	5.1			
	1888	9.7			
	1889	6.6			
5-year median	1885–9	6.5			
	1890	6.6	1.3		
	1891	6.8	1.2		
	1892	6.5	1.2		
	1893	6.2	1.9		
	1894	5.6	1.8		
5-year median	1890–4	6.3	1.5		
	1895	4.6	1.5	46	68
	1896	5.2	1.5	36	84
	1897	4.8	1.7	41	69
	1898	4.8	1.7	45	68
	1899	4.9	1.6	45	83
5-year median	1895–9	4.9	1.6	43	76
	1900	5.4	2.0	47	73
	1901	5.4	2.1	51	62
	1902	5.9	1.5	49	98
	1903	7.0	1.7	53	71
	1904	5.3	2.6	62	49
5-year median	1900–4	5.7	2.0	53	66
	1905	6.1	1.8	54	66
	1906	6.4	2.5	57	53
	1907	5.6	2.0	47	57
	1908	5.2	1.7	50	48
	1909	5.8	1.8	50	58
5-year median	1905–9	5.8	1.9	52	55
	1910	5.8	1.9	52	51
	1911	5.8	2.1	52	43
	1912	5.2	1.8	49	55
	1913	4.8	1.8	42	65
	1914	5.2	1.9	45	60
5-year median	1910–4	5.4	1.9	49	53
	1915	2.5	1.5	34	84
	1916	3.3	1.3	34	109
	1917	3.6	1.8	60	126
	1918	3.7	1.6	60	113
	1919	6.8	2.7	76	62
5-year median	1915–9	5.1	2.2	64	78
	1920	7.8	2.9	71	52
	1921	8.4	1.7	62	100
	1922	5.8	1.5	50	107

Table 3 (*continued*)

		Median duration (in days)	Median number of establish-ments per strike	Median plant participation rate (strikers/100 workers employed in struck establishment)	Median number of workers in establishments on strike
	1923	6.7	1.7	56	80
	1924	6.5	1.9	62	64
5-year median	1920–4	7.1	2.1	62	69
	1925	5.8	1.6	59	70
	1926	6.2	2.0	64	54
	1927	5.0	1.7	52	69
	1928	5.2	1.8	50	69
	1929	4.8	1.7	50	77
5-year median	1925–9	5.5	1.8	56	66
	1930	5.5	1.6	51	90
	1931	4.9	1.5	53	72
	1932	4.8	1.2	53	99
	1933	5.8	1.4	51	100
	1934	7.0	1.3	50	102
	1935	5.5	1.3	53	144
6-year median	1930–5	5.6	1.4	52	97

NOTES

The 'median' is in all cases the geometric mean, not the true median. Yet in these data the two are virtually interchangeable. On this procedure see notes to fig. 3.10, p. 73.

In calculations of strikers/100 workers employed in struck establishments, the total plant labor force, rather than the labor force of the specific craft on strike (in the case of craft strikes within industrial plants), has been taken as the rate's denominator.

In strikes with more than one establishment participating, 'size of establishments on strike' was computed by dividing the total number of workers employed by the total number of establishments. That figure was then used in computing the annual median size of establish-ments on strike.

Table 4: *Percent of strikes over worker organization issues, 1830–1965*

	Number of strikes over worker organization issues	Total number of strikes for which grievance is known	% of strikes over worker organization
1830–4	1	72	1.4
1835–9	2	44	4.6
1840–4	1	82	1.2
1845–7	3	66	4.6
1830–47	7	264	2.6
1871–90	457	4,560	10.2
1885	6	108	5.6
1886	16	161	9.9
1887	14	104	13.5
1888	13	107	12.1
1889	42	306	13.7

Table 4 (*continued*)

		Number of strikes over worker organization issues	Total number of strikes for which grievance is known	% of strikes over worker organization
5-year total	1885–9	91	786	11.6
	1890	49	327	15.0
	1891	54	276	19.6
	1892	62	307	20.2
	1893	105	820	12.8
	1894	85	448	19.0
5-year total	1890–4	355	2,178	16.3
	1895	90	496	18.1
	1896	111	626	17.7
	1897	80	443	18.0
	1898	69	474	14.6
	1899	149	1,014	14.7
5-year total	1895–9	499	3,053	16.3
	1900	197	1,229	16.0
	1901	139	751	18.5
	1902	90	640	14.1
	1903	154	788	19.5
	1904	250	1,523	16.4
5-year total	1900–4	830	4,931	16.8
	1905	278	1,346	20.6
	1906	305	2,102	14.5
	1907	318	1,780	17.9
	1908	289	1,464	19.7
	1909	335	1,477	22.7
5-year total	1905–9	1,525	8,169	18.7
	1910	436	2,045	21.3
	1911	383	1,928	19.9
	1912	312	1,508	20.7
	1913	278	1,351	20.6
	1914	172	845	20.4
5-year total	1910–14	1,581	7,677	20.6
	1915	11	98	11.2
	1916	21	312	6.7
	1917	16	683	2.3
	1918	41	496	8.3
	1919	149	2,025	7.4
5-year total	1915–19	238	3,614	6.6
	1920	185	1,858	10.0
	1921	74	565	13.1
	1922	142	694	20.5
	1923	129	1,093	11.8
	1924	89	1,067	8.3
5-year total	1920–4	619	5,277	11.7
	1925	140	907	15.4
	1926	145	1,644	8.8
	1927	59	393	15.0
	1928	91	787	11.6
	1929	151	1,188	12.7

Table 4 (*continued*)

		Number of strikes over worker organization issues	Total number of strikes for which grievance is known	% of strikes over worker organization
5-year total	1925–9	586	4,919	11.9
	1930	115	1,071	10.7
	1031	48	276	17.4
	1932	73	360	20.3
	1933	56	335	16.7
	1934	68	383	17.8
	1935	22	361	6.1
6-year total	1930–5	382	2,786	13.7
	1946	31	528	5.9
	1947	109	1,525	7.1
	1948	48	888	5.4
	1949	154	1,432	10.8
4-year total	1946–9	342	4,373	7.8
	1950	162	2,586	6.3
	1951	228	1,995	11.4
	1952	279	1,749	16.0
	1953	141	749	18.8
	1954	—	—	—
5-year total	1950–4	810	7,079	11.4
	1955	—	—	—
	1956	196	1,832	10.7
	1957	—	—	—
	1958	—	—	—
	1959	156	1,512	10.3
5-year total	1955–9	352	3,344	10.5
	1960	127	1,494	8.5
	1961	137	1,963	7.0
	1962	—	—	—
	1963	120	2,382	5.0
	1964	190	2,281	8.3
	1965	148	1,674	8.8
6-year total	1960–5	722	9,794	7.4

NOTES

Data from 1830–47 are from our own coding of Aguet; data on 1871–90 come from Michelle Perrot's *Ouvriers en grève*, pp. 360–2; data from 1885–9 have been taken from our coding of the *Statistique annuelle*.

For the years 1890–1914 we relied on the aggregate tables of grievances at the end of each volume of the *SG*. We took the following categories of *tableau IV* to mean strikes over 'worker organization': i, j, *renvois, réintegration des ouvriers, employés, etc*; k, *renvois des femmes*; l, *limitation sur le nombre des apprentis*. These categories do not coincide exactly with our 'worker organization' classification for other years, but the discrepancies are not large. The denominator of the percentage for 1890–1914 is the total number of *causes principales*, not the total of strikes.

Data from 1915–35 are from our own coding of the *SG*. In these years we had only one field for coding grievances, and if more than one demand was voiced in the strike (which is to say, if the official statisticians thought more than one demand was important) we would code the two grievances as a specific combination; for example, the combination grievance that hours be decreased, wages increased would receive a certain 'complex cause' code, the demand that pay be increased and paid out weekly another such code.

Data on stated grievances after 1946 come from the *RFT*. We considered the two grievance categories *embauchage*, *licenciement*, and *conventions collectives* to represent worker organization matters. Doubtless some disputes that in previous years we would have coded 'worker organization' are buried within the *RFT* residual category *autres*. Yet invariably the category contains but a small number of cases, and the omission of these few strikes after 1946 cannot change notably our conclusions about post-Second World War trends. The *RFT* published no grievance data for the years 1954, 1955, 1957, 1958 and 1962.

We could, of course, have drawn upon our own coding of the *SG* for at least part of the prewar period, the years 1895–9 and 1910–14. We decided to take official aggregate statistics in order to supply a uniform series. Yet to give the reader an exact sense of the kinds of demands advanced under 'worker organization' we reproduce as follows the specific grievances in that category, and the number of times each surfaced in 1910–14:

	Number	%
Worker organization and solidarity, discipline and hiring issues, otherwise unclassifiable	177	10
Demands for union recognition	36	2
Demands for closed shop or formal policy of hiring only union members	54	3
Demands that fired or striking workers be rehired	699	40
Demands that fired personnel be rehired	64	4
Demands that workers be fired	307	17
Demands that personnel be fired	348	20
Sympathy strikes	72	4
Jurisdictional disputes	4	—
	1,761	100%

The *APO* often gives stated grievance in the strikes it reports. We have not felt confident enough in the representativeness of *APO* material to report the results in the text; we reproduce here for the interested reader the percent of strikes with worker organization the main grievance, as reported in *APO* (number of strikes in parentheses):

	%	(number)
1848–9	11	(1)
1850–4	0	
1855–9	21	(4)
1860–4	13	(4)
1865-9	2	(1)
1870–4	4	(1)
1875–9	0	
1880–4	4	(3)

Table 5: *The outcome of strikes, 1830–1965*

		% success	% compromise	% failure	% strikes ending with dismissal of strikers (included in 'failure')
	1830–4	28	9	62	6
	1835–9	17	26	56	4
	1840–4	29	24	47	3
	1845–7	21	36	43	0
		% success + compromise			
	1865	53	47		
	1866	50	50		
	1867	54	46		
	1868	72	28		
	1869	81	19		
5-year average	1865–9	64	36		
	1870	78	22		
	1871	53	47		
	1872	74	26		
	1873	58	42		
	1874	33	67		
5-year average	1870–4	64	36		
	1875	50	50		
	1876	62	38		
	1877	44	56		
	1878	29	71		
	1879	36	64		
5-year average	1875–9	45	55		
	1880	60	40		
	1881	58	42		
	1882	58	42		
	1883	50	50		
	1884	30	70		
5-year average	1880–4	53	47		
	1885	29	71		
	1886	46	54		
	1887	49	51		
	1888	51	49		
	1889	60	40		
5-year average	1885–9	49	51		
	1890	27	21	52	
	1891	34	25	40	
	1892	22	32	46	
	1893	25	32	43	
	1894	22	33	46	
5-year average	1890–4	25	30	45	
	1895	25	29	46	15
	1896	25	26	50	12
	1897	19	34	47	17
	1898	20	33	46	15
		24	38	38	10
5-year average	1895–9	23	33	44	13
	1900	23	40	37	
	1901	22	37	41	

Table 5 (*continued*)

		% success	% compromise	% failure	% strikes ending with dismissal of strikers (included in 'failure')
	1902	22	36	42	
	1903	22	39	39	
	1904	29	38	33	
5-year average	1900–4	24	38	38	
	1905	22	44	34	
	1906	21	41	38	
	1907	21	38	41	
	1908	17	30	53	
	1909	21	38	41	
5-year average	1905–9	20	38	42	
	1910	20	40	40	7
	1911	18	36	46	10
	1912	17	34	48	9
	1913	17	35	48	13
	1914	19	32	48	9
5-year average	1910–14	18	36	46	9
	1915	24	32	45	13
	1916	23	37	40	10
	1917	28	56	16	2
	1918	22	53	25	3
	1919	25	53	22	1
5-year average	1915–19	25	52	23	2
	1920	25	43	32	1
	1921	24	26	50	7
	1922	25	27	49	6
	1923	20	28	52	6
	1924	20	34	46	5
5-year average	1920–4	23	34	43	4
	1925	26	32	42	4
	1926	26	38	35	5
	1927	21	30	49	11
	1928	16	38	46	10
	1929	17	40	43	10
5-year average	1925–9	22	37	41	7
	1930	14	35	51	7
	1931	16	26	58	1
	1932	20	23	57	6
	1933	20	29	51	7
	1934	16	30	54	8
	1935	24	34	42	4
6-year average	1930–5	17	31	52	6
	1946	26	65	8	
	1947	22	64	15	
	1948	14	54	32	
	1949	9	50	42	
4-year average	1946–9	17	58	26	
	1950	8	57	35	
	1951	20	48	32	
	1952	9	42	48	
	1953	8	37	55	
	1954	—	—	—	

Table 5 (*continued*)

		% success	% compromise	% failure
5-year average	1950–4	12	49	40
	1955	—	—	—
	1956	14	43	43
	1957	—	—	—
	1958	—	—	—
	1959	11	41	48
5-year average	1955–9	13	42	45
	1960	9	45	46
	1961	10	43	47
	1962	—	—	—
	1963	12	37	51
	1964	7	36	57
	1965	7	32	60
6-year average	1960–5	9	38	52

NOTES
1830–47 data from our coding of Aguet.
1865–89 data from Michelle Perrot, *Ouvriers en grève*, p. 82.
1895–9, 1910–14, 1915–35 data on percent of strikes in which strikers were fired are taken from our own coding of SG (strikes in which ⅔ or more of workers did not return to job).
1890–1935 data on outcome from *SG*, as reported in the *Annuaire statistique*, 1966, p. 120.
1946–65 data from *RFT*, yearly volumes.

Table 6: *Union membership and participation in strikes, 1884–1937*

		Worker–union involvement		Number of union members	
		% of strikes with *existence* *d'un syndicat* *pour les ouvriers*	% of strikes with mention of union in *remarques*	APO	*Annuaire des* *syndicats*
	1884			72,000	
	1885			91,000	
	1886			111,000	
	1887			125,000	
	1888			140,000	
	1889			174,000	
6-year average	1884–9			119,000	
	1890			232,000	140,000
	1891			305,000	205,000
	1892			366,000	289,000
	1893	67		453,000	402,000
	1894	58		435,000	403,000
5-year average	1890–4	64		358,000	288,000
	1895	52	21	434,000	420,000
	1896	49	6	435,000	423,000

Table 6 (*continued*)

		Worker–union involvement		Number of union members	
		% of strikes with *existence d'un syndicat pour les ouvriers*	% of strikes with mention of union in *remarques*	*APO*	*Annuaire des syndicats*
	1897	59	10		430,000[a]
	1898	57	22	430,000	438,000
	1899	60	16		420,000
5-year average	1895–9	56	15	433,000	426,000
	1900	61			492,000
	1901	69			589,000
	1902	59			614,000
	1903	73			644,000
	1904	75			716,000
5-year average	1900–4	68			611,000
	1905	82			781,000
	1906	77			836,000
	1907	75			896,000
	1908	78			957,000
	1909	78			945,000
5-year average	1905–9	78			883,000
	1910	83	11		977,000
	1911	75	11		1,029,000
	1912	76	13		1,064,000
	1913	72	15		1,027,000
	1914	62	12		1,026,000
5-year average	1910–14	74	12		1,025,000

		% of strikes with worker–union involvement: mention of union in *remarques*		Other sources	
	1915	4			
	1916	8			
	1917	7			
	1918	4			
	1919	16			
5-year average	1915–19	12			
	1920	9		1,053,000	(1,135,000)
	1921	3		838,000	
	1922	4			
	1923	4			
	1924	7			
5-year average	1920–4	6			
	1925	7			
	1926	10		956,000	(1,074,000)
	1927	16		941,000[a]	
	1928	10		925,000	
	1929	12		912,000[a]	
5-year average	1925–9	11	4-yr. avg. 1926–9	934,000	
	1930	5		900,000	

Table 6 (*continued*)

		% of strikes with worker–union involvement: mention of union in *remarques*			Other sources	
	1931	6			846,000[a]	
	1932	5			791,000	
	1933	4			773,000[a]	
	1934	3			755,000	(910,000)
	1935	3				
6-year average	1930–5	5	5-year average	1930–4	813,000	
				1935	786,000	
				1936	4,749,000	
				1937	4,989,000	
				1938	4,330,000	
			4-year average	1935–8	3,713,000	

[a]Interpolated.

NOTES
APO union membership data are hand-computed totals of yearly membership figures by industrial sector. Women included.

Annuaire statistique data from *AS*, 1938, p. 58*. *Membres syndicats ouvriers.*

1920–1 union membership data from Annie Kriegel, *La Croissance de la C.G.T.*, p. 22.

1926–35 union membership data include both CGT and CGTU, from Antoine Prost, *La C.G.T. à l'époque du front populaire*, pp. 177–94.

1936–8 union membership data from 'Gringoire,' as cited in Prost, p. 196.

Figures in parentheses represent estimated membership in the CFTC, plus the CGT–CGTU. CFTC membership statistics taken from Prost, pp. 49–50, and from *Annuaire statistique*, 1951, p. 100*.

Existence d'un syndicat pour les ouvriers data taken from aggregate figures published yearly in *SG*, 1893–1914.

'Mention of union in *remarques*' data on union participation in strikes computed from our own coding of *SG*. The *SG* compilers' references to unions seem to have been rather haphazard, and the reliability of these data is low. We include them because they constitute the only time series on union participation in industrial conflict in the interwar period.

Table 7: *Yearly average strike rates per 100,000 active population, cross-tabulated by region and industry, 1915–35*

	Agriculture	Mining-quarrying	Food industries	Chemicals	Printing-paper	Leather-hides	Textiles-garments	Metal production	Metalworking	General construction	Transport-tertiary	Total
Alsace												
Strike rate	0.1	10.2	6.1	18.3	7.4	6.7	11.3	450.4	10.4	17.7	1.3	5.5
Number of strikes	3	24	17	17	10	10	180	17	76	159	42	555
Aquitaine												
Strike rate	0.2	18.3	5.9	15.5	9.8	19.6	2.0	27.1	10.9	8.2	2.2	2.3
Number of strikes	30	9	32	34	14	50	30	20	97	155	136	607
Auvergne												
Strike rate	—	12.7	5.2	2.5	9.0	8.9	2.2	16.1	6.8	11.3	0.5	1.7
Number of strikes	—	28	15	9	6	8	22	13	36	101	15	253
Burgundy												
Strike rate	0.1	7.3	1.7	18.5	25.7	10.6	2.8	29.0	6.2	11.0	0.5	2.1
Number of strikes	6	26	6	16	16	16	24	11	65	128	19	333
Brittany												
Strike rate	0.0	30.4	6.9	31.2	13.4	14.7	1.8	38.8	12.2	18.6	1.9	2.4
Number of strikes	9	29	37	21	14	54	25	18	63	277	103	650
Center												
Strike rate	0.1	17.5	1.7	9.4	17.4	7.7	2.9	—	7.6	9.6	0.5	1.7
Number of strikes	8	7	8	14	22	24	41	—	57	136	26	343
Champagne												
Strike rate	0.3	33.3	2.6	11.5	19.4	4.9	9.7	31.4	6.4	7.5	0.7	3.4
Number of strikes	11	22	10	6	18	6	132	20	75	83	26	409
Corsica												
Strike rate	0.4	138.2	29.5	21.6	—	2.4	1.4	—	3.8	16.0	6.3	3.4
Number of strikes	5	4	8	2	—	1	1	—	1	14	32	68
Provence												
Strike rate	0.1	26.3	12.7	15.2	11.3	9.0	3.6	67.0	6.3	10.9	1.6	3.4
Number of strikes	8	45	82	78	23	27	50	13	64	209	157	756
Franche-Comté												
Strike rate	—	17.7	3.0	23.7	18.4	4.6	12.4	58.5	8.9	7.9	0.7	3.6
Number of strikes	—	10	6	10	16	3	95	14	116	67	16	353
Languedoc												
Strike rate	3.7	8.6	12.5	22.7	21.2	10.1	8.0	120.4	7.4	14.2	2.4	5.0
Number of strikes	203	42	37	28	12	18	79	14	35	135	96	799

Limousin												
Strike rate	—	42.1	3.5	9.3	19.5	35.5	10.4	21.0	11.6	17.9	1.0	3.4
Number of strikes	—	24	5	2	16	91	41	1	21	127	15	343
Lorraine												
Strike rate	0.0	6.3	1.4	4.9	6.8	9.6	7.8	3.6	7.0	5.8	0.2	2.8
Number of strikes	1	65	5	8	14	19	168	43	58	105	13	499
Midi-Pyrénées												
Strike rate	—	10.0	3.2	15.5	6.9	12.1	6.8	5.4	6.3	8.8	0.3	1.6
Number of strikes	—	34	12	13	9	43	85	8	39	114	13	370
Nord												
Strike rate	0.4	2.2	9.2	19.3	18.2	8.6	15.0	18.0	12.1	17.3	3.9	7.9
Number of strikes	21	73	79	68	52	31	823	89	270	516	320	2,342
Upper Normandy												
Strike rate	0.1	—	3.6	11.1	11.6	6.7	8.0	36.1	7.7	15.9	3.4	5.0
Number of strikes	5	—	13	30	13	10	159	33	64	174	164	665
Lower Normandy												
Strike rate	—	8.9	1.7	16.1	4.1	4.3	3.1	6.9	4.0	5.8	1.5	1.4
Number of strikes	—	9	5	8	2	5	29	7	14	50	48	177
Paris												
Strike rate	1.4	32.4	8.5	5.9	8.4	19.6	4.0	39.0	13.6	18.6	1.1	5.7
Number of strikes	45	44	152	107	165	272	290	56	1,197	1,264	403	3,995
Loire												
Strike rate	0.1	17.4	6.0	13.4	20.0	14.2	2.8	20.0	10.2	9.6	1.9	2.4
Number of strikes	10	43	35	18	25	50	55	19	118	146	109	628
Picardy												
Strike rate	0.1	6.6	4.6	8.0	8.9	10.9	9.3	26.8	8.6	5.8	0.6	3.2
Number of strikes	5	4	18	9	7	20	150	13	81	116	23	446
Charente												
Strike rate	0.1	27.1	4.3	11.3	10.0	2.9	1.0	138.0	4.6	5.9	1.2	1.2
Number of strikes	8	12	13	9	14	5	8	5	20	53	54	201
Rhône–Alpes												
Strike rate	0.0	11.1	3.7	8.6	15.4	13.9	8.2	32.2	11.2	19.2	1.1	4.6
Number of strikes	2	77	31	38	77	105	469	92	318	521	112	1,842
Number of strikes occurring in more than 1 department	2	9	—	1	—	—	2	1	—	2	8	25
Total												
Strike rate	0.3	8.1	6.1	10.4	11.5	13.7	7.1	17.0	10.4	13.2	1.5	3.7
Number of strikes	482	640	626	546	545	868	2,958	507	2,885	4,652	1,950	16,659

continued overleaf

NOTES
Please note that, whereas the strike rate is a yearly *average* for 1915–35, the absolute number of strikes is a *total* for the 1915–35 period.

Technical considerations of file handling and computer data processing resulted in the following procedure for calculating the labor-force denominators: the active population of each industry within each department was interpolated for each year on the basis of census data for 1911, 1921, 1926 and 1931. (1936 census data were unavailable to us, so we took the 1931 figure for the years 1932–5). We then summed these yearly figures and divided by 21, to produce a yearly average active population for 1915–35.

The rate in the far right-hand column is strikes/100,000 total active population (agriculture included).

The final row, 'strikes occurring in more than 1 department,' is reserved for those disputes in which the *SG* specifically mentioned two or more departments.

Industrial categories

We have relabeled and collapsed the *SG* industrial classifications as follows:

Our label	SG industries
Agriculture	*Agriculture, forêts et pêche*
Mining–quarrying	*Industries extractives: (A) Mines, (B) Carrières*
Food industries	*Produits alimentaires*
Chemicals	*Produits chimiques*
Printing–paper	*Papiers, cartons et industries polygraphiques*
Leather–hides	*Cuirs et peaux*
Textiles–garments	*Textiles: (A) Industries textiles proprement dites, (B) Travail des étoffes, nettoyage*
Metal production	*Métaux: (A) Usines métallurgiques*
Metalworking	*Métaux: (B) Travail des métaux ordinaires, (C) Travail des métaux fins*
General construction[a]	*Industries du bois: (A) Bois et tabletterie, (B) Bâtiment + Travail des pierres et des terres: (A) Taille et polissage, travail des pierres au feu, (B) Bâtiment*
Transport–tertiary	*Transport et manutention + XI bis*

[a] When the need arose, we were able to break general construction down into its component parts of:
— 'wood industries' (*bois et tabletterie*, and [wood] *bâtiment*)
— 'building materials and ceramics' (*taille et polissage, travail des pierres et terres au feu*)
— 'construction proper' (*bâtiment*)

Notes

Chapter 1. The significance of industrial conflict

1. Archives Nationales, BB¹⁸ 1186, 12 August 1830.
2. *Notre arme c'est la grève* (Paris: Maspéro, 1968), pp. 17–18. The book is authored by an anonymous collective of workers who took part in the strike.
3. J.-C. Toutain, *La Population de la France de 1700 à 1959* (Paris: Institut de science économique appliquée, 1963; Cahiers de l'ISEA, AF3), pp. 135, 161.
4. Mancur Olson Jr., *The Logic of Collective Action* (Cambridge, Mass.: Harvard University Press, 1965).
5. *Social Change in the Industrial Revolution* (Chicago: University of Chicago Press, 1959).
6. Clark Kerr, 'Changing Social Structures' in Wilbert E. Moore and Arnold S. Feldman (eds.), *Labor Commitment and Social Change in Developing Areas* (New York: Social Science Research Council, 1960), p. 353.
7. E. P. Thompson, *The Making of the English Working Class* (New York: Pantheon, 1963).
8. Touraine first explained the development of these stages of production in *L'Evolution du travail ouvrier aux usines Renault* (Paris, 1955), esp. pp. 173–83; he confined his discussion to artisans in factories, omitting the craft system as such. Serge Mallet has taken up the typology and related it to different stages of union activity and worker mentality. See his *La Nouvelle Classe ouvrière* (Paris, 1963), pp. 27–74, and his contribution to a discussion in Léo Hamon (ed.), *Les Nouveaux Comportements politiques de la classe ouvrière* (Paris, 1962), pp. 145–73. The following pages are a synthesis of the two authors' views.
9. On glassmaking see Joan W. Scott, 'The Glassworkers of Carmaux, 1850–1900' in Stephan Thernstrom and Richard Sennett (eds.), *Nineteenth-Century Cities: Essays in the New Urban History* (New Haven: Yale University Press, 1969), pp. 3–48; these features appear in an 1892 strike of glassworkers in the Ardèche, reported in *SG*, 1892, pp. 147–50; see below, p. 179.
10. See Georges Friedmann, *Industrial Society: The Emergence of the Human Problems of Automation* (Glencoe, Ill., 1955), pp. 261–90.
11. Jean-Pierre Aguet, *Contribution à l'étude du mouvement ouvrier français: Les Grèves sous la Monarchie di Juillet* (Geneva: Droz, 1954), pp. 131–2.
12. *SG*, 1903, pp. 405–6.
13. *Le Monde*, 22 March 1963, p. 2.

Chapter 2. The parties and the rules

1. *APO*, I, p. 12.
2. For the April 1803 law and the February 1810 penal code see *APO*, I, pp. 17–20; for the April 1834 law, *ibid.*, p. 26.
3. The relevant articles of the 25 May 1864 law are reprinted in *APO*, I, p. 38.
4. *APO*, I, pp. 45–7.
5. *APO* I, pp. 50–63, for the text and background of the 1884 law.
6. On the 1946 Constitution and law of 11 February 1950 see Hélène Sinay, *La Grève* (Paris, 1966; Traité de droit du travail, 6), pp. 177–218.
7. On events to 1901 see Georges Lefranc, *Mouvement syndical sous la Troisième République* (Paris, 1967), pp. 158–9.

8. Sinay discusses the complicated regulations on strikes in the nationalized industries and government service in *La Grève*, pp. 373–419.
9. Of course in practice the government intervened in many strikes. But before 1892 there was no regular administrative machinery to make intervention a routine, non-partisan matter.
10. The text of the 27 December 1892 law was reprinted often in the *SG*, as for example in *SG*, 1919, pp. 344–7.
11. On the 1919 law see Gérard Dehove, *Le Contrôle ouvrier en France. L'Elaboration de sa notion. Ses Conceptions.* (Paris, 1937), pp. 267–9.
12. *Les Expériences syndicales en France de 1939 à 1950* (Paris, 1950), p. 267.
13. *Ibid.*, pp. 274–81.
14. The 26 July 1957 law on labor relations introduced some of these features. For a careful juridical account of postwar collective bargaining legislation see Sinay, *La Grève*, pp. 434–87.
15. The reality of postwar collective bargaining is described in Jean-Daniel Reynaud, *Les Syndicats en France* (Paris, 1966), pp. 162–7.
   Only in the public sector have shop-floor relations been radically transformed by a North American-style bargaining system. Since the Second World War public enterprises have received a hierarchy of parity commissions for grievance settling, their capstone the Toutée report of 1 January 1964.
16. In prewar grievance data we made provision for coding a second principal demand; in interwar strikes we were able to code but a single demand, putting multigrievance strikes under the category 'complex cause'; thus in a small proportion of 1915–35 strikes it is impossible for us to sort out the exact grievance. The 1895–9 and 1910–14 results, however, demonstrate the insignificance of demands for union recognition.
17. On worker eagerness for government intervention in strikes, see Peter N. Stearns, *Revolutionary Syndicalism and French Labor: A Cause without Rebels* (New Brunswick, N.J., 1971), pp. 66–7; and Michelle Perrot, *Les Ouvriers en grève (France, 1871–1890)* (Paris I, *thèse*, 1971), *passim*. Perrot writes of the late nineteenth century: 'Les lettres adressées aux autorités notamment aux prèfets, ont et garderont longtemps une autre tonalité [than the letters from workers to employers]. Plus confiantes, elles sont plus solennelles usant volontiers du papier timbré, caution de l'acte officiel aux yeux des ouvriers qui en ont la révérence, presque la superstition... Ces textes s'allongent; circonstanciés et descriptifs, ils évoquent les cahiers des doléances; ils ont la saveur triste et douce que donne l'espoir d'être lu d'un regard bienveillant. Longtemps les ouvriers conserveront la foi dans les pouvoirs médiateurs du Préfet' (p. 354).
18. Information taken from *SG*, 1910, p. xiv.
19. *SG*, 1900, pp. 414–15.
20. Only a small proportion of strikes actually involved violence, according to Michelle Perrot only 3.6 percent of the total between 1870 and 1890. We have estimated the proportion of violent strikes at 3.2 percent for 1890–1914, and at scarcely 0.5 percent for 1915–35. Perrot, *Ouvriers en grève*, p. 819. Charles Tilly and Edward Shorter, 'Le Déclin de la grève violente en France de 1890 à 1935,' *Le Mouvement social*, no. 76 (July–Sept. 1971), pp. 95–118.
21. *SG*, 1893, pp. 377–9.
22. The conventional wisdom survives undamaged in even the most recent historiography. Stearns suggests that government intervention normally aimed at repression and defeat of strikes. And Perrot argues that in 1870–90 the rule was prefectoral sympathy with employers and against strikers, except for a few exceptional officials. She admits, however, that the years around 1880 may have represented a turning point, after which official hostility to the strike movement moderated considerably. Stearns, *Revolutionary Syndicalism*, pp. 13–16. Perrot, *Ouvriers en grève*, pp. 34, 253–72, 1002–33. Rolande Trempé's work on the miners of Carmaux, however, shows brilliantly how the government pursued its own objectives by intervening in strikes, refusing to ally with employers against workers. *Les Mineurs de Carmaux, 1848–1914* (Paris, 1971), p. 671 and *passim*. And Val Lorwin had already pointed

out for the period around 1900: 'Often the public officials got better terms for the workers than their economic strength would have won.' *The French Labor Movement* (Cambridge, Mass., 1954), p. 26.

23. Peter Stearns has in fact conducted such a study for the *belle époque*; see his important article, 'Against the Strike Threat: Employer Policy toward Labor Agitation in France, 1900–1914,' *Journal of Modern History*, 40 (1958): 474–500. Stearns emphasizes the hostility which met challenges to patronal authority. See also his *Revolutionary Syndicalism, passim*.

24. This finding goes against Peter Stearns's assertion that 'large manufacturers were much more closely united than were small manufacturers.' (*Revolutionary Syndicalism*, p. 83). Perhaps in various informal and subtle ways they were. Yet the crude *SG* categories that reported the organization of the participants do not reflect such a propensity. The table shows no tendency for larger firms to have better employer organization than smaller firms.

Percent of strikes having syndicat pour les patrons, *1910–14*.

Size of firm	(%)
1–10 workers	48
11–20	53
21–100	47
101–500	46
+500	53
All	48

SOURCE: Coding of individual strikes.

25. Source of 1893–1909 data is *SG*, 1910, pp. xiv–xv.
26. *SG*, 1902, p. 368.
27. *SG*, 1910, no. 503.
28. *SG*, 1894, pp. 206–7.
29. *SG*, 1900, pp. 442–3.
30. *SG*, 1893, pp. 176–8.
31. In a strike of *plombiers–zingueurs* in Nevers, as one example among many, the employers refused to take back the five workers 'considérés ... comme les promoteurs du conflit ... ' *SG*, 1897, pp. 245–6.
32. *SG*, 1892, pp. 115–29. On this strike see also Trempé's exhaustive account, *Les Mineurs de Carmaux*, p. 551ff.
33. *SG*, 1900, p. 422.
34. Landes, 'French Entrepreneurship and Industrial Growth in the Nineteenth Century,' *Journal of Economic History*, 9 (1949), pp. 45–61. Stearns calls the French employers 'unusually harsh' compared to others in Europe. *Revolutionary Syndicalism*, p. 20.
35. See, for example, Henri Dubief's discussion of Briand's role in the 1910 railway workers' strike ('Briand brisa en 1910 les grèves des cheminots ... avec une brutalité qui valait celle de Clemenceau et d'une façon encore plus démoralisante puisque dans des apostolats successifs il avait commencé par celui de la grève générale') *Le Syndicalisme révolutionnaire* (Paris, 1969), p. 49. Or take the hostility to Briand running through Harvey Goldberg's *The Life of Jean Jaurès* (Madison, Wisc., 1968), p. 411; for instance: 'Once committed t › his act of strike-breaking, Briand yielded not an inch. Ignoring the concrete issues in the dispute, he denounced the aims of syndicalism as sabotage and revolution.'
36. On Waldeck-Rousseau's attitude toward strike activity, and the hostility it evoked in employer circles, see Pierre Sorlin, *Waldeck-Rousseau* (Paris, 1966), pp. 461–80. See also Trempé on Carmaux, p. 671 and *passim*.
37. Aside from Stearns (*Revolutionary Syndicalism*), Trempé (*Les Mineurs de Carmaux*) and Perrot (*Ouvriers en grève*), the major archival investigations concerning the government's response to strike activity are Jacques Julliard's *Clemenceau, briseur de*

grèves: L'Affaire de Draveil-Villeneuve-Saint-Georges (1908) (Paris, 1965); Leo Loubère's 'Coal Miners, Strikes and Politics in the Lower Languedoc, 1880–1914,' *Journal of Social History*, 2 (1968), pp. 25–50; and Jean Néré's 'Aspects du déroulement des grèves en France durant la période 1883–1889,' *Revue d'histoire économique et sociale*, 34 (1956), pp. 286–302. Néré found administrative practice highly interventionist in strikes, often on the side of the workers (pp. 295–9).

38. *SG*, 1893, p. 350.
39. The entire story is in *SG*, 1893, pp. 337–54.
40. *SG*, 1896, p. 260.
41. The long view makes dubious Peter Stearns's assertion that the *belle époque* saw a widespread acceptance of routine collective bargaining procedures. Private employers in France have never accustomed themselves either to negotiating with unions or to comprehensive collective contracts. The evidence of the *SG* on these matters indicates growing employer hostility to organized labor between 1900 and 1914. Stearns, 'Against the Strike Threat,' pp. 452ff, and *Revolutionary Syndicalism, passim*.

Chapter 3. The transformation of the strike

1. Michelle Perrot and Peter Stearns both comment on the take-off of the strike movement in the 1890s and early 1900s, noting a later lengthy decline in strikes after 1910. Their explanations for this rise and fall diverge substantially. Stearns considers the acceleration of conflict in 1900–10 a result of declining (or stagnating) real wages and of deteriorating living conditions, a process arrested only after 1910. Hence strikes were a direct function of worsening living standards. (*Revolutionary Syndicalism*, pp. 18, 79.) Perrot believes the post-1900 strike increase a result of economic growth and prosperity: 'Le climat de la grève est la prosperité: la tiédeur du printemps, le feu de la "presse" lui sont favorables. C'est pourquoi son développement a été, après 1896, si vigoureux. A la tendance séculaire, au trend fondamental de croissance, s'ajoute l'impulsion d'un nouveau "Konradtieff" de hausse.' (*Ouvriers en grève*, p. 203.) Unlike Stearns, Perrot attributes the 1910–13 decline in strikes to the creation of alternative forms of collective action. As the workers became increasingly integrated into the social order, they developed more routine means of political participation and shop-floor militancy (pp. 88–9).
   We find this whole set of explanations, both for the 1896–1910 rise in strikes and the 1910–13 fall, slightly implausible. In later chapters we suggest that the essential motors of working-class militancy are the organizational ability to mount collective protest, and the receptiveness of the political *conjoncture* to worker demonstrations. And when strike statistics are seen over the long haul, the much-explained 'decline' in the movement after 1910 is a minor, short-term fluctuation, for the overall level of conflict in 1915–35 was just as high as for 1890–1914.
2. This section comes, with little alteration, from our article 'The Shape of Strikes in France, 1830–1960,' *Comparative Studies in Society and History*, 13 (1971), pp. 60–86; that article also discusses variations in strike shapes by industry, and compares French strike shapes with those of a number of other countries. John V. Spielmans represented strikes in two-dimensional form in 'Strike Profiles,' *Journal of Political Economy*, 52 (1944), pp. 319–39.
3. Millard Cass assumes in his work on U.S. firm size that strikes with large numbers of participants occur in large firms. That would be true only if each strike were limited to a single establishment. 'The Relationship of Size of Firm and Strike Activity,' *Monthly Labor Review*, 80 (1957), pp. 1330–4.
4. *Wildcat Strike: A Study in Worker–Management Relationships* (Yellow Springs, Ohio, 1954).
5. Perrot remarks on the large number of strikes against the fines that employers levied against workers, and on the many demands that foremen be fired, or otherwise restrained. Both, in her view, are signs that an essentially peasant labor force is being broken in to factory discipline and to the work habits of a modern labor force. *Ouvriers en grève*, pp. 416–19.
6. Whereas in 1915–35, 40 percent of all strikes ended in failure, 70 percent of those strikes over worker organization questions did so.

7. The CGT's interwar efforts to persuade employers to accept worker control seem to have caused few strikes within manufacturing, where the CGT was not, in any event, strongly implanted. The confederation more representative of the semi-skilled proletarian – the CGTU – was indifferent to job control issues, and demanded pay hikes plus revolution.

8. Perrot, *Ouvriers en grève*, p. 80; see also p. 350. Stearns, *Revolutionary Syndicalism*, pp. 36, 39, 74. Trempé, *Les Mineurs de Carmaux*, p. 743.

9. In 1895–9, 16 percent of all grievances were defensive, 4 percent in 1910–14 and 13 percent (of all strikes) in 1915–35.

10. Robert Gubbels, for example, advances this interpretation for postwar Belgian strikes. '*La grève est devenue ni plus ni moins qu'un mode d'expression* [italics in original]: c'est une façon de manifester une opinion, de la faire connaître et de lui donner tout le poids nécessaire. Elle intervient pour remettre en place les mécanismes faussés du régime démocratique.

   '*Ceci* revient à dire que la question de savoir si, quant à ses objectifs immédiats, un mouvement réussit ou échoue, est un point secondaire. Une grève peut avoir été utile (du point de vue de ceux qui l'ont déclenché s'entend) même si les objectifs mis en avant lors de son déclenchement n'ont pas été atteints; elle aura joué un rôle essentiel: elle aura permis au groupe de faire entendre sa voix, de faire connaître son point de vue.' *La Grève, phénomène de civilisation* (Brussels, 1962), p. 288.

11. Whereas in 1915–35, 60 percent of all strikes ended either in success or compromise, only 57 percent of those lasting 6 days or less did so – a tiny percentage difference from which only the inference may be drawn that if French strikes were short, it wasn't because the employers were the first to surrender. The longer a strike lasts, the greater becomes the chance that it will end in compromise. The likelihood of both success and failure declines with lengthening duration.

12. In 1915–35, for example, 9.7 percent of all strikes lasted 30 days or more; 17.7 percent of strikes in which worker unions were involved did so, and 23.8 percent of strikes in which the employers were organized lasted a month or longer.

13. This falling off of strike length is not owing merely to an upsurge of brief political strikes, the non-political ones remaining at their interwar duration. Even after conflicts of a day or less are removed from the data, strikes in general had become significantly shorter after the Second World War. Witness the following table:

	% of all strikes lasting			
Years	2–6 days	7–30 days	+30 days	Total
1890–1914	46	41	14	101
1915–35	43	45	12	100
1946–9	66	31[a]	2[b]	99
1960–5	56	39	4	99

[a] 7–25 days.
[b] +25 days.

Chapter 4. Year-to-year variation in strike activity

1. Michelle Perrot, *Ouvriers en grève*; Edgard Andréani, *Les Grèves et les fluctuations de l'activité économique de 1890 à 1914 en France* (Faculté de droit de Paris, *thèse*, 1965); Robert Goetz-Girey, *Le Mouvement des grèves en France, 1919–1962* (Paris, 1965). For some analyses we have to modify the period somewhat for lack of data covering the entire set of years. We have, for example, been able to discover usable data on the number of union members only for 1885–1915, 1920, 1921 and 1926–38. Yet we have been unwilling to abandon the analysis of relationships between unionization and strike activity for the interwar years; hence some analyses of 1920–38 actually treat the years 1920–1 and 1926–38 only. In each such case we

indicate clearly that a different set of years is involved. Readers who are already familiar with the sort of statistical analysis employed in this chapter will notice a good deal of redundancy in the presentation of results. We move step by step from zero-order correlation matrices to path diagrams which simply represent the basic relationships implicit in the earlier matrices. We have several compelling reasons for reporting all these overlapping analyses: (1) our inability to carry some of the variables over into the multiple regressions and path analyses because of the incompleteness of the time series involved; (2) our hope to communicate the basic findings to those readers who are not familiar with the more complicated statistical models used later in the chapter; (3) our desire to report results directly comparable to those already published, which tend to be in the form of simple correlation coefficients, balanced against (4) our interest in controlling for spurious relationships due to long trends and/or the intercorrelations of the explanatory variables.

2. Sources for variables: (1) unemployment: *Annuaire statistique*, 1966, p. 117; *Annuaire statistique*, 1968, p. 77; (2) cost of living: Jeanne Singer-Kérel, *Le Coût de la vie à Paris de 1840 à 1954* (Paris: Colin, 1961), pp. 536–7; *Annuaire statistique*, 1968, p. 653; (3) wholesale prices: *Annuaire statistique*, 1966, p. 373; *Annuaire statistique*, 1968, p. 653; (4) wholesale/retail ratio: computation of (3)/(4); (5) money wage: Singer-Kérel, pp. 536–7; (6) real wage: Singer-Kérel, pp. 538–41; (7) industrial production: François Crouzet, 'Essai de construction d'un indice de la production industrielle,' *Annales: ESC*, 25 (1970), pp. 56–99; *Annuaire statistique*, 1968, p. 653; (8) unionization: *Annuaire statistique*, 1938, p. 58*; Annie Kriegel, *La Croissance de la C.G.T., 1918–1921* (Paris, 1966), p. 22; Antoine Prost, *La C.G.T. à l'époque du front populaire* (Paris, 1964), pp. 177–96; (9) cabinet changes: compilation from multiple historical works; (10) violent conflicts: our General Sample, enumerated by reading of two national newspapers for each day from 1930 through 1960, and each day of three randomly selected months per year from 1870 through 1929; (11) participants: our estimates from analysis of newspaper accounts and (where available) published historical work dealing with the events.

3. See Tilly and Shorter, 'Le Déclin de la grève violente.'

4. We have attempted to make a case for that conclusion in many other reports of our research, e.g. Charles Tilly, 'The Changing Place of Collective Violence' in Melvin Richter (ed.), *Essays in Social and Political History* (Cambridge, Mass., 1970), pp. 139–64. But our evidence for other forms of political conflict is neither so full nor so systematic as our evidence concerning collective violence.

5. These findings fail to confirm Peter Stearns's assertion that syndicalist 'enthusiasm' correlates positively with unemployment. As we argue at the end of this chapter, an economic crisis may trigger a major worker outburst, yet it is fundamentally prosperity rather than hardship that is tied with industrial conflict. (*Revolutionary Syndicalism*, p. 16.) Michelle Perrot's discussion of strikes and economic activity is much closer to our own, as she stresses employer prosperity, high conjuncture and rising real wages as determinants of increased conflict. (*Ouvriers en grève*, pp. 163–83.)

6. Our findings on this point do not agree completely with those of Robert Goetz-Girey. He reported substantial positive correlations between the number of strikes and industrial production from 1921 to 1935 and 1948 to 1957. With respect to prices, our pattern agrees with his, but our coefficients are much lower. For example, he reports a correlation between strikes and wholesale prices over the period 1926–35 of +0·72; our computations produce a coefficient of +0·21; since the data are essentially the same, we suspect a computational error in Goetz-Girey's analysis.

We have not been able to recompute all of Goetz-Girey's correlations, because in a number of cases he neither reports the series in full nor offers a citation from which the series could be recovered. Where we are able to reuse precisely the same data as he employed, we ordinarily arrive at similar coefficients; for example, he computes the correlation between the industrial production index and strikes from 1921 to 1935 as +0.41, while our recomputation from the data reported in his book produces a coefficient of +0·48. Where we employ our own best measurements of the variables in question with Goetz-Girey's, however, the discrepancies run larger. For example, the following correlations with number of strikes:

Variable	Period	Goetz-Girey	Shorter–Tilly
Unemployment	1930–5	−0.74	−0.22
Unemployment	1948–57	−0.57	−0.15
Unemployment	1958–62	−0.44	−0.41
Industrial production	1948–57	+0.56	−0.14
Industrial production	1958–62	−0.29	+0.67
National income	1949–57	+0.47	+0.18
National income	1958–62	+0.86	+0.67

The experienced reader will notice immediately that the periods involved are very short, the number of observation points ridiculously few and the coefficients therefore likely to swing as the result of minor errors. In fact, most of the discrepancy between the two sets of coefficients appears to result from the fact that Goetz-Girey adopted the annual strike figures reported in the *Annuaire statistique de la France*. Those figures are not grossly inaccurate. Over the period 1921–35, they correlate 0.998 with our own series. Nevertheless, they have two weaknesses: (1) they include strikes occurring in Algeria, (2) they often lump together as a single strike a whole set of strikes occurring simultaneously in the same region and/or industry. In our own series, we have eliminated the Algerian strikes and counted separately each individual strike described as such in the *SG*.

7. Strikes ending with the workers' dismissal, normally considered 'failure' in this study, were removed as possibly ambiguous cases from the time-series analysis. They represented 7 percent of the total number of strikes.

8. Instead of removing the effect of trend by means of the regression of the number of strikes on time, we can detrend via the method of first differences: transforming all variables into their change from the previous year to the present one. In the periods for which we have been able to perform the analysis, the unstandardized results are:

1890–1913
strikes = 25.02 + 10503 (wholesale/retail) + 4.3 (violent conflicts)
$$R^2 = 0.493$$

1920, 1921, 1926–38
strikes = 2613 − 94.8 (nominal wage) − 152.6 (real wage)
    + 193.0 (industrial production)
    + 0.23 × 10^{-3} (union members)
$$R^2 = 0.835$$

1920–38, 1946–54
strikes = 157.08 − 166.5 (real wage)
$$R^2 = 0.559$$

1890–1913, 1920, 1921, 1926–38
strikes = 411.5 − 30918 (wholesale/retail) − 65.8 (nominal wage) − 150.0 (real wage) + 171.6 (industrial production)
$$R^2 = 0.699$$

These equations differ somewhat from those containing a linear detrending term. None of the relationships change direction, but some variables which came out with weak relationships to strike activity after linear detrending now come out strongly enough to be included in the first-difference equations, and some variables which are strongly related to strike activity in the linear-detrending equations fade to statistical insignificance in the first-difference equations. The survivors of both methods are:

1890–1913: wholesale/retail (+)

1920, 1921, 1926–38: real wage (–), industrial production (+), union members (+)

1920–38, 1946–54: none

1890–1913, 1920, 1921, 1926–38: wholesale/retail (−), nominal wage (−), real wage (−), industrial production (+)

The chief casualty of the further analysis may be our political variable, the number of violent conflicts; it appears in four of the eight equations being compared, but never twice in a pair for the same period. We apparently have brushed against a relationship between strike activity and violent conflict, but have specified its timing badly. Aside from that, the strongest conclusions of the multivariate analysis remain in place.

Chapter 5. Strike waves

1. Michelle Perrot has also emphasized the role of politics in the timing of strike waves, yet, unlike us, accounts for their diffusion with an electric-tension model. She speaks, for example, of 'grèves éruptives, qui crèvent comme les bulles d'un magma en ébullition, et qui se diffusent comme une épidémie' (p. 584). Yet on strike waves and politics we all agree: 'La conjoncture économique ne saurait seule expliquer la profondeur de certaines retraites [of strikes], l'ampleur de certains offensives. Les circonstances politiques pèsent ici très lourd et fournissent la clef des poussées majeures.' *Ouvriers en grève*, p. 278.
2. This relationship between technology and forms of protest is explored in detail in Chapter 8. We have built upon the preliminary work of Alain Touraine and Serge Mallet in identifying three distinct phases of technological change and militancy, the third of which harks back in some ways to the first. See above also, pp. 11–15. The basic texts are Mallet's *Nouvelle Classe ouvrière* and Touraine's *Evolution du travail ouvrier*.
3. An excellent treatment of strikes in the July Monarchy, emphasizing organizational reasons for the preponderance of artisans and underrepresentation of factory workers, is Peter N. Stearns's 'Patterns of Industrial Strike Activity in France during the July Monarchy,' *American Historical Review*, 70 (1965), pp. 371–94.
4. On the Lyon uprisings see Fernand Rude, *L'Insurrection lyonnaise de novembre 1831, le mouvement ouvrier à Lyon de 1827–1832*, 2nd ed. (Paris: Editions anthropos, 1969); Aguet, pp. 44–9; Robert Bezucha, 'The "Preindustrial" Worker Movement: the *Canuts* of Lyon' in Bezucha (ed.), *Modern European Social History* (Lexington, Mass.: D. C. Heath, 1972), pp. 93–123. For the political background we have relied on Paul Thureau-Dangin, *Histoire de la Monarchie de Juillet*, 5 vols. (Paris: Plon, 1884–92), II, pp. 205–21.
5. Aguet, p. 51.
6. Aguet, p. 47 and *passim*; Bezucha, '"Preindustrial" Worker Movement,' pp. 111–12.
7. *Histoire de la Monarchie de Juillet*, IV, pp. 283–5.
8. Pp. 195, 210.
9. Perrot, drawing upon archival data, has identified a strike wave in 1864–5, touched off by the 1864 law legalizing strikes. Principal participants were the established skilled trades, striking for economic gains. *Ouvriers en grève*, pp. 92–7.
10. Fernand L'Huillier, *La Lutte ouvrière à la fin du Second Empire* (Paris, 1957; Cahiers des Annales, 12), p. 20. Roland Trempé has studied the 1869 strikes in *Les Mineurs de Carmaux*, pp. 544–51 and *passim*.

11. L'Huillier, *La Lutte ouvrière*, p. 24.
12. See Pétrus Faure, *Histoire du mouvement ouvrier dans le département de la Loire* (St-Etienne, 1956), pp. 164–78.
13. P. 67. In 1869 a *Chambre fédérale des sociétés ouvrières de Paris* was established at the instigation of the bronze workers and in conformity with a resolution of the Third Congress of the International at Brussels in September 1868. According to *APO*, this *Chambre fédérale* supported and organized many of the 1869 strikes: "L'action de la Chambre fédérale s'était exercée, dans toutes les grèves de Paris et des départements, par le lancement de souscriptions et souvent par l'envoi de délégués spéciaux dans les localités en grève. Ce mouvement, en dehors de l'Internationale, par des hommes qui étaient tous membres de cette association, contribuait à donner à celle-ci une réputation de puissance considérable.' *APO*, I, p. 233.
14. L'Huillier omits the Paris region from his study. It must be noted that half of the strikes registered in *APO* in 1869 and a third in 1870 occurred in the Seine department; yet this source has a strong bias towards overreporting Paris and neglecting the provinces. In any case, disputes in Alsace, Normandy and the area around Lyon clearly had a life of their own. See L'Huillier for a map of the principal provincial strikes, p. 58.
15. For the political background we have relied on Goldberg, *Jaurès*, pp. 107–9, and on Jacques Chastenet, *Histoire de la Troisième République*, 7 vols. (Paris: Hachette, 1952–63), II, pp. 324–6.
16. *SG*, 1893, p. 292. Fifty-five of these spring strikes must be attributed to worker protests over the cutting of working time by employers in conformity with the November 1892 law on female and child labor. One might argue that in such disputes workers were taking advantage of political events at the center to improve their local positions. Such strikes were, in effect, demands for pay increases. But the timing of these walkouts was not determined by the electoral campaign. See *SG*, 1893, p. 331; 1894, p. 229.
17. Sorlin, *Waldeck-Rousseau*, p. 471.
18. *Ibid.*, pp. 475–7, on relations of strikers and employers with government.
19. Sorlin notes the exceptional coordination of the movement; *ibid.*, p. 464.
20. On these events see Edouard Dolléans, *Histoire du mouvement ouvrier*, 7th ed., 3 vols. (Paris, 1967), II, pp. 48–9.
21. Goldberg, *Jaurès*, pp. 257–70. On the divided Socialist response to a bloody clash between strikers and troops in April 1900 in the Saône-et-Loire, see Aaron Noland, *The Foundling of the French Socialist Party, 1893–1905* (Cambridge, Mass.: Harvard University Press, 1956), pp. 118–23.
22. We have taken this characterization of politics in 1906 from Goldberg, *Jaurès*, pp. 352–4, and Chastenet, *Histoire de la Troisième République*, III, pp. 294–9.
23. Miners invariably translate protests about the ghastliness of their work situation into demands for pay increases. See Norman Dennis *et al.*, *Coal is Our Life: An Analysis of a Yorkshire Mining Community* (London: Eyre, 1956), p. 65. Token differentials in piece rates for different jobs are no real compensation for the added peril, but the miners feel they are receiving at least some recognition for the risks they take.
    Jacques Julliard mentioned the *jeune syndicat's* role in the strike. *Clemenceau*, p. 22.
24. The largest previous strike effort in the Parisian construction industry amounted to 44,000 strikers in 1898, compared to 72,000 in 1906.
25. The first hesitant automobile strikes in France occurred in Paris in the 1899 wave, involving scarcely a thousand strikers. Between 1900 and 1905 a few more disputes broke out here and there in the automobile industry, none of them including more than a thousand participants.
26. The logarithms of the rates were used in the actual computations; there were 283 industry–department units.
27. The best narrative history of the 1906 strike wave is Georges Lefranc, *Mouvement syndical sous la Troisième République*, pp. 125–46.
28. *Aux origines du communisme français, 1914–1920: Contribution à l'histoire du*

mouvement ouvrier français, 2 vols. (Paris, 1964), I, p. 351. Kriegel provides the best account of the politics of this period, I, pp. 235–53; but see also Robert Wohl, *French Communism in the Making, 1914–1924* (Stanford, Cal., 1966), pp. 114–237.

29. On strikes in general during these years see Dolléans, *Mouvement ouvrier*, II, pp. 299–334; Lefranc, *Mouvement syndical sous la Troisième République*, pp. 213–37.

30. Lefranc, *ibid.*, pp. 234–5.

31. In processing the data we scaled down this faceless mass by a factor of four-fifths so that it would not completely distort the contributions of individual departments and industries during 1920. The true total of strikers in 1920 is, therefore, 1,444,000.

32. On the rail strikes see Kriegel, *Origines du communisme français*, I, pp. 359–547.

33. The conventional wisdom says that these new workers struck blindly and spontaneously, folding quickly. See, for example, Wohl, *French Communism in the Making*, p. 121: 'The new recruits had no staying power; though quick to attack, they were also quick to surrender.' In fact, the new recruits were exceptionally tenacious in their strike activity, a function not of their personal qualities but of the determination of the unions with which they found themselves allied. Strikes in 1919 as a whole were exceptionally long-lasting: 7 days at the median, compared to a normal duration of 6 days; and the sectors with large numbers of new workers had strikes unusually long for 1919: 8 days at the median for metalworking; and those places where metalworking had the most new personnel, had the *longest strikes of all*: metalworking in the department of the Seine in 1919 had a median duration of 15 days. So much for irresoluteness of the new workers. (These figures are genuine medians, not geometric means.)

34. The statistics may be found in Georges Dupeux, *Le Front populaire et les élections de 1936* (Paris: Colin, 1959; FNSP, 99), p. 139.

35. This sequence of events is narrated by Daniel R. Brower, *The New Jacobins: The French Communist Party and the Popular Front* (Ithaca, N.Y., 1968), pp. 145–6.

36. The basis of the estimate for each department was the assumption that a department's ratio of sitdown strikers (an unknown quantity) to total strikers (a known quantity) would be the same as its ratio of sitdown strikes to total strikes (both known quantities). The source of 1936 strike data is the *Bulletin du Ministère du travail*, nos. 4–12 (1936) and nos. 1–3 (1937).

37. *La C.G.T. à l'époque du front populaire*, pp. 90–117. Prost erroneously rejects the variable of establishment size as a determinant of geographical unionization patterns, and thereby makes his argument more complicated than it need be. He was led astray by taking as an indicator of large establishment size the percentage of the workforce employed in establishments of more than *10* workers (pp. 107–9); this correlated with almost nothing because it lumped small and medium establishments in with the large ones. Only a high threshold of 'large,' such as 500 or more, will catch the impact of industrial scale.

38. *Mouvement syndical sous la Troisième République*, p. 346. 'Pivertistes' were followers of Marceau Pivert's *gauche révolutionnaire*.

39. 'Les Origines de la crise ouvrière de 1936,' *Le Musée social*, N.S., 44 (1937), pp. 121–39, 153–65, 185–200, esp. pp. 165, 199.

40. There are high zero-order correlation coefficients between the unionization of the industrial labor force across departments in 1937 and such indices of industrial advance as the departmental production of electricity (in 1931), or the average size of industrial establishment in 1936. Unionization in 1937 correlates most highly with the departmental distribution of strikers in 1936. Similar results were obtained with the increase in unionization in 1935–7 as the dependent variable. (82 departments were used in these analyses; logarithms of the labor force, electricity and striker variables were employed in place of absolute numbers.) These results reinforce the hypothesis that the rush of unionism in 1936–7 came in areas of industrial modernization, and specifically within those made militant by the 1936 strike waves.

41. See for examples of this Georges Lefranc, *Juin 36: L'Explosion sociale du front populaire* (Paris, 1966), pp. 167–8, 211–12. Pierre Delon describes sitdowns in the

department stores and insurance companies in *Les Employés de la plume d'oie à l'or-dinateur: Un Siècle de lutte: Origines et activité de la fédération C.G.T.* (Paris, 1969), pp. 109–20. A thoughtful summary is Michel Crozier, 'White-Collar Unions–The Case of France' in Adolf Sturmthal (ed.), *White-Collar Trade Unions: Contemporary Developments in Industrialized Societies* (Urbana, Ill., 1966), pp. 106–9.
42. On the importance of *contrôle ouvrier* in worker demands see Henri Prouteau, *Les Occupations d'usines en Italie et en France (1920–1936)* (Paris, 1937), p. 118.
43. Lefranc, *Mouvement syndical sous la Troisième République*, pp. 344–5.
44. This interpretation diverges from the view that the 1936 explosions were entirely apolitical. Daniel Brower has written, 'As far as can be judged, the movement in June was not politically motivated, nor was it in any way under the control of political organizations' (*New Jacobins*, p. 151). And Henry Ehrmann dismisses the possible influence of 'extremist plotters, such as the anarchists and Trotskyites [who] had no influence whatever with the masses' (*French Labor from Popular Front to Liberation* [New York: Oxford University Press, 1947], p. 38).
45. *France, 1940–1955* (Boston: Beacon Press, 1956), p. 353.
46. *Le Mouvement syndical de la Libération aux événements de Mai–Juin 1968* (Paris, 1969), pp. 56, 58.
47. This account of the 1947 events is based on *RFT*, 2 (1947), pp. 619–24, 818–22, 1121–4, and 3 (1948), pp. 95–100; also on Lefranc, *Mouvement syndical de la Libéra-tion*, pp. 47–61, and on Herbert Luethy, *France against Herself* (New York: Praeger, 1955), pp. 137–57. The CFTC, it must be pointed out, opposed the strike, as did other small 'islands of resistance' in the worker movement, to use Lefranc's phrase.
48. Description of miners' strike from *RFT*, 4 (1949), pp. 92–4; and Lefranc, *Mouvement syndical de la Libération*, pp. 73–6.
49. For this account we depend on Lefranc, *Mouvement syndical de la Libération*, pp. 118–19 and Werth, *France*, pp. 608–37. *RFT* failed to chronicle the strikes of August 1953.
50. The strike section of the *Annuaire statistique de la France*, 1969, has no entries in the columns for May and June 1968; similarly blank is the Ministère d'état chargé des affaires sociales, *Bulletin mensuel de statistiques sociales*, issue of February 1969, p. 24, which reports 1968 strike returns.
51. On white-collar participation see, for example, Alain Touraine, *Le Mouvement de mai ou le communisme utopique* (Paris, 1968), pp. 24–5.
52. The three *modèles de déclenchement des grèves* were: (1) the *modéle syndical*, in which local organizations directed events from the beginning; (2) the *modèle spontané pro-syndical*, in which local unions captured control shortly after the initial walkout; and (3) the *modèle spontané anti-syndical* in which the workers were hostile to the local union throughout the strike; the few establishments of this third type to appear in the survey data were *de pointe sur le plan professionnel* in which the demands of the established unions had been completely irrelevant to the concerns of the workforce. Sabine Erbès-Seguin, 'Le Déclenchement des grèves de mai: Spontanéité des masses et rôle des syndicats,' *Sociologie du travail*, 12 (1970), pp. 177–89.
53. Several articles have studied the pattern of demands and issues in the plants, as in the *Sociologie du travail*, 12 (1970): Sami Dassa, 'La Mouvement de mai et le système de relations professionnelles,' pp. 244–60; Claude Durand and Sonia Cazes, 'La Signification politique du mouvement de mai: Analyse de tracts syndicaux et gauchistes,' pp. 293–308; Roger Cornu and Marc Maurice, 'Revendications, orienta-tions syndicales et participation des cadres à la grève,' pp. 328–37; and Pierre Dubois, "Nouvelles Pratiques de mobilisation dans la classe ouvrière," pp. 338–44.
54. 'L'Après-mai 1968: Grèves pour le contrôle ouvrier,' *ibid.*, pp. 309–27.
55. Uncorrected 1915–35 data; in 1910–14 the figures were 65 percent and 58 percent for mini-wave and non-wave respectively.
56. Lefranc sees the Chamber acting under the pressure of events in the eight-hour-day law. *Le Mouvement syndical sous la Troisième République*, pp. 221–2.
57. Val Lorwin has suggested to us that 1936 represented an even greater advance, however, for the unions' 'near-pariah' status before the Popular Front was com-pletely altered by the Matignon agreements and the 1936 legislation.

Chapter 6. The unionization of France

1. The best analysis of unions in the tertiary sector is Michel Crozier's 'White-Collar Unions.' For specific accounts of white-collar unions see Georges Frischmann, *Histoire de la fédération C.G.T. des P.T.T.: Des origines au statut des fonctionnaires (1672–1946)* (Paris, 1967), and Pierre Delon, *Employés de la plume d'oie à l'ordinateur.*

2. Serge Mallet, in *La Nouvelle Classe ouvrière*, pp. 49–69, was among the first to see the strategic importance of unionism among the new professionals. Other writers have tended to discuss increases in the unionization of 'cadres' rather than of science-sector professionals as such. The former are distinguished by their authority in the enterprise, the latter by the technology they use; yet considerable overlap between the two exists. On the growth of unionism among the cadres see Georges Lefranc, *Mouvement syndical de la Libération*, pp. 220–1; Jean-Daniel Reynaud, *Les Syndicats en France*, pp. 99–102; and François Sellier and André Tiano, *Economie du travail* (Paris, 1962), pp. 406–11.

3. See the section 'L'O.S. étranger au syndicat' in Collinet's *L'Ouvrier français, I: Esprit du syndicalisme (Essai)* (Paris, 1951), pp. 53–7.

4. Peter Stearns has identified this trend towards increasingly effective coordination among trades within a given municipality. 'Significantly, strikes that went beyond the usual framework were more often city-wide, cutting across industrial lines, than industry-wide and national.' (*Revolutionary syndicalism*, p. 30.) Stearns believes the reverse was true of Britain.

   On the role of Bourses du travail in organizing agricultural laborers in surrounding rural areas, see Philippe Gratton, *Les Luttes de classes dans les campagnes* (Paris, 1971), p. 409 and *passim*. This variety of cross-industry linkage within the same territory remains largely unexplored in the literature.

5. For this summary of the Bourse du travail movement we have relied on Georges Lefranc, *Mouvement syndical sous la Troisième République*, pp. 49–63; *APO*, I, pp. 259–61, and on the *Annuaire statistique*, 58 (1961), p. 101*.

6. We have this chronicle of miners' organizations from the CGT's publication *La Confédération générale du travail et le mouvement syndical* (Paris, 1925), pp. 430–3. (Hereafter cited as CGT, 1925.)

7. The story of the CGT's formation is told well in Lefranc, *Mouvement syndical sous la Troisième République*, pp. 33–4, 64–84.

8. Marjorie Ruth Clark, *A History of the French Labor Movement (1910–1928)* (Berkeley, Cal., 1930), example from pp. 24–5. Pp. 24–39 of this book are a good summary of the CGT's structure just before the First World War. For later years, see Val Lorwin's excellent account, *The French Labor Movement*, pp 145–75.

9. *APO* estimated that half of all *syndicats ouvriers* were *rattachées à unions locales ou nationales* around 1900 (I, p. 271). The government placed CGT membership in 1912 at 600,000 *membres*, which means males only. An estimated 60,000 female unionists would bring total CGT membership in 1912 to 660,000. This 660,000 was 57 percent of the total membership in all *syndicats ouvriers* of 1,064,000 males the government reported for 1912 plus an estimated 100,000 females. For these statistics see *Annuaire statistique*, 58 (1951), p. 100*; for male–female ratios *Annuaire des syndicats*, 17 (1911), p. xxxviii.

10. Edouard Dolléans, *Histoire du mouvement ouvrier*, 6th ed., I", p. 276.

11. Prost wrote of the Popular Front era: 'La réunification de la C.G.T. ne laissait subsister en dehors d'elle que des minorités très faibles.' (*La C.G.T. à l'époque du front populaire*, p. 8.) And Lefranc said that in 1966 four-fifths of all organized workers belonged to one of the three great confederations. (*Mouvement syndical de la Libération*, pp. 206–7.) Those belonging to the fourth confederation, the CGC, were largely unorganized before 1936.

12. Michelle Perrot stresses the overlapping of political and unionist personnel in the late 1870s: 'Partout, des hommes jeunes, à la mentalité bien plus combative conduisent le mouvement. Ces hommes sont souvent les mêmes qui organisent les premiers cercles d'études sociales envisagés au congrès de Marseille. Il existe à cette époque une grande confusion entre le syndical et le politique.' *Ouvriers en grève*, p. 116; see also pp. 614–19.

13. For a clear portrayal of anarcho-syndicalist ideology, making explicit contrasts with Marxism, see F. F. Ridley, *Revolutionary Syndicalism in France. The Direct Action of Its Time* (Cambridge, 1970), *passim*.

14. Yves Lequin, 'Classe ouvrière et idéologie dans la région lyonnaise à la fin du XIXe siècle,' *Mouvement social*, no. 69 (Oct.–Dec. 1969), pp. 3–20.

15. From Lefranc, *Le Mouvement socialiste sous la Troisième République* (Paris, 1963), p. 104.

16. This account of socialist party history taken from Lefranc, *ibid.*, pp. 49–133; a good summary in English is Aaron Noland's *The Founding of the French Socialist Party (1893–1905)* (Cambridge, Mass.: Harvard University Press, 1956). A convenient guide to events is the chart of *congrès ouvriers nationaux et internationaux de 1876 à 1898* in *APO*, I, facing p. 270.

17. The Charter of Amiens stated that in addition to the 'day-to-day demands,' the goal of syndicalism was 'complete emancipation, which can be achieved only by expropriating the capitalist class. [The Convention of Amiens] endorses the general strike as a means of action to that end. It holds that the trade union, which is today a fighting organization, will in the future be an organization for production and distribution, and the basis of social reorganization.' From the translation by Val Lorwin, *French Labor Movement*, 312–13.

Chapter 7. Unions and strikes

1. In this typology we have borrowed from pioneering treatments of the impact of industrial technology upon worker organization and militancy by Alain Touraine and Serge Mallet. We remind the reader that what they call 'phase A' is for us 'craft,' or 'artisanal,' unionism; their 'phase B' is our 'proletarian,' 'assembly-line,' 'mass-production' or 'semi-skilled' unionism; and their 'phase C' is our 'science sector.' Touraine's original study was *L'Evolution du travail ouvrier*; Mallet widened and generalized Touraine's basic ideas in *Nouvelle Classe ouvrière*, esp. pp. 7–74. For a discussion of the question in which both men participated see Léo Hamon (ed.), *Nouveaux Comportements*, pp. 145–80.

2. William H. Sewell Jr has demonstrated how pervasive these associations were among the skilled artisans of Marseille in the 1840s. See his 'La Classe ouvrière de Marseille sous la Seconde République: Structure sociale et comportement politique,' *Mouvement social*, no. 76 (July–Sept. 1971), pp. 27–65; Joan Scott's article in the same issue, 'Les Verriers de Carmaux, 1856–1895,' pp. 67–93, is another good local study of artisanal organization. Robert J. Bezucha's portrait of the Lyon silkweavers shows in the troubles of 1831–4 an established group of skilled craftsmen struggling desperately to maintain their former power and prestige against capitalistic merchant–enterpreneurs and against the state. 'What bound them together were the shared goals of winning for the *canuts* (particularly the master weavers) the respect they felt due them, and of wresting from the merchants the social and economic power that they wielded by their absolute control over the weaving rates' (p. 108). Bezucha explains that an arsenal of political controls over the weavers were available as well to the merchants. 'The "Preindustrial" Worker Movement: the *Canuts* of Lyon' in Bezucha (ed.), *Modern European Social History* (Lexington, Mass.: D. C. Heath, 1972), pp. 93–123.

To illustrate the strength of horizontal craft ties, Perrot writes of the leather workers: 'Ces habitudes de clandestinité permettent aux ouvriers du cuirs de conserver intact un réseau d'institutions et de relations étendues à l'échelle nationale. Entre les sites bien localisés de leur industrie – Paris, Grenoble, Lyon, Chaumont, Annonay, Bruxelles, ces itinérants tressent les liens d'une véritable franc-maçonnerie. En cas de conflits, on échange correspondance et secours. La solidarité de métier, si menacée verticalement par les divisions catégorielles, fonctionne exceptionnellement bien au niveau géogrphique.' *Ouvriers en grève*, pp. 558–9.

3. *APO*, I, pp. 278–9.

4. *APO*, I, pp. 278–9. *APO* stated: 'Le nombre des sociétés de secours mutuels qui ont joué le role de sociétés de défense professionnelle est, en effet, assez retreint; cependant, il va de soi que les réunions périodiques de ces sociétés ont facilité, souvent hors séance, le concert entre ouvriers d'une même profession à une époque

où les réunions ayant pour objet de traiter des conditions du travail n'étaient jamais autorisées' (I, p. 199).

5. The *compagnonnage* was an archaic form of journeyman organization without practical importance in the nineteenth-century strike movement. Michelle Perrot notes their lack of involvement in collective agitation. *Ouvriers en grève*, pp. 604–6.

6. *APO*, III, pp. 333–52.

7. This account taken from *APO*, IV, pp. 171–89, esp. pp. 180–1.

8. CGT, 1925, pp. 367–8, 457–62.

9. Seymour Martin Lipset *et al.*, *Union Democracy: The Internal Politics of the International Typographical Union* (Glencoe, Ill., 1956); Hubert Sales, *Les Relations industrielles dans l'imprimerie française* (Paris, 1967).

10. 'Naissance d'une conscience de classe dans le proletariat textile du Nord: 1830–1870,' *Revue économique*, 8 (1957), pp. 114–39. See also Peter Stearns, 'Industrial Strike Activity during the July Monarchy,' *American Historical Review*, 70 (1965), pp. 371–94.

11. *SG*, 1892, pp. 147–50.

12. Perrot writes that little solidarity existed in strikes between skilled and unskilled workers. Only later was mechanization and its dequalification of the artisan to bring the two groups together. *Ouvriers en grève*, pp. 730–1.

13. Noteworthy among the general literature are Robert Blauner, *Alienation and Freedom: The Factory Worker and His Industry* (Chicago: University of Chicago Press, 1964); Daniel Bell, *Work and Its Discontents* (New York: League for Industrial Democracy reprint, 1970); and John H. Goldthorpe *et al.*, *The Affluent Worker: Industrial Attitudes and Behaviour* (Cambride, 1968), and *The Affluent Worker: Political Attitudes and Behaviour* (Cambridge, 1968). On France see Michel Collinet, *Esprit du syndicalisme*; Georges Friedmann, *Industrial Society*; Alain Touraine, *Evolution du travail*. For a case study of radicalism and large-plant metalworking see Daniel Vasseur, *Les Débuts du mouvement ouvrier dans la région de Belfort–Montbéliard (1870–1914)* (Paris, 1967).

14. Reliance upon unpaid militants reinforces the revolutionary aspect of the union movement. As Michel Crozier explains: 'Unpaid millitants are the key men in the situation. Without their relentless efforts, unions would crumble; in order to survive, the unions must do their utmost to attract and retain these people. This dependence upon militants makes constructive leadership extremely difficult. Militants are motivated only by idealistic incentives, and the leaders are prisoners of the demagogic appeal that seems to be the only way to keep the militants active. The primacy of these idealistic incentives imposes revolutionary dogmas upon the organizations, fostering division and internal quarrel...' 'White-Collar Trade Unions,' p. 120.

15. Prost, *La C.G.T. à l'époque du front populaire*, p. 53 for influx, p. 45 for outflow. A similar test could be done for the union explosion of 1918–20, but Annie Kriegel could supply no data on the number of adherents (as opposed to the number of unions) before the September 1920 CGT congress, and by that time the great defections had already occurred. *Croissance de la C.G.T.*

16. These percentages are not true unionization rates, for the denominator includes many workers who would not have joined unions, such as *employés, chefs, isolés* and *chomeurs*. Yet the comparisons this index facilitates from one industry to another are quite valid. For exact unionization statistics by industry, see Prost, *La C.G.T. à l'époque du front populaire*, pp. 205–8.

17. *Esprit du syndicalisme*, p. 12.

18. This account is based on CGT, 1925, pp. 405–8, and Collinet, *Esprit du syndicalisme*, pp. 31–6 and *passim*.

19. Val R. Lorwin asks: 'Will workers achieve a unionism that can recover the best in their traditions and represent them constructively in an industrial nation's life? Again, one can only ask the question. They may see through the CGT's cloak of militant unionism to the realities of political subservience. They may develop a freely consented discipline to democratic labor organizations rather than alternating between anarchistic individualism and abdication of responsibility into the hands of totalitarians.' (*The French Labor Movement*, p. 306.) Collinet's own hostility to the PCF distorts his treatment of the matter.

20. See the discussion in Chapter 8 of the relationship between large establishment size and high rates of failure in strikes. At several points in time, the percent of strikes that failed was highly correlated with the presence of steam engines in the department:
    1910–14: +0.59
    1920–4: +0.64
    1925–9: +0.62
    1915–35: +0.65
21. 'White-Collar Trade Unions,' p. 116.
22. *Nouvelle Classe ouvrière*, pp. 160–1.
23. *Ibid.*, pp. 172–3.
24. Crozier, 'White-Collar Trade Unions,' p. 118.
25. For the years 1871–90 Michelle Perrot discovered that unions took charge of only 28 percent of all strikes; they were represented in some form or another in all together 46 percent of the strikes; the additional 13 percent of all strikes organized by some non-*syndicat* form of worker organization elevates the total percentage of strikes with formal organization to 59 percent. (*Ouvriers en grève*, pp. 598–607.) These data suggest that the apparent trough in union participation shown by fig. 7.3 (p. 188) for 1895–9 is an artifact born of our artificially inflated *APO* data for earlier years. If Perrot's figures are accurate, a steady upward movement of union involvement in strikes occurred from the early 1880s to the First World War.
26. Many establishments/strike with unions could be an artifact, for if enough establishments go out, there is bound to be a union somewhere. We must assume that when the *SG* reported union involvement for multi-establishment disputes, it meant that the union played a prominent coordinating role, and not merely that a few unionized workers happened to join in.
27. See Stearns's *Revolutionary Syndicalism*, pp. 30, 74, 87, 93 and *passim*. For prestrike negotiations in 1871–90 see Perrot, p. 596. For the years 1915–35 we coded the number of different communes the *SG* indicated were involved in a single strike; we did not take notice of this datum for the prewar period, and so are unable to confront Stearns directly on this question. Yet surely the tendency of unions to generalize conflicts territorially did not begin first after the war.

Chapter 8. Industrialization and strikes

1. See, for example, E. A. Wrigley, 'Industrialization and Modernization,' paper delivered at 1971 annual meeting of Organization of American Historians.
2. Michelle Perrot found few dramatic changes in the industrial distribution of conflict in the 1871–90 period: the share of textiles and construction grew a little smaller, that of transport and metals a little larger, presaging post-1890 developments. See p. 492.
3. See, for example, Hubert Sales, *Relations industrielles*, pp. 131–9 and *passim*.
4. Whenever possible, we have calculated the rate of strikes per 100,000 workers for these individual occupations. The strike data are from 1910–14, the labor force denominator is the number of *ouvriers* who were part of the *Personnel des établissements* in 1906. This labor-force information was taken from the three-to-five digit industrial codes in vol. I, part 2 of the 1906 census.
   Two problems make perilous the matching of strikes in the numerator to workers in the denominator. (1) In many strikes several different occupations within the same sector went out simultaneously, each contributing an unspecified part of the total. It proved impossible to do justice to this complexity in the coding and aggregating of the data, so we have identified such strikes by what appeared to be their main occupational component. The implication of this is that the strike propensities of the accompanying but unmentioned crafts will appear in our statistics artificially depressed. (2) Labor-force reporting categories in the census often do not coincide with occupational categories in the *SG*. Weaving and machine-building are cases in point. The *SG* reports endless strings of conflicts among *tisseurs* and *mécaniciens–constructeurs*, yet the census gives only the number of workers active by type of textile fabric (rather than by function in the production of the fabric), and by type of metal product (rather than by job status). So strike rates for these two occupations may not be computed, nor for many others.
   Finally, the reader should note that the labor-force denominator in these occupa-

tion-specific rates is the number of employed workers in establishments, rather than the total active population in a given sector, which is, of course, our customary denominator in industrial rate computations. These former rates, encompassing only the potentially strikable population within the occupation, will thus be typically much higher than the rates for the larger sectors of which these specific occupations are a part. The sectoral and occupational rates are not at all comparable.

The sources for changes in industrial concentration mentioned throughout this section are:

For 1906–26, Marcel de Ville-Chabrolle, 'La Concentration des entreprises en France avant et depuis la guerre (d'après les recensements généraux de mars 1906, 1921 et 1926),' *Bulletin de la statistique générale de la France*, 22 (1933), pp. 391–462, esp. p. 423.

For 1926–36, R. C. Marchand, 'La Concentration du personnel dans les entreprises en France entre les deux guerres,' *Bulletin de la statistique générale de la France*, Jan.–March 1945, pp. 77–100.

5. *Cordonniers* is the word used in the July Monarchy; its functional equivalent, the category *ouvriers en chaussures*, does not appear in Aguet.

6. *Relations industrielles*, pp. 84–7.

7. Our knowledge of conditions within metalworking comes principally from Michel Collinet, *Esprit du syndicalisme*, *passim*; and from R. Dufraisse, 'Rapports entre organisations ouvrières et organisations patronales de la métallurgie française durant la dépression économique (1929–1939)' in Denise Fauvel-Rouif (ed.), *Mouvements ouvriers et dépression économique de 1929 à 1939* (Assen, the Netherlands, 1966), pp. 189–219.

8. On the disarray of organization among Marseille dockworkers around 1890, for example, see Mireille Vecchie Lartigue, 'Les Grèves des dockers à Marseille de 1890 â 1903,' *Provence historique*, 10 (1960), pp. 146–79.

9. *SG* reporting conventions cause the occupational composition of metals production, mining–quarrying and agriculture to appear homogeneous. A multitude of trades and products are buried beneath the labels *métallurgistes, mineurs* and *ouvriers agricoles et viticoles*. But a lack of consistent supplementary information kept us from analyzing the three sectors in detail. Agricultural strikes, however, for the 1890–1921 period are treated at length in Philippe Gratton, *Luttes de classes dans les campagnes*, pp. 383–401.

10. In Michelle Perrot's view as well artisanal workers have better organization in strikes, endure longer and take the offensive more frequently than unorganized workers. Semi-skilled workers find themselves in between these two poles (p. 405). 'Elle [the artisanal strike] s'oppose presque en tous points à la grève de manoeuvres, subite, fruste, brutale, isolée, et massivement décue... Au triptyque des qualifications correspond une trilogie de l'action: la plume, la voix, le poing.' *Ouvriers en grève*, p. 487.

We disagree with her conclusions about skill level and strike activity in only two respects, one minor and one major. We are unable to discover in 1910–14 the differences in strike outcome Perrot sees in 1871–90. She claims the higher the skill level, the more successful the strike tended to be. But the principal skilled trades had, in 1910–14, the same percentage of totally successful strikes (16.8 percent) as the unskilled (16.0 percent). And the skilled trades had a 'happy outcome' rate (success + compromise) only marginally higher than the unskilled trades': 56.9 percent opposed to 49.4 percent.

A more serious shortcoming in the Perrot analysis is the attribution of strike differentials among skill levels to differences in 'passion.' Perrot argues that skilled workers were less exploited, therefore less aggrieved, less likely to erupt in fits of rage and more calculating about conflict. Unskilled workers, on the other hand, would explode in directionless, leaderless wildcat strikes because exploitation, combined with the deadening, unpleasant nature of their work, created antagonism and frustration that only conflict could ventilate. We, of course, lay differences in the strike activity of various skill levels to differences in their ability to organize.

11. After the First World War the percent of strikes over worker organization issues dropped sharply among *mécaniciens–constructeurs*, a sign, in our opinion, of the abandonment of the job control struggle.

*Percent of strikes over worker organization issues
among* mécaniciens–constructeurs

1895–9	40
1910–14	40
1915–19	13
1920–4	16
1925–9	12

12. On the organizational inconstancy of factory spinners and weavers in the Nord, see Jean-Paul Courtheoux, 'Naissance d'une conscience de classe,' pp. 114–39. Perrot considers textile disputes the archetype of wildcat strikes (*Ouvriers en grève*, pp. 500–1).

13. René Michaud's memoirs recall conditions in shoe factories around the turn of the century. *J'avais vingt ans: Un Jeune Ouvrier au début du siècle* (Paris, 1967). P. Cousteix follows the history of the shoe industry around Limoges in 'Le Mouvement ouvrier limousin de 1870 à 1939,' *L'Actualité de l'histoire*, nos. 20–21 (Dec. 1957), pp. 27–96; the Goodyear welt machine, though invented around 1875, was introduced in the region only at the turn of the century.

14. The national federation of *chapellerie* noted in 1925: 'Depuis sa fondation (1879) cette Fédération a changé complètement d'aspect. Elle est composée aujourd'hui presque exclusivement de chapeliers confectionnant le chapeau de paille et l'article pour dames. Les fondateurs, c'est à dire les "feutriers," à part une centaine, sont complètement désorganisés.' CGT, 1925, p. 343.

15. Ingham, *Size of Industrial Organization and Worker Behaviour* (Cambridge, 1970), pp. 116, 141–50. Hamilton, *Affluence and the French Worker in the Fourth Republic* (Princeton, N.J., 1967), pp. 205–28. Hamilton finds, moreover, that workers in small towns are more radical than those in big cities. This may be, but data presented in Chapter 10 show that collective action is more solidary and effective in big cities than in small towns, even if, as Hamilton claims, small-town workers are more 'alienated.'

16. The computations were done with logarithms. Strikes occurred – and large establishments existed – during both periods in some 278 department–industry units. The unpartialed zero-order correlations between the number of strikes and number of large establishments were very much higher.

17. Jerome F. Scott and George C. Homans explain the high percentage of wildcat strikes over worker organization questions in Detroit during the Second World War as a consequence of a conflict between small-group loyalties and 'the aims of the organization as a whole [the automobile factories].' This conflict arises from what the authors call a failure in 'communications,' by which term they seem to mean the failure of management to acknowledge appropriately the status and influence of the workers. We had considered this analysis inappropriate to France, because large-plant French workers seem to intend little communication of any sort with management when they go on strike. Yet if detailed research should demonstrate active informal bargaining and communication between, say, auto factory work groups and management representatives, the Scott–Homans analysis might account for semi-skilled concern over worker organization questions. 'Reflections on the Wildcat strikes,' *American Sociological Review*, 12 (1947), pp. 278–87.

18. The reader might wonder how many of these apparent consequences of plant size are really due to differences in the level of unionization. If, for example, larger plants in 1910–14 had lower participation rates (strikers/workers employed) than small plants, might that not be because large plants generally had higher levels of unionization? After all, the unions likely to be present among semi-skilled proletarians were highly politicized, and often divided the labor force in strike calls. The answer to this particular question, and to the general query about unionization as the master variable lurking beneath the surface, is no.

Almost none of the differences between large and small plants reported in table 8.14 disappear, or even flatten out, when union membership is controlled for. Small plants continue to have longer durations than large ones, even after the data have been filtered through union membership. Plant participation rates in small plants continue to be higher than in large plants, whether a union is present or not. And so on. Only in preventing large-plant strikers from being fired does a union matter, for whereas only 3.4 percent of all large-plant strikes with unions ended in worker dismissal during 1910–14, 9.3 percent of those strikes *without unions* did so.

19. We are not entirely satisfied with either of two recent explanations for the high strike propensity of large plants. Peter Stearns claims that industrial concentration promoted militancy by endangering artisanal solidarity and ways of life. And we are sympathetic to the notion that in many factories skilled workers were the principal militants. Yet enough big-plant industries without artisanal contingents in them, such as textiles, experienced high strike rates to discourage Stearns's argument as a general explanation of the relationship between militancy and scale.

Michelle Perrot suggests that the particular style of authority prevailing within a big plant may have infuriated the workers to the point of revolt. She discusses 'le grand patronat, anonyme et concentré,' unapproachable and unbending in negotiation. 'A des degrès divers, la grande entreprise, anonyme ou familiale, apparaît donc comme un noeud de conflits . . . asservissante, frustrante, véritablement castratrice de la liberté.' *Ouvriers en grève*, pp. 971, 972, 984.

Chapter 9. Territorial differences in strike activity

1. To study inequality we plotted for various periods the cumulative percent of strikes in France on the vertical axis of a graph, the cumulative percent of all communes having strikes on the horizontal. The more the real curve deviated from the lower-left to upper-right diagonal (representing perfect equality), the greater the inequality of the distribution.

2. Only two departments could not be classed within larger regions of conflict: the Gironde and the Haute-Vienne. For the sake of completeness, we should glance briefly at their contribution to French aggregate strike activity.

   –The Gironde means in practice Bordeaux, for the port had three-quarters of the department's strikes and nine-tenths of its strikers during 1915–35. Of the participants, a third were in transportation, a quarter in metalworking and the remainder scattered among the other sectors, an industrial distribution similar to the Breton maritime departments.

   –To an almost equal degree, Limoges dominated strikes in the Haute-Vienne (69 percent of strikes, 78 percent of strikers). The department's disputes were divided among the two major industries of ceramics (30 percent of all strikers – ceramics differentiated here from 'general construction') and leather goods (45 percent of all strikers). Thus in the vast stretches of France south of the Loire and west of the Saône, only the two big cities of Limoges and Bordeaux made themselves felt on the national scene.

3. See the section 'Etude des dimensions des établissements industriels,' in Gabriel Dessus *et al.*, *Matériaux pour une géographie volontaire de l'industrie française* (Paris, 1949), pp. 109–43; quote from p. 134.

4. On industrial relations in interwar coalmining see 'The Lens Mining Company' in International Labour Office, *Studies on Industrial Relations* (Geneva: ILO, 1930; Studies and Reports, Series A, no. 33), pp. 63–99.

Chapter 10. Cities, urbanization and strikes

1. 'Esquisse d'une théorie du syndicalisme,' *Sociologie du travail*, 10 (1968), pp. 362–92.

2. For a statement of this case see John C. Leggett, *Class, Race, and Labor: Working-Class Consciousness in Detroit* (New York: Oxford University Press, 1968), pp. 62–75.

3. Perrot makes a similar point about stability as a prerequisite for collective action: 'La phase de constitution du prolétariat, temps du déracinement, de la dépossession, de la "rébellion primitive" pour reprendre l'expression d'Eric Hobsbawm, précède la formation du mouvement ouvrier. Celle-ci requiert une certaine stabilisation, une continuité: elle est le fait des heritiers.' *Ouvriers en grève*, p. 70.

4. Almost all these cities grew in population between 1872 and 1911. Most of the increase in such cases, it has been established, comes not from the natural excess of urban births over deaths, but from immigration. See Philippe Pinchemel; *France: A Geographical Survey*, Eng. trans. (New York: Praeger, 1969), p. 391.

5. Maurice Agulhon's work on sociability in the Midi is brilliantly suggestive; the same *chambrées* and *bars* that launched lower-class political action in the Var during 1848 might well later have formed springboards for industrial conflict as well. The question awaits monographic research. See 'Les Chambrées en Basse-Provence: histoire et ethnologie,' *Revue historique*, 498 (1971), pp. 337–68, and *La République au village: les populations du Var de la Révolution à la Seconde République* (Paris: Plon, 1970). Similar regional traditions of informal organization perhaps lay behind other regional differentials in conflict.

6. Philippe Gratton points out how aggressive urban Bourses du travail helped export militancy to agricultural workers in the surrounding countryside. *Luttes de classes dans les campagnes*, p. 409.

7. Yet it must have been this weak relationship that nonetheless was responsible for giving big cities higher striker rates and strike sizes than small towns had, because at the level of zero-order correlations, at least, the other two possible mobilizing mechanisms involved in strike size – size of establishment and percent of establishment workforce actually on strike – wash out completely. The zero-order correlation between size of town in 1911 and strikers/100 workers employed in struck establishments was −0.09. The correlation between establishments/strike and town size was still modest, yet at 0.25 considerably higher than the first two mentioned. The same kind of zero-order correlations turn up between the three mobilizing variables in 1915–35 and town size in 1921. (Logarithms of all values were used in these computations. The 128 communes larger than 20,000 in 1911 were the unit of analysis.)

8. Michelle Perrot comments on the uniqueness of worker organization and conflict in Paris, identifying leaders 'typiquement' Parisian, and finding 'une note d'exotisme' in the 'univers plus riant des petits ateliers parisiens.' (*Ouvriers en grève*, p. 676.) Her sensitive filtering of impressionistic kinds of evidence reinforces a conviction we reached with hard quantitative data: strikes in the metropolis had an air all their own.

Chapter 11. The interplay of organization, location and industrial conflict

1. In Arthur Kornhauser *et al.* (eds.), *Industrial Conflict* (New York, 1954), pp. 189–212.

2. 'This hypothesis explains a good many of the facts but not quite so neatly as the first' (p. 195). Militant French bank employees will smile at this point. Lucien Karpik's account of the psychological origins of industrial discontent seems more promising. He suggests that urbanity is responsible for political and economic aspects of job dissatisfaction; the city, however, shares the blame with mono-industrial communities for 'socio-professional' aspects of discontent. 'Urbanisation et satisfactions du travail,' *Sociologie du travail*, 8 (1966), pp. 179–214.

3. This conclusion coincides with John Foster's argument that territorial variations of class consciousness among English towns may be partly explained by whether the local employers live in the city; labor will retain its solidarity if the 'enemy' is clearly visible as a resident economic elite. 'Nineteenth-Century Towns: A Class Dimension' in H. J. Dyos (ed.), *The Study of Urban History* (London: Edward Arnold, 1968), pp. 281–99.

4. William Sewell has recently pointed to the corporate tradition among French skilled workers as the launching pad of their modern class consciousness. 'Social Mobility in a Nineteenth-Century European City [Marseille]: Some Findings and Implications,' paper delivered at the annual meeting of the American Sociological Association, 1971.

5. *La C.G.T. à l'époque du front populaire*, pp. 95–6.

Chapter 12. French strikes in international perspective

1. Arthur M. Ross and Paul T. Hartman, *Changing Patterns of Industrial Conflict* (New York, 1960), remains the standard discussion of international differences in strike activity. The argument presented in these pages differs from that book's in two ways:

(a) we suggest different – and fewer – groupings of countries into international patterns, because we emphasize the number of strikes per 100,000 workers as a measure of militancy, rather than the number of strikes per 100,000 unionists, which is the Ross–Hartman measure; (b) we treat politics as the truly strategic variable in international differences, and are reluctant to regard a country's labor relations system as having, in its own right, an important independent influence in shaping conflict; similarly, we feel that fragmentation of the labor movement into rival confederations is more a consequence than a creation of fundamental international differences in political mobilization and participation. Ross and Hartman give these and several other factors prominent mention in explaining why nations differ. This multiplicity of variables leads them towards *ad hoc* explanations which stress different factors for different countries, and away from predictive models.

Three articles by K. Forchheimer compose the classic study of international strike differences. Forchheimer spotted the fall in propensity through the twenties, the secular decline in duration and the rise in size, though he offered no accounting of these developments. We go beyond Forchheimer's description of events mainly by presenting data for the post-Second World War period. 'Some International Aspects of the Strike Movement,' *Bulletin of the Oxford University Institute of Statistics*, 10 (1948), pp. 9–24 and 294–304, and 'Some International Aspects of Strikes,' *ibid.*, 11 (1949), pp. 279–86.

2. We first employed this device to compare strikes among western industrial nations in 'The Shape of Strikes in France, 1830–1960,' pp. 60–86.

3. Val Lorwin, for example, writes: 'Britain developed a labor movement of class solidarity and class organization without class hatred,' and suggests that these organizational features may be in part related to economic structures. 'Working-Class Politics and Economic Development in Western Europe,' *American Historical Review*, 63 (1958), pp. 335–51, esp. p. 347.

4. John I. Griffin, *Strikes: A Study in Quantitative Economics* (New York, 1939), p. 87.

5. On strikes in Italian politics see Guido Baglioni, *Il Conflitto industriale e l'azione del sindacato* (Bologna, 1966).

6. The causes of the 'quickies' have received little scholarly attention in Britain. H. A. Turner, however, writes: 'The great majority of strikes constitute reactions to, or protests against, some change in the work context: they are refusals to continue work on the same terms as previously when the conditions previously assumed no longer apply. As such, they very commonly amount to a demonstration against some managerial action.' *Is Britain Really Strike-Prone? A Review of the Incidence, Character & Costs of Industrial Conflict* (Cambridge, 1969), pp. 21–2.

Richard A. Lester has called attention to the lack of formal union organization at the plant level in Britain. 'Reflections on Collective Bargaining in Britain and Sweden,' *Industrial and Labor Relations Review*, 10 (1956–7), pp. 375–401. P. Galambos and E. W. Evans have traced the postwar evolution of the characteristics of British strikes in 'Work-Stoppages in the United Kingdom, 1951–1964: A Quantitative Study,' *Bulletin of the Oxford University Institute of Statistics*, 28 (1966), pp. 33–57.

7. A recent work on Belgian strikes stresses their role in working-class political protest. Robert Gubbels, *La Grève*, see also Guy Spitaels, *Le Mouvement syndical en Belgique* (Brussels: Université libre de Bruxelles, Institut de sociologie, 1969), and B. S. Chlepner, *Cent ans d'histoire sociale* (Brussels: Université libre de Bruxelles, Institut de sociologie, 1958).

8. Arthur M. Ross emphasizes worker representation in the works council rather than in the government: 'The fact that so many important matters are lodged with works councils, rather than unions, and that works councils are forbidden to strike, helps to explain the almost complete disappearance of strikes in Germany during the postwar period.' 'Prosperity and Labor Relations in Europe: The Case of West Germany,' *Quarterly Journal of Economics*, 76 (1962), pp. 331–58, esp. p. 345.

9. Thomas A. Krueger describes such new orientations in 'American Labor Historiography, Old and New: A Review Essay,' *Journal of Social History*, 4 (1970–1), pp. 277–85. And S. M. Lipset mentions the shift from 'social or socialist unionism to business unionism' in 'Trade Unions and Social Structure,' *Industrial Relations*, I, i (Oct. 1961), pp. 75–89, and I, ii (Feb. 1962), pp. 89–110, esp. ii, p. 90.

10. John H. M. Laslett has recently studied political activity within a number of American industrial federations late in the nineteenth century, the U.S. counterpart of France's 'great mobilization' period. He argues that in the United States a substantial socialist movement flourished within labor after 1880, launched by politicized skilled workers attempting to protect themselves against technological change. Manifestly, the American rank and file commitment to the ideology of socialism was not as strong as the European. Yet from Laslett's work it becomes clear that in the United States the masses of workers wanted to see the labor movement undertake independent political action. *Labor and the Left: A Study of Socialist and Radical Influences in the American Labor Movement, 1881–1924* (New York, 1970), esp. pp. 293–304.

Among other recent research, J. David Greenstone has described labor's turn in the 1930s from independent action in the cause of its working-class clientele to affiliation with the Democratic Party in a broad political coalition. *Labor in American Politics* (New York: Knopf, 1969). Neither he, nor any other writer to our knowledge, has considered possible changes in the role of American strikes.

11. We endorse fully the conclusion of Peter Stearns's essay 'The European Labor Movement and the Working Classes, 1890–1914' that industrial conflict and worker organization were essentially similar from country to country. Stearns writes: '[The] protest orientation of any large group of workers was largely determined by economic factors and relationships on the job, and these factors were fundamentally comparable in all the mature industrial countries.' (In Harvey Mitchell and Stearns (eds.), *The European Labor Movement* [Itasca, Ill., 1971], p. 214.) See also Stearns, 'National Character and European Labor History,' *Journal of Social History*, 4 (1970–1), pp. 95–124.

12. For an example of this stereotype, see most recently F. F. Ridley, *Revolutionary Syndicalism in France*, pp. 11–12: 'One might conclude that the French worker, seeking an outlet for his enthusiasm in politics, would naturally incline to extremist and revolutionary doctrines. Syndicalism provided an outlet for his *élan*, an opportunity for explosive action.'

13. H. A. Turner and W. E. J. McCarthy have recently debated differences in reporting criteria as a barrier to international comparisons of strikes. Turner, *Is Britain Really Strike-Prone?* and McCarthy, 'The Nature of Britain's Strike Problem,' *British Journal of Industrial Relations*, 8 (1970), pp. 224–36.

14. There are not many such disputes in the U.S. Strikes lasting less than a full working day have been estimated at less than 5 percent of the total in 1901–5, for example. See Griffin, *Strikes*, p. 88.

15. National recording procedures are noted in the ILO's *Year Book of Labour Statistics*. We used the 1967 edition, pp. 713–23. One other factor affecting the international comparability of strike data is whether the country records just the number of strikers, or the number of workers in the struck establishments put out of work as well. France has published the latter figure since the Second World War. Other countries, however, exclude workers indirectly affected by the strike from the data they give to the International Labour Office, particularly Belgium, Italy and Norway. We know from prewar French data that the number of workers indirectly affected by strikes does not inflate the actual number of strikers greatly if added to it. Of the 277,000 'strikers' in 1895–8, for example, only 11 percent were non-strikers forced out of work.

Chapter 13. Conclusion

1. The principal authors of both views have succinctly resumed their arguments in Hugh Davis Graham and Ted Robert Gurr (eds.), *Violence in America: Historical and Comparative Perspectives* (New York: Bantam Books, 1969); see Gurr, 'A Comparative Study of Civil Strife,' pp. 572–632, and James C. Davies, 'The J-Curve of Rising and Declining Satisfactions as a Cause of Some Great Revolutions and Contained Rebellion,' pp. 690–731. See also Gurr, *Why Men Rebel* (Princeton, N.J.: University Press, 1970).

2. 'A Theoretical Setting for the Study and Treatment of Strikes,' *Occupational Psychology*, 32 (1958), pp. 1–20.

3. *Revolutionary Syndicalism*, p. 28.

4. *Ouvriers en grève*, p. 1058.
5. Collinet, *L'Ouvrier français*, I, pp. 119–20; quoted matter: II, p. 72.
6. F. F. Ridley ascribes important consequences to 'the Latin temper' in one part of his book and in another asserts: 'Certain workers found in the strike an outlet for their naturally combative temperament – in earlier times they would have run to the barricades at every call.' *Revolutionary Syndicalism in France*, pp. 11–13, 110.
7. The few French studies on short-term economic fluctuations and strikes are not entirely comparable because different periods and indicators have been selected. Of these the most sophisticated is no doubt Edgard Andréani, *Les Grèves et les fluctuations de l'activité économique de 1890 à 1914 en France* (Paris, Faculté de droit, *thèse*, 1965). Also to be mentioned are Jean Bouvier, 'Mouvement ouvrier et conjonctures économiques,' *Le Mouvement social*, no. 48 (July–Sept. 1964), pp. 3–28; Robert Goetz-Girey, *Mouvement des grèves*, esp. pp. 96–103, 119–40; Michelle Perrot, *Ouvriers en grève* esp. pp. 148–200; and Peter N. Stearns, *Revolutionary Syndicalism*, pp. 16, 18, 44.
8. K. G. J. C. Knowles argues that wage demands are not to be taken at their face value. 'Since wages stand for more than can be bought with them, wage strikes tend to be symbolic of wider grievances.' *Strikes* (Oxford, 1952), p. 219.
9. Representative statements and supporting evidence appear in Lynn Lees and Charles Tilly, 'The People of June, 1848,' Working Paper 70, Center for Research on Social Organization, University of Michigan, 1972 (French version forthcoming in *Annales; Economies, Sociétés, Civilisations*); James Rule and Charles Tilly '1830 and the Unnatural History of Revolution,' *Journal of Social Issues* 28 (1972), pp. 49–76; David Snyder and Charles Tilly, 'Hardship and Collective Violence in France, 1830–1960,' *American Sociological Review* 37 (1972), pp. 520–32; Charles Tilly, 'How Protest Modernized in France, 1845 to 1855' in Robert Fogel (ed.), *The Dimensions of Quantitative Research in History* (Princeton, N.J.: University Press, 1972).
10. Cited from Marx's letter to F. Bolte of 23 November 1871, in *Karl Marx and Friedrich Engels: Selected Works in One Volume* (New York: International Publishers, 1968), p. 683. For a recent analysis of Marx's views of class and industrial conflict, see J. A. Banks, *Marxist Sociology in Action: A Sociological Critique of the Marxist Approach to Industrial Relations* (London: Faber and Faber, 1970).

Appendix A

1. Mentioned in a circular of 20 November 1892, reprinted in *SG*, 1890–1, p. 8.
2. *SG*, 1890–1, p. 6.
3. Circular of 3 July 1885, mentioned in *SG*, 1891–1 p. 5.
4. Circular of 10 December 1895 in *SG*, 1895, pp. 326–8.
5. Circular of 4 July 1894 in *SG*, 1893, pp. 414–15.
6. This estimate of 90 percent coverage stems from a sampling of strikes we collected from a source independent of officialdom: newspaper accounts of violent strikes. Nine of the 98 violent strikes spotted in *Le Temps* and other journals could not be found in *SG*. Accordingly we conclude that 9 percent of the strike movement as a whole was not caught up in the official sieve. We consider somewhat over-optimistic Robert Goetz-Girey's estimate that post-Second World War strike reporting is 99 percent complete. *Mouvement des grèves*, p. 59.
7. These procedures are summarized in Goetz-Girey, *Mouvement des grèves*, pp. 59–61. He prints a sample *fiche* on p. 182, and reproduces the circular of 4 April 1956, which definitively established modes of reporting, on p. 195–200.
8. See Hélène Sinay, *La Grève*, p.76.
9. *SG*, 1893, pp. 414–15; see Goetz-Girey's reprint of the circular of 4 April 1956, esp. p. 196.
10. Fortunately, the statistical division seems to have counted a worker separately each time he went on strike in the figures it sent to the International Labour Office. So we may consult data from the *Year Book of Labour Statistics* to ensure comparability between postwar and interwar figures on the number of strikers.
11. *SG*, 1890–1, p. 6, n. 1.
12. International Labour Office, *The International Standardization of Labour Statistics* (Geneva: ILO, 1959), p. 108; the text is taken from the 1926 Resolution concerning Statistics of Industrial Disputes.

13. *Grèves sous la Monarchie de Juillet.*
14. *Statistique générale de la France,* vol. 15: *Statistique annuelle, 1885* (Paris: Berger-Levrault, 1888), pp. 72–83; vol. 18–19: *Statistique annuelle, 1888–89,* pp. 134–9.
15. The prominence of strikes which found their way into *APO* may be seen from their high median duration of 40 days. The median duration of strikes reported in the *Statistique annuelle* for the same period, presumably conflicts of greater typicality, is 6 days.
16. Ministère du commerce, Office du travail, *Les Associations professionnelles ouvrières,* 4 vols. (Paris: Imprimerie nationale, 1894–1904); an explanation of the work's origin is found in I, pp. i–iv.
17. Ministère du commerce, Office du travail, *Statistique des grèves et des recours à la conciliation et à l'arbitrage,* 1890–1935 (Paris: Imprimerie nationale, 1892–1939).
18. *SG* also listed strikes in the three Algerian departments belonging to France. We, however, have rigorously excluded these conflicts from our data file.
19. In this study we often use the median as a measure of central tendency. Unless otherwise indicated, the figure we call the median is in fact not the true median (the half-way point on a frequency distribution of cases), but the geometric mean. We have chosen the geometric over the arithmetic mean because it helps to discount the distorting influence of extreme cases upon the central tendency. We have chosen the geometric mean over the plain old median because it is much easier to compute, either by hand or by computer. (Finding the median of a frequency distribution with 36,000-odd cases is complicated even by computer, and when one must do this hundreds of times in dozens and dozens of different runs, the technical tedium is acute.)

    In most arrays of our own data, certainly in those with large numbers of cases, the geometric mean will be *the same* as the median.
20. Some scholars combine these separate strike series in composite indices of conflict by producing index numbers which represent through various weighting schemes strikes, strikers and man-days lost. See P. Galambos and E. W. Evans, 'Work-Stoppages in the United Kingdom,' pp. 33–57, the 'Comment' by K. G. J. C. Knowles, pp. 59–62, and the authors' 'Reply,' pp. 283–4. While suitable for some purposes, these composite indices conceal the separate development of the three essential components of the strike movement, the relative frequency of strikes, their average size and their normal duration, and we accordingly avoid them.
21. An alternative denominator occasionally appears in the literature, the number of strikers per 100 union members. Arthur M. Ross and Paul T. Hartman call this the 'membership involvement ratio.' *Changing Patterns of Industrial Conflict,* pp. 11–12. In countries where almost all strikers are union members this may give a more exact idea of the pool from which the strikers are drawn. Yet in France most strikers may well *not* belong to unions, although they follow union leadership in industrial conflict; therefore employing such a denominator would misleadingly inflate French strike rates.

    These labor-force data were taken from the *Statistique générale*'s published censuses, which appeared every five years between 1886 and 1936 except for 1916. The 1936 volumes were not available to us, but for every other census year we preserved on punchcards the active civilian population in each industrial sector within each department of France. We kept special note of the number of unemployed, reported after 1896, so that they could be subtracted from the population. The active population includes such groups as the self-employed ('isolated workers') who would not have participated in strikes, yet because they are present consistently they will not affect the relative results. In order to derive yearly labor-force figures we have interpolated the five-year census returns. And to make up for the lacking 1936 census, we let the active population in 1931 stand as the labor-force base in 1932–5. (Extrapolating earlier trends seemed dangerous in view of the Depression's impact.) We may rely on the internal consistency of French census data only after 1896, for the principles and categories of the 1891 and 1886 censuses were somewhat at variance with those of later years. J.-C. Toutain describes the evolution of censuses in *La Population de la France de 1700 à 1959* (J. Marczewski (ed.), *Histoire quantitative de l'économie française,* vol. III), in Cahiers de l'Institut de Sciences économiques appliquées, Series AF, pp. 83–103.

For the censuses see Statistique générale de la France, *Résultats statistiques du dénombrement de* ... (1886, 1891, 1896); *Résultats statistiques de recensement générale de la population effectué le* ... (1901, 1906, 1911, 1921, 1926, 1931).

To ensure consistency, labor-force data for France used in international comparisons are taken not from the Statistique générale de la France or the Institut national de la statistique et des études économiques, but from P. Bairoch, *The Working Population and Its Structure* (New York: Gordon and Breach, 1968).

Bibliography

This list includes only the secondary literature we have found useful. Sources of strike data are enumerated in Appendix A; sources of 'background' quantitative data are given in the notes of Chapters 5 and 11. Some works cited in the footnotes have not been incorporated in the bibliography.

Industrial conflict in France

Andréani, Edgard. *Les Grèves et les fluctuations de l'activité économique de 1890 à 1914 en France*. Faculté de droit de Paris, *thèse*, 1965. A careful quantitative analysis.

Aron, Raymond. *Le Révolution introuvable: Réflexions sur la révolution de mai*. Paris: Fayard, 1968.

Barrier-Lynn, Christiane. *Nouvelles Couches salariées dans une entreprise national-isée: Leur potentiel revendicatif à la veille du mouvement de mai 1968*. Paris: CNRS, Centre d'études sociologiques, n.d.

'Techniciens et grèves à l'électricité de France,' *Sociologie du travail*, 10 (1968): 50–71.

Bartoli, Henri. 'Emploi et industrialisation,' *Economie appliquée: Archives de l'I.S.E.A.*, 21, no. 1 (1968): 123–236. Compares postwar and interwar strike activity by industry.

Brécy, Robert. *La Grève générale en France*. Paris: Etudes et documentation inter-nationales, 1969.

Cornu, Roger and Marc Maurice. 'Revendications, orientations syndicales et participation des cadres à la grève,' *Sociologie du travail*, 12 (1970): 328–37.

Dubois, Pierre. 'Les Types de revendications dans l'industrie textile,' *Revue fran-çaise des affaires sociales*, 24 (1970): 25–40.

Durand, Claude and Sonia Cazes. 'La Signification politique du mouvement de mai: analyse de tracts syndicaux et gauchistes,' *Sociologie du travail*, 12 (1970): 293–308.

Erbès-Seguin, Sabine. 'Relations entre travailleurs dans l'entreprise en grève: Le Cas de mai–juin 1968,' *Revue française de sociologie*, 11 (1970): 339–50.

'Le Déclenchement des grèves de mai: spontanéité des masses et rôle des syn-dicats,' *Sociologie du travail*, 12 (1970): 177–89.

Goetz-Girey, Robert. *Le Mouvement des grèves en France, 1919–1962*. Paris: Sirey, 1965. An important study, concentrating on the relationship between strikes and economic fluctuations.

Gratton, Philippe. *Les Luttes de classes dans les campagnes*. Paris: Editions anthropos, 1971. Based on both archives and *SG*.

Guillaume, P. 'Grèves et organisation ouvrière chez les mineurs de la Loire au milieu du XIXe siécle,' *Le Mouvement social*, no. 43 (April–June 1963): 5–18.

Lapierre, J.-W. 'La Violence dans les conflits sociaux' in Centre d'études de la civilisation contemporaine (ed.), *La Violence dans le monde actuel* (Paris: Desclée de Brouwer, 1968), pp. 129–58.

Lefranc, Georges. *Histoire du front populaire (1934–1938)*. Paris: Payot, 1965.

Juin 36: L'Explosion sociale du front populaire. Paris: Julliard, 1966.

Grèves d'hier et d'aujourd'hui: Histoire du travail et de la vie économique. Paris: Aubier–Montaigne, 1970. Chronicles some major conflicts.

Léon, Pierre, 'Les Grèves de 1867–1870 dans le département de l'Isère,' *Revue d'histoire moderne et contemporaine*, 1 (1954): 272–300.

Lequin, Yves. 'Sources et méthodes de l'histoire des grèves dans la seconde moitié du XIXe siècle: L'Exemple de l'Isère (1848–1914),' *Cahiers d'histoire*, 12 (1967): 215–31.

L'Huillier, Fernand. *La Lutte ouvrière à la fin du Second Empire*. Paris: Colin, 1957; Cahiers des Annales, 12.

Lorcin, Jean. 'Un Essai de stratigraphie sociale: Chefs d'ateliers et compagnons dans la grève des passementiers de Saint-Etienne en 1900,' *Cahiers d'histoire*, 12 (1968): 179–92.

Loubère, Leo. 'Coal Miners, Strikes and Politics in the Lower Languedoc, 1880–1914,' *Journal of Social History*, 2 (1968): 25–50.

Mallet, Serge. 'L'Après-mai 1968: Grèves pour le contrôle ouvrier,' *Sociologie du travail*, 12 (1970): 309–27.

March, Lucien. 'Mouvements du commerce et du crédit, mouvement ouvrier, en relation avec le mouvement des prix,' *Bulletin de la statistique générale*, 1 (1912): 188–222.

Masse, Jean. 'Les Grèves des mineurs et carriers du Var de 1871 à 1921,' *Annales du Midi*, 79 (1967): 196–218.

Monpied, Ernest. 'Le Mouvement des métayers de l'Adour (1919–1920),' *Le Mouvement social*, no. 67 (April–June 1969): 111–21.

Néré, Jean. 'Aspect du déroulement des grèves en France durant la période 1883–1889,' *Revue d'histoire économique et sociale*, 34 (1956): 286–302.

Perrot, Michelle. 'Grèves, grèvistes et conjoncture. Vieux problèmes, travaux neufs,' *Le Mouvement social*, no. 63 (April–June 1968): 109–24.

Les Ouvriers en grève (France, 1871–1890). Paris I, *thèse*, 1971. A magisterial treatment of worker life and conflict.

Picquenard, C. 'Le Bilan financier des grèves,' *Revue d'économie politique*, 22 (1908): 356–77.

Prouteau, Henri. *Les Occupations d'usines en Italie et en France (1920–1936)*. Paris: Librairie technique et économique, 1937.

Rist, Charles. 'La Progression des grèves en France et sa valeur symptomatique,' *Revue d'économie politique*, 21 (1907): 161–93.

'Relation entre les variations annuelles du chômage, des grèves et des prix,' *Revue d'économie politique*, 26 (1912): 748–58.

Schulz, Marcel. 'Les Origines de la crise ouvrière de 1936,' *Le Musée social*, N.S., 44 (1937): 121–39, 153–65, 185–200.

Sellier, François and André Tiano. *Economie du travail.* Paris: PUF, 1962. Analyzes postwar strikes.

Sinay, Hélène. *La Grève.* Paris: Dalloz, 1966. Analysis of strike legislation, plus chronicle of major disputes after 1955.

Sorlin, Pierre. *Waldeck-Rousseau.* Paris: Colin, 1966. Invaluable for the political background of the strike movement in the 1890s.

Stearns, Peter N. 'Patterns of Industrial Strike Activity in France during the July Monarchy,' *American Historical Review,* 70, (1965): 371–94.

'Against the Strike Threat: Employer Policy toward Labor Agitation in France, 1900–1914,' *Journal of Modern History,* 40 (1968): 474–500.

'The European Labor Movement and the Working Classes, 1890–1914' in Harvey Mitchell and Stearns (eds.), *Workers and Protest: The European Labor Movement, the Working Classes and the Origins of Social Democracy, 1890–1914* (Itasca, Ill.: F. E. Peacock, 1971), pp. 120–221.

'National Character and European Labor History,' *Journal of Social History,* 4 (1970–1): 95–124.

Revolutionary Syndicalism and French Labor: A Cause without Rebels. New Brunswick, N. J.: Rutgers University Press, 1971. Sharply downplays the role of syndicalism in the strike movement, 1890–1914.

Tarlé, E. 'La Grande Coalition des mineurs de Rive-de-Gier en 1844,' *Revue historique,* 177 (1936): 249–78.

Tilly, Charles. 'Collective Violence in European Perspective' in Hugh Davis Graham and Ted Robert Gurr (eds.), *Violence in America: Historical and Comparative Perspectives* (New York: Bantam, 1969), pp. 4–45.

'A Travers le chaos des vivantes cités' in Paul Meadows and Ephraim H. Mizruchi (eds.), *Urbanism, Urbanization, and Change: Comparative Perspectives* (Reading, Mass.: Addison–Wesley, 1969), pp. 379–94.

'The Changing Place of Collective Violence' in Melvin Richter (ed.), *Essays in Theory and History: An Approach to the Social Sciences* (Cambridge, Mass.: Harvard University Press, 1970), pp. 139–64.

Tilly, Charles and Edward Shorter. 'Le Déclin de la grève violente en France de 1890 à 1935,' *Le Mouvement social,* no. 76 (July–Sept. 1971): 95–118.

'The Shape of Strikes in France, 1830–1960,' *Comparative Studies in Society and History,* 13 (1971): 60–86.

Touraine, Alain. *Le Mouvement de mai ou le communisme utopique.* Paris: Seuil, 1968.

Turquan, Victor. 'Les Grèves en France depuis 1874. Leurs causes et leurs résultats,' *Journal de la société de statistique de Paris,* 30 (1889): 290–7.

Worker organization and labor relations

Baker, Robert P. 'Socialism in the Nord, 1880–1914: A Regional View of the French Socialist Movement,' *International Review of Social History,* 12 (1967): 357–89.

Bartuel, Casimir *et al. La Mine aux mineurs.* Paris: Doin, 1927.

Berthon, Jean. 'Les Militants de la C.F.T.C.,' *Sociologie du travail,* 4 (1962): 174–84.

Braque, René. 'Aux origines du syndicalisme dans les milieux ruraux du centre de la France (Allier–Cher–Nièvre–sud du Loiret),' *Le Mouvement social,* no. 42 (Jan.–March 1963): 79–116.

Brécy, Robert. *Le Mouvement syndical en France, 1871–1921: Essai bibliographique.* Paris: Mouton, 1963.

Bron, Jean. *Histoire du mouvement ouvrier français*, 2 vols. Paris: Editions ouvrières, 1968–70. A popular account.

Brower, Daniel R. *The New Jacobins: The French Communist Party and the Popular Front.* Ithaca, N.Y.: Cornell University Press, 1968.

Charles, Jean. 'Les Débuts de l'organisation ouvrière à Besançon, 1874–1904,' *Le Mouvement social*, no. 40 (July–Sept. 1962): 19–38.

Les Débuts du mouvement syndical à Besançon. La Fédération ouvrière (1891– 1914). Paris: Editions sociales, 1962. An important local study.

Clark, Marjorie Ruth. *A History of the French Labor Movement (1910–1928).* Berkeley: University of California Press, 1930. Still of value for interwar years.

Confédération Générale du Travail. *La Confédération générale du travail et le mouvement syndical.* Paris: CGT, 1925. (Cited as CGT, 1925.) Gives a brief history of each federation and departmental *union des syndicats* affiliated with interwar CGT.

Cousteix, P. 'Le Mouvement ouvrier limousin de 1870 à 1939,' *L'Actualité de l'histoire*, nos. 20–21 (Dec. 1957): 27–96.

Crozier, Michel. *The Bureaucratic Phenomenon.* Chicago: University of Chicago Press, 1964.

'Sociologie du syndicalisme' in Georges Friedmann and Pierre Naville (eds.), *Traité du sociologie du travail*, 2 vols. (Paris: Colin, 1964), II, pp. 170–93.

'White-Collar Unions – The Case of France' in Adolf Sturmthal (ed.), *White-Collar Trade-Unions: Contemporary Developments in Industrialized Societies* (Urbana: University of Illinois Press, 1967), pp. 90–126.

Dehove, Gérard. *Le Contrôle ouvrier en France. L'Elaboration de sa notion. Ses conceptions.* Paris: Sirey, 1937.

Delon, Pierre. *Les Employés de la plume d'oie à l'ordinateur: Un Siècle de lutte. Origines et activité de la fédération C.G.T.* Paris: Editions sociales, 1969. Written by a union official.

Dolléans, Edouard. *Histoire du mouvement ouvrier*, 7th ed., 3 vols. Paris: Colin, 1967. A classic text.

Dubief, Henri (ed.). *Le Syndicalisme révolutionnaire.* Paris: Colin, 1969. Introduction to union ideologies before 1914, followed by selected texts and thumbnail biographies of worker leaders.

Dubois, Pierre. 'Nouvelles pratiques de mobilisation dans la classe ouvrière,' *Sociologie du travail*, 12 (1970): 338–44.

Dufraisse, R. 'Le Mouvement ouvrier français "rouge" devant la grande dépression économique de 1929 à 1933' in Denise Fauvel-Rouif (ed.), *Mouvements ouvriers et dépression économique de 1929 à 1939* (Assen, the Netherlands: Van Gorcum, 1966), pp. 163–88.

'Rapports entre organisations ouvrières et organisations patronales de la métallurgie française durant la dépression économique (1929–1939)' in *ibid.*, pp. 189– 219.

Durand, Claude. 'Dynamique sociale et évolution du syndicalisme,' *Sociologie du travail*, 6 (1964): 296–300.

Faure, Pétrus. *Histoire du mouvement ouvrier dans le département de la Loire.* St-Etienne: Imprimerie Dumas, 1956. A massive chronicle.

Flonneau, Jean-Marie. 'Crise de vie chère et mouvement syndical, 1910–1914,' *Le Mouvement social*, no. 72 (July–Sept. 1970): 49–81.

Frischmann, Georges. *Histoire de la fédération C.G.T. des P.T. T.: Des origines au statut des fonctionnaires (1672–1946)*. Paris: Editions sociales, 1967.

Gallagher, Orvoell R. 'Voluntary Associations in France,' *Social Forces*, 36 (1957–8): 153–60.

Gallard, Jeanne. 'Les Usines Cail et les ouvriers métallurgistes de Grenelle,' *Le Mouvement social*, nos. 33–34 (Oct. 1960–March 1961): 35–53.

Gallo, Max. 'Quelques aspects de la mentalité et du comportement ouvrier dans les usines de guerre–1914–1918,' *Le Mouvement social*, no. 56 (July–Sept. 1966): 3–33.

Georges, Bernard and Denise Tintant. *Léon Jouhaux, cinquante ans de syndicalisme*, vol. I: *Des origines à 1921*. Paris: PUF, 1962.

Girault, Jacques. 'Le Rôle du socialisme dans le révolte des vignerons de l'Aube,' *Le Mouvement social*, no. 67 (April–June 1969): 89–109.

Goetz-Girey, Robert. *La Pensée syndicale française: Militants et théoriciens*. Paris: Colin, 1948.

Goldberg, Harvey. *The Life of Jean Jaurès*. Madison: University of Wisconsin Press, 1962.

Greene, Nathanael. *Crisis and Decline: The French Socialist Party in the Popular Front Era*. Ithaca, N.Y.: Cornell University Press, 1969.

Guilbert, Madeleine. *Les Femmes et l'organisation syndicale avant 1914. Présentation et commentaires des documents pour une étude du syndicalisme féminin*. Paris: CNRS, 1966.

Hardy-Hémery, Odette. 'Rationalisation technique et rationalisation du travail à la compagnie des mines d'Anzin (1927–1938),' *Le Mouvement social*, no. 72 (July–Sept. 1970): 3–48.

Huard, R. 'Aspects du mouvement ouvrier gardois pendant la guerre de 1914–18,' *Annales du Midi*, 80 (1968): 305–18.

Joran, Raymond. *L'Organisation syndicale dans l'industrie du batîment*. Paris: Arthur Savaéte, 1914. Among the few studies of industrial federations.

Julliard, Jacques. 'Jeune et vieux syndicat chez les mineurs du Pas-de-Calais (à travers les papiers de Pierre Monatte),' *Le Mouvement social*, no. 47 (April–June 1964): 7–30.

Clemenceau, briseur de grèves: L'Affaire de Draveil–Villeneuve–Saint–Georges (1908). Paris: Julliard, 1965. Contains both important archival material on strikes and an analysis of the political background.

'Théorie syndicaliste révolutionnaire et pratique grèviste,' *Le Mouvement social*, no. 65 (Oct.–Dec. 1968): 55–69.

'Fernand Pelloutier et les origines du syndicalisme d'action directe,' *Le Mouvement social*, no. 75 (April–June 1971): 3–32.

Kriegel, Annie. *Aux origines du communisme français, 1914–1920: Contribution à l'histoire du mouvement ouvrier français*, 2 vols. Paris: Mouton, 1964. Fundamental for relationship between strikes and politics.

La Croissance de la C.G.T., 1918–1921: Essai statistique. Paris: Mouton, 1966. Analysis of local membership figures as reported at CGT congresses.

'A la conquête du prolétariat rural: Les Bûcherons et leurs syndicats au tournant du siècle' in Kriegel (ed.), *Le Pain et les roses: Jalons pour une histoire des socialismes* (Paris: PUF, 1968), pp. 51–60. Volume contains other important Kriegel essays too.

Les Communistes français: Essai d'ethnographie politique. Paris: Seuil, 1968.

Kulstein, David I. 'Bonapartist Workers during the Second Empire,' *International Review of Social History*, 9 (1964): 226–36.

Landauer, Carl. 'The Origin of Socialist Reformism in France,' *International Review of Social History*, 12 (1967): 81–107.

Laroque, Pierre. *Les Rapports entre patrons et ouvriers.* Paris: Montaigne, 1938.

Laubier, Patrick de. 'Esquisse d'une théorie du syndicalisme,' *Sociologie du travail*, 10 (1968): 362–92. Provocative.

Launay, Michel. 'Le Syndicalisme chrétien dans un grand conflit du travail,' *Le Mouvement social*, no. 73 (Oct.–Dec. 1970): 39–78.

Lebrun, François. 'Ludovic Ménard et la naissance du syndicalisme ardoisier,' *L'Actualité de l'histoire*, no. 29 (Oct.–Dec. 1959): 2–46.

Lefranc, Georges. *Les Expériences syndicales en France de 1939 à 1950.* Paris: Aubier, 1950.

Le Mouvement socialiste sous la Troisième République (1875–1940). Paris: Payot, 1963.

Le Mouvement syndical sous la Troisième République. Paris: Payot, 1967. This, and the volume following, represent the standard history of modern French unionism.

Le Mouvement syndical de la Libération aux événements de mai–juin 1968. Paris: Payot, 1969.

Lorwin, Val R. *The French Labor Movement.* Cambridge, Mass.: Harvard University Press, 1954. The best historical account in English, plus a careful treatment of industrial relations in the early 1950s.

'Reflections on the History of French and American Labor Movements,' *Journal of Economic History*, 17 (1957): 25–44.

Loubère, Leo A. 'Les Radicaux d'extrême-gauche en France et les rapports entre patrons et ouvriers,' *Revue d'histoire économique et sociale*, 42 (1964): 89–103.

Maitron, Jean. 'La Personalité du militant ouvrier français dans la seconde moitié du XIX siècle,' *Le Mouvement social*, no. 33–34 (Oct. 1960–March 1961): 68–86.

Maurice, Marc. 'Déterminants du militantisme et projet syndical des ouvriers et des techniciens,' *Sociologie du travail*, 7 (1965): 254–72.

Meyers, Frédéric. 'Deux aspects du rôle des négociations collectives en France,' *Sociologie du travail*, 7 (1965): 1–33, 113–50.

Perrot, Michelle. 'Le Problème des sources pour l'étude du militant ouvrier au XIXe siècle,' *Le Mouvement social*, nos. 33–34 (Oct. 1960–March 1961): 21–34.

Polet, Jean. 'Les Militants anarchistes dans le département du Nord au début du XXe siècle,' *Revue du Nord*, 51 (1969): 629–40.

Poperen, Maurice. 'Création des bourses du travail en Anjou, 1892–1894,' *Le Mouvement social*, no. 40 (July–Sept. 1962): 39–55.

Prost, Antoine. *La C.G.T. à l'époque du front populaire, 1934–1939: Essai de description numérique.* Paris: Colin, 1964. A pioneering analysis.

Reynaud, Jean-Daniel. *Les Syndicats en France.* Paris: Colin, 1966. The best guide to contemporary unionism.

Ridley, F. F. *Revolutionary Syndicalism in France: The Direct Action of Its Time.* Cambridge: University Press, 1970. A useful summary of CGT ideology before the First World War.

Sainsaulieu, Renaud. 'Pouvoirs et stratégies de groupes ouvriers dans l'atelier,' *Sociologie du travail*, 7 (1965): 162–74.

Sales, Hubert. *Les Relations industrielles dans l'imprimerie française.* Paris: Cujas, 1966.

Spitzer, Alan B. 'Anarchy and Culture: Fernand Pelloutier and the Dilemma of Revolutionary Syndicalism,' *International Review of Social History*, 8 (1963): 379–88.

Stafford, David. *From Anarchism to Reformism: A Study of the Political Activities of Paul Brousse within the First International and the French Socialist Movement, 1870–90.* Toronto: University of Toronto Press, 1971.

Sturmthal, Adolf. 'Collective Bargaining in France' in Sturmthal (ed.), *Contemporary Collective Bargaining in Seven Countries.* Ithaca, N.Y.: Cornell University Press, 1957, pp. 127–67.

Thomas, G. 'Le Socialisme et le syndicalisme dans l'Indre: Des origines à 1920–1922,' *L'Actualité de l'histoire*, nos. 20–21 (Dec. 1957): 1–26.

Tiano, André. 'L'Action des syndicats ouvriers: Etat des travaux,' *Revue française de science politique*, 10 (1960): 912–30.

Touraine, Alain. 'Contribution à la sociologie du mouvement ouvrier, Le Syndicalisme de contrôle,' *Cahiers internationaux de sociologie*, N.S., 28 (1960): 57–88.

Trempé, Rolande. *Les Mineurs de Carmaux, 1848–1914.* Paris: Editions ouvrières, 1971. A massive, imaginative monograph.

Vasseur, Daniel. *Les Débuts du mouvement ouvrier dans la région de Belfort–Montbéliard (1870–1914).* Paris: Les Belles Lettres, 1967. An important local study.

Vial, Jean. *La Coutume chapelière: Histoire du mouvement ouvrier dans la chapellerie.* Paris: Domat, 1941. Notable among the few existing works on industrial federations.

Willard, Claude. *Le Mouvement socialiste en France (1893–1905): Les Guesdistes.* Paris: Editions sociales, 1965.

Winock, M. 'La Scission de Châtellerault et la naissance du parti "allemaniste" (1890–1891),' *Le Mouvement social*, no. 75 (April–June 1971): 33–62.

Wohl, Robert. *French Communism in the Making, 1914–1924.* Stanford, Cal.: University Press, 1966.

French working-class life

Belleville, Pierre. *Une Nouvelle Classe ouvrière.* Paris: Julliard, 1963.

Bonnet, R. P. Serge. 'Political Alignments and Religious Attitudes within the Italian Immigration to the Metallurgical Districts of Lorraine,' *Journal of Social History*, 2 (1968): 123–55.

Caron, F. 'Essai d'analyse historique d'une psychologie du travail: Les Mécaniciens et chauffeurs de locomotives du réseau du Nord de 1850 à 1910,' *Le Mouvement social*, no. 50 (Jan.–March 1965): 3–40.

Collinet, Michel. *L'Ouvrier français*, I: *Essai sur la condition ouvrière (1900–1950)*; II: *Esprit du syndicalisme (Essai).* Paris: Editions ouvrières, 1951. Good on the world of the shop floor.

Courtheoux, Jean-Paul. 'Naissance d'une conscience de classe dans le proletariat textile du Nord, 1830–1870,' *Revue économique*, 8 (1957): 114–39.

Durand, Claude. 'Participation et conflit: Orientations de la recherche,' *Sociologie du travail*, 4 (1962): 64–74.

Gavi, Philippe. *Les Ouvriers*. Paris: Mercure de France, 1970.

Girod, Roger. *Etudes sociologiques sur les couches salariées: Ouvriers et employés*. Paris: Marcel Rivière, 1961.

Hamilton, Richard F. *Affluence and the French Worker in the Fourth Republic*. Princeton: University Press, 1967. A skillful analysis of extensive survey data.

Hamon, Léo (ed.). *Les Nouveaux Comportements politiques de la classe ouvrière*. Paris: PUF, 1962.

Idiart, Pierre. 'Phénomène ouvrier et phénomène de classe,' *Cahiers internationaux de sociologie*, 32 (1962): 105–24.

Kriegel, Annie, Remi Gossez and Jacques Rougerie. 'Sources et méthodes pour une histoire sociale de la classe ouvrière,' *Le Mouvement social*, no. 40 (July–Sept. 1962): 1–18.

'L'Histoire ouvrière du XXe siècle,' *Bulletin historique*, 230 (1963): 447–78; 235 (1966): 455–90.

Lequin, Yves. 'Classe ouvrière et idéologie dans la région lyonnaise à la fin du XIXe siècle (vers 1870–1914),' *Le Mouvement social*, no. 69 (Oct.–Dec. 1969): 3–20.

Louis, Paul. *La Condition ouvrière en France depuis cent ans*. Paris: PUF, 1950.

Mallet, Serge. *La Nouvelle Classe ouvrière*. Paris: Seuil, 1963. An important hypothesis about industrial technology and conflict.

'La Nouvelle Classe ouvrière en France,' *Cahiers internationaux de sociologie*, 38 (1965): 57–72.

Mathieu, Gilbert. 'La Réponse des chiffres . . .' [to issue: abundance or pauperization], *Les Temps modernes*, 18 (1962): 403–58.

Michaud, René, *J'avais vingt ans. Un Jeune Ouvrier au début du siècle*. Paris: Editions syndicalistes, 1967.

Parent-Lardeur, Françoise. *Les Demoiselles de magasin*. Paris: Editions ouvrières, 1970.

Rainville, Jean-Marie. *Condition ouvrière et intégration sociale*. Paris: Editions ouvrières, 1967.

Sewell, William H., Jr. 'Working-Class History Beyond Marxism: The Case of Marseille in the Nineteenth Century.' Paper delivered at 1971 meeting of the American Historical Association.

Touraine, Alain. *La Conscience ouvrière*, Paris: Seuil, 1966.

Post-industrial Society. New York: Random House, 1971.

Vial, J. 'L'Ouvrier métallurgiste français,' *Droit social*, 13 (1950): 58–68.

Industrial conflict in other countries

Abrate, M. *La Lotta sindicale nella industrializzazione in Italia, 1906–1926*. Turin: Franco Angeli, 1968.

Baglione, Guido. *Il Conflitto industriale e l'azione del sindicato*. Bologna: Societa Editrice Il Mulino, 1966.

Cameron, G. C. 'Post-War Strikes in the North-East Shipbuilding and Ship-Repairing Industry,' *British Journal of Industrial Relations*, 2 (1964): 1–22.

Cass, Millard. 'The Relationship of Size of Firm and Strike Activity,' *Monthly Labor Review*, 80 (1957): 1330–4.

Chaumont, Maurice. 'Grèves, syndicalisme et attitudes ouvrières: Les Grèves belges de décembre 1960–janvier 1961,' *Sociologie du travail*, 4 (1962): 142–58.

Dubin, Robert. 'Industrial Conflict: The Power of Prediction,' *Industrial and Labor Relations Review*, 18 (1964–5): 352–63.

Eldridge, J. E. T. *Industrial Disputes: Essays in the Sociology of Industrial Relations.* London: Routledge & Kegan Paul, 1968. Of special interest is Chapter 1, 'Explanations of Strikes: A Critical Review.'

Féaux, Valmy. *Cinq semaines de lutte sociale: La Grève de l'hiver, 1960–1961.* Brussels: Editions de l'institut de sociologie, Université libre de Bruxelles, 1963.

Forchheimer, K. 'Some International Aspects of the Strike Movement,' *Bulletin of the Oxford University Institute of Statistics*, 10 (1948): 9–24, 294–304.

'Some International Aspects of Strikes: The Effectiveness of Large and of Long Strikes, with Special Reference to Sweden,' *Bulletin of the Oxford University Institute of Statistics*, 11 (1949): 279–86. Forchheimer pioneered in international comparisons.

Galambos, P. and E. W. Evans. 'Work-Stoppages in the United Kingdom, 1951–1964: A Quantitative Study,' *Bulletin of the Oxford University Institute of Statistics*, 28 (1966): 33–57. In the same issue are a comment by K. G. J. C. Knowles and a reply by Galambos.

Giugni, Gino. 'Bargaining Units and Labor Organization in Italy,' *Industrial and Labor Relations Review*, 10 (1956–7): 424–39.

Goldberg, Joseph P. and Bernard Yabroff. 'Analysis of Strikes, 1927–49,' [U.S.] *Monthly Labor Review*, 72 (1951): 1–7.

Goodman, J. F. B. 'Strikes in the United Kingdom: Recent Statistics,' *International Labour Review*, 96 (1967): 465–81.

Gouldner, Alvin W. *Wildcat Strike: A Study in Worker–Management Relationships.* Yellow Springs, Ohio: Antioch Press, 1954. New York: Harper and Row, 1965. A classic case study.

'Les Grèves sauvages en Europe occidentale,' *Analyse et documents*, N.S., nos. 182–3 (March 1970). Special issue.

Griffin, John I. *Strikes: A Study in Quantitative Economics.* New York: Columbia University Press, 1939. The standard work on U.S. strike history.

Gubbels, Robert. *La Grève, Phénomène de civilisation.* Brussels: Université libre de Bruxelles, Institut de sociologie, 1962. Interprets post-1945 Belgian strikes as principally a *phénomène sociologique*.

Hobsbawm, E. J. 'Economic Fluctuations and Some Social Movements' in Hobsbawm (ed.), *Labouring Men: Studies in the History of Labour* (New York: Basic Books, 1964), pp. 126–57.

International Labour Office. 'Industrial Disputes, 1937–54,' *International Labour Review*, 72 (1955): 78–91.

'The Incidence of Industrial Disputes by Industry,' *International Labour Review*, 74 (1956): 290–302.

'The Incidence and Duration of Industrial Disputes,' *International Labour Review*, 77, (1958): 455–68.

Knowles, K. G. J. C. *Strikes.* Oxford: University Press, 1952. On Great Britain. The most detailed national study to date of the history and character of industrial conflict.

Kuhn, James W. *Bargaining in Grievance Settlement: The Power of Industrial Work Groups.* New York: Columbia University Press, 1961.

Lester, Richard A. 'Reflections on Collective Bargaining in Britain and Sweden,' *Industrial and Labor Relations Review*, 10 (1956–7): 375–401.

Levitt, Theodore. 'Prosperity versus Strikes,' *Industrial and Labor Relations Review*, 6 (1952–3): 220–6.

McCarthy, W. E. J. 'The Nature of Britain's Strike Problem: A Reassessment of the Arguments in the Donovan Report and a Reply to H. A. Turner,' *British Journal of Industrial Relations*, 8 (1970): 224–36.

McCord, Norman. 'The Seamen's Strike of 1815 in North-East England,' *Economic History Review*, 2nd ser., 21 (1968): 127–43.

Mertens, Clément. 'Grèves et vieillissement de la population,' *La Revue nouvelle*, 33, iii (March 1961): 245–50.

Pencavel, John H. 'An Investigation into Industrial Strike Activity in Britain,' *Economica*, 37 (1970): 239–56.

Peterson, Florence. 'Strikes in the United States, 1880–1936,' *U. S. Bureau of Labor Statistics, Bulletin*, no. 651 (Aug. 1937): 1–183.

Pope, Liston. *Millhands and Preachers: A Study of Gastonia.* New Haven, Conn.: Yale University Press, 1942; rev. ed., 1967. Last third of book concerns Loray textile strike.

Rimlinger, Gaston V. 'International Differences in the Strike Propensity of Coal Miners: Experience in Four Countries,' *Industrial and Labor Relations Review*, 12 (1959): 389–405.

'The Legitimation of Protest: A Comparative Study in Labor History,' *Comparative Studies in Society and History*, 2 (1960): 329–43.

Ross, Arthur M. and Donald Irwin. 'Strike Experience in Five Countries, 1927–47: An Interpretation,' *Industrial and Labor Relations Review*, 4 (1951): 323–42.

Ross, Arthur M. and Paul T. Hartman. *Changing Patterns of Industrial Conflict.* New York: Wiley, 1960. The standard work on international differences in styles of organization and conflict.

'Prosperity and Labor Relations in Western Europe: Italy and France,' *Industrial and Labor Relations Review*, 16 (1962–3): 63–85.

Scott, Jerome F. and George C. Homans. 'Reflections on the Wildcat Strikes,' *American Sociological Review*, 12 (1947): 278–87.

Spielmans, John V. 'Strike Profiles,' *Journal of Political Economy*, 52 (1944): 319–39. Represents two dimensions of strike activity simultaneously with rectangles.

Turner, Herbert Arthur. *Labour Relations in the Motor Industry: A Study of Industrial Unrest and an International Comparison.* London: Allen & Unwin, 1967.

Is Britain Really Strike-Prone? A Review of the Incidence, Character and Costs of Industrial Conflict. Cambridge: University Press, 1969. University of Cambridge, Department of Applied Economics, Occasional Papers, 20.

Weintraub, Andrew R. 'Prosperity versus Strikes: An Empirical Approach,' *Industrial and Labor Relations Review*, 19 (1965–6): 231–8.

Woodbury, Robert Morse. 'The Incidence of Industrial Disputes: Rates of Time-Loss, 1927–47,' *International Labour Review*, 60 (1949): 451–66.

Yoder, Dale. 'Economic Change and Industrial Unrest in the United States,' *Journal of Political Economy*, 48 (1940): 222–37.

Other literature

Blum, Albert A. 'Why Unions Grow,' *Labor History*, 9 (1968): 39–72.

Delcourt, Jacques and Gérard Lamarque. *Un Faux Dilemme: Embourgeoisement ou proletarisation de la classe ouvrière*. Paris: La Pensée catholique, 1963. A useful survey.

Derber, Milton. *The American Ideal of Industrial Democracy, 1865–1965*. Urbana: University of Illinois Press, 1970.

Dessus, Gabriel, Pierre George and Jacques Weulersse. *Matériaux pour une géographie volontaire de l'industrie française*. Paris: Colin, 1949. See esp. pp. 109–43 on differences in establishment size by industry within department.

Dubin, Robert. 'A Theory of Conflict and Power in Union–Management Relations,' *Industrial and Labor Relations Review*, 13 (1959–60): 501–18.

Friedmann, Georges. *Industrial Society: The Emergence of the Human Problems of Automation*. Glencoe, Ill.: Free Press, 1955.

Galenson, Walter. *Trade Union Democracy in Western Europe*. Berkeley: University of California Press, 1962.

Gibrat, Robert. 'Une Loi des répartitions économiques: L'Effet proportionnel (Applications à la concentration des entreprises . . .),' *Bulletin de la statistique générale*, 19 (July–Sept. 1930): 469–513.

Goldthorpe, John H. *et al. The Affluent Worker: Industrial Attitudes and Behaviour*. Cambridge: University Press, 1968.
  The Affluent Worker: Political Attitudes and Behaviour. Cambridge: University Press, 1968.

Greenstone, J. David. *Labor in American Politics*. New York: Knopf, 1968

Ingham, Geoffrey K. *Size of Industrial Organization and Worker Behaviour*. Cambridge: University Press, 1970.

Kornhauser, Arthur *et al.* (eds.). *Industrial Conflict*. New York: McGraw–Hill, 1954. A reader containing numerous important essays, including Clark Kerr and Abraham Siegel, 'The Interindustry Propensity to Strike – An International Comparison,' pp. 189–212.

Krueger, Thomas A. 'American Labor Historiography, Old and New: A Review Essay,' *Journal of Social History*, (1970–1): 277–85.

Lambert, Jean. *Le Patron: De l'avènement à la contestation*. Paris: Bloud et Gay, 1969.

Laslett, John H. M. *Labor and the Left: A Study of Socialist and Radical Influences in the American Labor Movement, 1881–1924*. New York: Basic Books, 1970.

Lipset, Seymour Martin. 'Trade Unions and Social Structure,' *Industrial Relations*, I, i (Oct. 1961): 75–89, and I, ii (Feb. 1962): 89–110.

Lipset, Seymour Martin *et al. Union Democracy: The Internal Politics of the International Typographical Union*. Glencoe, Ill.: Free Press, 1956.

Neufeld, Maurice F. 'The Inevitability of Political Unionism in Underdeveloped Countries: Italy, the Exemplar,' *Industrial and Labor Relations Review*, 13 (1959–60): 363–86.

'Quelques résultats essentiels du recensement de l'industrie [of 1963],' *Etudes et conjonctures*, 22 (1967): 119–47.

Revans, R. W. 'Industrial Morale and Size of Unit,' *Political Quarterly*, 27 (1956): 303–11.

Statistique générale de la France. 'La Concentration de personnel dans les entreprises en France entre les deux guerres,' *Bulletin de la statistique générale de la France* (Jan.–March 1945): 77–100.

Touraine, Alain. *L'Evolution du travail ouvrier aux usines Renault*. Paris: CNRS, 1955.

Ville-Chabrolle, Marcel de. 'La Concentration des entreprises en France avant et depuis la guerre (d'après les recensements généraux de mars 1906, 1921 et 1926),' *Bulletin de la statistique générale de la France*, 22 (1933): 391–462.

Windmuller, John P. *Labor Relations in the Netherlands*. Ithaca, N. Y.: Cornell University Press, 1969.

Index

f—figure
m—map
n—note
t—table

APO, 49n, 60n, 69n, 73n, 148f, 149n, 150n, 151n, 176, 196, 212, 218, 354, 355, 363n, 368n, 371–3t, 377, 385, 388, 389, 390, 391, 399
agriculture and agricultural workers, 5, 77, 112, 176, 194, 202, 213, 227, 234, 257, 277n, 287, 293n, 331, 359, 392, 395; strikes, 115, 119t, 120, 124t, 125, 128, 195t, 197f, 201t, 238, 250, 252, 253t, 264, 289, 374–6t, 392; unions, 149n, 150, 388
Aguet, Jean-Pierre, 49n, 61, 73n, 108, 110, 176, 196, 208, 345, 351, 354, 363n, 367n, 371n, 377, 384, 392
Agulhon, Maurice, 3, 395
Ain, 120, 160n, 293n
aircraft industry and workers, 2, 15, 123, 140
Aisne, 116, 293n
Alès, 249, 276m, 293n
Algeria, 49n, 149n, 363n, 383, 399
Allemanists, 171, 172
Alpes-Maritimes, 264
Alsace, 111, 237, 242m, 243m, 247, 248, 252, 253t, 256, 274, 374–5t, 385
Ambès, 185
Amiens, 112, 247, 276m, 293n
ammunition industry, 23
anarchists, 61, 114, 119, 133, 167, 171, 172, 183, 387, 389
Andréani, Edgard, 78, 79, 80, 81n, 82, 84, 90, 94, 381, 398
Angers, 30
Annuaire des syndicats, 148f, 149n, 160n, 371–3t
Annuaire statistique, 49n, 63n, 64n, 65n, 106n, 149n, 232, 332, 363n, 371n, 373n, 382, 383, 387, 388
Anzin, 108, 109m, 167
Aquitaine, 128, 242m, 243m, 253t, 374–5t
arbitration, 25, 26, 29, 34, 114; *see also* collective bargaining
Ardèche, 112, 160n, 179, 268t, 269t, 270t, 377
Ardennes, 125, 132, 156, 256, 293n
Argenteuil, 250
Armentières, 247

army, 17, 38, 42, 43, 110, 138, 385
arrests, 1, 43, 74, 122, 123
arrondissements, 290–4
artisanal industries and artisans, 12, 105, 116, 174, 180, 182, 184, 185, 200, 202–4, 206, 207, 209, 212, 216–18, 336, 346–9, 377, 394; industrialization and, 216–27, 234; strikes, 17, 41, 63n, 66, 72, 74–5, 107, 110, 111, 114, 120, 200, 203–4, 208, 210, 216–27, 230, 235, 338–9, 345, 384, 392; unions and guilds, 12, 13, 15–16, 64, 67, 142, 148–9, 150, 152, 160, 161, 167, 174–9, 182, 183, 215–27, 235, 389, 392; *see also* dequalification, professional
artisanal phase, 11–15, 16, 105, 107, 112, 175–9, 198, 285–6
Artois, 247
assembly line, *see* mass production phase
Aube, 116, 125, 128, 156, 237, 247, 248, 257, 293n
Aubin, 111
Aude, 237, 250, 256, 264
authority on the shop floor, *see* grievances, job control; job control
automation, *see* science sector phase
automobile industry and workers, 14, 15, 68, 202, 208, 209, 348; strikes, 1, 120, 122, 128, 137, 140, 197, 385, 393; unions, 151, 179, 183
Auvergne, 242m, 243m, 253t, 374–5t
Aveyron, 132
aviation industry and workers, *see* aircraft industry and workers

Baglioni, Guido, 396
Bairoch, P., 331, 400
bakers, 110, 152t, 167, 206–7, 249; helpers of, 228
Banks, J. A., 398
banks and bank employees, 15, 136, 137, 138, 186, 199, 213, 214, 232n, 395
bargaining, *see* collective bargaining
Bas-Rhin, 47, 125, 246, 248, 355
Basly, Emile-Joseph, 119, 167
Basse Normandie, 237, 242m, 243m, 253t,

413